PREACHING CHRIST
FROM THE OLD TESTAMENT

PREACHING CHRIST FROM THE OLD TESTAMENT

A Contemporary Hermeneutical Method

SIDNEY GREIDANUS

WILLIAM B. EERDMANS PUBLISHING COMPANY
GRAND RAPIDS, MICHIGAN / CAMBRIDGE, U.K.

© 1999 Sidney Greidanus

First published 1999 by Wm. B. Eerdmans Publishing Co.
255 Jefferson Ave. S.E., Grand Rapids, Michigan 49503 /
P.O. Box 163, Cambridge CB3 9PU U.K.
All rights reserved

Printed in the United States of America

04 03 02 01 00   7 6 5 4 3 2

Library of Congress Cataloging-in-Publication Data

ISBN 0-8028-4449-9

CONTENTS

Preface   xii

Acknowledgments   xv

List of Abbreviations   xvii

1. PREACHING CHRIST AND PREACHING
THE OLD TESTAMENT   1

THE NECESSITY OF PREACHING CHRIST   1

    Confusion about the Meaning of "Preaching Christ "   2

    The New Testament on "Preaching Christ "   4

    The Meaning of "Preaching Christ "   8

    Reasons for Preaching Christ Today   10

THE NECESSITY OF PREACHING FROM
THE OLD TESTAMENT   15

    Reasons for the Lack of Preaching from the Old Testament   16

    Reasons for Preaching from the Old Testament as well as
        the New   25

2. THE NECESSITY OF PREACHING CHRIST
FROM THE OLD TESTAMENT   33

THE LACK OF PREACHING CHRIST FROM
THE OLD TESTAMENT   33

    The Temptation of Human-Centered Preaching   34

The Concern about Forced Interpretation 36

The Separation of the Old Testament from the New 37

THE UNIQUE CHARACTER OF THE OLD TESTAMENT 39

The Old Testament Is Sub-Christian 39

The Old Testament Is Non-Christian 39

The Old Testament Is Pre-Christian 40

The Old Testament Is Christian 44

THE RELATION OF THE OLD TESTAMENT TO THE NEW 46

The Old Testament Is Open to the Future 46

A Single Redemptive History Underlies Both Testaments 48

Jesus Christ Is the Link between the Two Testaments 49

The New Testament Writers Fused Their Writings
with the Old Testament 50

The Old Testament Must Be Interpreted
from the Perspective of the New 51

THE OLD TESTAMENT'S WITNESS TO CHRIST 53

Various Options in Preaching Christ
from the Old Testament 54

New Testament Insights into Preaching Christ
from the Old Testament 55

BENEFITS OF PREACHING CHRIST FROM THE OLD
TESTAMENT 62

Acquainting People with the Old Testament 63

Providing a Fuller Understanding of Christ 63

3. THE HISTORY OF PREACHING CHRIST
FROM THE OLD TESTAMENT (I) 69

ALLEGORICAL INTERPRETATION 70

Background 70

The Apostolic Fathers 73

The School of Alexandria   80

Evaluation of Allegorical Interpretation   87

TYPOLOGICAL INTERPRETATION   90

Background   90

The School of Antioch   91

Evaluation of Typological Interpretation   96

FOURFOLD INTERPRETATION   98

Background   98

The Four Senses of Scripture   98

Evaluation of Fourfold Interpretation   107

4. **THE HISTORY OF PREACHING CHRIST
   FROM THE OLD TESTAMENT (II)**   **111**

CHRISTOLOGICAL INTERPRETATION   111

The Young Luther   111

Luther's Hermeneutical Method   113

Luther's Christological Interpretation of the Old Testament   119

Luther's Preaching of Christ   121

Evaluation of Luther's Christological Interpretation   124

THEOCENTRIC INTERPRETATION   127

Calvin   127

Calvin's Hermeneutical Method   128

Calvin's Theocentric Interpretation of the Old Testament   137

Calvin's Theocentric Preaching   145

Evaluation of Calvin's Theocentric Interpretation   148

MODERN CHRISTOLOGICAL INTERPRETATIONS   151

Spurgeon   151

Wilhelm Vischer   163

5. **NEW TESTAMENT PRINCIPLES FOR PREACHING
   CHRIST FROM THE OLD TESTAMENT**   **177**

CHRIST-CENTERED PREACHING IS TO BE
   GOD-CENTERED   178

The Danger of Christomonism   178

Preaching Christ to the Glory of God   179

Concern about Preaching the Holy Spirit   181

INTERPRET THE OLD TESTAMENT FROM
   THE REALITY OF CHRIST   182

Understanding the Old Testament from
   the Reality of Christ   184

New Testament Use of the Old Testament   185

New Testament Presuppositions for Interpreting
   the Old Testament   191

MANY ROADS LEAD FROM THE OLD TESTAMENT
   TO CHRIST   203

The Way of Redemptive-Historical Progression   203

The Way of Promise-Fulfillment   206

The Way of Typology   212

The Way of Analogy   220

The Way of Longitudinal Themes   222

The Way of Contrast   224

6. **THE CHRISTOCENTRIC METHOD**   **227**

REDEMPTIVE-HISTORICAL CHRISTOCENTRIC
   INTERPRETATION   227

First, Understand the Passage in Its Own
   Historical Context   228

Next, Understand the Message in the Contexts
   of Canon and Redemptive History   230

THE WAY OF REDEMPTIVE-HISTORICAL PROGRESSION   234
Pivotal Points in Redemptive History   235
Characteristics of Redemptive History   235
The Way of Redemptive-Historical Progression   237

THE WAY OF PROMISE-FULFILLMENT   240
Special Rules for Promise-Fulfillment   242
Promises in the Prophets   242
Promises in the Psalms   244
Promises in Narrative   245
The Relevance of Using the Way of Promise-Fulfillment 248

THE WAY OF TYPOLOGY   249
Typology and Exegesis   250
Dangers along the Way of Typology   252
Typology Defined   254
Characteristics of Types   255
Rules for Using Typology   257
Examples of Types in Various Genres of Literature   260

THE WAY OF ANALOGY   261
The Way of Analogy for Preaching Christ
  from the Old Testament   262
Examples of Using Analogy in Various
  Genres of Literature   263

THE WAY OF LONGITUDINAL THEMES   266
Biblical Theology   266
Examples of Longitudinal Themes   267

THE WAY OF NEW TESTAMENT REFERENCES   269
The Use of New Testament References   269
Examples of Using New Testament References   269

THE WAY OF CONTRAST   271

  The Way of Contrast Centers in Christ   272

  Examples of the Way of Contrast in
    Various Genres of Literature   273

7. **STEPS FROM OLD TESTAMENT TEXT TO
   CHRISTOCENTRIC SERMON**   **279**

  TEN STEPS FROM OLD TESTAMENT TEXT TO
    CHRISTOCENTRIC SERMON   280

  First, Select a Textual Unit with an Eye to
    Congregational Needs   280

  Second, Read and Reread the Text in Its
    Literary Context   282

  Third, Outline the Structure of the Text   283

  Fourth, Interpret the Text in Its Own Historical Setting 284

  Fifth, Formulate the Text's Theme and Goal   286

  Sixth, Understand the Message in the Contexts
    of Canon and Redemptive History   287

  Seventh, Formulate the Sermon Theme and Goal   288

  Eighth, Select a Suitable Sermon Form   289

  Ninth, Prepare the Sermon Outline   290

  Tenth, Write the Sermon in Oral Style   292

  THE STEPS APPLIED TO GENESIS 22   292

8. **PRACTICING THE CHRISTOCENTRIC METHOD**   **319**

  TESTING THE CHRISTOCENTRIC METHOD
    AGAINST THE ALLEGORICAL   319

  Preaching on Noah and the Flood (Gen 6:9–8:22)   320

  Preaching on Israel and the Water of Marah
    (Exod 15:22-27)   325

  Preaching on Israel's Battle with Amalek
    (Exod 17:8-16)   328

Preaching on the Ceremony of the Red Heifer
(Numbers 19)   332

Preaching on the Destruction of Jericho and
the Salvation of Rahab (Joshua 2 and 6)   337

EXERCISES IN USING THE CHRISTOCENTRIC METHOD   345

APPENDICES   347
1. Steps from Text to Sermon   347
2. An Expository Sermon Model   349

Select Bibliography   351
Scripture Index   367
Subject Index   369

PREFACE

WHEN, after a twenty-five-year absence, I returned to my alma mater to teach preaching, I polled the faculty regarding the elective courses I should prepare. Of the six suggestions offered, the highest number of votes by far went for a proposed course entitled "Christocentric Preaching from the Old Testament." Unfortunately, I was unable to find a suitable textbook that explored this particular topic in depth. In fact, I was surprised to discover that since Wilhelm Vischer published *Das Christus Zeugnis des Alten Testaments* in 1936 very few authors have written books on the topic of preaching Christ from the Old Testament. Was it because Vischer strayed into the minefield of allegorizing that biblical scholars became disenchanted with this topic? Or did biblical scholarship turn against any form of christological interpretation of the Old Testament? Or were contemporary methods in biblical studies more appealing?

Since the late 1960s, biblical scholars have been exploring the Bible using exciting new methods such as rhetorical criticism, narrative criticism, and canonical criticism. They have been, and still are, gaining many new insights into the meaning of biblical texts. Although I much appreciate the value of these new methods for biblical preaching (see *The Modern Preacher and the Ancient Text*, 48-79), I am increasingly concerned that the exclusive use of these new tools for interpretation will cause us to miss the heart of Scripture. Preachers trained in these methods may know how to say many interesting truths about biblical texts, but will they know how to preach the Truth, Jesus Christ? The primary aim of this book is to provide seminary students and preachers with a responsible, contemporary method for preaching Christ from the Old Testament. A secondary, but no less important, aim is to challenge Old Testament scholars to broaden their focus and to understand the Old Testament not only in its own historical context but also in the context of the New Testament.

While I am aware that it has become fashionable in scholarly circles to designate the Old Testament as the "Hebrew Bible," I will continue to use the traditional term "Old Testament" for several reasons. First, we need not use the adjective "old" in the pejorative sense of antiquated and obsolete but will use it in the positive sense of venerable and valuable — like an *old* treasure that retains its value. Second, the term "Hebrew Bible" is not suitable for identifying the Scriptures cited by New Testament authors since they customarily used not Hebrew Scriptures but their Greek translation, the Septuagint. Third, and more substantively, I will continue to use the term "Old Testament" because the traditional distinction between the Old and New Testaments rests on a distinction made in the Old Testament itself between the old covenant and the new covenant (Jer 31:31-33; cf. 2 Cor 3:14). Finally, the terms "Old Testament" and "New Testament" indicate not only the relation of these two canonical collections to the historical old and new covenants God made with his people (*testamentum* being the Latin translation in the Vulgate of the Greek word *diathēkē*, that is, covenant) but also the relation of these two collections to each other, signifying their continuity ("Testament") as well as their discontinuity ("old" and "new"). These biblical and confessional connections are too important to lose by replacing "Old Testament" with the fashionable but inaccurate term "Hebrew Bible."[1]

We are about to embark on a journey of discovery. Our voyage will take us from the necessity of preaching Christ to the necessity of preaching from the Old Testament (Chapter 1), to the necessity of preaching Christ from the Old Testament (Chapter 2), to the struggles in church history to attain this requirement (Chapters 3 and 4). We expect to learn from the failures as well as the triumphs. Meanwhile, we will have to sort through many fundamental issues on which there is no agreement among contemporary scholars. For example: What do we mean precisely by preaching *Christ*? Is God-centered preaching of the Old Testament sufficient, or should preachers aim for explicitly Christ-centered sermons? Is the Old Testament a sub-Christian, a pre-Christian, or a Christian book? Should the Old Testament be interpreted in its own context, in the context of the New Testament, or both? Does or does not the Old Testament witness to Christ, and, if so, how? Is typological interpretation in the same league with allegorical interpretation? Is the New Testament use of the

---

1. A few other technical details: I have generally followed the latest *Chicago Manual of Style* (1993). Wherever I have added italics in quotations, I have so indicated, except for biblical quotations, where it is self-evident that I added the italics. To keep the footnotes short but functional, I usually provide only the author's name, key word(s) of the title, and pages. Complete information can be found in the Bibliography. Where an article or book is not selected for the Bibliography, I have supplied full information in the first reference to this article or book.

Old Testament normative for preachers today, or is this "precritical" interpretation outdated (Chapter 5)? And how, specifically, does one go about preaching Christ from the Old Testament in a responsible manner (Chapter 6)? We will conclude our journey by suggesting specific steps for moving from Old Testament text to Christian sermon (Chapter 7) and by providing concrete examples of ways of preaching Christ from the Old Testament (Chapter 8).

Grand Rapids, Michigan   SIDNEY GREIDANUS

ACKNOWLEDGMENTS

AT THE beginning of this book I wish to express my deep appreciation to all who contributed to its publication. I thank the Calvin Alumni Association for funding my travel to South Africa in 1993 for five months of research at three major Reformed universities. I also wish to thank the staff of the libraries in Stellenbosch, Bloemfontein, and Potchefstroom for their courteous service.

I am also grateful to the Calvin Seminary Heritage Fund for underwriting further research in Europe in 1997, especially at Tyndale House, Cambridge, England. I thank the staff of Tyndale House and its supporters for providing an ideal atmosphere for conducting biblical research.

In North America, the splendid library of Calvin College and Seminary also served me very well. I am grateful to the Calvin library staff for its helpful service, for tracking down articles and books, and for ordering some by way of inter-library loan.

I also want to express my gratitude to my student assistants: Cindy Holtrop, particularly for typing the original, lengthy bibliography in proper form, and David Vroege, particularly for proofreading the entire manuscript and working on the subject and text indexes. I further thank the staff at Eerdmans for their capable work.

I especially wish to thank a few experts in Old Testament interpretation and theology who took time out of their busy schedules to proofread part or all of the manuscript. Richard A. Muller, Professor of Historical Theology at Calvin Seminary, checked the historical chapters, while Ronald J. Feenstra, Professor of Systematic and Philosophical Theology, and John H. Stek, Professor (Emeritus) of Old Testament, at the Seminary, checked and commented on the entire manuscript. Family members were also involved in this project: my sister, Janice Greidanus Baker, teacher of French in Sarnia, Ontario, read the whole manuscript for readability, and my brother-in-law, George Vandervelde, Senior Member in Systematic

Theology at the Institute for Christian Studies in Toronto, offered numerous worthwhile suggestions.

A special word of thanks is due to my faithful wife and best friend, Marie. She not only encouraged me in this major project but accompanied me on many trips to libraries on various continents, took notes, typed bibliographical entries, searched the stacks for books and articles, copied relevant pages, filed and refiled books and articles in my study, and never complained.

Above all, I am thankful to the Lord for providing so much encouragement for this project through relatives and friends, fellow church members, and scholars in different countries. I also thank the Lord for providing me with good health during the years of research, for sudden flashes of insight for solving perplexing problems, and for constant joy in working on this important project.

The Board of Trustees of Calvin Theological Seminary granted me not only a sabbatical leave but also a publication leave to finish this book. I thank the board members for their confidence in me. And I thank my colleagues and students for their helpful comments. I dedicate this book to all involved in the mission of Calvin Seminary.

To the Students, Staff, and Supporters
of Calvin Theological Seminary
Grand Rapids, Michigan

ABBREVIATIONS

BSac	Bibliotheca Sacra
CBQ	Catholic Biblical Quarterly
CO	Calvini Opera — Corpus Reformatorum
Comm.	Calvin's Commentaries
CR	Corpus Reformatorum
CTJ	Calvin Theological Journal
CTM	Concordia Theological Monthly
CurTM	Currents in Theology and Mission
EvQ	Evangelical Quarterly
ExpT	Expository Times
GTJ	Grace Theological Journal
HorBT	Horizons of Biblical Theology
Int	Interpretation
ISBE	International Standard Bible Encyclopedia
JETS	Journal of the Evangelical Theological Society
JSOT	Journal for the Study of the Old Testament
LuthQ	Lutheran Quarterly
LW	Luther's Works — American Edition
NGTT	Nederduitse Gereformeerde Teologiese Tydskrif
NTS	New Testament Studies
PG	Patrologia Graeca
PL	Patrologia Latina
RevExp	Review and Expositor
SJT	Scottish Journal of Theology
TDNT	Theological Dictionary of the New Testament
Th	Theology
TynBul	Tyndale Bulletin
WA	Weimarer Ausgabe, Luther's Werke
WTJ	Westminster Theological Journal

CHAPTER 1

Preaching Christ and Preaching the Old Testament

"We preach Christ crucified . . . , Christ the power of God and the wisdom of God."

Paul, 1 Corinthians 1:23-24 (NIV)

THIS BOOK deals with preaching Christ from the Old Testament. Before we turn our attention specifically to this topic, we need to lay the foundations on which to build subsequently. In this opening chapter, we shall discuss two distinct topics: (1) the necessity of preaching *Christ*, and (2) the necessity of preaching from the *Old Testament*. In Chapter 2 we shall merge the results of our discoveries as we discuss the necessity of preaching *Christ from the Old Testament*.

THE NECESSITY OF PREACHING CHRIST

Homileticians from a wide variety of Christian traditions advocate the preaching of Christ. For example, the Roman Catholic author Domenico Grasso states, "The object and content of preaching is Christ, the Word in which the Father expresses Himself and communicates His will to man."[1] The Eastern Orthodox Georges Florovsky asserts, "Ministers are commissioned and ordained in the church precisely to preach the Word of God.

1. Grasso, *Proclaiming*, 6.

1

They are given some fixed terms of reference — namely, the gospel of Jesus Christ — and they are committed to this sole and perennial message."[2] The Lutheran homiletician M. Reu contends, "It is necessary that the sermon be Christocentric, have no one and nothing else for its centre and content than Christ Jesus."[3] The Reformed homiletician T. Hoekstra maintains, "In expositing Scripture for the congregation, the preacher . . . must show that there is a way to the center even from the farthest point on the periphery. For a sermon without Christ is no sermon."[4] And the Baptist preacher Charles Spurgeon says, "Preach Christ, always and everywhere. He is the whole gospel. His person, offices, and work must be our one great, all-comprehending theme."[5] Authors from a broad spectrum of traditions, therefore, testify to the necessity of preaching Christ.[6]

Confusion about the Meaning of "Preaching Christ"

Unfortunately, one could make a similar list of people complaining that the actual practice of preaching Christ falls far short of the ideal. One reason for this failure may be the difficulty of preaching Christ from the Old Testament. This problem is compounded by the lack of concrete directions in textbooks on Old Testament interpretation and preaching. Horror stories abound of preachers twisting an Old Testament text in order to land miraculously at Calvary. But subverting the Scriptures in order to preach Christ only undermines the authority of the message.

To some, the notion of "preaching Christ" also seems rather narrow and confining, far removed from that other ideal of Christian preachers, namely, preaching "the whole counsel of God" (Acts 20:27). Does one

2. Florovsky, *Bible*, 9.

3. Reu, *Homiletics*, 57.

4. Hoekstra, *Homiletiek*, 172 (my translation). Cf. Abraham Kuyper, quoted by C. Veenhof, *Predik*, 20 (my translation), "Believers rightly require that every sermon present the Christ."

5. Spurgeon, *Lectures to My Students*, 194.

6. See also, e.g., James Stewart, *Heralds*, 54, "If we are not determined that in every sermon Christ is to be preached, it were better that we should resign our commission forthwith and seek some other vocation." R. B. Kuiper, "Scriptural Preaching," 239, "Truly Scriptural preaching, therefore, cannot but be christocentric." Edmund Clowney, *Preaching and Biblical Theology*, 74, "He who would preach the Word must preach Christ." Jay Adams, *Preaching with Purpose*, 152, "Preach Christ in all the Scriptures: He is the subject matter of the whole Bible. He is there. Until you have found Him in your preaching portion, you are not ready to preach." David Larsen, *Anatomy of Preaching*, 163, "The Christian proclaimer, whether preaching from the Old Testament or the New, must present Christ as the ultimate frame of reference."

preach Christ, for example, at the expense of preaching other Christian doctrines, Christian living, or social justice concerns?

But there are other reasons as well for the general failure to preach Christ. Strange as it may seem, we are not at all clear on what it means to "preach Christ." Although the meaning seems simple on the surface, it is complicated by several factors, not the least of which is that Christ is both the eternal Logos, who is present from the beginning (John 1:1), and Christ incarnate, who is present only after Old Testament times (John 1:14). This complexity reveals itself in the wide variety of meanings that have attached themselves to the phrase "preaching Christ."[7] For some, preaching Christ means preaching "Christ crucified" in the sense of linking every text to Calvary and Christ's atoning work on the cross. Others broaden the meaning to preaching "Christ's death and resurrection." Still others seek to link the text to the work of the eternal Logos, who is active in Old Testament times especially as the Angel of Yahweh, the Commander of the Lord's army, and the Wisdom of God. Others broaden the meaning even further to preaching sermons that center on God, for, it is argued, since Christ is the second person of the Trinity and fully God, a God-centered sermon is Christ-centered. Still others argue that "the Lord Jesus Christ is recognized as Jehovah," and therefore we can substitute the name of Christ wherever we see "Jehovah" in the Old Testament.[8]

At the beginning of this book on preaching Christ from the Old Testament, it would be well to come to clarity on what we mean by "preaching Christ." But instead of adding another definition to a long list, we will find it far more valuable to examine the New Testament regarding the meaning of "preaching Christ." After all, the apostles first coined the phrase.

---

7. Note a similar confusion in systematic theology. "Theologians as different from each other as Luther and Socinus, Karl Barth and Paul Tillich speak of Christ being the center of the Scriptures," but what they mean by this is different for each. Robert D. Preus, "A Response to the Unity of the Bible," 677.

8. William Robinson, "Jesus Christ Is Jehovah," *EvQ* 5 (1933) 145. Cf. T. W. Calloway, *Christ in the Old Testament* (New York: Loizeaux, 1950), e.g., chap. 1, "'Jehovah' of the Old Testament the Christ of the New." Also Howard A. Hanke, *Christ and the Church in the Old Testament* (Grand Rapids: Zondervan, 1957), e.g., p. 173, "In the Old Testament our Lord was revealed to man under the name of Christ (Jehovah); in the New Testament He revealed Himself in the name of Yahshua or Christ (Jesus)."

The New Testament on "Preaching Christ"

The Heart of Apostolic Preaching

The heart of apostolic preaching is Jesus Christ. Richard Lischer notes, "A cursory review of the objects of the New Testament verbs for 'preach' shows how saturated with Christ that early proclamation was. Some of the objects are: Jesus, Lord Jesus, Christ, Jesus Christ as Lord, Christ crucified, Christ as raised from the dead, Jesus and the resurrection, good news about the Kingdom, Jesus as the Son of God, the gospel of God, Word of the Lord, the forgiveness of sins, and Christ in you — the hope of glory."[9] As the objects of the verbs for preaching demonstrate, there can be no doubt that Christ is the heart of apostolic preaching. Yet this result does not resolve our predicament. Does "Christ" refer to Christ as the Second Person of the Trinity? Or to Christ as the eternal Logos? Or to Christ crucified? Or to the risen and exalted Lord? Or to all of the above? To find the answer, we will have to explore the New Testament further.

In his book *The Apostolic Preaching and Its Development*, C. H. Dodd concludes that the first four speeches of Peter in Acts provide "a comprehensive view of the content of the early *kerygma*." He summarizes the contents of this preaching under six heads: First, "the age of fulfillment has dawned." Second, "this has taken place through the ministry, death, and resurrection of Jesus, of which a brief account is given." Third, "by virtue of the resurrection, Jesus has been exalted at the right hand of God, as Messianic head of the new Israel." Fourth, "the Holy Spirit in the Church is the sign of Christ's present power and glory." Fifth, "the Messianic Age will shortly reach its consummation in the return of Christ." And finally, "the *kerygma* always closes with an appeal for repentance, the offer of forgiveness and of the Holy Spirit, and the promise of 'salvation.'"[10]

A quick scrutiny of these six elements indicates that preaching in the New Testament church indeed centered on Jesus Christ — but not in the narrow sense of focussing only on Christ crucified, nor in the broadest sense of focussing only on the Second Person of the Trinity or the eternal Logos. The New Testament church preached the birth, ministry, death, resurrection, and exaltation of Jesus of Nazareth as the fulfillment of God's old covenant promises, his presence today in the Spirit, and his imminent return. In short, "preaching Christ" meant preaching Christ incarnate in the context of the full sweep of redemptive history.

9. Lischer, *Theology of Preaching*, 73.
10. Dodd, *Apostolic Preaching*, 38-43.

The Breadth of Preaching Christ

We can observe the tremendous breadth of the concept "preaching Christ" by following the apostles from preaching Christ crucified, to preaching Christ risen, to preaching the kingdom of God.

Jesus' Cross

Defenders of the narrow view that "preaching Christ" means only preaching the cross often appeal to the explicit statements of the apostle Paul. In 1 Corinthians 1:23 Paul reminds the church in Corinth, "We preach Christ crucified . . ." (NIV); and again in the next chapter, "I decided to know nothing among you except Jesus Christ, and him crucified" (1 Cor 2:2). However, Reu rightly cautions that the preacher should not "divorce the cross of Christ from His life, teaching and works, as preachers of the 'old faith' were accused of doing."[11] For Paul, preaching "Christ crucified" has a much broader meaning than focussing every sermon on Jesus' suffering on the cross. The cross of Christ is indeed the focal point for Paul's preaching, but, as Paul's sermons and letters demonstrate, the cross of Christ reveals much more than the suffering of Jesus. It also provides a viewpoint on the perfect justice of God (Rom 3:25-26) and the dreadful catastrophe of human sin. "The cross . . . signifies as nothing else could possibly do the awful seriousness of our sin, and therefore the depth and quality of the penitence that is required of us and that only the remembrance of it and the appropriation of its meaning can create in us."[12]

But much more than the depth of sin and penitence is seen in the light of the cross. The cross of Christ also provides a view of the wondrous love of God for his creatures and creation (Rom 5:9-10; 8:32-34). "What the first Christians came to see was this — that God was there as nowhere else. This thing occurred, declared Peter in the first Christian sermon, . . . 'by the determinate counsel and foreknowledge of God.' They never preached the Cross without saying, 'This is God's deed, God's purpose in action, God's way of bringing a mad and ruined world back to health and sanity and peace.'"[13]

On a time line, the cross is but a point in the sweep of redemptive history from creation to the new creation. But exactly in the sweep of redemptive history, the cross is such a pivotal point that its impact echoes

11. Reu, *Homiletics,* 59.
12. John Knox, *Chapters,* 126.
13. Stewart, *Faith to Proclaim,* 98.

all the way back to the fall of humanity and God's penalty of *death* (Gen 3:19), even while it thrusts kingdom history forward to its full perfection — when all the nations will come in, there will be no more death and tears, and God will be all and in all (Rev 21:1-4). For, says Paul, "In Christ God was reconciling the world to himself, not counting their trespasses against them" (2 Cor 5:19).

Jesus' Resurrection

In addition to bringing to view the vast vistas provided by the cross of Christ, Paul's preaching focusses equally on the resurrection of Christ. Even the seemingly limited focus found in 1 Corinthians 2:2 of Paul knowing "nothing among you except Jesus Christ, and him crucified" may contain a much broader perspective. John Knox helpfully explains, "At first sight this last phrase ['and him crucified'] seems to leave out the Resurrection entirely. But it seems to do so only because we suppose Paul's thought was moving, as ours customarily does, in a forward direction. . . . But when Paul wrote the phrase, he was thinking first of all of the risen, exalted Christ, and his thought moved *backward* to the cross. . . . Thus, far from omitting reference to the Resurrection, Paul's phrase takes its start from it; the word *Christ* means primarily the one now known as living and present Lord."[14]

Other passages state more directly that Paul focusses equally on the resurrection of Christ. For example, when Paul and Barnabas preached in the synagogue of Antioch of Pisidia, Paul proclaimed, "God raised him from the dead. . . . And we bring you the good news that what God promised to our ancestors he has fulfilled for us, their children, by raising Jesus . . ." (Acts 13:30, 32; cf. Acts 17:31). Again, "Remember Jesus Christ, raised from the dead, a descendant of David — that is my gospel" (2 Tim 2:8). Consequently, James Stewart advises preachers, "I would urge you to preach the Resurrection as the one fact above all others which vitally concerns, not only the life of the individual Christian but the entire human scene and the destiny of the race. It is the break-through of the eternal order into this world of suffering and confusion and sin and death. . . . It is the vindication of eternal righteousness, the declaration that the heart of the universe is spiritual. It is the Kingdom of God made visible."[15]

---

14. Knox, *Chapters*, 109. Cf. Stewart, *Faith to Proclaim*, 111, "'Knowing Christ' means here what it means regularly in Paul: the primary reference is not to the Jesus of history but to the exalted, ever present Lord. . . . to preach 'Christ and Him crucified' is emphatically a Resurrection *kerygma*."

15. Stewart, *Heralds*, 89.

But we ought not to play the crucifixion and the resurrection off against each other. "The death and resurrection of Jesus are from the very beginning inseparably interconnected in the kerygma. They are the two aspects of *one* salvatory happening, continually calling each other to mind."[16] In fact, in the very letter in which Paul states that he preaches "Christ crucified" (1 Cor 1:23; 2:2), he reminds the Corinthians "of the good news that I proclaimed to you. . . . For I handed on to you as of first importance what I in turn had received: that Christ died for our sins in accordance with the scriptures, and that he was buried, and that he was raised on the third day in accordance with the scriptures . . ." (1 Cor 15:1-4; cf. 15:12).

The Kingdom of God

Preaching the death and resurrection of Christ, we have seen, was more than recounting the facts concerning Jesus of Nazareth.[17] These two events provided remarkably profound insights into God's justice, love, and final victory and into human sin, punishment, and salvation.[18] But they also provided viewpoints for perceiving the grand sweep of God's plan of salvation as it unfolded in redemptive history.[19] The early Christian preachers proclaimed that "in these two shattering events, now seen to be one, the Kingdom of God had broken in with power. . . . What had formerly been pure eschatology was there before their eyes: the supernatural made visible, the Word made flesh. No longer were they dreaming of the Kingdom age: they were living in it. It had arrived."[20]

Accordingly, preaching Christ was intimately related to preaching the kingdom of God. Paul acknowledged that he also preached "Jesus Christ as Lord" (2 Cor 4:5), that is, as the Ruler who has received "all authority" (Matt 28:18). In Jesus Christ the kingdom of God had come. The

---

16. J. Kahmann, *Bible*, 82. Cf. Raymond Brown, *Biblical Exegesis*, 141, "If one cannot understand the resurrection properly without the cross, one cannot understand either the cross or the resurrection without understanding the Jesus who reached out to heal the sick . . . who proclaimed God's blessing to the poor and the oppressed."

17. It was proclaiming these events, too, of course. See, e.g., 1 Cor 15:12-20 and 2 Pet 1:16. "It was the announcement of certain concrete facts of history, the heralding of real, objective events. Its keynote was, 'That which we have seen and heard declare we unto you.'" Stewart, *Heralds*, 62-64.

18. For example, Paul marveled that to him was given the grace "to preach to the Gentiles the unsearchable riches of Christ" (Eph 3:8, NIV).

19. Note Paul's emphasis (repetition) in 1 Corinthians 15 on "in accordance with the scriptures."

20. Stewart, *Heralds*, 64.

book of Acts ends with the stirring picture of Paul in custody in Rome —
the kingdom of God has not yet arrived in perfection. But the great Apostle is in Rome, the center of the world, "proclaiming the kingdom of God
and teaching about the Lord Jesus Christ" (Acts 28:31; cf. Acts 20:25).

The Meaning of "Preaching Christ"

On the basis of this New Testament testimony, we can sketch the contours
of what "preaching Christ" means. To clear the deck, it may be well to
state first what it is not. Preaching Christ is not, of course, merely men-
tioning the name of Jesus or Christ in the sermon. It is not identifying
Christ with Yahweh in the Old Testament, or the Angel of Yahweh, or the
Commander of the Lord's army, or the Wisdom of God. It is not simply
pointing to Christ from a distance or "drawing lines to Christ" by way of
typology.

Positively, preaching Christ is as broad as preaching the gospel of
the kingdom of God. One has only to look at a concordance to see how often the New Testament speaks of "the gospel of the kingdom," "the gospel of Christ," "the gospel of Jesus Christ," "the gospel of the grace of
God," and "the gospel of peace." In these terms two characteristics stand
out. Preaching Christ is good news for people, and preaching Christ is as
broad as preaching the gospel of the kingdom — as long as this kingdom
is related to its King, Jesus.

More specifically, to preach Christ is to proclaim some facet of the
person, work, or *teaching* of Jesus of Nazareth so that people may believe
him, trust him, love him, and obey him. We shall take a closer look at
each of these aspects.

The Person of Christ

The distinction between the person and the work of Christ is fairly common (and controversial) in systematic theology[21] and in the literature
about preaching Christ. The distinction should never lead to a separation
between the person and the work of Christ, of course, for the two are inseparably intertwined.[22] Still, the distinction has merit in highlighting
certain facets of the Messiah. Jesus himself asked his disciples, "Who do

21. See G. C. Berkouwer, *Person of Christ,* 101-6.
22. "Not to know who he is means: not to understand what his work is; and not
to see his work in the right perspective is not to understand his person. . . . Therefore
the revelation of God illumines both Christ's person and work." Berkouwer, ibid., 105.

you say that I am?" Peter's answer, "You are the Messiah, the Son of the living God," was a revelation from God himself, Jesus said (Matt 16:16-17). Knowing who Jesus was (Messiah, Son of God) helped the disciples understand somewhat the profound significance of his work of preaching and healing and dying and rising.

In fact, John *begins* his Gospel with the identity of the person of Christ. He writes, "No one has ever seen God. It is God the only Son, who is close to the Father's heart, who has made him known" (John 1:18). The person of Jesus Christ, God's only Son, is the climax of God's revelation about himself. In Jesus we see God. He has made God known. Similarly, the letter to the Hebrews begins with the identity of the person of Christ: "He is the reflection of God's glory and the exact imprint of God's very being" (1:3).

In preaching Christ from the Old Testament, we can often link the Old Testament message to some facet of the person of Christ: the Son of God, the Messiah, our Prophet, Priest, and King.

The Work of Christ

In preaching Christ, we can also focus on a facet of the work of Christ. The Gospel writer John moves from the person of Jesus to some of the "signs" (works) he did, "so that you may come to believe that Jesus is the Messiah, the Son of God, and that through believing you may have life in his name" (John 20:31).

Usually the work of Christ is associated with his work of reconciling us to God (atonement) through his suffering and death. But we can also think of his miracles of healing (signs of the presence of the kingdom), his resurrection (victory over death), his ascension (the enthronement of the King), and his coming again (the coming kingdom). In preaching Christ from the Old Testament, we can often link the message of the text with the redeeming work of our Savior and the just rule of our Lord.

The Teaching of Christ

Although the teaching of Christ could be considered part of the work of Christ, Jesus' teaching is often overlooked in discussions on preaching Christ from the Old Testament.[23] Because of its significance for our topic, we shall consider the teaching of Christ separately.

23. Perhaps in reaction to liberal theology and social gospel preaching in the early 1900s with its almost exclusive focus on the *teaching* of Christ. See Meade Williams, *Princeton Theological Review* 4 (1906) 191-95.

The importance of Jesus' teaching rises to the surface with Jesus' own statement, "If you hold to my teaching, you are really my disciples. Then you will know the truth, and the truth will set you free" (John 8:31-32, NIV). The crucial importance of the teaching of Christ shows up especially in Christ's mandate to his disciples to "make disciples of all nations, baptizing them . . . , and teaching them to observe everything *I have commanded you*" (Matt 28:19-20). The teaching of Jesus is an indispensable component for preaching Christ from the Old Testament, for the Old Testament was Jesus' Bible, and he based his teaching on it. Jesus' teaching includes not only teachings about himself (Son of Man, Messiah), his mission, and his coming again but also teachings about God, God's kingdom, God's covenant, God's law (e.g., Matt 5–7), and the like.

Summing up this section, we can define "preaching Christ" as *preaching sermons which authentically integrate the message of the text with the climax of God's revelation in the person, work, and/or teaching of Jesus Christ as revealed in the New Testament.*

Reasons for Preaching Christ Today

In response to the question why we should preach Christ today, many might respond by pointing to the example of the apostles: If Peter and Paul preached Christ, then preachers today must preach Christ. But this argument from imitation is rather superficial and flawed. To imitate Paul in preaching Christ is rather selective imitation, for most of us do not imitate Paul in going on missionary journeys to do our preaching. Nor do we imitate Paul in going first to the synagogues to do our preaching. Nor do we imitate Paul in literally making tents to support a "tentmaking ministry." In all these and other instances we realize that biblical *description* of what Paul was doing does not necessarily translate into biblical *prescription* for us today.[24] So we must dig deeper to make the case for preaching Christ today. We must ask ourselves: What were the underlying reasons for Paul and the other apostles to preach Christ? And do these reasons still hold for preachers today?

---

24. Reading biblical description as biblical prescription is a common form of the genre mistake, i.e., reading the genre of historical or autobiographical narrative as if it were the genre of law or exhortation. See my *Modern Preacher*, 17, 165.

Jesus' Command: "Go . . . and Make Disciples of All Nations. . . ."

A frequently overlooked but obvious reason why the apostles preached Christ was Jesus' parting command: "Go . . . and make disciples of all nations, baptizing them in the name of the Father and of the Son and of the Holy Spirit, and teaching them to obey everything that I have commanded you. And remember, I am with you always, to the end of the age" (Matt 28:19-20). Although the baptismal formula is trinitarian, the command to make "disciples [of Jesus]" and to "teach . . . them to obey everything that I have commanded you," and the promise of Jesus' presence — all focus specifically on Jesus Christ. The apostle Peter later recalls, "He commanded us to preach to the people and to testify that he is the one ordained by God as judge of the living and the dead" (Acts 10:42).

Even the apostle Paul, who did not receive the original mandate, would later receive the specific command to preach Christ. While he was on the way to Damascus to persecute Christians, the living Lord intercepted him: "I am Jesus, whom you are persecuting. But get up and enter the city, and you will be told what you are to do." Then Jesus told Ananias to meet Paul, "for he is an instrument whom I have chosen to bring my name before the Gentiles and kings and before the people of Israel" (Acts 9:5-6, 15).

The apostles, then, were commanded by their risen Lord to preach his "name" (the revelation concerning Jesus) among the nations, and they responded by preaching Jesus Christ. A few decades later, the Gospel writers accepted this original mandate as their mandate. For example, in writing his Gospel, Mark reveals his central concern in his opening verse: "The beginning of the good news of Jesus Christ, the Son of God." Christian preachers today also live under the command to preach the "name" of Jesus Christ, for the command to preach Christ reaches far beyond the first apostles and Gospel writers — it reaches "to the end of the age."

Exciting News: The King Has Come!

In addition to obedience to Jesus' mandate, another major reason for preaching Christ lies in the message itself. Even today when a President or a Queen visits a city, the arrival itself is a newsworthy event. No one needs to command broadcasters to tell the story, for the story itself begs to be told. If this is true for the arrival of a President or a Queen, how much more for the arrival of "the King of Kings." After centuries of waiting for God's promised Messiah, after many high expectations and more dashed hopes, the story of his arrival simply has to be proclaimed.

For example, when Peter's brother Andrew met Jesus, he found a natural outlet for his excitement: "The first thing Andrew did was to find his brother Simon and tell him, 'We have found the Messiah'. . . . And he brought him to Jesus" (John 1:41-42, NIV). Andrew's need to tell was but a small foretaste of the church's missionary zeal after Jesus' resurrection. This story simply has to be told: God has fulfilled his promises; his salvation has become a reality; the kingdom of God has broken into this world in a wonderful new way; the King has come!

Life-Giving News: "Believe on the Lord Jesus, and You Will Be Saved."

Another major reason for preaching Christ lies in the life-saving character of the message. When there was an outbreak of polio in British Columbia, Canada, in the 1970s, the government wasted no time getting out the message to all parents to have their children inoculated against polio. It was a vital message; it needed to be broadcast immediately. The need to tell was obvious in the light of the disease and the availability of an antidote.

Ever since the fall into sin, humanity has been alienated from God and under the penalty of death. Everyone with discernment can recognize the disease, but not all know the cure. People need to be told about the cure. When the Philippian jailer cried out, "What must I do to be saved?" Paul answered, "Believe on the Lord Jesus, and you will be saved, you and your household" (Acts 16:30-31). As Paul put it a few years later, "If you confess with your lips that Jesus is Lord and believe in your heart that God raised him from the dead, you will be saved" (Rom 10:9). Faith in Jesus Christ is the antidote for eternal death. In a world dead in sin, alienated from God, headed for death, the life-giving message of Jesus Christ is so urgent that it simply must be told. For it is a message of hope, of reconciliation, of peace with God, of healing, of restoration, of salvation, of eternal life.

Exclusive News: "There Is Salvation in No One Else."

A further stimulus for preaching Christ is that Christ is the only way of salvation. As Peter puts it, "There is salvation in no one else, for there is no other name under heaven given among mortals by which we must be saved" (Acts 4:12). Peter's hopeful but exclusive message echoes the message of Jesus himself, "I am the way, and the truth, and the life. No one comes to the Father except through me."[25] Eternal life is to be found only in Jesus Christ.

25. John 14:6; cf. John 15:5; 17; Matt 11:27; 2 Cor 5:20-21; 2 Tim 2:5.

If Jesus were one of many ways of salvation, the church could relax a bit, hoping that people might find some other way to be saved from death. But now that Christ is the only way, the urgency of preaching Christ is all the more pressing. There is salvation in no one else but Jesus.[26]

All of the above reasons for preaching Christ hold today as much as they did in the times of the New Testament church, for Jesus' command is valid "till the end of the age." In a century which counts more Christian martyrs than in all of church history, the good news that the King has come is as significant and encouraging as ever; in a materialistic age in which people despair of the meaning of human life, the vital news that there is salvation from death through faith in Christ is as crucial as ever; and in our relativistic, pluralistic society with its many so-called saviors, the exclusive news that there is salvation in no one else but Jesus Christ is as essential as ever.

Hearers in a Non-Christian Culture

The final reason for preaching Christ is that our hearers are living in a non-Christian culture. The early church, in the nature of the case, addressed people living in a non-Christian culture. People needed to hear about Christ and the difference he makes. But contemporary preachers equally address people living in a non-Christian or post-Christian culture. If contemporary hearers were living in a culture saturated with Christian thinking and action, one might perhaps take for granted that people hearing a sermon would sense how it is related to Christ. For all of life is related to Christ. As Paul writes, "He [Christ] is the image of the invisible God . . . ; for in him all things in heaven and on earth were created . . . — all things have been created through him and for him. He himself is before all things, and in him all things hold together" (Col 1:15-17). But preachers today cannot assume that their hearers will see these connections; they cannot even assume that their hearers will know the meaning of words like "gospel" and "God" and "Christ."

Non-Christian Hearers

Europe and North America have become mission fields. People have lost their way and are searching for the Ultimate, for meaning to their brief existence on earth. Church services are fast moving from Christian wor-

---

26. See, e.g., Allan Harman, "No Other Name," *Theological Forum* 24 (November 1996) 43-53.

ship to "seeker services." Today, both in Christian worship (seeker sensitive, one would hope) and in seeker services, Christ needs to be preached. "One of the most fascinating of all the preacher's tasks," John Stott writes, "is to explore both the emptiness of fallen man and the fullness of Jesus Christ, in order then to demonstrate how he can fill our emptiness, lighten our darkness, enrich our poverty, and bring our human aspirations to fulfillment."[27] For "to encounter Christ is to touch reality and experience transcendence. He gives us a sense of self-worth or personal significance, because he assures us of God's love for us. He sets us free from guilt because he died for us, from the prison of our own self-centredness by the power of his resurrection, and from paralyzing fear because he reigns. . . . He gives meaning to marriage and home, work and leisure, personhood and citizenship."[28]

Christian Hearers

Committed Christians as well as non-Christians will benefit from explicitly Christ-centered preaching today. In a post-Christian culture such preaching will enable Christians to sense the centrality of Christ in their lives and in the world. It will help them to distinguish their specific faith from that of Judaism, Eastern religions, the new age movement, the health-and-wealth gospel, and other competing faiths. It will continually build their faith in Jesus, their Savior and Lord. Preaching Christ in a non-Christian culture sustains Christians as water sustains nomads in the desert. Reu claims, "Genuine Christian faith and life can exist only so long as it remains a daily appropriation of Christ."[29] Even those committed to Christ must continually learn and relearn what it means to serve Jesus their Savior as Lord of their life.

Preaching in a post-Christian culture places a tremendous responsibility on contemporary preachers to preach Christ plainly, genuinely, and perceptively. Preachers can no longer assume that their hearers will discern the connections of the message with Christ in the context of a Christian mind-set and in the context of Christian worship. These connections need to be intentionally exposed for all to see. John Stott brings the goal into focus for contemporary preachers: "The main objective of preaching is to expound Scripture so faithfully and relevantly that Jesus Christ is perceived in all his adequacy to meet human need."[30] William Hull adds

27. Stott, *Between Two Worlds*, 154.
28. *Ibid.*
29. Reu, *Homiletics*, 57.
30. Stott, *Between Two Worlds*, 325.

this sound advice, "Let us not mount the pulpit to debate peripheral questions or to speculate on esoteric curiosities. . . . We are there to preach Jesus Christ as Lord. . . . That is our awesome assignment: to put into words, in such a way that our hearers will put into deeds, the new day that is ours in Jesus Christ our Lord."[31]

THE NECESSITY OF PREACHING
FROM THE OLD TESTAMENT

Before we focus our discussion of preaching Christ specifically on preaching Christ from the Old Testament (Chapter 2), we must first consider the general question of preaching from the *Old* Testament. It is no secret that the Old Testament is like a lost treasure in the church today. Comments like "the Old Testament was a closed book in my experience"[32] are indicative of a trend. W. A. Criswell claims that the Old Testament is "perhaps the most neglected area of the Bible in modern preaching," and that, when the Old Testament is used, "it is often only the text for some topical treatise that soon departs from its context."[33] Gleason Archer muses, "Curious to observe and hard to understand is the relative neglect of the Old Testament by Christians in our day as Sunday after Sunday the average church attendant in the average evangelical, Bible-believing church hears no message at all from the Hebrew Scriptures." And he asks, "How can Christian pastors hope to feed their flock on a well-balanced spiritual diet if they completely neglect the 39 books of Holy Scripture on which Christ and all the New Testament authors received their own spiritual nourishment?"[34]

Statistics are hard to come by, but from reports of several denominations it is safe to conclude that fewer than 20 percent of the sermons the average church member hears are based on an Old Testament text.[35] This figure is all the more telling when we remember that the Old Testament constitutes about three-fourths of the Christian canon. The editor of an

31. Hull, "Called to Preach," 47-48.
32. Thomas Ridenhour, "Old Testament and Preaching," 254.
33. Criswell, "Preaching from the Old Testament," 293.
34. Gleason L. Archer Jr., "A New Look at the Old Testament," *Decision,* August 1972, 5.
35. Cf. Herbert Mayer, "The Old Testament in the Pulpit," *CTM* 35 (1964) 603, "The Lutheran Church — Missouri Synod reveals an average of four or five New Testament studies for each Old Testament text." Cf. John Stapert, *Church Herald* [Reformed Church in America], July 13, 1979, 9, "The great majority of the sermons I have heard were exclusively or almost exclusively from the New Testament."

evangelical journal for preachers laments, "I annually receive hundreds of sermon manuscripts from ministers in a variety of Protestant denominations. . . . Less than one-tenth of the sermons submitted to *Preaching* are based on Old Testament texts."[36]

Reasons for the Lack of Preaching from the Old Testament

There may be many individual reasons for the lack of preaching from the Old Testament. We shall discuss four of the major ones: the use of lectionaries, critical Old Testament scholarship, the rejection of the Old Testament, and the difficulties of preaching from the Old Testament.

The Use of Lectionaries

The use of lectionaries has had both a positive and a negative impact on preaching from the Old Testament. Positively, by including Old Testament readings, lectionaries have certainly contributed to the Old Testament being heard again in Christian worship services. Foster McCurley acknowledges, "In my own Lutheran tradition it was not until . . . 1958 . . . that an Old Testament lesson was prescribed for weekly reading at the Service. Until this date in most American Lutheran churches only an Epistle and a Gospel had been read. . . ."[37]

Reading an "Old Testament lesson," however, does not necessarily translate into preaching it, for most pastors will select their preaching-text from the New Testament readings. This preference for a New Testament text is dictated partly by the predilections of pastors, but it is also built into most lectionaries. In following the church year (the life of Christ) from Advent to Christmas to Epiphany to Lent to Easter to Pentecost, the continuous readings tend to come from one of the Gospels. Consequently, the Old Testament readings provide at most a supportive role. What is more, "the Old Testament readings . . . have little if any continuity from Sunday to Sunday."[38] Thus by following the church year and providing continuity in the Gospel readings, lectionaries tilt the selection of preaching-texts in favor of the New Testament.

36. Michael Duduit, "The Church's Need for Old Testament Preaching," 10.

37. McCurley, *Proclaiming*, 3. Presenting a few lectures in Norway in 1997, I was surprised to discover that the Lutheran church in Norway did not really preach from the Old Testament until the 1980s, when two Old Testament passages were placed on their lectionary.

38. Calvin Storley, "Reclaiming the Old Testament," 490.

Dennis Olson raises another concern. He observes that "most lectionaries use readings from a quite limited body of Old Testament material" — mainly Isaiah, Jeremiah, Genesis, Exodus, and Deuteronomy. "Citations from other Old Testament books rapidly fall off. . . . In the present shape of most lectionaries, eighty percent of the Old Testament witness is never even read in congregational worship, much less preached. It is like taking the Boston Symphony Orchestra and stripping it of all but twenty percent of its players. . . . What happens when we strip down the Old Testament to twenty percent of its full voice? What theological emphases are lost?"[39]

Critical Old Testament Scholarship

A more serious reason for the lack of preaching from the Old Testament is the kind of training in Old Testament many preachers receive in various theological seminaries and universities. "By the beginning of the twentieth century, theological exegesis as the paramount concern of biblical scholarship had been supplanted by the scientific-historical conception of the scholar's task."[40] Higher criticism concentrated on source criticism, form criticism, and history of religion. The Old Testament was studied only to recover the history of Israel, the history of its literature, and the history of its religion — and future preachers were left without a word from God to preach. Illustrative of the sterility of theological training was the resignation of Julius Wellhausen (of source-criticism fame) as professor of theology at Greifswald University and his acceptance of the position of professor of Semitic languages at Halle. He explained the reason for his switch from theology to Semitic languages as follows: "I became a theologian because I was interested in the scientific treatment of the Bible; it has only gradually dawned upon me that a professor of theology likewise has the practical task of preparing students for service in the Evangelical Church, and that I was not fulfilling this practical task, but rather, in spite of all reserve on my part, was *incapacitating* my hearers for their office."[41] Some fifty years later, training for preaching from the Old Testament had not improved, at least not in Germany. Von Rad observes that "Old Testament scholarship . . . with an almost religious earnestness, . . . had trained people to the ethic of an incorruptible historical discern-

39. Olson, "Rediscovering," 3.

40. Herbert F. Hahn, *The Old Testament in Modern Research* (Philadelphia: Fortress, 1966), 10.

41. Wellhausen as cited in Alfred Jepsen, "The Scientific Study of the Old Testament," in *Essays on Old Testament Hermeneutics*, ed. Claus Westermann (Richmond, VA: John Knox, 1964), 247, my emphasis.

ment; but it had not trained them to acknowledge the Old Testament publicly . . . — what theologians call *in statu confessionis*."[42] The recent rise of redaction criticism, rhetorical criticism, narrative criticism, and the canonical approach holds greater promise of biblical scholars focussing their energy on understanding the message of Old Testament literature for Israel and thus helping prepare students for their task of preaching from the Old Testament.[43]

Rejection of the Old Testament

Still another reason for the lack of preaching from the Old Testament is the outright rejection of the Old Testament. Rejection of the Old Testament has a long history, going back all the way to Marcion. To get an idea of the reasons why people reject the Old Testament, we shall briefly review the positions of four theologians: Marcion, Schleiermacher, von Harnack, and Bultmann.

Marcion (ca. 85-160)

Marcion was a wealthy shipowner on the southern shore of the Black Sea. Around the year A.D. 140 he moved to Rome, where he became a member of the church. "While in Rome, he succumbed to the influence of the un-orthodox Syrian teacher Cerdo, from whom he derived the basis of his teaching, the differentiation between the God portrayed in the Old Testament and the God portrayed in the New."[44] When Marcion was excommunicated in 144, he founded his own church and spread his peculiar views far and wide.

Like the Gnostics,[45] Marcion held to a dualistic view of the universe: the material world is evil and the spiritual world is good. A good God (pure Spirit) could not possibly have created this material world. Since the God of the Old Testament is the Creator God, he must be an inferior deity, a demiurge. We also meet him in the Old Testament as the God of the law, a God of wrath, a God of war, a stern judge. The God revealed in the New Testament, by contrast, is a God of love, grace, and peace. The true God sent Jesus Christ to rescue us from this evil world. Because he started with a

42. Von Rad, "Gerhard von Rad über von Rad," in *Probleme biblischer Theologie*, ed. H. W. Wolff (Munich, 1971), 660, as cited in Rendtorff, *Canon*, 76.

43. See my *Modern Preacher*, 55-79.

44. A. J. B. Higgins, *Christian Significance of the Old Testament*, 14.

45. On the debate regarding Marcion's dependence on gnosticism, see John Bright, *Authority*, 62, n. 4.

different God in each of the Testaments and because he saw seeming contradictions between the Testaments, Marcion rejected the Old Testament and tried to purge the New Testament of all references to the Old Testament. Marcion's wholesale rejection of the Old Testament forced the Christian church to reflect on its canon. The church concluded that the Old Testament belonged to its canon as much as the New — the two were one.[46]

The church's official declaration in A.D. 382[47] that the books of the Hebrew Old Testament also belonged to its canon should have settled the matter. Regrettably, this was not the end of the story. It is hard for independent thinkers to submit to the biblical canon (the rule, standard), to bring every thought captive to the Scriptures. Or, to put it another way, it is extremely difficult to enter the hermeneutical circle for interpreting the Old Testament with genuine biblical presuppositions. It is all too easy to start with nonbiblical presuppositions and make them the rule (canon) by which we judge the Scriptures. Marcion's nonbiblical starting point was two Gods — and the Bible was torn apart. Instead of respectful submission to the Scriptures as the word of God, Marcion ruled over the Scriptures.

Others have followed in Marcion's footsteps. Scholars need not, like Marcion, start out with two Gods. They only have to subscribe to a new definition of revelation or a new view of religion or a new norm of ethics — and instead of submitting to the canon, they rule over the canon and begin to cut out certain parts as inferior and unworthy. Throughout church history Marcionism, in the sense of rejecting or ignoring the Old Testament, kept resurfacing. We need not review the whole story;[48] a few quotations from recent influential scholars will be sufficient to make the point.

46. The church may well have changed the order of the Hebrew Bible from Torah–Prophets–Writings to Torah–Writings–Prophets in order to express this unity of the two Testaments by highlighting that Christ is the fulfillment of Old Testament prophecy. But scholars are not agreed on this point. Otto Eissfeldt, *The Old Testament: An Introduction,* trans. Peter R. Ackroyd (New York: Harper and Row, 1965), 570, claims that this change took place in "the tradition represented in LXX. . . . The arrangements of the books here is clearly determined by the principle that there stand first the historical books which deal with the past, then the poetic and didactic writings, understood as being in a special sense books of edification and instruction for contemporary life, and the prophetic writings directed towards the future provide the ending."

47. This Council, probably held in Rome, "gave a complete list of the canonical books of both the OT and the NT (also known as the 'Gelasian Decree' because it was reproduced by Gelasius in 495) which is identical with the list given at the Council of Trent." *The Oxford Dictionary of the Christian Church* (3d ed.; New York: Oxford University Press, 1997), 279.

48. See, e.g., A. H. J. Gunneweg, *Understanding the Old Testament;* Emil G. Kraeling, *The Old Testament since the Reformation;* Foster McCurley, *Proclaiming the Promise;* and Alan Richardson, "Is the Old Testament the Propaedeutic to Christian Faith?"

Friedrich Schleiermacher (1768-1834)

Schleiermacher is famous for his new definition of religion as the "feeling of absolute dependence on God." He further "defines revelation as something new in the sphere of religious feelings that is basic for a certain religious community's life. . . ."[49] With this subjectivistic spin on revelation, the Old Testament comes to be regarded not just as pre-Christian but as sub-Christian. Schleiermacher sees no continuity between Judaism and Christianity; instead he argues that "the relations of Christianity to Judaism and Heathenism are the same, inasmuch as the transition from either of these to Christianity is a transition to another religion."[50] He also suggests that it might be better "if the Old Testament were put after the New as an appendix. . . ."[51] Kraeling, an admirer, writes, "The greatest theologian of nineteenth-century Protestantism was thus in favour of putting the Old Testament in an extremely subordinate position. But he hesitates to draw the full consequences of his standpoint by joining the Marcionite group."[52]

Adolf von Harnack (1851-1930)

Harnack was an influential exponent of Liberal Protestantism. He wrote the classic work on Marcion. "He concedes that Marcion went too far in considering the Creator God and the Christian God two entirely different gods. . . . But that, he argues, cannot save the Old Testament." He asks Christians to "consider the harm the Old Testament does to their cause. Much of the opposition to Christianity in the modern world is based on the Old Testament, which affords so much opportunity to people to attack and ridicule the Bible. . . ."[53] Harnack suggests that the Old Testament should be included with the Apocrypha, "the books which are useful to read but not authoritative."[54] This is his considered opinion: "To have cast aside the Old Testament in the second century was an error which the church rightly rejected; to have retained it in the sixteenth century was a fate which the Reformation was not yet able to avoid; but still to keep it after the nineteenth century as a canonical doc-

---

49. Kraeling, *Old Testament*, 59.
50. Schleiermacher, *The Christian Faith*, 60-62, as cited in McCurley, *Proclaiming the Promise*, 9.
51. Kraeling, *Old Testament*, 66.
52. Ibid.
53. Ibid., 148.
54. Ibid., 149.

ument within Protestantism results from a religious and ecclesiastical paralysis."[55]

Rudolf Bultmann (1884-1976)

We could consider many other persons,[56] but we shall move straight to the influential Rudolf Bultmann. Scholars have debated whether Bultmann should be classified as a Marcionite, for he does not reject the Old Testament outright.[57] But it cannot be denied that he accepts its value for the church in a very restricted and negative sense. In "The Significance of the Old Testament for the Christian Faith," he acknowledges that "the New Testament presupposes the Old, the Gospel presupposes the Law." But then he goes right on to say, "It can be only for pedagogical reasons that the Christian Church uses the Old Testament to make man conscious of standing under God's demand."[58] That is the "positive" side.

But these minimal, qualified statements regarding the significance of the Old Testament for the Christian must be weighed against Bultmann's perturbing negative statements in the same article: "To the Christian faith the Old Testament is no longer revelation as it has been, and still is, for the Jews. For the person who stands within the Church the history of Israel is a closed chapter. . . . Israel's history is not our history, and in so far as God has shown his grace in that history, such grace is not meant for us. . . . To us the history of Israel is not history of revelation. The events which meant something for Israel, which were God's Word, mean nothing more to us. . . . To the Christian faith the Old Testament is not in the true sense God's Word."[59]

The Old Testament is still maligned and slighted. Today Marcionism may not be promoted as blatantly as it was by the theologians who just passed

55. Harnack, *Marcion: Das Evangelium vom fremden Gott* (1924), 221-22. Quotation taken from Bright, *Authority,* 65.

56. See Bright, *Authority,* 67-75.

57. See, e.g., Bernard Anderson in his "Introduction" to *The Old Testament and Christian Faith* (New York: Harper & Row, 1963), 7; and in the same volume, Carl Michaelson, "Bultmann against Marcion," 49-63.

58. Bultmann, "Significance," 17. Cf. pp. 34-35: "If . . . the Old Testament is taken up into the Church's proclamation as God's word, then the inviolable conditions are: (1) that the Old Testament is used in its original sense . . . ; (2) that the Old Testament is adopted only in so far as it is actually promise — that is, preparation for the Christian understanding of existence." Cf. Friedrich Baumgärtel, "The Hermeneutical Problem of the Old Testament," in *Essays on Old Testament Hermeneutics,* 135, "For this understanding we cannot eliminate the fact, derived from study of the history of religion, that the Old Testament is a witness out of a non-Christian religion. . . ."

59. Ibid., 31-32.

our review, but ideas have wings, and even in distant places these perni-
cious ideas have tainted the image of the Old Testament.[60] Moreover, today Marcionism is fostered by default by preachers who bypass or pay
only lip-service to the Old Testament. It is also fostered by preachers who
use the Old Testament only "as a foil for heightening the uniqueness of
the teachings of Jesus."[61]

Sadly, even today the question is being raised whether the God of
the Old Testament is the God of the New Testament. It is a question that
has troubled the church for centuries and muddied the waters of theological debate. But it is a foolhardy question, for it does not arise from the
Scriptures themselves. Every morning and evening the Israelites were reminded: "Hear, O Israel: The LORD our God, the LORD is one" (Deut 6:4,
NIV). Jesus, the true Israelite, revealed this one Lord and called him Father. We may raise questions about different emphases in and tensions
between the two Testaments, but to contemplate the question of different
Gods is to take one's starting point outside the canon in an alien religion.

Difficulties in Preaching from the Old Testament

Beginning with the biblical presuppositions of one God and one Bible
does not alleviate all the difficulties of preaching from the Old Testament, of course, but it does allow us to address them within the context
of the historic Christian faith. For there is no doubt that another major
reason for slighting the Old Testament is the genuine difficulty the
preacher faces in preaching from the Old Testament. We can distinguish
at least four sets of difficulties: historical-cultural, theological, ethical,
and practical.

Historical-Cultural Difficulties

The Old Testament is an ancient book set in a Middle Eastern, agricul-
tural society. We enter a foreign world of temples and animal sacrifices, of
sabbatical years and dietary laws. This world is far removed from the
modern church in a Western, postindustrial, urban setting. Preaching
from the Old Testament, the preacher comes face-to-face with the histori-

---

60. For example, in August 1962, the London *Times* published a series of letters
regarding the reading of the Old Testament in public worship. Dr. Leslie Weatherhead,
Minister Emeritus of London's City Temple, wrote, "Again and again, one would like
to rise in church after the Old Testament lesson and say, 'My dear friends, do not pay
any heed to the irrelevant nonsense which has just been read to you. It has no bearing
whatever on the Christian religion.'" See *Christianity Today*, September 28, 1962, 54.

61. Bright, *Authority*, 74.

cal-cultural gap. It seems impossible to preach relevant sermons from this ancient book.

The immense historical-cultural gap appears to be the main reason for the lack of preaching from the Old Testament today. Donald Gowan in his book *Reclaiming the Old Testament for the Christian Pulpit* claims that "the central problem which has faced modern preachers who attempt to use the Old Testament faithfully is *discontinuity*."[62] The Old Testament seems to have little to say to Christians living in an entirely different era from that of Israel. Approaching this issue from a different angle, Walter Kaiser comes to the same conclusion: "Overriding all of the reasons for neglect of the Old Testament . . . is the issue of the Bible's historical particularity; that is, its words are most frequently, if not always in the Old Testament, directed to a *specific* people in a *specific* situation at a *specific* time and in a *specific* culture. That is the real difficulty."[63]

Granted that it presents a major problem for preaching relevantly from the Old Testament today, the historical-cultural gap need not be viewed entirely negatively. For the fact that we, from our times, discern a historical-cultural gap discloses the fact that the Old Testament addressed its own time relevantly: God's word did not float high above Israel as an eternal word but entered Israel's culture in a relevant way. Instead of an obstacle, therefore, the historical-cultural gap can become a challenge for preachers to discern this past relevance and to preach the message of the Old Testament just as relevantly today as it addressed Israel in the past.[64]

Theological Difficulties

More than eighteen hundred years ago Marcion confronted the church with some major theological difficulties in preaching from the Old Testament. For example, he noted differences between the God revealed in the Old Testament and in the New Testament: in the Old Testament God commanded Israel to "exterminate" the Canaanites without mercy (Josh 11:20), "but Christ forbade all force and preached mercy and peace"; "the Creator sends down fire at the demand of Elijah (2 Kings 1:9-12), but Christ forbids the disciples to ask for fire from heaven"; "The Old Testament God is mighty in war; Christ brings peace."[65]

62. Gowan, *Reclaiming*, 6.
63. Kaiser, *Exegetical Theology*, 37.
64. For some suggestions and references, see my *Modern Preacher*, 157-87.
65. Marcion, as recounted by Tertullian, *Against Marcion*, respectively 2.18, 4.23, and 3.21, as quoted by Higgins, *Christian Significance*, 16.

One does not have to begin with two different Gods to notice that there are differences between the Old Testament revelation of God and that of the New Testament. The Old Testament at times presents God as a stern, judging God, "punishing children for the iniquity of parents to the third and the fourth generation of those who reject me" (Exod 20:5), while the New Testament presents God as the one who "so loved the world that he gave his only Son" (John 3:16) and who is quick to forgive (1 John 1:9). The Old Testament presents God's blessings in the area of material wealth (many children, livestock, harvests — Deut 30:9), while the New Testament sees God's greatest blessing as "eternal life" (John 3:16). The Old Testament seems to present salvation by works (e.g., "If you obey the commandments . . . , then you shall live. . ."; Deut 30:16), while the New Testament presents salvation by faith (Rom 5:1). In preaching from the Old Testament, preachers need to resolve these and many other tensions. In Chapters 3 and 4 we shall see how the church sought to address these issues with the idea of progressive revelation.

Ethical Difficulties

In addition to the historical-cultural and theological problems, preachers will be confronted with ethical difficulties. Eighteen hundred years ago already Marcion tripped over some of these ethical obstacles: "In the Law it says: 'An eye for an eye, a tooth for a tooth.' The Lord, however, the good, says in the Gospel: 'If any strike thee on one cheek, offer him the other also.' In the Law God (the Creator) says: 'Thou shalt love him who loveth thee, and hate thine enemy.' But our Lord, the good, says: 'Love your enemies, and pray for those who persecute you.'"[66]

These particular problems have been highlighted throughout church history by detractors of the Old Testament. But preachers will be confronted by many other ethical difficulties as well. For example, the law of Moses demanded the execution not only of murderers but also of witches (Exod 22:18), idolaters (Deut 13:6-10; 16:2-7), and even of a "stubborn and rebellious son" (Deut 21:18-21). And some of the Psalms beg God to annihilate the enemy and more: "Happy shall they be who take your little ones and dash them against the rock!" (Ps 137:9; cf. Ps 109:6-13).[67]

Sensitive Christians can easily be offended by certain parts of the

---

66. Ibid., 4.16, as quoted by Higgins, *Christian Significance*, 16.
67. On the so-called "imprecatory Psalms," see pp. 274-75 below. Also see Walter Kaiser, *Old Testament Ethics*, 292-97.

Old Testament. In this connection John Bright raises the interesting question as to why, "although the Old Testament on occasion offends our Christian feelings, it did not apparently offend Christ's 'Christian feelings'! Could it really be that we are ethically and religiously more sensitive than he? Or is it perhaps that we do not view the Old Testament — and its God — as he did?"[68]

Practical Difficulties

In addition to the historical-cultural, theological, and ethical difficulties, there are also some obvious practical difficulties in preaching from the Old Testament. Foster McCurley describes the challenges: "The Old Testament is so broad; it requires a staggering breadth of knowledge of history, literature, and theology. . . . Rather than covering one century as does the New Testament, the Old Testament spans twelve centuries of literature and approximately eighteen of history. . . . The breadth of Old Testament study . . . itself is frightening and demanding for the interpreter."[69]

Reasons for Preaching from the Old Testament as well as the New

In spite of these major hurdles, there are many reasons why pastors must preach from the Old Testament: (1) the Old Testament is part of the Christian canon, (2) it discloses the history of redemption leading to Christ, (3) it proclaims truths not found in the New Testament, (4) it helps us understand the New Testament, (5) it prevents misunderstanding the New Testament, and (6) it provides a fuller understanding of Christ. In concluding this chapter, we shall discuss the first five reasons.

The Old Testament Is Part of the Christian Canon

The first reason for preaching from the Old Testament is that the church has accepted this collection of books as part of its canon. To accept a document as part of one's canon only to let this "standard for faith and life" gather dust makes little sense. If the Old Testament is part of the Christian canon, then it should be used in the church. Paul instructs Timothy to "give attention to the public reading of scripture [that is, the Old Testa-

68. Bright, *Authority*, 77-78.
69. McCurley, *Proclaiming*, 5.

ment], to exhorting, to teaching" (1 Tim 4:13). Later Paul makes the argument that the Old Testament is inspired ("God-breathed") to be used. He writes, "All scripture is inspired by God and useful for teaching, for reproof, for correction, and for training in righteousness, so that everyone who belongs to God may be proficient, equipped for every good work" (2 Tim 3:16-17). The Old Testament, says Paul, is useful for teaching Christians. It contains teachings which the New Testament simply assumes but does not necessarily repeat (see examples below). In fact, in the preceding verse (15), Paul claims that "the sacred writings . . . are able to instruct you [literally, "make you wise"] for salvation through faith in Christ Jesus." The Old Testament is also useful for "reproof," that is, for showing sinners the error of their ways so that they may return to holy living (think of the moral law and of wisdom literature). It is also useful for "correction," that is, "setting straight that which had become bent or twisted." Finally, says Paul, it is useful for "training in righteousness," that is, instruction that will lead to a state of being upright.[70] In Romans 15:4 Paul adds the element of hope we can receive from the Old Testament: "Whatever was written in former days was written for our instruction, so that by steadfastness and by the encouragement of the scriptures we might have hope."

The apostle Peter agrees with Paul that Christians are to use the Old Testament. He writes to the dispersed Christians, "It was revealed to them [the prophets] that they were serving not themselves but you, in regard to the things that have now been announced to you . . ." (1 Pet 1:12). Every Christian church today needs to hear the Old Testament for its function of teaching, reproof, correction, and training in righteousness, as well as for the hope it brings and the instruction it offers for "salvation through faith in Christ Jesus" (2 Tim 3:15).

The Old Testament Discloses the History of Redemption Leading to Christ

The second reason for preaching from the Old Testament is that it reveals the long history of redemption which culminates in the coming of Jesus Christ.[71] The Old Testament discloses God's acts of redemption in a history that stretches from the creation to just prior to the coming of Christ.

---

70. Some of these explanations were gleaned from Kaiser, *Rediscovering*, 26-32.

71. Although the Old Testament contains a rich treasure of biblical truths (doctrines), we should first consider redemptive history. For redemptive history precedes biblical doctrines. Redemptive history, we could say, forms the indispensable foundation of biblical doctrine.

It reveals how God, after the fall into sin, seeks to save his people and restore his kingdom (rule) on earth. It reveals God's redemptive acts over many centuries as well as God's promises and their fulfillments. We do not find this long history of God's acts of salvation in the New Testament; it simply assumes and builds on this history. Since only the Old Testament reveals this redemptive history, it is indispensable for the Christian church.

We can liken redemptive history to a drama with many acts. The first act shows God creating a beautiful kingdom where he will be honored as King. The second act is about an attempted coup in the kingdom when human beings join Satan and rebel against God. It ends not only with God's punishment of death but also with God's assurance that he will not give up on his kingdom, for God breaks up the evil alliance and sets enmity between the "seed of the woman" and the seed of the evil one. Act 2 is followed by countless acts in which God saves his people. A high point is the call of Abraham in which God promises him many offspring, land, and (note God's universal design) "in you all the families of the earth shall be blessed" (Gen 12:3; cf. Isa 2:3 = Mic 4:2). Other high points are the exodus from Egypt, the rule of King David, and the return of the exiles. But still the climax has not been reached. The climax comes in the New Testament with God sending his own Son to save the world. Accordingly, just as one cannot understand the last act of a drama without knowing the earlier acts, so this climactic act of God sending his Son cannot be understood without knowing the foregoing acts of God. Since these acts are recorded only in the Old Testament, preaching the Old Testament story is indispensable for the Christian church.

The Old Testament Proclaims Truths Not Found in the New Testament

A third reason for preaching from the Old Testament is that it reveals truths we know from no other source. When Jesus was asked which was the great commandment of the law, he could use the Old Testament to show that it was the love commandment (Mark 12:29-32). But the New Testament does not repeat everything the Old Testament teaches; it can simply assume Old Testament teaching because it was accepted as God's word.

For example, only in the Old Testament do we receive the comprehensive revelation of God as the sovereign Creator, wholly other than his creation yet involved in it. Only in the Old Testament do we learn that God created human beings in his image for fellowship with him and with each other, and with the mandate to develop and care for the earth. Only in the Old Testament do we receive a picture of the human fall into sin, resulting in death, brokenness, and enmity between the seed of the woman and the seed of the serpent. Only in the Old Testament do we hear of God electing Abraham/Israel as a beachhead for restoring his kingdom on earth. Only in the Old Testament do we find details about God's covenant with Israel, the ten words of the covenant (Decalogue), the blessings and the curses. Only in the Old Testament do we hear of the coming Messiah and the Day of the Lord.

The various teachings of the Old Testament are sufficient to form a comprehensive worldview, namely, the interrelationship between God, human beings, and the world.

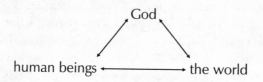

A worldview is crucial, for it acts as a grid which sorts and interprets information and helps us make sense of the world and our place and task in it.[72] The Old Testament worldview is quite distinct from other worldviews such as polytheism, pantheism, gnosticism, deism, atheism, and naturalism. The New Testament does not provide another worldview but simply assumes the one taught in the Old Testament.

Besides these foundational teachings, the Old Testament offers a host of other teachings which may or may not be echoed in the New Testament. Some of these are the sovereignty of God over all nations (Isa 10:5-19; Habakkuk), the incomparability of God (Isa 40:12-31), the problem of the suffering of God's people (Job, Psalms), human responsibility for promoting social justice (Deuteronomy 15, Amos, Micah, Isaiah), the gift of sexual love (Gen 2:18-28; Song of Songs), and a hopeful view of the new earth (Isa 11:6-9; 65:17-25). Bereft of these Old Testament teachings, preaching becomes anemic. Michael Duduit judges, "For us to neglect these books in our preaching is to abandon our congregations to theological shallowness and mediocrity."[73]

72. See Albert M. Wolters, *Creation Regained: Biblical Basis for a Reformational Worldview* (Grand Rapids: Eerdmans, 1985).

73. Duduit, "Church's Need," 12. See also Achtemeier, *Preaching*, 21-26.

The Old Testament Helps Us to
Understand the New Testament

The night before Jesus' death, he celebrated the Passover with his disciples. But a strange thing happened. Matthew tells us that Jesus took a cup and said, "This is my blood of the covenant, which is poured out for many for the forgiveness of sins" (26:28). We may have heard these words so often that we do not find them strange anymore, but what is this talk about "blood" and "covenant"? We would never know unless we knew the Old Testament teaching about Passover and about God's covenant with his people and the blood sacrifices required to atone for their sins.

Or consider the concept of church. Without the Old Testament we cannot know what the church is, for the New Testament describes the church in images from the Old Testament. Paul portrays the church as "the temple of the living God" (2 Cor 6:16) and "the Israel of God" (Gal 6:16). Peter also describes the church in Old Testament concepts: "a chosen race, a royal priesthood, a holy nation, God's own people, in order that you may proclaim the mighty acts [the praises, NIV] of him who called you out of darkness into his marvelous light" (1 Pet 2:9). Even the way Peter describes the task of the church derives from the Old Testament, where we read: "The people whom I formed for myself so that they might declare my praise" (Isa 43:21). When Jesus gave his church the great commission to "make disciples of all nations" (Matt 28:18-20), he reiterated the task of Israel: "I will give you as a light to the nations, that my salvation may reach the end of the earth" (Isa 49:6; cf. Gen 12:3). John Bright's summary reveals many of these Old Testament concepts: "The New Testament understood . . . [the church] as the true Israel, God's covenant and servant people, called to exhibit the righteousness of his Kingdom before the world, charged with proclaiming that Kingdom in the world and summoning men to its covenant fellowship."[74]

The New Testament is filled with many other images and concepts whose meaning we cannot know without the Old Testament. Think, for example, of such concepts as God, the kingdom of God, salvation, prophet, priest, king, atonement, law, faith, hope, love, Christ, Son of Man, good shepherd, and servant of God. Preaching from the Old Testament, therefore, helps a congregation understand the New Testament.

---

74. Bright, *Kingdom*, 259.

The Old Testament Prevents
Misunderstanding the New Testament

An even more important reason for preaching from the Old Testament is that it prevents misunderstanding the New Testament. For example, the first thing we read about Jesus' ministry is that he began to preach, "Repent, for the kingdom of heaven has come near" (Matt 4:17). What is "the kingdom of heaven"? Without the Old Testament we wonder: Is this a kingdom in heaven, far away from this evil world? We seem to find confirmation of this view later when Jesus says to Pilate, "My kingdom is not of this world" (John 18:36, NIV). Consequently, many Christians look forward to escaping this wicked world and occupying their "mansion in heaven." Without realizing it, they have adopted the Marcionistic/Gnostic view of salvation, which is to escape from this evil, material world. But is Jesus really saying that his kingdom is in heaven only?

F. F. Bruce writes that Jesus "used language which must have rung a loud bell, or several loud bells, in the minds of those hearers who had some consciousness of their people's heritage [the Old Testament]. The kingship of Yahweh, the God of Israel, had been for centuries a dominant theme in the national worship. . . . Yahweh's mighty acts in creation and history alike prefigured that coming day when He would be obeyed as King over all the earth."[75] According to the clear expectation of the Old Testament, God's kingdom (reign) would be returning to this *earth*. Did Jesus change this expectation from earth to heaven? A clearer translation of Jesus' words to Pilate is, "My kingdom is not *from* this world" (John 18:36, NRSV), implying that Jesus' kingdom originates in heaven. But Jesus continues the Old Testament expectation that the kingdom of heaven (= kingdom of God) is coming to this earth. In fact, with his presence and miracles, Jesus says, "the kingdom of God has come to you" (Luke 11:20). But it is not yet complete. Therefore Jesus teaches his people to pray, "Your kingdom come. Your will be done, on *earth* as it is in heaven" (Matt 6:10). When Jesus comes again — and that will be the final act in this redemptive drama — he will bring God's perfect kingdom to this earth. "In accordance with his promise, we wait for new heavens and a new earth, where righteousness is at home" (2 Pet 3:13; cf. Rev 21:1).

Clearly, one of the dangers of reading the New Testament without its Old Testament background is a serious misunderstanding of the teaching of the New Testament. Marvin Wilson has written a sobering chapter on "Where the Church Went Wrong." He notes that "the Church paid little heed to the exhortation of Paul to continue in what it had learned and

---

75. Bruce, *New Testament Development*, 22, 24.

believed in the context of its Hebrew beginnings. Rather, as it became more and more Hellenized. . . , it began to be led away into strange teachings (cf. Heb. 13:9)."[76] At the root of these strange teachings lay a Greek dualistic way of thinking (worldview) which held to a higher, invisible spiritual world and an inferior, visible material world. These two worlds, it was thought, are also present in each person as the higher, spiritual soul and the lower, material body. According to Plato, the body is the prison of the soul, and salvation is the escape of the soul at death to the realm of pure spirit. Reading the New Testament through these dualistic glasses, the church at various times devalued the material world and our human bodies by promoting asceticism (though rejected by Paul — Col 2:20-23), celibacy, otherworldliness, and salvation as escape from the world.[77]

A. J. B. Higgins observes, "We have in Marcion's treatment a perfect example of what can happen to the New Testament when the Old is cast on one side as of little or no importance for Christianity."[78] Marcion may have been rejected by the church, but his dualistic views keep cropping up to the present day. "In various ways this old enemy [gnosticism] has returned in various guises: new age religion, various eastern religions, but also in the church itself. . . . If we present a Christian faith that is of no earthly use, that has no implications for the practice of life in every realm, and that has no demonstration of the power of the gospel to renew life here and now, then we have succumbed to a future-oriented gnostic reduction of the gospel."[79]

Since we all have our presuppositions and prejudices, no one can claim to have a perfect understanding of the New Testament. But there is one presupposition that is indispensable for a good interpretation of the New Testament. That presupposition is the unity of the Bible and, therefore, the necessity of understanding the New Testament in the context of

---

76. Wilson, *Our Father Abraham*, 166.

77. Wilson, ibid., 173, writes, "The Scriptures view both humanity and the world in terms of dynamic unity, not dualistically. But gradually unwholesome and unbiblical attitudes became embedded in Christian thought. Consequently, the Church's perspective on the enjoying of material and physical pleasures, and on the affirming of the goodness of marriage and the family, became distorted. . . ." On pp. 182-90 Wilson deals with the Western view of faith as intellectual assent instead of faithfulness or trust, and individualism at the cost of community.

78. Higgins, *Christian Significance*, 21. Cf. D. Moody Smith, "Where the Old Testament is ignored, such an understanding of man as creature, indeed as historical and societal creature, usually disappears, and the New Testament is wrongly regarded as only a handbook of personal piety and religion." "The Use of the Old Testament," 65.

79. Raymond Van Leeuwen, "No Other Gods," 42.

the Old, and vice versa. "The Old Testament holds the gospel to history. It is the surest bulwark against assimilation with alien philosophies and ideologies, against a flight into a sentimental and purely otherworldly piety, and against that disintegrating individualism that so easily besets us."[80]

The Old Testament Provides a
Fuller Understanding of Christ

A final reason for preaching from the Old Testament is that it provides a fuller understanding of the person, work, and teaching of Christ than does preaching only from the New Testament. For Jesus not only taught that the Old Testament witnessed to him, but in his life he also lived out of, fulfilled, and taught the Scriptures. A discussion of this reason, however, is more appropriate at the end of the next chapter.

---

80. Bright, *Authority*, 78.

The Necessity of Preaching Christ from the Old Testament

"Beginning with Moses and all the prophets, he [Jesus] interpreted to them the things about himself in all the scriptures."

Luke 24:27

HAVING CONSIDERED both the necessity of preaching Christ and the necessity of preaching from the Old Testament, we shall now seek to merge the results of our discoveries by examining the necessity of preaching Christ from the Old Testament. Although this may seem like a logical outcome, this blending of two distinct topics confronts us with a whole new set of issues: the non-Christian or Christian character of the Old Testament, the relation of the Old Testament to the New, the way in which the Old Testament witnesses to Christ, and the benefits of preaching Christ specifically from the Old Testament. We will need to work our way through all these issues, but we shall start with an examination of the reasons for the frequent failure to preach Christ from the Old Testament.

THE LACK OF PREACHING CHRIST
FROM THE OLD TESTAMENT

There are probably many reasons for the lack of preaching Christ from the Old Testament, ranging from the difficulty of doing so to a lack of interest. We shall analyze three sets of possible reasons: (1) the temptation of human-centered preaching, (2) the concern about forced interpretation, and (3) the separation of the Old Testament from the New.

The Temptation of Human-Centered Preaching

A textbook on preaching states unequivocally: "The first and most vivid value of the Old Testament for the preacher may be in the figures it portrays."[1] The colorful characters roaming the Old Testament are a powerful attraction for preachers. Especially for busy pastors, the temptation is great simply to retell the story of one of these characters and relate it to the lives of their parishioners. William Willimon asserts, "Most of the preaching I hear and too much that I do attempts to build upon 'common human experience.' 'Are you depressed? Everyone has been depressed at one time or another. Down in the dumps. There is a story of someone who was down in the dumps, in the pit, so to speak. His name was Joseph. He was thrown into a pit. . . .'"[2] The result of such biblical character preaching is tragic: "Unable to preach Christ and him crucified, we preach humanity and it improved."[3]

Biographical Preaching

Much of human-centered preaching is promoted by what is called "biographical preaching" or "character preaching." Since I have dealt extensively with this topic elsewhere,[4] we shall here examine only a recent text entitled *Guide to Biographical Preaching* (1988). In this book, Roy De Brand advocates preaching biographical sermons not only because they are "easy to prepare and preach" but especially "because they have tremendous preaching value." He promotes the value of biographical sermons as follows:

> They carry the automatic bonus of example. . . . We learn from others. Sometimes the lessons are positive and we emulate them. Other times we learn what not to do, think, or say from the example of others. Often both positive and negative lessons can be learned from the same Bible

---

1. Walter Russell Bowie, *Preaching: Why Preach, What to Preach, How to Preach* (Nashville: Abingdon, 1954), 99.

2. Willimon, *Peculiar Speech*, 13.

3. Ibid., 9.

4. See my *Sola Scriptura*, 56-120, and *Modern Preacher*, 116-18, 161-66, 216-17. Regarding "identification" with biblical characters, see my *Modern Preacher*, 175-81.

character. For example, we could benefit by learning from King David's noble deeds, high aspirations, and deep worship of God. We can also learn much about what to avoid from the examples of his terrible sins against Uriah and Bathsheba. . . . Hold forth the virtues to be imitated and expose the vices to be eliminated by preaching the tremendous examples found in lives of Bible characters.[5]

De Brand continues by illustrating his method. Suppose one preaches on Genesis 32:22-32. A typical biographical sermon might look like this:

> Title: "When Jacob Wrestled with the Angel."
> Main points:
> 1. Jacob struggled (32:22-25).
> 2. Jacob was changed (32:26-28).
> 3. Jacob was blessed (32:29-32).

De Brand rightly senses that this development leaves the message in the past. In order to relate the message to the present hearers, he suggests the following improvement:

> Title: "When God Confronts Us."
> Main points:
> 1. When God confronts us it sometimes causes struggle (32:22-25).
> 2. God's confrontation calls us to change (32:26-28).
> 3. We receive God's blessing when he confronts us (32:29-32).[6]

The new outline is a vast improvement over the old one. Instead of being human-centered, the new outline is more God-centered. Moreover, it is relevant. But at what cost? Notice that in point 1 Jacob's unique struggle is turned into every person's struggle — that is the error of generalizing or universalizing.[7] Notice further that Jacob's physical struggle is turned into our spiritual struggle with God — that is the error of spiritualizing. Notice that in point 2 Jacob's change becomes our call to change

---

5. Roy E. De Brand, *Guide to Biographical Preaching* (Nashville: Broadman, 1988), 23-24. For a similar approach, see, e.g., Paul R. House, "Ancient Allies in the Culture Wars: Preaching the Former Prophets Today," *Faith & Mission* 13/1 (Fall 1995) 24-36. On p. 30, e.g., House asserts, "It is the preacher's task to make these positive and negative role models seem real to people who live thousands of years later."

6. Ibid., 35.

7. On the error of universalizing, see Ernest Best, *From Text to Sermon*, 86-89.

— that is the error of moralizing.[8] It is also a "genre mistake" in turning a narrative *description* into a *prescription* for us, as if this were the legal genre. Finally, notice that in point 3 Jacob being blessed is turned into an assurance that all of us will be blessed — generalizing again.

Problems of Biographical Preaching

The problems of this kind of preaching are evident in the attempt at application: generalizing, spiritualizing, and moralizing. But these problems in application are only indicative of underlying problems, problems in hermeneutical approach and exposition. For it is evident that biographical preaching does not interpret each story in the context of the one underlying story of the coming kingdom of God. Instead, it tends to isolate each story from its redemptive-historical and literary contexts. Biographical preaching also fails to inquire after the intention of the author: What was the author's message for Israel?[9] Instead, it imposes an interpretative grid on the story that equates biblical characters with the people in the pew and then inquires how we ought to imitate or learn from their examples. Because biographical preaching shortchanges the contexts of the biblical story and the biblical author's intention, it is unable to produce genuine Christ-centered sermons.

The Concern about Forced Interpretation

For many years I have personally been ambivalent about the necessity of preaching Christ from every text. My main concern was that such a strict requirement would lead to forced interpretation, as one finds in allegorizing and typologizing. Consequently, I thought and taught that with some texts preachers may have to be satisfied with the broader category of *God*-centered preaching, noting that God-centered preaching is implicitly Christ-centered since Christ is God. I imagine that many other preachers have the same fear of forced interpretation and therefore do not always preach Christ explicitly when preaching from the Old Testament.

---

8. On the error of spiritualizing, see my *Modern Preacher*, 160-61; on moralizing, see pp. 116-19, and 163-66.

9. See John Bright, *Authority*, 153-54, "If all we can do is to salvage a few stray morals from the story. . . . we have succeeded only in drawing from it something its author had no intention of giving, for it was simply not his aim to present either David or Nathan as an example to follow."

On the basis of the evidence of the New Testament (see Chapter 1), however, I am arguing in this book not merely for the general category of God-centered preaching but for the more specific category of explicitly Christ-centered preaching. But we must still be watchful that we do not force the text and make it say things it does not say. A popular radio preacher, for example, presented the following interpretation of Genesis 2:18-25:

> While Adam slept, God created from his wounded side a wife, who was part of himself, and he paid for her by the shedding of his blood. . . . Now all is clear. Adam is a picture of the Lord Jesus, who left His Father's house to gain His bride at the price of His own life. Jesus, the last Adam, like the first, must be put to sleep to purchase His Bride, the Church, and Jesus died on the cross and slept in the tomb for three days and three nights. His side too was opened after He had fallen asleep, and from that wounded side redemption flowed.[10]

The message is ingenious, interesting, and Christ-centered. But it preaches Christ at the cost of misusing the Old Testament text. This, clearly, is a case of allegorizing, for this message about Christ has no basis in the text itself. The preacher simply reads Christ, as we know him from the New Testament, back into the Old Testament text. It has nothing whatsoever to do with the author's intended message; not even a "fuller sense" can arrive at this kind of interpretation. And, sadly, in the process of allegorizing the text, its real message is left behind. For the text is about God in the beginning making a partner for the lonely man. The author's message for Israel is about God's wonderful gift of marriage. Since Israel lived in a culture where polygamy was normal and where women were not valued as true partners, this message of God's original design for marriage taught Israel about God's norm for marriage. That message should have been preached, for it is still good news for women and men today. And it could have been reinforced by Jesus' own teaching based on this passage: "Therefore what God has joined together, let no one separate" (Mark 10:9).

The Separation of the Old Testament from the New

For other preachers, the failure to preach Christ from the Old Testament derives from their view of the Old Testament. Simply put, many preachers separate the Old Testament from the New and view the Old Testament as a

10. Martin R. DeHaan, *Portraits of Christ in Genesis* (Grand Rapids: Zondervan, 1966), 32-33.

non-Christian book. Consequently, they are opposed to any kind of "christological interpretation" from the outset. R. N. Whybray, for example, argues that "the Old Testament can only be properly understood if it is studied independently."[11] He asserts that "it is necessary to rule out the traditional christological principle of interpretation, whereby the Old Testament is understood as looking forward to, or as in some way foreshadowing, the Christian dispensation. That this was the way in which the New Testament writers understood it . . . is irrelevant for the interpretation of the Old Testament. . . ." He urges us "to admit frankly that the New Testament interpretation of the Old is not acceptable to modern scholarship."[12] Clearly, Whybray argues for understanding the Old Testament as a non-Christian book. The combination of separating the Old Testament from the New and employing a rigid historical-critical method which focusses at best only on the original message for Israel undermines the very possibility of preaching Christ from the Old Testament.

James Barr, though more moderate, also ends up opposed to "christological interpretation" of the Old Testament: "Our decision against a 'Christological' kind of interpretation here is not primarily founded on historical-critical method, though this is not without importance. Theologically, it rests upon the fact that, though the God of the Old Testament is the Father of our Lord, the Old Testament is the time in which our Lord is not yet come. It is as the time in which he is not yet come that we ought to understand it."[13]

It seems to me that Barr's reason is not so much theological as it is chronological. However that may be, if the term "Christ" refers specifically to the incarnate Christ, we must agree with Barr that "the Old Testament is the time in which our Lord is not yet come." To think otherwise is anachronistic. Yet this important sensitivity to the uniqueness of historical development does not preclude preaching Christ from the Old Testament. One of the main clues, I think, lies in the way we view the relation of the Old Testament and the New Testament.[14] Therefore, we shall next

---

11. R. N. Whybray, "Old Testament Theology — A Non-existent Beast," in *Scripture: Meaning and Method*, ed. Barry P. Thompson (Hull: Hull University Press, 1987), 172. Cf. Gunneweg, *Understanding*, 222, "It is impossible to give a Christian interpretation of something that is not Christian; Christian interpretation of something that is not Christian is pseudo-interpretation. Proper interpretation is concerned, rather, to let the OT have its own say and to interpret it and understand it in the light of the present."

12. Whybray, "Old Testament Theology," 170, 171.

13. Barr, *Old and New*, 152.

14. Cf. Merrill Unger, *Principles*, 156, "Perhaps no single factor is more detrimental to Biblical exposition in our day than a widespread failure to recognize that the Bi-

explore three foundational issues on which we need a measure of clarity before we can authentically preach Christ from the Old Testament: the unique character of the Old Testament, the relation of the Old Testament to the New, and the Old Testament's witness to Christ.

THE UNIQUE CHARACTER OF THE OLD TESTAMENT

A person's view of the Old Testament is so decisive hermeneutically that it governs all subsequent interpretation. In contemporary views, we can distinguish at least four different positions on the character of the Old Testament: (1) the Old Testament is sub-Christian, (2) the Old Testament is non-Christian, (3) the Old Testament is pre-Christian, and (4) the Old Testament is Christian.

The Old Testament Is Sub-Christian

We need not spend much time on the position that the Old Testament is sub-Christian. We met some of its representatives in Chapter 1, people who rejected the Old Testament outright or had minimal use for it: Marcion, Schleiermacher, Harnack, Delitzsch, Bultmann, Baumgärtel, Weatherhead, and many others. In North America one can think of some social gospel preachers who produced their messages within the framework of Liberal Theology and used the Old Testament selectively. They rejected much of the Old Testament as sub-Christian, but they did find some worthwhile nuggets here and there, especially the call for social justice by the prophets.

The Old Testament Is Non-Christian

The position that the Old Testament is non-Christian is represented by biblical scholars (Jews and Christians) who read the Old Testament independently of the New Testament (see Whybray, Gunneweg, and Barr above). They wish to be objective and will generally see the Old Testament as *Tanakh* (an acronym for the Jewish Scriptures Torah–Prophets–Writings). One of its representatives, Leonard Thompson, argues that in

---

ble is a unity, and in order to be adequately interpreted must be treated as such. In many circles this unity is lost sight of in a tendency to emphasize the diversity of the content of the Bible."

teaching the Hebrew Scriptures, one should emphasize "that Hebrew Scriptures are a complete work and do not need the New Testament to complete them."[15] The resulting interpretation deliberately ignores the New Testament. Commenting on the Immanuel passage, he writes, "When Isaiah is read in the context of *Tanakh* . . . , the connection with Jesus is inconceivable. Within the immediate context, the message in Isaiah 7:14 is given as a sign to Ahaz, the reigning king of Judah, that he should not be afraid of a military coalition between Syria and northern Israel that threatens him. . . . From a historical perspective the Christian [Matthew's] reading becomes impossible, for Jesus was born several centuries after Ahaz was king, whereas the sign is directed at a particular situation in his reign."[16] The outcome of this position is an exclusively non-Christian Jewish interpretation of the Old Testament.

It should be clear that the question is not, Whose book is the Old Testament? The Jews claim *Tanakh* as their holy Scriptures; Christians claim the Old Testament as part of their canon; Mormons claim the Old Testament alongside their Book of Mormon;[17] Muslims claim parts of the Old Testament for their Koran. In the course of history, this sacred book has been accepted as Scripture by a wide variety of faiths. However, the question is not whose book it is. The question is rather, In which context does it find its final interpretation?

For Christians, that context cannot be anything but the New Testament. In his day already Paul had to deal with the issue of non-Christian Jewish interpretation of the Old Testament. He writes in 2 Corinthians 3:15-16, "Indeed, to this very day, whenever Moses is read, a veil lies over their minds; but when one turns to the Lord, the veil is removed." Surely Christian preachers do not desire to interpret the Old Testament with "a veil over their minds." A better option is to see the Old Testament as pre-Christian.

The Old Testament Is Pre-Christian

We can best illustrate the position that the Old Testament is pre-Christian by summarizing the views of two well-known biblical scholars.

---

15. Leonard L. Thompson, "From *Tanakh* to Old Testament," in *Approaches to Teaching Hebrew Bible as Literature in Translation* (New York: Modern Language Association, 1983), 52.

16. Ibid., 45-46.

17. As well as sections of Isaiah within the Book of Mormon.

The Old Testament Is B.C.

In his thorough book *The Authority of the Old Testament*, John Bright struggles earnestly with the relationship between the Old and New Testaments and the hermeneutical significance of this relationship for preaching from the Old Testament. On the one hand, he rightly posits that "we can preach no sermons save Christian sermons."[18] On the other hand, he holds that the message of the Old Testament "is not *of and by itself* a Christian message."[19] And therein lies the dilemma. Bright sees the Old Testament as a pre-Christian book, or, as he likes to put it, a "B.C." book. "The Old Testament . . . stands in discontinuity with the New because it speaks a B.C. word, not an A.D. word."[20] Again, "The basic problem with the Old Testament is that, in all its texts, it occupies a perspective that is not, and cannot be, our own. It stands on the other side of Christ. . . ."[21]

Hermeneutically this position puts Bright in a real bind. On the one hand, he asserts, "We must proclaim it from an A.D. perspective, in its Christian significance, or the Old Testament will, quite frankly, be of little use to us in the pulpit." On the other hand, he rightly posits as a first principle of hermeneutics that "we may not impose Christian meanings on its texts either through exegetical skulduggery or homiletical irresponsibility: honest and sound method forbids it."[22]

Bright has a difficult time working his way out of this dilemma. He does offer a good suggestion (coming close to what is known as a "fuller sense"): "One can very well see retrospectively in past events a deeper significance than was apparent at the time, and that without in the least attributing to the actors in those events insights that they did not have."[23] But this promising suggestion is scuttled by a disappointing solution: "Precisely because it has this B.C. perspective, the Old Testament can address us with an unusual immediacy, for we live — all of us — to some degree in B.C." — B.C. now meaning "not fully subject to the messianic kingdom of Christ."[24] Since Bright has posited too much of a qualitative

---

18. Bright, *Authority*, 197.
19. Ibid., 183.
20. Ibid., 207.
21. Ibid., 183-84.
22. Ibid., 184.
23. Ibid., 203. Cf. p. 200.
24. Ibid., 206. For a similar solution, see Rudolf Bultmann, "Prophecy and Fulfillment," in *Essays on Old Testament Hermeneutics*, ed. Claus Westermann (Richmond: John Knox, 1963), 50-75, and in the same volume, Friedrich Baumgärtel, "The Hermeneutical Problem of the Old Testament," 134-59.

difference between the Old Testament and the New, his difficulty in finding a solution is partly of his own making.

The Old Testament Is Directed to Israel

Another person whom we should hear briefly is Elizabeth Achtemeier. Achtemeier has written a helpful book for preachers: *Preaching from the Old Testament*. But, like Bright, she takes the position that the Old Testament is pre-Christian. She writes, "The fact is . . . that apart from the New Testament, the Old Testament does not belong to the Christian church and is not its book. The Old Testament is the word of God to Israel. . . ."[25] Or, as she puts it elsewhere, "The . . . basic presupposition that we must hold as we preach from the Old Testament is that the Old Testament is directed to Israel. . . . Unless we therefore have some connection with Israel, the Old Testament is not our book, and it is not revelation spoken to us."[26] Happily, there is such a connection with Israel through Christ. "As Ephesians 2 states, Christ 'has made us both one,' and the Church now has become a member of the 'commonwealth of Israel.' Or, as in Romans 11, we wild gentile branches have been grafted into the root of Israel."[27]

Yet this connection with Israel alone is not sufficient for us to receive a Christian message from the Old Testament. Achtemeier states, "It must be emphasized that no sermon can become the Word of God for the Christian church if it deals only with the Old Testament apart from the New. In every sermon rising out of an Old Testament text there must be reference to the New Testament outcome of the Old Testament's word."[28] So how can we preach a Christian message from the Old Testament? In contrast to Bright's hermeneutical struggles with this issue, Achtemeier has a simple homiletical solution: "If the preacher chooses an Old Testament text first, then he must also choose a New Testament text to go with it."[29] Elsewhere she reiterates, "We must never preach only from an Old Testament text, without pairing that text with one from the New Testament."[30]

---

25. Achtemeier, *Preaching*, 56. Cf. Reu, *Homiletics*, 57, "To preach the Old Testament alone would be a deplorable relapse to the stage of pre-Christian preparation."

26. Achtemeier, "From Exegesis to Proclamation," 50.

27. Ibid. Cf. *Preaching*, 56.

28. Achtemeier, *Old Testament*, 142.

29. Ibid. Cf. *Preaching*, 56-59.

30. Achtemeier, *RevExp* 72/4 (1975) 474.

The Requirement of "Pairing"

Homiletically, "pairing" is a valid option, of course. Although there are many good reasons for "textual preaching" (that is, preaching on a single text), there is no law that restricts preachers to only one text. Yet "pairing," in my opinion, is not a good option. For one, it adds several complications to the preacher's task: preachers will have to do justice to expositing not one but two texts in two entirely different historical-cultural settings.[31] Also, sermons will tend to be dualistic, with an Old Testament part and a New Testament part. What is more, the significance of the Old Testament text is presented through the lens of a single New Testament text instead of the entire New Testament. If the New Testament text is not well chosen, this procedure can distort the message of the Old Testament text. For example, for Epiphany 4B the lectionary pairs the healing of Naaman (2 Kings 5:1-14) with Jesus' healing of a leper (Mark 1:40-45) — a rather superficial parallel at the level of two lepers being healed. But the *message* of 2 Kings 5:1-27 (the whole story) has to do with God's free healing (grace) of a Gentile being hindered by an Israelite (Gehazi). This specific message is not carried through in Mark 1:40-45. A more supportive New Testament passage would be Jesus' sermon in Nazareth in which he recalls this incident of God's grace for Gentiles, and "all in the synagogue were filled with rage" (Luke 4:27-30).

As the last example shows, one can often confirm or reinforce or deepen the Old Testament message by referring to one or more New Testament passages, but that is quite different from *requiring* "pairing" the Old Testament text with one from the New Testament in order that thereby the sermon "become the Word of God for the Christian church." This requirement degrades the Old Testament, for the Old Testament is God's word in its own right. It is true, of course, that we must read the Old Testament in the light of God's later revelation in the New Testament. But this context will bring to light many Old Testament teachings which the New Testament reiterates or simply assumes (see the list on pp. 27-28 above). Where the teaching of an Old Testament text is in full agreement with New Testament teaching, there is no need for "pairing." To establish a link with the present, or to confirm that this is also the teaching of the New Testament, the preacher may still refer to a New Testament incident or quote one or more New Testament texts, but this move is not re-

---

31. Cf. Achtemeier, *Old Testament*, 146, "Not until he fully understands the Old Testament lesson can he join a New Testament passage to it. And obviously he is going to have to bring the same study to the chosen New Testament pericope that he did to the Old."

quired to make the message "Christian." For example, one can preach on
Psalm 23, the Lord is my shepherd, and have a Christian message without "pairing" the Psalm with a New Testament text. In the sermon, one
should point out, of course, that this Lord is our shepherd only through
Christ, but "pairing" is not required to make the message Christian.

Consequently, I conclude that "pairing" is superfluous where there
is strong continuity between the message of the Old Testament and the
teaching of the New Testament. In cases where the Old Testament passage contains a promise which is fulfilled in the New Testament, the
preacher should naturally move on in the sermon to the fulfillment. But
this move to the New Testament can be done by statement, quotation, or
allusion, and does not require "pairing." The only time some kind of
"pairing" may be required is when there is strong *dis*continuity between
the message of the Old Testament text and the New Testament. For example, when preaching on Genesis 17:9-14, "Circumcise every male among
you as a sign of God's covenant," one must necessarily move on in the
sermon to an exposition of Acts, where the first Christian assembly dealt
with the issue of circumcision. But as a rule, "pairing" is not necessary
because the Old Testament, understood in the context of the New Testament, is also the word of God for his people today.

The Old Testament Is Christian

There is a sense in which we can call the Old Testament "pre-Christian,"
but then we are speaking chronologically, that is, we are saying that the
Old Testament existed before Christianity. But this description does not
say anything about its character. We could also call the foundations of a
house "pre-house," but all along we know that these foundations are an
integral part of the house. In like manner, we could say that the Old Testament is "pre-Christian," but all along we know that its essence is not
"pre-Christian" but "Christian." "Christian" describes the *character* of the
Old Testament, its nature.

If we have any doubts about the Old Testament being Christian, we
should recall that the Old Testament was the Bible of Jesus Christ himself.
It was also the Bible of Paul and the other apostles. Paul had the Old Testament in mind when he wrote, "All scripture is inspired by God and is
useful for teaching, for reproof, for correction, and for training in righteousness" (2 Tim 3:16). The Old Testament was the Bible of the authors
of the New Testament. The (Jewish) Christian church accepted the Old
Testament as its Bible as a matter of course: it had been theirs all along.
There never was any doubt about the Old Testament being (part of) the

Christian Bible[32] — until Marcion came along. Then the church made it official (A.D. 382).[33] Later creeds reiterated this position. For example, one creed of the Reformation reads: "We include in the Holy Scriptures the two volumes of the Old and New Testaments. . . . We receive all these [66] books and these only as holy and canonical, for the regulating, founding, and establishing of our faith."[34] And Vatican Council II declared, "The plan of salvation, foretold by the sacred authors, recounted and explained by them, is found as the true word of God in the books of the Old Testament: these books, therefore, written under divine inspiration, remain permanently valuable."[35]

Consequently, the dilemma of how to get a Christian message out of a "non-Christian" or "pre-Christian" book is a predicament of our own making, for it does not arise out of the Scriptures themselves. Of course, as we move from the Old Testament to the New Testament, we notice progression in redemptive history as well as in revelation. But progression does not make the Old Testament non-Christian or pre-Christian. The headwaters of a river are not "non-river" or "pre-river"; they are an essential part of the river as it flows downstream. Moreover, as a river moves forward even while remaining where it has always been, so the progression in redemptive history and revelation takes place without disqualifying the past. For progression takes place within the larger framework of continuity. Jesus, the person who moved redemptive history and revelation forward as no one else, said in Matthew 5:17, "Do not think that I have come to abolish the law or the prophets [that is, the Old Testament]; I have not come to abolish but to fulfill" — that is, to reveal its full meaning and bring it to its consummation.

The point is that we ought not to create a breach between the Old Testament and the New and then scurry about to find some kind of continuity in order to bring a Christian message. Instead, we ought to start with the continuity of a unified history of redemption which progresses from the old covenant to the new, and a single Scripture consisting of two Testaments. The Old Testament and the New are both parts of the Chris-

32. Cf. Oscar Cullmann, *Christ and Time,* 132, who, referring to the *Epistle of Barnabas,* makes the point that "the first Christians in their services of worship read the Old Testament and regard it as the canon of the Christian community; they thus treat it in practice as a *Christian* book."

33. See p. 19 above, n. 47.

34. *The Belgic Confession,* arts. 4 and 5. Cf. Berkouwer, *Person of Christ,* 117, "One can boil down the church's credo regarding the Scriptures into the statement that it is no anachronism to say that the Old Testament is Christian."

35. *Constitution on Divine Revelation,* 4.14, as cited in Bruce, *New Testament Development,* 12.

tian Bible; both reveal the same covenant-making God; both reveal the gospel of God's grace; both show God reaching out to his disobedient children with the promise, "I will be your God, and you will be my people"; both reveal God's acts of redemption. With this foundation of continuity firmly in mind, we are prepared to detect discontinuities, for we know that the God of the Bible is not a static God but a God who moves along with his people through history, meeting them where they are, revealing ever more of his plan of redemption even as he moves history forward to the perfection of his kingdom.

THE RELATION OF THE OLD TESTAMENT TO THE NEW

The relation of the Old and New Testaments is a much explored topic. Someone has calculated that "from 1869 to 1960 more than five hundred major works on the subject have been published."[36] The high interest in the relation of the Old and New Testaments indicates the pivotal importance of this topic. A. H. J. Gunneweg maintains, "The association of the Old and New Testament in the canon is itself the real hermeneutical problem."[37]

The Old Testament Is Open to the Future

Earlier we heard a professor of religion declare that the "Hebrew Scriptures are a complete work and do not need the New Testament to complete them." "If one stops reading at the end of the Hebrew Bible, there is no sense of incompleteness."[38] But this claim is patently false. As a matter of fact, many non-Christian Jews themselves continued to look for the final fulfillment of God's promises. N. T. Wright observes that "the great story of the Hebrew Scriptures was . . . inevitably read in the second-temple period as a story in search of a conclusion. This ending would have to incorporate the full liberation and redemption of Israel. . . ." He notes the different endings proposed by Josephus, Sirach 44–50, and the Maccabees. "These three examples of the many retellings of Israel's story

---

36. William Cosser, *Preaching*, 9. For a fine review of current positions on this issue, see David L. Baker, *Two Testaments, One Bible: A Study of Some Modern Solutions to the Theological Problem of the Relationship between the Old and New Testaments.*

37. Gunneweg, *Understanding*, 219.

38. Thompson, "From *Tanakh*," 52, 46 (see p. 40 above).

show that Jews of the period . . . were able to conceive of the story as a whole, and to be regularly looking for its proper conclusion. . . ."[39] Wright concludes, "On virtually all sides there is a sense that the history of the creator, his world and his covenant people is going somewhere, but that it has not yet arrived there. The creator will act again, as he did in the past, to deliver Israel from her plight and to deal with the evil in the world."[40]

Bernhard Anderson concedes, "The Old Testament does not necessarily lead to the New: it could, and did, lead to the Talmud and continuing rabbinical tradition; or it could lead to the Koran and to the religion of radical monotheism." But "seen in the perspective of Christian faith, the whole biblical story, which extends from creation to consummation, reaches its climax in the life, death, and resurrection of Jesus Christ and the new age in human history that he introduced."[41]

Taking our cue from Irenaeus and Chrysostom, we can liken the Old Testament to a painting which God is sketching on the canvass of history. As long as the painting is incomplete, it can be developed in various ways — that is, it is open to various interpretations. But when the painting has received its definitive shape and hues with New Testament teachings about a first and second coming of Christ, the ambiguity inherent in the Old Testament is resolved. Now every part of the Old Testament must be seen in its relation to the complete picture; every part must be seen in its relation to Jesus Christ.

---

39. Wright, *New Testament*, 217, 218. Cf. Bright, *Authority*, 199, "It is an unfinished *Heilsgeschichte*, a *Heilsgeschichte* that does not arrive at *Heil*. . . . One turns its [the Old Testament's] last page to find Israel still in a posture of waiting — for God's future." Cf. von Rad, *Old Testament Theology*, 2.319, "The Old Testament can only be read as a book of ever increasing anticipation."

40. Ibid., 219. Cf. Shires, *Finding*, 31, "Both Jews and Christians recognized that because the Scriptures were inspired writings their unfulfilled prophecies demanded some kind of fulfillment. The O.T. everywhere looks toward a future in which God will reign over all mankind and there will be peace and happiness on earth. There is in the Jewish Scriptures an inescapable incompleteness and a deep longing for the coming of God in power and right to correct man's evils and failings." Cf. Toombs, *Old Testament*, 27, "Seen through Christian eyes, the Old Testament is an incomplete book. Repeatedly it points beyond itself to something still to come. Longings, hopes, and aspirations are raised, but never fulfilled."

41. Anderson, "Bible as Shared Story," 32, 33.

A Single Redemptive History Underlies Both Testaments

The Old Testament proclaims God's mighty acts of redemption. These acts reach a climax in the New Testament when God sends his Son. Redemptive history is the mighty river that runs from the old covenant to the new and holds the two together. It is true, of course, that there is progression in redemptive history, but it is one redemptive history. It is true that there is an old covenant and a new covenant, but it is one covenant of grace.[42] It is true that the sacrifice of Christ brought an end to Old Testament temple worship with its blood sacrifices, but Christians are still required to bring sacrifices to the same God.[43] Progression in redemptive history takes place within the continuity of a single redemptive history.

Along with progression in redemptive history, we notice progression in revelation. This progression results in discontinuities between the teachings of the Old Testament and those of the New (see the list on pp. 23-25 above). But in revelation, too, the progression takes place within the framework of underlying continuity. Although the New Testament shows many discontinuities with the Old Testament, it reveals even more continuities; and these continuities are more fundamental. The New Testament authors repeat over and over the connections: Old Testament promises come to fulfillment in the New Testament; Old Testament types find their fulfillment in New Testament antitypes; and Old Testament themes, such as the kingdom of God, covenant, and redemption, even while undergoing dramatic transformation, are continued into the New Testament. All of these links demonstrate the unity of the Old and New Testaments. And all of these links are based, ultimately, on the fact that God's redemptive history is of one piece. For the connections between promise and fulfillment, between type and antitype, and the continuity of themes in the Bible are possible only because of God's covenant faithfulness in redemptive history. In other words, a single, God-guided, redemptive history is the basis, the foundation, of the unity of the Old and New Testaments.

---

42. On the continuity between the old and the new covenant as it comes to expression in Jeremiah 31, see Bernhard W. Anderson, "The New Covenant and the Old," in *The Old Testament and Christian Faith* (New York: Harper & Row, 1963), 225-42.

43. For example, Rom 12:1, "Present your bodies as a living sacrifice, holy and acceptable to God. . . ."

Jesus Christ Is the Link between the Two Testaments

Although a single redemptive history is crucial for establishing the unity between Old and New Testaments, more can be said. We usually think of Jesus as a New Testament figure. However, T. C. Vriezen strikingly points out that "like the authors of the apocrypha and of the Qumran-literature, and like John the Baptist, He belongs to the world of the Old Testament. . . ."[44] A little reflection will show that this statement is true. Jesus was eight days old when he received the sign of the old covenant (Luke 2:21). After forty days, Joseph and Mary brought him to the temple to be dedicated to God, "as it is written in the law of the Lord, 'Every firstborn male shall be designated as holy to the Lord'" (Luke 2:23). Jesus studied the Old Testament, went to the synagogue on the sabbath ("as was his custom," Luke 4:16), sang the Psalms, prayed in the temple, and celebrated Passover. "Like John the Baptist, He belongs to the world of the Old Testament, and simultaneously," Vriezen continues, "He is the creator of the events of which the New Testament is full and thus the head of the new community of the Kingdom of God. In this way there is a fundamental connection between the two Testaments in the person of Jesus Christ."[45]

Jesus Christ is the link between the Old Testament and the New. God's revelation reaches its climax in the New Testament — and this climax is not a new teaching or a new law, but a person, God's own Son. The Old and New Testaments are related, therefore, not as law-gospel but as promise-fulfillment (a person).[46] The writer to the Hebrews proclaims, "Long ago God spoke to our ancestors in many and various ways by the prophets, but in these last days he has spoken to us by a Son . . ." (Heb 1:1-2). The author underscores the continuity of God speaking throughout the ages, even while he marvels at the new way God is speaking in these last days: God "has spoken to us by a Son."

This speaking by a Son is unheard of; no other religion makes this claim. Yet the author of Hebrews is not the first to make this claim; he simply passes on the teaching of Jesus himself. For Jesus disclosed the astounding progression in revelation that took place with his coming: "Whoever has seen me has seen the Father," he said

---

44. Vriezen, *Outline of Old Testament Theology*, 123.

45. Ibid. Cf. Gustaf Wingren, *Living Word*, 57, "The unity of the Bible . . . depends on the fact that Christ is Lord. Christ is the living Lord who rises up between the two Covenants, the two 'Testaments,' fulfilling the one and laying the foundation of the other."

46. See Herman Bavinck, *Magnalia Dei: Onderwijzing in de Christelijke Religie naar Gereformeerde Belijdenis* (Kampen: Kok, 1909), 94.

(John 14:9).[47] Paul also underscores this momentous progression in revelation with the coming of God's Son. For example, he writes about "the revelation of the mystery that was kept secret for long ages but is now disclosed, and through the prophetic writings is made known to all the Gentiles . . ." (Rom 16:25-26). Notice how Paul ties this progression (the "mystery" now disclosed) to the past ("through the prophetic writings") and thus reiterates the unity in God's revelation even as it progresses. What is this "mystery" that has now been disclosed? In 1 Timothy 3:16 Paul answers this question with an early Christian hymn. He writes,

> Without any doubt, the mystery of our religion is great:
> He was revealed in flesh,
>   vindicated by the Spirit,[48]
>   seen by angels,
> proclaimed among Gentiles,
>   believed in throughout the world,
>   taken up in glory.

The mystery is Jesus Christ, God in human flesh, raised from the dead by the Spirit,[49] ascended into heaven ("seen by angels"). Christ incarnate is both the "mystery" revealed in the New Testament and the link between the Old Testament and the New.

The New Testament Writers Fused Their Writings with the Old Testament

In writing their Gospels and letters, the writers of the New Testament deliberately connected their work to the Old Testament. In Chapter 5 we shall examine the various ways in which they used the Old Testament, but at this point it is sufficient to note that they used the Old Testament as their preaching-text, so to speak, for proclaiming the gospel of Jesus Christ. Hence they linked the New Testament to the Old Testament. They did this not only by way of promise-fulfillment, typology, and Old Testament themes (see above) but also by frequently quoting the Old Testament or alluding to it. Biblical scholars are not agreed on the number of quotations and allusions. Depending on the criteria used, the number of quotations ranges from 250 to some 600, and the number of allusions

---

47. Cf. John 1:18, "No one has ever seen God. It is God the only Son, who is close to the Father's heart, who has made him known."

48. NRSV alternate translation; NIV only translation.

49. See, e.g., Rom 1:4.

from 650 to some 4,000.[50] In addition, the New Testament authors carried forward into the New Testament countless images and concepts from the Old Testament. Clearly they saw the Old Testament as the book of God's promises, which find their fulfillment in Jesus Christ. The church subsequently recognized this unity of Old Testament and New Testament and received both as its canon.

The Old Testament Must Be Interpreted from the Perspective of the New

We have looked at the relation of the Old Testament and the New from different angles: the Old Testament is incomplete without the New, a single redemptive history is the river that holds the Old and New Testaments together, the person of Jesus Christ unites the two Testaments, and the writers of the New Testament intentionally fuse their writings with the Old Testament. These considerations lead to the fundamentally decisive conclusion that the two Testaments are not two books but one. And this conclusion, in turn, leads to the equally fundamental hermeneutical conclusion that *the Old Testament must be interpreted not only in its own context but also in the context of the New Testament.*

This conclusion is but an application of the standard hermeneutical principle that every text must be understood in its context. Since the literary context of the Old Testament in the Christian canon is the New Testament, this means that the Old Testament must be understood in the context of the New Testament. And since the heart of the New Testament is Jesus Christ, this means that every message from the Old Testament must be seen in the light of Jesus Christ.[51]

---

50. See Walter Kaiser, *Rediscovering*, 168; Kaiser, *Introduction*, 216; and Klaas Runia, *CTJ* 24 (1989) 305.

51. Many Christian scholars agree on this hermeneutical principle. For example, Toombs, *Old Testament*, 26, "The preacher must be able to take his stand squarely in the New Testament faith, so that, although he may preach *from* the Old Testament, he will never be preaching the Old Testament, but always his own distinctive Christian gospel." Cf. Kuiper, "Scriptural Preaching," 228, "In the new dispensation no preacher may be satisfied to occupy the standpoint of the old. A sermon on an Old Testament text must always be a New Testament sermon." Cf. Clowney, *Preaching*, 75, "The Christian proclamation of an Old Testament text is not the preaching of an Old Testament sermon." Cf. also Carl Graesser, "Preaching," 529, "The Old Testament looks forward to the goal of the coming of the kingdom of God. Because that kingdom has come in Jesus Christ, the Old Testament can be preached only in the light of that fulfillment and completeness of the New Testament event of Jesus Christ."

The necessity to read the Old Testament from the perspective of the New also follows from the progressive nature of redemptive history. The arrival of Jesus in the "fullness of time" and God's final revelation in him calls for reading the Old Testament from the perspective of this final revelation. John Stek clarifies this point: "The fact of progression in salvation history demands an ever *new* hearing of the word of the Lord spoken at an earlier moment in salvation history. The hearing must be new because it is a hearing in the context of the later events and circumstances in salvation history, and in the light of the word of the Lord spoken later in salvation history."[52]

Paul wrote about this new hearing of the Old Testament in 2 Corinthians 3:15-16, "Whenever Moses is read, a veil lies over their minds; but when one turns to the Lord, the veil is removed." A Christian who knows the Lord Jesus from God's revelation in the New Testament has a "new reader-competence"[53] for understanding the Old Testament.

Earlier we saw that the Old Testament by itself is like an incomplete painting. The revelation in and of Christ in the New Testament completes this painting, and we must now see every part of the Old Testament in the light of the whole painting. This analogy is nothing other than a form of the standard hermeneutical circle: one cannot really know the meaning of a part until one knows the whole, and one cannot know the whole until one knows its parts.

Hermeneutical Circle

Old Testament passages (parts)

New Testament passages (parts)

Jesus Christ

Given the unity of the two Testaments in the Christian canon, the widely accepted hermeneutical circle informs us that one can really understand Old Testament passages only in the light of the New Testament

52. Stek, *CTJ* 4/1 (1969) 47-48.
53. Richard Hays, *Echoes*, 124.

and its testimony to Jesus Christ.[54] But the reverse also holds: one cannot really understand Jesus Christ until one knows the Old Testament parts. We will get back to this idea later, but first we need to discuss one more key issue in preaching Christ from the Old Testament.

THE OLD TESTAMENT'S WITNESS TO CHRIST

Another major issue we face in preaching Christ from the Old Testament is whether Christ is present in the Old Testament. If Christ is not in some way present in the Old Testament, how can we authentically preach him from the Old Testament? As we shall see in Chapter 4, von Rad opposed Wilhelm Vischer on this issue. Von Rad warned against the temptation "to speak of a 'personal presence' of Christ in the Old Testament, that is, that Christ was 'in Isaac,' 'in David,' 'in the one who prayed Psalm 22.'" Von Rad could not accept such a personal presence of Christ in the Old Testament.[55] More recently James Mays stated, "The Old Testament texts do not speak about Jesus of Nazareth, at least in readings that will pass muster in our modern intellectual climate. The Jesus of history was not there as a reference for these texts."[56] Earlier we heard James Barr make the same point: "The Old Testament is the time in which our Lord is not yet come."[57] Preachers are, therefore, faced with a dilemma: How does one preach Christ from a book that was written long before he was born?

54. Cf. Herbert Mayer, *CTM* 35 (1964) 607, "The Old Testament can be Christologically understood and preached in harmony with its own purposes only by the Christian. Only that man who looks at the Old Testament with his back to the cross and the tomb [the resurrection, ascension, and second coming] can appreciate what God is doing and saying." The words in brackets are my additions to Mayer's narrow view (see Chapter 1). Cf. Kuyper, *Scripture Unbroken*, 56, "To present the Old in isolation from the New is to run the risk of offering a truncated understanding of the faith. . . . Every Old Testament passage should be brought under the light of the New for correction, improvement, and enlargement. . . ."

55. Martin Kuske, *Old Testament*, 67, referring to von Rad's *Fragen der Schriftauslegung im Alten Testament* (1938), 7ff.

56. Mays, *The Lord Reigns*, 99.

57. See p. 38 above.

Various Options in Preaching Christ from the Old Testament

Christ Is the Eternal Logos Working in Old Testament Times

Some respond to this dilemma by pointing out that the New Testament reveals Christ as the eternal Logos, present at creation and, therefore, also in Old Testament times (e.g., John 1:1-3). Although this understanding of Christ is true and has been used to preach Christ from the Old Testament, it avoids the real issue. Von Rad rejects a "personal presence of Christ in the Old Testament," by which he means Jesus of Nazareth. Mays and Barr are also speaking of the historical Jesus. To appeal to Christ as the eternal Logos is to sidestep the real issue for preachers, for the challenge is to preach Christ *incarnate* as the climax of God's revelation. As incarnate, we should all agree, Christ was not physically present in Old Testament times. To claim otherwise is to deny the New Testament claim that Christ became incarnate only *after* the events recorded in the Old Testament. The issue, then, is how to preach the incarnate Christ from a book that predates his incarnation by many centuries. This way of putting the issue still leaves preachers with several options.

Reading Christ Back into the Old Testament

Some preachers simply read Jesus Christ back into the Old Testament. This has often been done in the history of preaching, as we shall see in the next two chapters. Allegorizing and typologizing are easy ways to preach the historical Jesus or his cross from Old Testament passages. Other preachers use the Old Testament text simply as a springboard to retell the New Testament story of Jesus. But in spite of its popularity historically, reading Christ back into the Old Testament is not a good option because it forces the text to say something it does not intend to say. In other words, it misuses the Old Testament text.

Move from the Old Testament Text to Christ in the New Testament

A better option is to start one's sermon with an Old Testament text and then move to the New Testament to preach Jesus Christ. Since every text should be interpreted in its literary context anyway, and since the Old and New Testaments are a unity, there is warrant for such a move. Of course, one ought not to move to the New Testament in an arbitrary manner. One must look for a clue, a feature, in the Old Testament text that warrants linking it with a particular New Testament event or one or more New Testament passages. In other words, one must look for a road that allows one to move meaningfully from the Old Testament to the New Testament.

The Old Testament Witnesses to Christ Incarnate

The New Testament offers us a similar option but grounds it firmly in the Old Testament. It proclaims that the Old Testament itself witnesses to Christ incarnate. If this is true, the ultimate form of interpreting the Old Testament is messianic interpretation or christocentric interpretation. Other forms of interpretation, such as literary, historical, and sociological, may discover aspects of the truth, but only messianic interpretation will uncover the vital truth of the Old Testament. Because of the significance of this option, and because messianic interpretation has many detractors in modern Old Testament scholarship,[58] we need to explore this option further with a survey of New Testament evidence.

New Testament Insights into Preaching Christ from the Old Testament

In Chapter 5 we shall analyze in depth how the New Testament preaches Christ from the Old Testament. For our purposes at this stage, it is sufficient to establish that we can preach Christ from the Old Testament because the Old Testament itself witnesses to Christ incarnate. We shall listen in turn to the preaching of Jesus, that of the apostles, and that of the Gospel writers.

The Preaching of Jesus

In one of his first sermons, in his hometown of Nazareth, Jesus read Isaiah 61:1-2, which alludes to the Year of Jubilee (Lev 25:8-55): "The Spirit of the Lord is upon me, because he has anointed me to bring good news to the poor. He has sent me to proclaim release to the captives and recovery of sight to the blind, to let the oppressed go free, to proclaim the year of the Lord's favor." Then he said, "Today this scripture has been fulfilled

---

58. Gordon McConville, "Messianic Interpretation," 2, judges, "Modern Old Testament scholarship has been largely informed by the belief that traditional Christian messianic interpretations of Old Testament passages have been exegetically indefensible." The book he introduces seeks to bring a solidly argued change in modern biases against messianic interpretation. See especially the excellent essay by Iain Provan, "The Messiah in the Book of Kings," in *The Lord's Anointed: Interpretation of Old Testament Messianic Texts*, 67-85.

in your hearing" (Luke 4:18-21). Notice that the fulfillment had to do with Jesus of Nazareth: the Spirit of the Lord was on him; he proclaimed good news to the poor; he healed the sick; he brought in the Year of Jubilee. According to Jesus, the Old Testament witnessed to him long before he was born.

This Old Testament witness to Jesus was difficult to detect, however. In one of his last "sermons," Jesus scolded two of his disciples on the way to Emmaus, "Oh, how foolish you are, and how slow of heart to believe all that the prophets have declared! Was it not necessary that the Messiah should suffer these things and then enter into his glory?" (Luke 24:25-26). The Jewish people were looking for a victorious Messiah, not a suffering Messiah. But, says Jesus, the prophets had predicted his suffering. "Then beginning with Moses and all the prophets, he interpreted to them the things about himself in all the scriptures" (Luke 24:27).[59] Jesus believed that Moses and all the prophets bore witness to him, the incarnate Christ. How, then, was Jesus present in the Old Testament centuries before he was born? He was "present" basically as promise.

The concept of "promise" turns out to be much broader, however, than the predictions in a few messianic prophecies. In his last "sermon" in Luke (24:44-49), Jesus says, ". . . everything written about me in the law of Moses, the prophets, and the psalms must be fulfilled." Notice, Jesus refers to the three main sections of the Old Testament; not just a few prophecies but the whole Old Testament speaks of Jesus Christ. And what does it reveal about Jesus? At a minimum, it speaks of his suffering, his resurrection, and his teaching. Jesus says, "Thus it is written, that the Messiah is to suffer and to rise from the dead on the third day, and that repentance and forgiveness of sins is to be proclaimed in his name to all nations, beginning from Jerusalem." In John 5:39, similarly, we hear Jesus say to the Jews, "You search the scriptures, because you think that in them you have eternal life; and it is they that testify on my behalf [about me, NIV]." Not just a few isolated messianic prophecies, but the whole Old Testament bears witness to Jesus.

The Preaching of the Apostles

Because Jesus is "present" in the Old Testament as promise, the apostles can preach Christ from the Old Testament. On the day of Pentecost, Peter

---

59. Clowney, "Preaching Christ," 164, notes, "The phrase 'beginning at Moses and all the prophets' and the use of the verb *diermeneuo* indicate reasoned interpretation. Jesus did not present a course in 'eisegesis.' He interpreted what the Scriptures *do* say and opened His disciples' minds to understand."

uses Joel and Psalms 16 and 110 to proclaim Christ (Acts 2:14-34). A few days later Peter is preaching in Solomon's portico (Acts 3:11-26) and says, "God fulfilled what he had foretold through all the prophets, that his Messiah would suffer" (v 18). Then he speaks of Jesus remaining in heaven "until the time of universal restoration that God announced long ago through his holy prophets" (v 21). Next he quotes Deuteronomy 15:15, 18, "Moses said, 'The Lord your God will raise up for you from your own people a prophet like me. . . .' And all the prophets, as many as have spoken, from Samuel and those after him, also predicted these days" (vv 22-24). And Peter concludes by quoting God's promise to Abraham in Genesis 12:3, "And in your descendants all the families of the earth shall be blessed," making the point that Jesus had come first to Abraham's descendants to bless them by turning them from their "wicked ways" (vv 25-26).

Later, Philip encounters an Ethiopian eunuch who was reading from Isaiah 53, "Like a sheep he was led to the slaughter . . . ," but did not understand the passage. "Then Philip began to speak, and starting with this scripture, he proclaimed to him the good news about Jesus" (Acts 8:35).

Preaching in Antioch of Pisidia, Paul briefly surveys the history of Israel from Egypt to King David, and then gets to the point: "Of this man's [David's] posterity God has brought to Israel a Savior, Jesus, as he promised" (Acts 13:23). Paul continues by speaking of the death and resurrection of Jesus, concluding with a remarkable string of quotations from the Old Testament (vv 32-35):

> And we bring you the good news that what God promised to our ancestors he has fulfilled for us, their children, by raising Jesus; as also it is written in the second psalm,
>
> "You are my Son; today I have begotten you."
>
> As to his raising him from the dead, no more to return to corruption, he has spoken in this way [Isa 55:3],
>
> "I will give you the holy promises made to David."
>
> Therefore he has also said in another psalm [16:10],
>
> "You will not let your Holy One experience corruption."

Reporting on Paul's preaching in Thessalonica, Luke writes, "On three sabbath days he argued with them from the scriptures [the Old Testament], explaining and proving that it was necessary for the Messiah to suffer and to rise from the dead, and saying, 'This is the Messiah, Jesus whom I am proclaiming to you'" (Acts 17:2-3). Some hearers were persuaded, but others wanted to harm Paul and Silas, so they had to flee to Beroea. Luke reports, "These Jews [in Beroea] were more receptive than those in Thessalonica, for they welcomed the message very eagerly and examined the scriptures [the Old Testament] every day to see whether these things were so" (v 11).

Later Paul reminds the Corinthians of his preaching of Christ and his dependence on the Old Testament in doing so. "For I handed on to you as of first importance . . . : that Christ died for our sins in accordance with the scriptures, and that he was buried, and that he was raised on the third day in accordance with the scriptures" (1 Cor 15:3-4).[60]

In their preaching, therefore, the apostles followed their Master by preaching Christ from the Old Testament.[61] There was no doubt in their minds that the Old Testament witnessed to Jesus. In fact, Herman Ridderbos notes that "one of the leading motifs of Paul's preaching is that his gospel is according to the scriptures."[62] He writes further, "Paul proclaims Christ as the fulfillment of the promise of God to Abraham, as the seed in which all the families of the earth shall be blessed (Gal. 3:8, 16, 29), the eschatological bringer of salvation whose all-embracing significance must be understood in the light of prophecy (Rom. 15:9-12), the fulfillment of God's redemptive counsel concerning the whole world and its future."[63]

The Preaching of the Gospel Writers

In addition to the testimony of Jesus and the apostles, it is instructive to see how the Gospel writers begin their presentations of Jesus.

Mark

This is how Mark begins his Gospel: "The beginning of the good news of Jesus Christ, the Son of God. As it is written in the prophet Isaiah, 'See, I

---

60. Luke also characterizes the preaching of Apollos as "showing by the scriptures that the Messiah is Jesus" (Acts 18:28).

61. Even the Sanhedrin, according to Luke, astonished at the bold preaching of Peter and John as "unschooled, ordinary men . . . , took note that these men had been with Jesus" (Acts 4:13, NIV).

62. Ridderbos, *Paul*, 51. This quotation is followed by "(Rom. 1:17; 3:28; cf. Rom. 4; Gal. 3:6ff.; 4:21ff.; 1 Cor. 10:1-10; Rom. 15:4; 1 Cor. 9:10; 2 Tim. 3:16, *et al.*)."

63. Ibid. Cf. ibid., "This fulfillment was not only foretold by the prophets, but signifies the execution of the divine plan of salvation that he purposed to himself with respect to the course of the ages and the end of the times (Eph. 1:9, 10; 3:11). This is the fundamental redemptive-historical and all-embracing character of Paul's preaching of Christ."

am sending my messenger ahead of you, who will prepare your way; the voice of one crying out in the wilderness. . . .' John the baptizer appeared in the wilderness, proclaiming . . ." (1:1-4). Mark links Jesus and his fore-runner John to the Old Testament by way of Malachi 3:1 and Isaiah 40:3 — prophecies concerning the coming of the Lord's messenger and the Lord himself. Soon Jesus begins his ministry. "Now after John was ar-rested, Jesus came to Galilee, proclaiming the good news of God, and saying, 'The time is fulfilled, and the kingdom of God has come near; re-pent, and believe the good news'" (1:14-15). Jack Kingsbury comments, "As Mark describes it, therefore, the appearance of John and of Jesus means that the age of Old Testament prophecy has passed and the escha-tological age of fulfillment has begun."[64] Kingsbury raises the question why Mark situates "his story of the earthly ministry of Jesus within a con-text of history that runs from the time of Old Testament prophecy to the end of time?" He answers, "Because . . . he wants to raise the claim that it is exactly the earthly ministry of Jesus that is pivotal to the whole of God's dealings with humankind."[65]

Matthew

Matthew begins his Gospel as follows: "An account of the genealogy of Jesus the Messiah, the son of David, the son of Abraham." Whereas Mark links Jesus to the prophets, Matthew links Jesus via the great king David all the way back to the patriarch Abraham. Matthew traces Jesus' roots all the way back to Abraham because with him God first established his cov-enant of grace, including the promises of offspring, land, and being a blessing to all families of the earth (Gen 12:2-3; 17:8; 22:17-18). On the sig-nificance of this link of Jesus to Abraham, David Holwerda comments: "By linking Jesus to Abraham, Matthew declares that God's promise of blessing for the nations is now being fulfilled through Jesus. The early hint of this fulfilled promise is given in the coming of the magi to wor-ship Jesus (Matthew 2). Later Jesus prophetically announces that 'many will come from east and west and will eat with Abraham and Isaac and Jacob in the kingdom of heaven' (8:11). Then at the conclusion of the Gos-pel Jesus commissions his disciples to 'make disciples of all nations' (28:19)."[66]

Matthew traces Jesus' roots also to the great king David. This is an-other person in Israel's history to whom God had given rich promises. In

64. Kingsbury, *Jesus Christ*, 29.
65. Ibid.
66. Holwerda, *Jesus and Israel*, 32-33.

fact, it was through Israel's king that God would fulfill his promise to Abraham to be a blessing to all nations: "May all nations be blessed in him" (Ps 72:17). But God had promised David specifically, "Your house and your kingdom shall be made sure forever before me; your throne shall be established forever" (2 Sam 7:16). Again Matthew's point is that Jesus is the ultimate fulfillment of God's promises to David; this son of David inaugurates a kingdom that will last forever. "The focus of Matthew's genealogy is clear. The significance of Jesus is deeply rooted in the history of Old Testament Israel, so deeply that the blessings promised to Old Testament Israel find their fulfillment only through him. He is Israel, the representative embodiment of true Israel and Israel's king."[67]

Luke

Whereas Matthew traces Jesus' roots to Abraham at the beginning of covenant history, Luke goes back even farther. In his genealogy of Jesus, he traces Jesus' roots all the way back to "Adam, son of God" (3:38). Luke goes back all the way to Adam because, in contrast to Matthew who is writing to Jews, he is writing to Gentiles. The history in which Luke views Jesus is all of human history — a history which includes Gentiles from the beginning. In case we miss the point, Luke records that Jesus was born in the days of Emperor Augustus, when "Quirinius was governor of Syria" (2:1-2). Luke continues the story of Jesus with the book of Acts, which ends with Paul in Rome, "proclaiming the kingdom of God and teaching about the Lord Jesus Christ with all boldness and unhindered" (Acts 28:31). Jesus, according to Luke, is the midpoint of human history.[68] He is the junction between B.C. and A.D..

Jack Kingsbury notes that "Luke distinguishes between the 'time of Israel' (1:54-55, 68), which is the 'time of prophecy' (1:70; 24:25-27, 44-45), and the 'time of fulfillment' (1:1; 24:44)."[69] The link between the two ages is Jesus. He is the one who fulfills prophecy and ushers in the new age. No wonder Luke is the writer who records Jesus' saying, "Everything written about me in the law of Moses, the prophets, and the psalms must be fulfilled" (24:44). According to Luke, Jesus is the one who fulfills the Old Testament.

---

67. Ibid., 34.
68. The title of Hans Conzelmann's commentary on Luke, *Die Mitte der Zeit*.
69. Kingsbury, *Jesus Christ*, 97.

John

John traces the good news of Jesus even further back than do Mark (the prophets), Matthew (Abraham), and Luke (Adam). John goes all the way back to the beginning, even before creation: "In the beginning was the Word. . . . All things came into being through him. . . . And the Word became flesh . . ." (1:1-14). With his "in the beginning," John obviously alludes to Genesis 1:1, "In the beginning when God created the heavens and the earth. . . ." John presents Jesus as the eternal Logos who is fully one with God but who at a certain point in history takes on human nature. John is the Gospel writer who presents the "I am" sayings, identifying Jesus with Yahweh, the "I AM" of the Old Testament.

But John also presents Jesus as the fulfillment of God's promises to Israel. He records Jesus' saying, "You search the scriptures because you think that in them you have eternal life; and it is they that testify on my behalf [about me, NIV]" (5:39). He further quotes Jesus' saying, "If you believed Moses, you would believe me, for he wrote about me" (5:46). Clearly, John also believed that the Old Testament witnessed to Jesus Christ.

*   *   *

From this brief survey of the New Testament, it is clear that the apostles and the Gospel writers preached Christ from the Old Testament.[70] It is also clear that they could do so with integrity because they believed that the Old Testament spoke of Christ.[71] Finally, it is evident that they learned this christological understanding of the Old Testament from no one other than Jesus himself, for Jesus not only modeled in his life his ful-

70. Cf. Karl Barth, *Church Dogmatics* 1/2, 72, "The New Testament writers are utterly unanimous in seeing . . . in the history of Israel attested in the Old Testament Canon the connecting point for their proclamation, doctrine and narrative of Christ; and *vice versa*, in seeing in their proclamation, doctrine and narrative of Christ the truth of the history of Israel, the fulfilment of the Holy Scripture read in the synagogue."

71. Cf. Brevard Childs, *Biblical Theology*, 480, "The overwhelming conviction of all of the New Testament is that in the incarnation of Jesus Christ both Old Testament lines of revelation, from 'above' and from 'below', were united in the one Lord and Saviour." Cf. William Cosser, *Preaching*, 13, "The Old Testament is the preparation, the prophecy and the promise, of which the incarnation is the realization and the fulfillment." See further H. L. Ellison, *The Centrality of the Messianic Idea for the Old Testament,* and Donald Juel, *Messianic Exegesis,* who argues that early Christianity applied 2 Samuel 7, Psalms 22, 69, 89, and 110, the Servant songs of Isaiah, and Daniel 7 to Jesus because these passages had already been understood as messianic by Jewish interpreters.

fillment of the Old Testament[72] but he also taught them "the things about himself in all the scriptures" (Luke 24:27).

The point for contemporary preachers is this: *if the Old Testament indeed witnesses to Christ, then we are faithful preachers only when we do justice to this dimension in our interpretation and preaching of the Old Testament.* The tragedy is that contemporary historical-critical exegesis, which tries so hard to recover the original meaning of the Old Testament, usually ignores this dimension. Although Christ is pictured in the Old Testament, contemporary Christian preachers frequently fail to notice it. This blind spot of ours makes it crucial that we, after establishing the original message of our text, view it again in the light of the New Testament, raising questions as to how this message connects with Jesus Christ. Does this passage witness to Christ by way of Old Testament expectations, predictions, promises, types, or themes which find their fulfillment in Christ in the New Testament? These questions are important questions to raise, for, according to the New Testament, if we fail to preach Christ from the Old Testament, we have missed its essence.[73]

BENEFITS OF PREACHING CHRIST FROM THE OLD TESTAMENT

One of the major benefits of preaching Christ is that such preaching saves people for eternity, "for there is no other name under heaven given among mortals by which we must be saved" (Acts 4:12). But in addition to this benefit of preaching Christ, we can discern others which arise specifically from preaching Christ from the *Old* Testament. We shall note two such benefits: acquainting people with the Old Testament and providing them a fuller understanding of Christ.

---

72. Cf. Martin Selman, "Messianic Mysteries," 283, "Jesus both fulfilled and expanded the messianic ideas of the Old Testament. He fulfilled all the qualities associated with anointed leaders in the Old Testament. . . ." Cf. James Dunn, "Messianic Ideas and Their Influence on the Jesus of History."

73. An interdenominational committee reported to the World Council of Churches in 1947, "In the two Testaments the same God offers the same salvation by the same Saviour." Quoted by Cosser, *Preaching*, 15. Cf. "The Chicago Statement on Biblical Hermeneutics," 1982: "The person and work of Jesus Christ are the central focus of the entire Bible. We deny that any method of interpretation which rejects or obscures the Christ-centeredness of the Bible is correct."

Acquainting People with the Old Testament

One of the major benefits of preaching Christ from the Old Testament is that the Old Testament will be heard in the Christian church. In Chapter 1 we have enumerated reasons for preaching from the Old Testament. Specific benefits accrue to the preacher as well as the congregation from a fuller understanding of God's revelation: the Old Testament discloses the history of redemption leading to Christ;[74] it proclaims truth not found in the New Testament; it helps us understand the New Testament; and it prevents misunderstanding the New Testament.

These benefits assume that preachers seek to cover the broad range of Old Testament literature and do not limit themselves to a narrow band of favorite passages. For a legitimate concern is that the goal of preaching *Christ* may lead preachers to select only messianic prophecies. With such a limited range, unfortunately, one would miss out on the expansive, broader themes of the Old Testament. For the Old Testament is the revelation of God's "faithfulness and his mercy, the disclosure of his covenant which is eternally sure and of the holy remnant saved by grace alone."[75] To avoid the selection of texts from only a narrow band of messianic texts, preachers should select their preaching-texts not with the primary goal of preaching Christ but with the primary goals of preaching the whole counsel of God and building up the faith of the church. How one preaches Christ from these texts is an important but later consideration.

Providing a Fuller Understanding of Christ

A second cluster of benefits of preaching Christ from the Old Testament involves a fuller understanding of Christ. Berkouwer observes that without the Old Testament "one will have left a Christ who is detached from the broad background of human misery and of divine redemptive action, the background of God's righteousness and his wrath, his love and his holiness."[76] Von Rad also maintains that "our knowledge of Christ is incom-

74. See, e.g., Clowney, "Preaching Christ from All the Scriptures," 183, "When the Old Testament is interpreted in the light of its own structure of promise and when that promise is seen as fulfilled in Jesus Christ, then the significance of the Old Testament can be preached in theological depth and in practical power. Preaching that does not center on Christ will always miss the dimension of depth in Old Testament revelation."

75. Berkouwer, *Person of Christ*, 139.

76. Ibid., 152. Vriezen, *Outline*, 9, states, "Christ's Messianic office cannot be confessed and maintained without the Old Testament."

plete without the witness of the Old Testament. Christ is given to us only through the double witness of the choir of those who await and those who remember."[77] We shall note this fuller understanding in three specific areas: the person of Christ, the work of Christ, and the teaching of Christ.

The Person of Christ

Matthew begins his Gospel with the familiar, "An account of the genealogy of Jesus the Messiah . . ." (1:1). For those unfamiliar with the Old Testament, questions immediately arise: Why begin with a genealogy? What is the meaning of the name "Jesus"? What is the meaning of the title "the Messiah," or, in its Greek translation, "the Christ"? Before we are even halfway into the first verse of the New Testament, we need the Old Testament for a right understanding of what Matthew is saying about Jesus. Bruce Birch maintains that "without the witness of the Old Testament, we frequently would have little idea of what the early church was saying about Jesus in the New Testament."[78]

Jesus speaks of himself most often as "the Son of Man."[79] Many think that this term describes Jesus in his human nature in distinction from his divine nature. Reading Mark 13:26 may jar this conception a bit, for here Jesus speaks of his second coming as "the Son of Man coming in clouds with great power and glory." But the misconception will remain unless the pastor preaches a sermon on Daniel 7:9-14: "I saw one like a human being [one like a son of man] coming with the clouds of heaven. . . . To him was given dominion and glory and kingship, that all peoples, nations, and languages should serve him. His dominion is an everlasting dominion that shall not pass away, and his kingship is one that shall never be destroyed."

Bright observes that "the New Testament hails him [Jesus] as Messiah and Son of man, and describes him as the suffering servant; yet it nowhere explains what these terms mean. . . . Apart from the Old Testament, indeed, it is impossible to understand the significance of our Lord's

---

77. Von Rad, "Typological Interpretation of the Old Testament," 39.

78. Bruce C. Birch, *What Does the Lord Require? The Old Testament Call to Social Witness* (Philadelphia: Westminster, 1985), 110.

79. Cf. Bright, *Kingdom,* 201, "This was the title which he [Jesus] applied to himself more often than any other." Strangely, Norman Perrin, *Rediscovering the Teaching of Jesus* (London, 1967), 198, claims that "Jesus could not have spoken of the coming of the Son of Man," presumably because this title has not been found in contemporary Judaism. F. F. Bruce, *Time Is Fulfilled,* 27, counters that the criterion of dissimilarity, which Perrin champions, "ought to be a powerful argument for the authenticity of the designation 'the Son of Man.'"

work as the New Testament writers saw it."[80] After examining the concepts of messianic king, Son of Man, and Suffering Servant, William LaSor concludes, "To the best of my knowledge, no one prior to the time of Jesus ever attempted to bring these three concepts together in one person. Jesus did."[81] Walter Burghardt summarizes, "If I am to preach Jesus as the apostolic Church did — the Messiah of Israel — it behooves me to understand the complex of beliefs and hopes that 'Messiah' signified in Judaism [better, in the Old Testament]."[82]

The Work of Christ

The Old Testament titles of Christ not only describe Jesus as a person but also recount his work. This is most evident in titles like "Son of Man" and "Servant of Yahweh." Although the New Testament links Jesus with the Old Testament Servant of Yahweh (e.g., Matt 12:18-21; Acts 8:32-35; 2 Cor 5:21), for the most part the references are so subtle that we would probably miss them if we did not know the Servant songs in Isaiah (42:1-9; 49:1-6; 50:4-11; 52:13–53:12). Yet a good case can be made that "Jesus interpreted his messianic mission in terms of the Suffering Servant of Yahweh."[83] Jesus said, "For the Son of Man came not to be served but to serve, and to give his life as a ransom for many" (Mark 10:45; cf. Isa 53:10-11). The night before his death, Jesus declared, "For the Son of Man goes as it is written of him" — presumably in Isaiah 53 (Mark 14:21). Then, changing the Passover into the Lord's Supper, Jesus said, "This is my blood of the covenant, which is poured out for many" (Mark 14:24; cf. Isa 53:5-6). Next Jesus was taken before the Sanhedrin, "but he was silent" (Mark 14:61); later, before Pilate, "Jesus made no further reply" (Mark 15:5; cf. Isa 53:7). Jesus was crucified with criminals on either side; then he prayed, "Father, forgive them . . ." (Luke 23:34; cf. Isa 53:12).[84] It is clear that we cannot understand Jesus' suffering and death without knowing the Servant of Yahweh from the Old Testament.[85]

---

80. Bright, *Authority*, 204.

81. LaSor, "Messiah," 90-91.

82. Burghardt, *Preaching: The Art and the Craft*, 143. For explanations on the titles of Jesus from an Old Testament perspective, see William Barclay, *Jesus As They Saw Him: New Testament Interpretation of Jesus* (New York: Harper & Row, 1962); Leopold Sabourin, *Bible and Christ*, 110-26; and F. F. Bruce, "Promise and Fulfilment," 38-50.

83. Bright, *Kingdom*, 267.

84. I have taken most of these parallels from Leopold Sabourin, *Bible and Christ*, 121-22.

85. Cf. Anders Nygren, *Significance*, 26, "The New Testament is necessary to unveil the deepest meaning of the Old Testament; but it is just as necessary that God's

The work of Christ includes Jesus' miracles. When we read about his miracles, we might conclude that Jesus was just another miracle worker — until we see these miracles against the background of God's redemptive miracles in Egypt (Yahweh versus the gods of Egypt) and the healing miracles of the prophets. Then we begin to see the deeper dimension of Jesus' miracles: the miracles are manifestations of the enmity between the Seed of the woman and the seed of the serpent; they are signs of the kingdom of God breaking into this world, setting straight what was crooked, healing diseases, redeeming lives. As Jesus himself said, "If it is by the finger of God that I cast out the demons, then the kingdom of God has come to you" (Luke 11:20).

The Teaching of Christ

One of the key teachings of Jesus is the kingdom of God. This is how Jesus began his ministry: "The time is fulfilled, and the kingdom of God has come near . . ." (Mark 1:15). We have already noted how easily we think of the kingdom of God as being future in heaven (Chapter 1). Knowing the Old Testament background of "the kingdom of God" makes us (and our congregations) more receptive to the idea that the kingdom of God is coming on this earth and that God expects us to be loyal citizens of this kingdom right now. That is also the teaching of Jesus in the Lord's Prayer: "Your kingdom come. Your will be done, on *earth* as it is in heaven" (Matt 6:10).

Similarly, Jesus teaches, "In my Father's house there are many dwelling places. . . . I go to prepare a place for you" (John 14:2). We might easily understand Jesus' teaching about the hereafter in the Gnostic sense of our souls escaping our bodies for some safe spiritual realm. However, knowing the Old Testament teaching about God's good creation and coming kingdom makes us (and our congregations) more receptive to the New Testament teaching that our foremost hope in the face of death is what we regularly confess in the words of the Apostles' Creed, "I believe the resurrection of the body." At his last supper, Jesus says to his disciples, "I tell you, I will never again drink of this fruit of the vine until that day when I drink it new with you in my Father's kingdom" (Matt 26:29). Although Christians may look forward to being with the Lord when they die (Phil 1:23), our ultimate hope is the Second Coming of Christ, when the dead in Christ shall be raised, the new Jerusalem will descend on

---

work in Christ be seen in the light of the Old Testament, in order that its deepest meaning may be comprehended. It is hard to see how the preaching of Christ's death on the cross could have been effective had not the Old Testament declaration regarding the Suffering Servant been available (Isa 53)."

earth, and God will be all and in all (1 Thess 4:16; Rev 21:3). Our ultimate hope in the face of death, according to Paul, is the resurrection of the body. Jesus was the first to experience this marvelous transformation. He is "the first fruits of those who have died. For since death came through a human being, the resurrection of the dead has also come through a human being" (1 Cor 15:20-21).

These are just two examples of how the teaching of Jesus can be understood better against the background of his Bible, the Old Testament. Christopher Wright frankly states his conviction that "the more you understand the Old Testament, the closer you will come to the heart of Jesus."[86]

In the next two chapters we shall investigate the history of Christian preaching to see how influential interpreters and preachers in successive centuries preached Christ from the Old Testament.

---

86. Wright, *Knowing Jesus*, 108. Cf. McKenzie, "The Significance of the Old Testament for Christian Faith in Roman Catholicism," 108, "The New Testament presents Jesus as the fullness of Israel.... It follows ... that one does not know Jesus Christ very well if one does not know Israel."

CHAPTER 3

The History of Preaching Christ
from the Old Testament (I)

> "Anyone who reads the Scriptures attentively will find in them
> the word concerning Christ. . . . For Christ is 'the treasure hidden
> in a field' . . . ; he was hidden, for he was signified by types and
> parabolic expressions which on the human level could not be un-
> derstood before the consummation of that which was prophesied
> had been reached, namely, the coming of Christ. . . ."
>
> Irenaeus, *Against Heresies*, 4.26.1

PREACHERS TODAY are being bombarded with new methods of interpretation following each other in quick succession. Most of these methods — such as source criticism, form criticism, structuralism, and
deconstructionism — light up the hermeneutical landscape briefly, only,
like falling stars, to burn out with surprising swiftness. In a time of rapid
change, it is well for us to take some distance from the contemporary
scene and search for stability for our method of interpretation in a long-
range, historical perspective. In the next two chapters we shall trace the
history of preaching Christ from the Old Testament, beginning with the
preaching of the early church and tracking it to contemporary christocentric preaching. For our purposes it is best to examine this history primarily in terms of methods of interpretation and to let the original authors speak for themselves as much as is feasible. In this chapter, we shall
cover the preaching of Christ from the early church to the Reformation
and focus on allegorical, typological, and fourfold interpretations.

ALLEGORICAL INTERPRETATION

Allegorical interpretation enables preachers to move beyond the literal, historical meaning of a passage to a supposed deeper sense. From the third century to the sixteenth, it was the primary method of preaching Christ from the Old Testament. Although some of the church fathers such as Irenaeus and Tertullian tried to stem the tide, in the long run the allegorical method won out.

Background

In order to appreciate the popularity of the allegorical method, we need to understand something of the background out of which it developed. The early church needed to defend the Christian character of the Old Testament against a variety of opponents. Non-Christian Gentiles, such as Celsus, attacked the Old Testament for its immorality and contradictions. Non-Christian Jewish opponents denied that Jesus Christ was the fulfillment of the Old Testament. This "polemic between church and synagogue necessitated an exegetical procedure and development that understood the Old Testament Christologically."[1] Then, too, Gnostic "Christians" separated the Old Testament from the New because they held that the Old Testament revealed an inferior Creator God and not the Father of Jesus Christ. Finally, Marcion (ca. 85-160) and his rival church considered the Old Testament an inferior, non-Christian book.

The predominant reason for the general adoption of the allegorical method was probably to defend the Christian character of the Old Testament over against Marcion and his influence. In his *Antitheses*, Marcion sought to accentuate the differences between the Old Testament and the New. For example, he writes:

(1) Joshua used force and cruelty to conquer the land, but Christ forbade all force and preached mercy and peace.
(2) In the Law it says: "An eye for an eye, a tooth for a tooth." The Lord, however, the good, says in the Gospel: "If any strike thee on one cheek, offer him the other also" (2.18; 4.16).
(3) The Creator sends down fire at the demand of Elijah (2 Kings 1:9-12); but Christ forbids the disciples to ask for fire from heaven (4.23).

---

1. Larry Chouinard, "History," 196.

(4) The Creator says: "Cursed is everyone who is hanged on the tree" (Deut 21:23); but Christ suffered the death of the Cross (3.18; 5.3)

(5) In the Law God (the Creator) says: "Thou shalt love him who loveth thee, and hate thine enemy." But our Lord, the good, says: "Love your enemies, and pray for those who persecute you."

(6) The Creator ordained the sabbath; Christ abolished it (4.12).

(7) The promises of the Creator were earthly, but Christ's heavenly (4.14).

(8) The Old Testament God is mighty in war; Christ brings peace (3.21).[2]

Marcion was a literalist. With his rigid literal interpretation he could show inconsistencies between the Old Testament and the New and reject the Old.[3] The rival church he started forced the Christian church into substantiating that the Old Testament is indeed a Christian book, that it speaks of Jesus Christ. And, as we shall see, the easiest way to demonstrate the presence of Christ in the Old Testament is the allegorical method.

The church fathers were not at all agreed on the legitimacy of allegorical interpretation. In spite of their differences, however, Geoffrey Bromiley reminds us of their fundamentally unified approach: "A cursory acquaintance with the Fathers quickly reveals that for all the exegetical variations, they undoubtedly shared the same basic understanding. . . . The Old Testament and the New Testament were seen together in indissoluble unity as the one book of the one God inspired by the one Spirit and testifying to the one Son."[4] David Dockery adds, "While there were definite differences among the Fathers regarding their understanding of the literal-historical sense of Scripture, as well as the typological and allegorical, there existed a general consensus that Scripture should be interpreted christologically."[5]

---

2. These examples are found in Tertullian, *Against Marcion*. They are quoted by A. J. B. Higgins, *Christian Significance*, 16, who took them from Harnack, *Marcion. Das Evangelium vom fremden Gott* (2d ed., 1924), 89ff.

3. Marcion also rejected much of the New Testament. He accepted only the Gospel of Luke and the ten letters of Paul (excluding the Pastorals and Hebrews). But even this remnant of the New Testament had to be purged. Marcion began by eliminating Luke's birth narratives, presumably because Christ could not have had a material body (docetism), and began the Gospel by combining Luke 3:1 and 4:31, "In the fifteenth year of the reign of Emperor Tiberius, He went down to Capernaum, a city in Galilee. . . ." Then, of course, Marcion had to expunge all references to the Old Testament — a difficult task because the New Testament is saturated with the Old.

4. Bromiley, "Church Fathers," 212.

5. Dockery, *Biblical Interpretation*, 157.

At first, Christian preachers seem to have preached Christ from the Old Testament by using the kind of typological interpretation we find in the New Testament. "Even in the second century the Apostolic Fathers largely 'follow this New Testament exegetical pattern and remain, like Paul, Christocentric and just to the historical sense.'"[6] One of the oldest extant Christian sermons is the *Paschal Homily* of Melito of Sardis (ca. 170). According to O. C. Edwards, "Essentially, the sermon is an interpretation of the account of the Passover in Exodus as a type of the death and resurrection of Christ. It begins with a long account of salvation history, showing the necessity for a redeemer. That is followed by a statement of the principles of typological interpretation, which leads into an identification of the salvation wrought through Christ with all that was prefigured in the exodus, especially the Passover."[7]

But alongside typological interpretation, we soon find allegorical interpretation as well.[8] Around A.D. 96, Bishop Clement of Rome wrote a pastoral letter to the church in Corinth. At one point he retells the story of Rahab in Jericho. The spies told her to prepare a sign: "She should hang a red cord from her house. By this they made it manifest that redemption for all who believe and hope in God will come through the blood of the Lord. You see, beloved, how there was not only faith but prophecy in this woman."[9] This kind of allegorical interpretation was subsequently repeated by Justin Martyr, Irenaeus, Origen, Ambrose, Augustine, and many other Christian preachers.[10]

The *Epistle of Barnabas,* probably written between A.D. 70 and 100, presents much more farfetched allegorical interpretations. "If anywhere in the Old Testament something is said concerning wood or a tree, he at once draws the conclusion that here the cross of Christ is meant. In doing so he pays no attention to the context in which that word appears in the

---

6. Chouinard, "History," 196-97, quoting J. N. S. Alexander, "The Interpretation of Scripture in the Ante-Nicene Period," *Int* 12 (1958) 273. The *Epistle of Barnabas* would be a clear exception.

7. Edwards, "History of Preaching," 188.

8. F. W. Farrar, *History,* 166-67, notes that "allegory was already a familiar method among the Jews, and just as the Alexandrians had adopted it in order to find in Moses an anticipation of Greek philosophy, so the Apostolic Fathers, before the full formation of the New Testament Canon, were driven to it in order to make the Old Testament an immediate witness for Christian truth."

9. *1 Clem* 12:7-8. There is very little about Christ in this letter. Instead, in Hellenistic fashion, the Old Testament characters, called "ancient examples" (5:1), are presented as examples of virtues to be imitated and vices to be avoided.

10. For documentation, see Farrar, *History,* 166, n. 4. For more discussion on the interpretation of Rahab, see pp. 337-44 below.

Old Testament."[11] But the *Epistle of Barnabas* goes on to even more elaborate allegorical interpretations. For example, *Barnabas* 8:1-7 interprets the ceremony of the red heifer which is to be burned with cedarwood (Num 19:1-10) as follows:

> Men already grown grey in sin shall offer a heifer, and slay and burn it; then little boys are to collect the ashes and put them into vessels, and tie around a piece of wood the scarlet wool and hyssop — note here again the type of the Cross [the wood] and the scarlet wool! . . . Observe how plainly he speaks to you! The calf is Jesus; the sinners who offer it are those who brought Him to the slaughter. . . . The little boys who did the sprinkling are those who brought us the good tidings of the forgiveness of sins and the sanctification of the heart — those whom He empowered to preach the Gospel. . . . But why are the sprinklers three boys? To represent Abraham, Isaac, and Jacob. . . . And why the wool around the wood? Because the kingdom of Jesus rests on the Wood. . . .[12]

In our survey of preaching Christ from the Old Testament, we shall look particularly at Old Testament interpretation as developed or practiced by the Apostolic Fathers Justin Martyr and Irenaeus.

The Apostolic Fathers

Justin Martyr (ca. 100-165)

Justin Martyr is usually designated as the church father who continued the "typological-Christological method of the apostles."[13] "From the time

---

11. Cullmann, *Christ and Time*, 132.

12. *Barn* 8:1-5, trans. James A. Kleist, *Ancient Christian Writers*, no. 6 (Westminster, MD: Newman, 1948). In 9:8-9, the author even manages to find the cross of Christ in the number of Abraham's servants recorded in Gen 14:14. He writes, "It says: *And Abraham circumcised eighteen and three hundred men of his household.* . . . Notice that it first says 'ten and eight,' and then, in a separate phrase, 'three hundred.' As to the 'ten and eight': 'ten' = I, 'eight' = H. There you have IESUS. But since the Cross, prefigured by a T, was to be the source of grace, it adds the 'three hundred.' It therefore points to Jesus in two letters, and to the Cross in the one. He who put in us the implanted gift of His teaching, well understands. No one has received from me a more reliable explanation; but I know you are entitled to it."

13. Dockery, "New Testament Interpretation," 43. Cf. Stanley N. Gundry, "Typology," 234, "This was the method of Justin in his *Dialogue with Trypho*. If the Old Testament was a book about Christ, typology was a means of discovering and interpreting that fact."

of his conversion probably at Ephesus ca. 130 until his death as a martyr in Rome in 165, he stood for an orthodoxy opposed alike to Gnosticism, Marcionism and Judaism, as well as to the pagan society he had rejected."[14] Justin's main purpose in interpreting the Old Testament is to show that it witnesses to Jesus Christ. He seeks to relate "the details of the text to details of the story of Christ's preexistence, birth, death, resurrection, and second coming."[15] For example, in his *Dialogue with Trypho* we read about his debate with the Jews:

> "But if you knew, Trypho," continued I, "who He is that is called at one time the Angel of Great Counsel (Isa. 9:6), and a Man by Ezekiel (40:3), and like the Son of Man by Daniel (7:13), and a child by Isaiah (9:6), and Christ and God to be worshipped by David (Ps. 2), and Christ and a Stone by many (Ps. 118:22f., Isa. 8:14, 28:16, 50:7, Dan. 2:34, 44f.), and wisdom by Solomon (Prov. 8:22ff.), and Joseph and Judah and a Star by Moses (Gen. 49, Num. 24:17), and the East by Zechariah (6:12), and the Suffering One and Jacob and Israel by Isaiah again (42, 43, 52–53), and a Rod, and Flower, and Cornerstone, and Son of God (Isa. 8:14, 28:16, 11:1), you would not have blasphemed Him who has now come, and been born, and suffered and ascended to heaven, who shall also come again, and then your twelve tribes shall mourn (Zech. 12:10). For if you had understood what has been written by the prophets, you would not have denied that He was God, Son of the only, unbegotten, unutterable God."[16]

To detect Christ in the Old Testament, Justin relies not only on promises and typology but also on the fact that Christ is the preexistent Logos. It was Christ as preexistent Logos who shut Noah in the ark (Gen 7:16), who came down to see the tower of Babel (Gen 11:5), who spoke to Abraham (Gen 18), who wrestled with Jacob (Gen 32), who spoke to Moses from the burning bush (Exod 3).[17]

R. P. C. Hanson notes that "Justin's exegesis is much more developed than that of any Christian writer before him. Not only does he use traditional types and images from the Old Testament christologically, such as that of Noah's flood and that of the promised land (*Dial.* 119.8), but he is

14. W. H. C. Frend, *SJT* 26 (1973) 139.

15. Rowan Greer, "Christian Bible," 146. Cf. Frend, *SJT* 26 (1973) 144, "The whole Old Testament was thus put under contribution to prove that Jesus was Messiah and that he fulfilled to the last detail what had been foretold about the Messiah."

16. Justin, *Dialogue*, 126, as quoted by Greer, ibid. Greer added "the probable scriptural allusions."

17. See Greer, "Christian Bible," 147, with references to *Dialogue*, 61-62 and 126-27.

prepared to identify any object or incident in the Old Testament as a prediction of the Christian dispensation."[18] This drive to find Christ in every text in the Old Testament results in a form of allegorical interpretation which parallels Justin's typological interpretation. Allegorizing is most evident when Justin looks in the Old Testament for the cross of Christ. For example, in the story of Noah and the ark, "the wood of the ark symbolizes the cross; the water symbolizes Christian baptism; and the eight people saved 'were a symbol of the eighth day, whereon Christ appeared when he rose from the dead.'"[19] Justin also discovers the cross in "the tree of life in paradise, Moses' rod, the tree that sweetened the bitter waters of Marah, Jacob's rod and his ladder, Aaron's rod, the oak of Mamre, the seventy willows of Ex. 15:27, Elisha's stick, and Judah's rod."[20] In addition, he detects the cross in "Moses' lifting up his hands in the battle with Amalek . . . and his lifting up the serpent to heal the people. . . ."[21]

Rowan Greer concludes that Justin uses three different methods in demonstrating that the Old Testament bears witness to Christ: "the proof from prophecy, typology, and allegorism. These methods are mixed with one another not only by being placed side by side but also by being used simultaneously on the same texts."[22] For good or ill, Justin Martyr set the tone for early Christian interpretation of the Old Testament. "We find first in Justin many 'proof-text' passages which occur again and again in later writers."[23]

Irenaeus (ca. 130-200)

Irenaeus, Bishop of Lyons, Gaul, was the first of the church fathers to refer to all of the books of the New Testament. In his exegesis of the Old Testament he largely follows the path of Justin.[24] Yet he moves far beyond Justin in developing biblical hermeneutics.

---

18. Hanson, "Biblical Exegesis," 415.

19. Greer, "Christian Bible," 148, citing *Dialogue,* 138. On Noah and the flood, see further pp. 320-25 below.

20. Greer, ibid. On "the tree that sweetened the bitter waters of Marah," see further pp. 325-28 below.

21. Ibid., respectively Exod 17:8-16, *Dialogue,* 90, 111, and Num 21:4-9, *Dialogue,* 91. For more examples, see J. L. Koole, *Overname,* 111-13. For further discussion on "Moses' lifting his hands in the battle with Amalek," see pp. 328-32 below.

22. Ibid., 151.

23. Hanson, "Biblical Exegesis," 415.

24. Cf. Greer, "Christian Bible," 172, "Chapters 42-85 of the *Demonstration of the Apostolic Preaching,* for example, include most of the prophecies and types that may be found in Justin's *Dialogue with Trypho.*"

"For Irenaeus the foundation-stone of hermeneutics is that Christ constitutes the heart of Scripture. The Bible is a book about the Saviour. The fundamental theme of the Biblical writers is the plan of salvation."[25] Irenaeus writes:

> Therefore, anyone who reads the Scriptures attentively will find in them the word concerning Christ and the prefiguration of the new calling. For Christ is "the treasure hidden in a field" . . . ; he was hidden, for he was signified by types and parabolic expressions which on the human level could not be understood before the consummation of that which was prophesied had been reached, namely, the coming of Christ. . . . Every prophecy is enigmatic and ambiguous for human minds before it is fulfilled. But when the time has arrived, and the prediction has come true, then prophecies find their clear and unambiguous interpretation. This is the reason that the law resembles a fable when it is read by Jews. . . . But when it is read by Christians, it is indeed a treasure hidden in the field but revealed and explained by the cross of Christ. It enriches human understanding, shows forth the wisdom of God, reveals God's dispensations concerning the human race, prefigures the kingdom of Christ, and proclaims the inheritance of holy Jerusalem in advance.[26]

As can be seen in this quotation, Irenaeus works with an overall view of Scripture which includes "dispensations," types and promises of Christ, fulfillment in the coming of Christ, the kingdom of Christ, and the consummation. In other words, he sees the unity of Old and New Testaments in their revelation of a single redemptive history which is centered in Christ.[27] Elsewhere he notes progression in God's revelation in the Scriptures. Greer provides a good summary of Irenaeus's views: "The Son of God . . . reveals the Father in the created order, in the Hebrew

---

25. A. S. Wood, *Principles of Biblical Interpretation*, 26.

26. Irenaeus, *Against Heresies*, 4.26.1. Translation in Karlfried Froelich, *Biblical Interpretation*, 44-45.

27. Cf. A. H. J. Gunneweg, 175, "The anti-Gnostic theologian Irenaeus worked out this conception [of salvation history] . . . in his book 'An Unmasking and Refutation of that which is wrongly called Knowledge.' In his view, one and the same God was at work in the mists of time and then especially in the history of Israel, before he revealed himself fully and universally in Christ. Regarded in this light, the Old Testament is no longer merely the prelude to the New; it is the written record of a salvation history which takes place in stages and extends over a long period. According to Irenaeus, it moves from stage to stage, from covenant to covenant, from Adam to Noah, to Moses, and then to the new covenant of Christ, in which the Word (Logos) becomes visible."

Scriptures, and in the incarnation. . . . Indeed, the incarnation, far from introducing the revelation of God for the first time, brings to focus God's self-disclosure in creation and in the Hebrew Scriptures. Thus, the history of the human race is one of the progressive revelation of God, a revelation that drives toward the final redemption of incorruption in the new age. . . . Christ's revelation of the Father in the Hebrew Scriptures takes place by stages. There are four covenants, under Adam, under Noah, under Moses, and the fourth 'which renovates man, and sums up all things in itself by means of the Gospel. . . .' "[28]

The idea of "dispensations" enables Irenaeus to move beyond the limited concern of simply discovering Christ in the Old Testament to considering also the meaning of the passage for Israel. He writes that God "raised up prophets upon earth . . . : sketching out, like an architect, the plan of salvation to those that pleased Him. And He did Himself furnish guidance to those who beheld Him not in Egypt, while to those who became unruly in the desert He promulgated a law very suitable [to their condition]."[29] Here we see Irenaeus take a first step toward what we today would call "historical interpretation."

According to A. S. Wood, Irenaeus deduced two hermeneutical principles from the unity of Scripture. "The first is the harmony of Scripture."[30] The second "is the principle of analogy by which Scripture is permitted to act as its own interpreter."[31] Irenaeus also developed other hermeneutical principles in opposition to arbitrary and atomistic Gnostic exegesis.[32] He insisted that every passage be understood in its own con-

28. Greer, "Christian Bible," 166-67, with references to *Against Heresies*, 4.6.6-7 and 3.11.8. Cf. Brevard Childs, *Biblical Theology*, 31, "Central for Irenaeus was the biblical emphasis that God's order for salvation had extended from creation to its fulfillment in Christ, as God progressively made himself known in creation, law, and prophecy through the divine Logos. Christian scripture bore witness to Jesus Christ as God's son and saviour who was from the beginning with God and fully active throughout this entire history (4.20.1ff.)."

29. Irenaeus, *Against Heresies*, 4.14.2.

30. Wood, *Principles of Biblical Interpretation*, 29. Cf. Irenaeus, *Against Heresies*, 2.28.3: "All Scripture, which has been given to us by God, shall be found by us perfectly consistent; and the parables shall harmonize with those passages which are perfectly plain; and those statements the meaning of which is clear, shall serve to explain the parables. . . ."

31. Ibid., 31. Cf. Irenaeus, *Against Heresies*, 3.12.9: "Proofs [of the things which are contained] in the Scriptures cannot be shown except from the Scriptures themselves."

32. Cf. ibid., 29, "Irenaeus protests most vigorously against the heretics who relied upon the atomistic application of isolated texts to support their misguided and fundamentally unbiblical opinions."

text,[33] and that every passage be interpreted in the framework of "the rule of the truth."[34] It appears that this "rule of the truth," also called "rule of faith," is a forerunner of the later creeds of the church.[35] The "rule of faith" also functions to center interpretation on Jesus Christ. As David Dockery notes, "With Irenaeus we discover the first clear evidence of a Christian Bible and also a framework of interpretation in the church's rule of faith. Continuing the Christological emphasis of the apostles, these early exegetes also emphasized that the rule of faith outlined the theological story that found its focus in the incarnate Lord."[36]

In opposition to Gnostic allegorical interpretation, Irenaeus suggests still another hermeneutical principle: preachers should aim for "the ordinary, simple, obvious interpretation of the text of the Bible."[37] This principle is later supported by Tertullian, who "formulates the dictum: 'But we prefer to find less meaning in the Bible, if possible, rather than the opposite.'"[38]

Like Justin before him, Irenaeus uses promises and types to uncover

---

33. Irenaeus, *Against Heresies*, 1.8.1, "They [the Valentinians] disregard the order and the connection of the Scriptures, and so far as in them lies, dismember and destroy the truth."

34. Ibid., 1.9.4, "He also who retains unchangeable in his heart *the rule of the truth* which he received by means of baptism, will doubtless recognize the names, the expressions, and the parables taken from the Scriptures, but will by no means acknowledge the blasphemous use which these men make of them. . . . But when he has restored every one of the expressions quoted to its proper position, and has *fitted it to the body of the truth*, he will lay bare, and prove to be without any foundation, the figment of these heretics" (my emphases).

35. Cf. ibid., 1.10.1. "The church . . . has received from the apostles and their disciples this faith: [She believes] in one God, the Father Almighty, Maker of heaven, and earth, and the sea, and all things that are in them; and in one Christ Jesus, the Son of God, who became incarnate for our salvation; and in the Holy Spirit. . . ." Cf. *Proof of the Apostolic Preaching*, 3, "The Rule of Faith," and 6, "The Three Articles of the Faith."

36. Dockery, "New Testament Interpretation," 43.

37. R. P. C. Hanson, "Biblical Exegesis," 427, referring to Irenaeus, *Against Heresies*, chaps. 39–41.

38. Ibid., quoting Tertullian's *De Pudicitia*, 9.22. Cf. Robert Daly, "Hermeneutics," 139, "Tertullian allowed allegory only when the literal meaning proved to be nonsensical or unacceptable; he refused to permit it when a passage appeared to be historically real. . . . *Figura* (roughly approximating the modern definition of typology) was Tertullian's favorite method of spiritual interpretation." Cf. J. H. Waszink, "Tertullian's Principles and Methods of Exegesis," in *Early Christian Literature and the Classical Intellectual Tradition*, ed. William R. Schoedel and Robert L. Wilken (Paris: Beauchesne, 1979), 28, "He [Tertullian] insists that whenever one supposes that the text contains a *parabola* or an *allegoria*, one has to stick to the *tertium comparationis* and not look for an allegorical interpretation of every detail which often only adorns or completes the metaphor. . . ."

the witness to Jesus Christ in the Old Testament.[39] And, like Justin, he utilizes the view that Christ as the eternal Logos is present throughout the Old Testament. For example, in Genesis 18:2 we read of Abraham meeting three men. Irenaeus interprets, "Moses says that the Son of God drew near to exchange speech with Abraham. . . . Two, then, of the three, were angels, but one the Son of God."[40] Later, "Jacob also, while journeying into Mesopotamia, sees Him, in a dream, standing at the ladder, that is, the tree, set up from earth even to heaven; for by it those who believe in Him mount to heaven, for His passion is our raising on high."[41] Again, the Son meets Moses: "He it was, who spoke with Moses in the bush, and said: 'I have indeed seen the affliction of my people in Egypt, and I am come down to deliver them.'"[42]

In spite of Irenaeus's opposition to Gnostic allegorizing, and in spite of his alternatives of preaching Christ by way of promises, types, and the eternal Logos, Irenaeus himself succumbs at times to the allegorical method.[43] For example, he sees Jesus on the cross in the figure of Moses praying with outstretched arms: "He [Jesus] too frees us from Amalec by the stretching forth of His hands, and takes us and bears us into the kingdom of the Father."[44] In the story of Rahab hiding the spies, Irenaeus talks about three spies, "which three were doubtless the Father, the Son and the Holy Spirit."[45] In his interpretation of clean and unclean animals, he suggests that the clean animals represent true Christians, "who make their way by faith steadily towards the Father and the Son; for this is denoted by the steadiness of those which divide the hoof; and they meditate day and night upon the words of God," as indicated by chewing the cud. The unclean animals fall into three classes: Gentiles, Jews, and heretics. For instance, "The unclean . . . are those which do neither divide the hoof nor ruminate; that is, those persons who have neither faith in God, nor do meditate on His words, and such is the abominations of the Gentiles."[46]

---

39. Cf. Childs, *Biblical Theology*, 31, "Through his use of 'types' (4.14.3) and prophecy (4.10.1) Irenaeus sought to demonstrate that the two covenants were of the selfsame substance and of the one divine author (4.9.1)."

40. Irenaeus, *Proof of the Apostolic Preaching*, 44.

41. Ibid., 45. Note the allusion to the standard allegorical interpretation of a tree being a symbol of Jesus' cross.

42. Ibid., 46.

43. Anthony Thiselton, *New Horizons*, 155, states that allegorical interpretation "arises because Irenaeus believes that every part of scripture carries significance and points ultimately to Christ, or serves the gospel."

44. Irenaeus, *Proof*, 46.

45. Ibid., *Against Heresies*, 4.20.12.

46. Ibid., 5.8.4.

Notwithstanding these and other lapses, Irenaeus stands out as a leader who, in countering Marcion and the Gnostics, laid the foundations for sound biblical interpretation. A quick review shows his valuable insights: the Old and New Testaments are a united whole; Christ is the heart of Scripture; Scripture is consistent with itself; Scripture must be allowed to be its own interpreter; Christian interpretation should take place in the framework of the "rule of faith"; interpret a passage in its context; understand the meaning of a passage for Israel in its various "dispensations," and aim for the ordinary, obvious interpretation.[47]

The School of Alexandria

Allegorical interpretation was first developed in Greece in the third century B.C. to make the embarrassing elements in Homer and Hesiod philosophically correct. "The stories of the gods, and the writings of the poets, were not to be taken *literally*. Rather underneath is the secret or real meaning. . . ."[48] This method of interpretation spread to Alexandria, Egypt, where the Jewish scholar Philo (ca. 20 B.C.-A.D. 54) used it to demonstrate that the Septuagint was consonant with Plato and the Stoics. And from Philo it spread to the Christian church via Clement of Alexandria and Origen.

John Breck shows how the Greek philosophical school which originated with Plato (ca. 429-347 B.C.) "inspired the allegorical interpretation favored by the Alexandrians": "By opposing the eternal realm of truth to the historical world of matter, the heirs of Platonic philosophy tended to devaluate the concept of history and, consequently, the historical framework of revelation. . . . Interpretation of historical events consists in discerning their 'spiritual sense'; that is, the deeper significance of the eternal, celestial reality which expresses itself within human life. Stated as a hermeneutic principle, the aim is to discern the 'hidden meaning' of an event by laying bare the eternal truth enshrined within it. The purely historical or 'literal sense' . . . while valuable for situating the revelation in its temporal context, is of merely secondary importance."[49] In our survey

---

47. Thiselton, *New Horizons,* 156, observes, "His appeal to the centrality of Christ as a hermeneutical principle or key, together with his concern about the wholeness of scripture, anticipates two of the fundamental concerns of Luther and the Reformers. His work, Skevington Wood concludes, leads on to the Reformation principle of scripture's being allowed to be 'its own interpreter.'"

48. Bernard Ramm, *Protestant Biblical Interpretation,* 25.

49. Breck, *Power,* 50, 51.

we shall focus on the two major representatives of the School of Alexandria, Clement and Origen.

Clement of Alexandria (ca. 150-215)

Clement was the first to add Philo's allegorical method to the existing methods of exegesis. Although we have seen evidence of allegorical interpretation before this time, according to R. P. C. Hanson, Philo's allegorical method was "something quite new."[50] Hanson explains: "In addition to conservative, Jewish-type allegory such as we find in the *Epistle of Barnabas* and Irenaeus and Tertullian, and to the primitive Christological types, there is now introduced a basically hellenistic, anti-historical kind of allegory which is designed to produce from the text to which it is applied general truths of morality, of psychology, of philosophy and, in the hands of Clement and of Origen, of a system of Christian doctrine which is steadily becoming more elaborate."[51]

Twofold Interpretation of Scripture

Whereas previously allegorical interpretation was employed rather sporadically, with Clement it becomes a method that is applied to all of Scripture. "Like Philo, Clement taught that Scripture has a twofold meaning. Analogous to a human being, it has a body (literal) meaning as well as a soul (spiritual) meaning hidden behind the literal sense. Clement regarded the hidden, spiritual sense as the more important one."[52] The literal meaning, he notes, "is meant to excite interest in understanding the deeper meaning."[53] Clement writes, "For many reasons the Scriptures hide the sense. . . . Wherefore the holy mysteries of the prophecies are veiled in parables."[54] The nature of Scripture, therefore, demands allegorical interpretation.

---

50. Hanson, "Biblical Exegesis," 436.

51. Ibid.

52. William Klein, Craig Blomberg, and Robert Hubbard, *Introduction*, 34.

53. Clement "laid down some principles of interpretation, namely that: (1) nothing is literally true which is unworthy of God; (2) no interpretation can be accepted which contradicts the Bible as a whole, and (3) literal meaning is meant to excite interest in understanding the deeper meaning." See Dan McCartney and Charles Clayton, *Let the Reader*, 87, with references to *Stromateis*, 6.15.126 and 7.16.96.

54. Clement, *Miscellanies*, 6.15, as quoted by Walter Kaiser and Moisés Silva, *Introduction*, 218. See p. 219 for a quotation from Clement's *Stromata* 6124.5-6 *(sic)*, "Almost the whole of Scripture is expressed in enigmas."

Finding Christ in the Old Testament

Clement also thinks that the allegorical method is necessary to discover Christ in the Old Testament. "Clement strives to show how Christ is the supreme source and content of knowledge in its most profound sense, and in using the Old Testament, his approach is that Christ has spoken in the Old Testament, and that what he said there was both anterior to, and the source for, all that was best in Greek philosophy."[55] Clement writes, "Our Instructor is the holy God Jesus, the Word, who is the guide of all humanity. The living God himself is our Instructor. . . ."[56]

In Clement's hands, the allegorical method leads to some strange interpretations of the Old Testament. For example, in the story of Abraham and Hagar, Abraham symbolizes the faithful man; Hagar, secular philosophy; and Sarah, true philosophy. "Clement understands by Abraham's preference for Hagar over Sarah that Abraham is 'choosing only what was profitable in secular philosophy'; and when he said to Sarah 'Behold thy maid is in thy hands' (Genesis 16:6) he 'manifestly' meant: 'I embrace secular culture as youthful, and a handmaid, but thy knowledge I honour and reverence as true wife.' "[57] He clearly exhibits no concern at all for the intention of the author of this story for Israel. Moreover, the historicity of the account plays no role in its interpretation. Using his allegorical method, Clement could have derived the same message from a story in an ancient *People* magazine.

Origen (ca. 185-254)

Origen has been called "probably the most influential theologian of the early Christian era."[58] He is seen in a much more favorable light today than he was a century ago. Of course, it is unfair to judge him as a clone of his teacher Clement, "as if he allegorized the two Testaments simply in a Philonic or infinitely polyvalent sense."[59] Thiselton argues that "Origen's approach is more deeply rooted in a *theology of the incarnation* and a 'sacramental' view of the world. . . . Christ the Logos communicates to us in three 'incarnational' modes: in his historical and risen body; in

---

55. John Rogerson, Christopher Rowland, and Barnabas Lindars, *Study*, 28-29.
56. Clement, *The Instructor*, 1.7, as quoted in ibid.
57. Rogerson, *et al.*, *Study*, 31, quoting Clement, *Miscellanies*, 1.21.
58. Froelich, *Biblical Interpretation*, 16.
59. Thiselton, *New Horizons*, 167.

his body, the church; and in his 'body' of the scriptures whose letters are brought to life by the Holy Spirit."[60]

Finding Christ in the Old Testament

Origen is concerned about preaching Christ from the Old Testament. Although Christ was foretold in the Old Testament, not until his incarnation was the veil lifted and the spiritual meaning behind the letter exposed.[61] Dockery notes that "the allegorical approach was an extension of the church's christological interpretation, for the deeper meaning that Origen sought was christocentric. For Origen, Christ was the center of history and the key to understanding the Old Testament. Christ had superseded the laws and ceremonies of the Old Testament, and the literal approach to its meaning had to be changed."[62]

Origen is convinced that mere literal interpretation can lead people astray. Had not Marcion rejected the Old Testament because of his literal understanding? And had not the Jews rejected Jesus because of their literal understanding? Origen writes: "Those advocates of circumcision . . . refused to believe in our Savior. It was their intention to follow the letter of the prophecies which spoke of him, but they did not see him physically 'proclaiming release to the captives' [Isa 61:1], or 'building the city' [Ps 46:4-5, LXX] . . . , or 'cutting off the chariots from Ephraim and the war horse from Jerusalem' [Zech 9:10]. . . . Failing to see any of this happening in a physical sense at the advent of the one whom we believe to be the Christ, they did not accept our Lord Jesus. . . ."[63] With reference to Jews, Gnostics, Marcionites, and simple Christians, Origen argues, "The reason for the false opinions, the impious attitudes, and the amateurish talk about God on the part of those groups just mentioned seems to be no other than that Scripture is not understood in its spiritual sense but is interpreted according to the mere letter."[64]

Letter or spirit is the issue for Origen.[65] In his Preface to his *First*

---

60. Ibid.

61. Origen, *First Principles*, 4.1.6, "Before the advent of Christ it was not altogether possible to exhibit manifest proofs of the divine inspiration of the ancient Scriptures; whereas His coming led those who might suspect the law and the prophets not to be divine, to the clear conviction that they were composed by the aid of heavenly grace."

62. Dockery, *Biblical Interpretation*, 93-94.

63. Origen, *First Principles*, 4.2.1.

64. Ibid., 4.2.2.

65. Greer, "Christian Bible," 180, notes that "he sets the stage for more complicated theories about the senses of Scripture, but the only distinction that really matters for him is the one between the letter and the spirit."

Principles, he asserts: "The Scriptures were written by the Spirit of God, and have a meaning, not only such as is apparent at first sight, but also another, which escapes the notice of most. For those words which are written are the forms of certain mysteries, and the images of divine things. Respecting which there is one opinion throughout the whole Church, that the whole law is indeed spiritual; but that the spiritual meaning which the law conveys is not known to all, but to those only on whom the grace of the Holy Spirit is bestowed in the word of wisdom and knowledge."[66]

Threefold Interpretation of Scripture

Corresponding with the view of a human person as body, soul, and spirit, Origen proposes three levels of meaning for biblical texts: "One should inscribe on one's soul the intentions of the holy literature in a threefold manner; the simpler person might be edified by the flesh of Scripture, as it were (flesh is our designation for the obvious understanding), the somewhat more advanced by its soul, as it were; but the person who is perfect . . . by the spiritual law which contains 'a shadow of the good things to come' (Heb. 10:1). For just as the human being consists of body, soul, and spirit, so does Scripture which God has arranged to be given for the salvation of humankind."[67]

The quotation above shows that Origen sometimes links his three levels of meaning to three kinds of people in the congregation: simple believers, the somewhat advanced, and the perfect. This connection reflects his pastoral concern. In fact, Thiselton argues, "At times 'allegorical interpretation' comes closer to representing what we should nowadays call pastoral application, and here Origen is at his best."[68] But at other times Origen uses the three senses of Scripture to obtain different levels of meaning (contents) from the same text. "The spiritual interpretation is that which relates to Christ and the great truths of God's saving dispensation, whereas the moral [soul] interpretation is one which relates to human experience." For example, "The spiritual meaning of Noah's building of the ark concerns Christ and the Church; the moral meaning applies to the man who turns

---

66. Origen, *First Principles,* Preface, 8.

67. Ibid., 4.2.4.

68. Thiselton, *New Horizons,* 171. Cf. p. 168: "Karen Torjesen interprets Origen's concern not as a philosophical or quasi-gnostic one but as a *pastoral* concern about the *reader-effects* of the biblical texts." Edwards, "History," 189, also reads Origen's levels of meaning as "application": "His [Origen's] methods of application he called moral and mystical. The moral sense looked for the meaning of the passage for the soul, and the mystical sense sought what the passage meant in regard to Christ and the church."

from the evil world around him and in obedience to the commands of God prepares an ark of salvation in his own heart."[69] And the bodily meaning refers to the historical event of Noah's building the ark.

Although Origen begins his interpretation with the "bodily sense," he clearly favors the spiritual. He writes, "With regard to divine Scripture as a whole we are of the opinion that all of it has a spiritual sense, but not all of it has a bodily sense."[70] In commentaries and sermons, he often spends very little time on the literal sense in order to move quickly to the spiritual sense. For example, in a commentary he writes, "These things seem to me to afford no profit to the reader as far as the story goes. . . . It is necessary, therefore, rather to give them all a spiritual meaning."[71] In a sermon on the sun standing still (Josh 10:1-16), Origen first summarizes the story and then proceeds: "These, according to the history, miraculous deeds of divine power preach to all ages; they need no interpretation from outside, for the light of factual reality shines in them. But let us now see what kind of spiritual understanding is contained in them."[72]

Jerome credits Origen with 444 published sermons on Old Testament texts and 130 on New Testament texts[73] — an interesting reversal of current text selection. Only about 200 of these sermons survive, but the evidence is sufficient to credit Origen with the "creation of the classical form of the homily."[74] His pattern was as follows, "After the reading, and with little or no introduction, Origen would begin to explain the scripture, verse by verse. He first dealt with the literal sense, then with any spiritual senses he discovered. He always tried to find a way for his hearers to apply the passage to their lives."[75]

Joseph Lienhard observes that "the continuous reading of the scriptures, without omissions, demanded courage — or, better, confidence in

---

69. M. F. Wiles, "Origen," 468. Cf. Origen's comment in the homily on the flood: "Let us try to join a third interpretation to the two preceding. The first, the historical, is the very foundation of the other two. The second, the mystical, is more elevated and noble. We shall try to add a third, the moral." *Homilies on Genesis*, 2.6; 36.18-25, as cited in Jean Daniélou, *From Shadows*, 110.

70. Origen, *First Principles*, 4.3.5.

71. Origen, *Commentary*, bk. 3, quoted in Roland Murphy, *CBQ* 43 (1981) 511. Cf. E. C. Blackman, *Biblical Interpretation*, 98, "Many times in his commentaries themselves he shows a curious insensitiveness to the plain meaning."

72. Origen, *Joshua Homilies*, 11.1, as quoted in Robert Daly, "Hermeneutics," 140.

73. Paul Wilson, *Concise History*, 36.

74. Edwards, "History," 189. Cf. ibid., "He went through the pericope a verse at a time, explaining it literally and then applying it to the lives of the people."

75. Joseph Lienhard, "Origen," 45.

the power of God's word. . . . Origen was convinced that the Holy Spirit was the author of the scriptures, and that the Holy Spirit could never compose carelessly or awkwardly; every word had to have profound meaning — or rather, a meaning that would profit the reader and the hearer."[76] For example, in Genesis 18:8 we read that Abraham "stood under a tree." Origen says, "We ought not to believe that it was of greatest concern to the Holy Spirit to write in the books of the Law where Abraham was standing. For what does it help me who have come to hear what the Holy Spirit teaches the human race, if I hear that 'Abraham was standing under a tree'?"[77]

To find this deeper meaning for every word or phrase, Origen employs allegorical interpretation. His sermons demonstrate what he means by allegorical interpretation. Preaching on Israel's battle against Amalek (Exod 17), Origen reads verse 9, "Moses said to Joshua, 'Choose some men for us and go out, fight with Amalek," and exclaims, "Up to this point the Scripture has never anywhere mentioned the blessed name of Jesus. Here for the first time the brightness of the name shines forth. For the first time Moses makes an appeal to Jesus and says to him, 'Choose men.' Moses calls on Jesus, the Law asks Christ to choose strong men from among the people. Moses cannot choose; it is Jesus alone who can choose strong men; he has said, 'You did not choose me, but I chose you.'"[78]

Preaching on Israel's journey to Moab (Num 21:16-18), Origen notes that the Lord commanded Moses to gather the people to the well and, "I will give them water." He observes how strange it is that the people did not go to the well of their own accord when they were thirsty but had to be gathered together. Then he continues: "The meanness of the literal sense drives us back to the richness of the spiritual interpretation. And so I think it convenient to collect from other parts of Scripture the mysteries of the wells, that by comparison of several texts the obscurities of this passage may be made plain." After a lengthy discussion on the meaning of many wells, Origen concludes, "To this well, to the faith of Christ, the Law bids us come; for He said, 'Moses spake of Me.'"[79] From the literal meaning of God gathering Israel by the well for a drink of water, Origen moves on to quite a different meaning: Moses is the Law and the well is Jesus Christ. The message of the passage, according to Origen, is that the

---

76. Ibid., 46.

77. Origen, *Homilies on Genesis*, 4.3 and 16.3, as cited in Lienhard, ibid.

78. Lucas Grollenberg, *Bible*, 63-64, citing Origen from *Sources Chrétiennes: Origène, Homélies sur l'Exode* (Paris, 1947) 334. See pp. 61-62 for Origen's allegorical interpretation applied to Exodus 2.

79. Origen, *Homily on Numbers*, 12, quoted by Arthur Hebert, *Authority*, 272-73.

Law calls us to Christ to drink. Ironically, the hermeneutical principle of comparing Scripture with Scripture begins to function for Origen as a servant of allegorical, Christ-centered interpretation.

Origen begins his series of sermons on the book of Joshua with an introduction on the significance of this book: "This significance is not so much to tell us the deeds of Jesus (Joshua) the son of Nun as rather to tell us the mysteries of Jesus my Lord. For it is he who after the death of Moses took over the leadership, he who commanded the camp and who fought against Amalek; and what was indicated there on the mountain, with those outstretched hands, he actualized on the cross, on which in his own person he triumphed over the powers and dominions."[80]

Preaching on the battle of Jericho (Josh 6), Origen says that "Joshua stands for Jesus, and Jericho for this world. The seven priests carrying trumpets represent Matthew, Mark, Luke, John, James, Jude and Peter. The prostitute Rahab stands for the Church, which consists of sinners; and the scarlet cord which she displayed to save herself and her household from the massacre stands for the redemptive blood of Christ."[81] And preaching on the sun standing still so that Joshua can defeat five kings who subsequently hide in a cave (Josh 10:1-16), Origen states that Joshua is Jesus, the five kings are the five senses of the flesh, and the cave represents "the earthly works of the body in which the senses are immersed."[82]

Evaluation of Allegorical Interpretation

Valuable Contributions

Since the allegorical method is frequently rejected out of hand today, let us begin by noting some positive features. First, the church fathers' use of allegorical interpretation was a genuine attempt to preach Christ from the Old Testament. Second, their preaching was generally not unbiblical,

---

80. Quoted in Grollenberg, *Bible*, 64.

81. Arthur Wainwright, *Beyond*, 87, with references to Origen, *In lib. Jesu Nave Hom.* 3.4-5; 6.3–7.7 (*PG* 12.839-42; 854-63). Origen also uses allegorical interpretation to solve "problem passages." For example, Ps 137:9 declares, "Happy shall they be who take your little ones [of Babylon] and dash them against the rock!" Origen comments: "The infants of Babylon, which means 'confusion,' are the confused thoughts caused by evil which have just been implanted and are growing up in the soul. The man who takes hold of them, so that he breaks their heads by the firmness and solidity of the Word, is dashing the infants of Babylon against the rock." *Against Celsus*, 7.22, as quoted by McCartney and Clayton, *Let the Reader*, 89.

82. Daly, "Hermeneutics," 140.

for they tended to use allegorical interpretation within the context of Scripture and the framework of the "rule of faith."[83] Third, with the allegorical method the church fathers were able to defend the Christian character of the Old Testament rather successfully against the charges of Marcionites, Gnostics, and non-Christians like Celsus. Finally, the allegorical method is indeed a good method for interpreting *allegories*. An allegory is an extended metaphor — that is, a number of elements in a story make up a string of metaphors which have a deeper, unified meaning. For example, Jesus' parable of the sower is really an allegory: the seed is the word, and the different places where the seed falls — the path, the rocky ground, the soil with thorns, and the good soil — represent different people and different snares (Mark 4:3-20). Bunyan's *Pilgrim's Progress* is also an allegory; we would miss its meaning if we did not interpret it allegorically. In the Old Testament we find various allegories: for example, the dreams of Joseph, Pharaoh, the royal butler and baker, Nebuchadnezzar, and Daniel. Other examples are the parable of the trees (Judg 9:8-15), the transplanted vine (Ps 80:8-16), the unfruitful vineyard (Isa 5:1-7), and the two eagles and the vine (Ezek 17:3-10, 22-24). All these passages require allegorical interpretation for proper understanding.

Shortcomings in Allegorical Interpretation

However, to use allegorical interpretation for other genres of literature, say historical narrative, is to make a genre mistake and to read alien ideas into the text. Clement and Origen read historical narratives as allegories, that is, as extended metaphor. They still acknowledge the historical sense as true, but this "bodily sense" hardly functions in their interpretation and preaching. The deeper level of meaning — Joshua is Jesus; Jericho, the world; Rahab, the church; the scarlet cord, the blood of Christ — makes the Old Testament word a Christian message. In looking for the real message at this "deeper" level, allegorical interpretation violates the historical nature of the biblical narrative and ultimately denies the value of redemptive history. As Oscar Cullmann writes, "The Old Testament here becomes a book of riddles, and its content, in so far as it is a revelation of a redemptive history which moves toward Christ as its goal, is deprived of its value."[84]

---

83. Cf. Ramm, *Protestant*, 29, "They did emphasize the truths of the Gospel in their fancies. If they had not done this, they would have become sectarian." The use of the allegorical method in Gnosticism did indeed lead to "sectarianism."

84. Cullmann, *Christ and Time*, 133. Cf. Thiselton, *New Horizons*, 171-72, "But in the end, as Duncan Ferguson also concludes, the Antiochene Fathers were right in

In distinction from the School of Alexandria, Justin and Irenaeus employ a different kind of allegorical interpretation. They generally do not read historical narrative as allegory, that is, as extended metaphor. They usually accept the story for what it is, but on occasion they use a single element of a story as a metaphor. For example, when a narrative mentions a tree or wood, this element tends to be read as a metaphor for the cross of Christ. Or the color scarlet tends to be isolated to refer to the blood of Christ. It almost appears as if there were lists that helped preachers identify the metaphors: wood = cross, scarlet = blood, Moses = law, Joshua = Jesus.[85] Even if there were no such lists, it would not have taken long in a church intent on preaching Christ from the Old Testament to establish such an oral tradition.

The problem with the allegorizing of Justin and Irenaeus is not so much that they fail to do justice to the historical nature of the narrative as that they suspend this nature momentarily for an easy, suprahistorical link to Jesus. The problem is that they look for this connection to Jesus in a rather incidental detail instead of in the *message* of the inspired author. If one can isolate one detail for treatment as a metaphor, why not others? "One danger of allegorizing is the tendency to press into service every detail of the narrative in order to minister to the homiletical cause."[86] But

---

their claim that Origen and the other Alexandrians failed to achieve an adequately *historical* understanding of the broad temporal unfolding of the divine purposes in word and deed in scripture." Cf. John Breck, *Power*, 64, "The real danger with the allegorical method, insofar as it transgressed the historical limits of typology, was to transform the divine economy from *Heilsgeschichte* into mythology."

85. Scholars have discovered a list of allegorical equivalents dating from the seventh century A.D., now known as Papyrus Michigan Inventory 3718. Froelich, *Biblical Interpretation*, 19, suggests that the contents "reflect longstanding school tradition. Lists of this kind may have been in the hands of preachers or teachers." A few samples from the translation by Froelich, ibid., 79-81, will be instructive to see how such lists could be used as an aid to preaching Christ from the Old Testament. "(Prov. 10:1) A wise son makes a glad father, but a foolish son is a sorrow to his mother. The wise son is Paul; the father, the Savior; the foolish, Judas; the mother, the church. . . . (Prov. 14:7) The weapons of knowledge are wise lips. The weapons are the apostles; the lips, Christ; wise, the gospels. . . . (Prov. 15:7) The lips of the wise are devoted to perception. The lips are the prophets; the wise, the apostles; perception, Christ. . . . (Prov. 16:26) A man troubles himself in his labors and drives out his perdition. The man is Christ; the labors, the afflictions which he underwent; the perdition, sin. . . ."

86. R. K. Harrison, *BSac* 146 (1989) 369. Some contemporary authors seem to think that homiletics can allow for allegorizing while exegesis cannot. For example, G. Lampe, "Typological Exegesis," *Th* 51 (1953) 206, "Pure allegory . . . may be edifying, and there may be a place for it in homiletics, but it is of no value for sound exegesis." Cf. Edwards, "History," 190. I can think of no possible reason why one should al-

even interpreting only one detail of historical narrative as a metaphor, unless so intended by the author, distorts the author's message.

Since allegorical interpretation is not guided by the inspired author's intention, its use leaves preachers wide open to the pitfall of arbitrary and subjective interpretations.[87] "Origen's allegorical interpretation was generally limited only by his imagination. There were, however, other parameters or safeguards that he established for himself: (1) the Scripture itself and (2) the church's rule of faith."[88] But not all preachers will observe these safeguards.[89] "The curse of the allegorical method," writes Bernard Ramm, "is that it obscures the true meaning of the Word of God. . . . The Bible treated allegorically becomes putty in the hand of the exegete."[90] Instead of preachers being ministers (servants) of the word, they become its masters. In spite of its long tradition, allegorical interpretation must be rejected as a viable method for preaching Christ from the Old Testament.

TYPOLOGICAL INTERPRETATION

Background

We need not spend much time on the background of typological interpretation since it shares much of this background with allegorical interpretation (see above). In distinction from the allegorical method, typological interpretation can trace its roots back to the Old Testament. For example, the prophets used the exodus from Egypt as a type of God's future deliverance from Babylon.[91] The New Testament also uses typological interpretation frequently, as we shall see in Chapter 5. The Apostolic Fathers

---

low in biblical preaching what is considered reprehensible in biblical exegesis, but I can think of many reasons why allegorizing should not be used in biblical preaching.

87. Cf. Blackman, *Biblical Interpretation*, 101, "Origen is not immune from the common criticism of allegory, that it opens too wide a door to fantasy; it turns away from the level ground of sober comment and embarks on imagination, a slope too slippery to permit a safe return."

88. Dockery, *Biblical Interpretation*, 94.

89. G. W. H. Lampe, *Th* 51 (1953) 206-7, provides a few examples and comments, "In such allegorism the reader is left at the mercy of any individual exegete with sufficient ingenuity to construct and solve artificial puzzles. The interpretation is wholly subjective and individualist, controlled neither by ecclesiastical tradition nor by any canons of exegesis whatever."

90. Ramm, *Protestant*, 30.

91. For example, Isa 11:11-12, 15-16; 43:16-21; 48:20-21; 51:9-11; 52:11-12; Jer 16:14-15.

such as Justin Martyr and Irenaeus largely carried on this tradition. With Irenaeus, especially, we observed the development of sound hermeneutical principles: the Old and New Testaments are a united whole; Christ is the heart of Scripture; Scripture is consistent with itself; Scripture must be its own interpreter; and one should interpret a passage in its own context and in the framework of the "rule of faith."

But then Clement and Origen of Alexandria adopted and spread the Greek method of allegorical interpretation. To counter this nonhistorical approach, a new school was started in the fourth century in Antioch, Syria.

The School of Antioch

Antioch rejected allegorical interpretation and instead emphasized literal interpretation. This interpretation was more than literalism, however (which was called Jewish interpretation). Wherever present, Antioch's literal interpretation acknowledged figures of speech such as metaphors, anthropomorphisms, and types.

The major difference between typological and allegorical interpretation is the way redemptive history functions in interpretation. Although allegorical interpretation may not deny redemptive history, it plays no role in interpreting Scripture. Typological interpretation, by contrast, requires redemptive history because the analogy and escalation between type and antitype are drawn within redemptive history. As K. J. Woollcombe puts it, "Typological exegesis is the search for linkages between events, persons or things *within the historical framework of revelation*, whereas allegorism is the search for a secondary and hidden meaning underlying the primary and obvious meaning of a narrative."[92] A related difference is that Clement and Origen saw at least two distinct senses in most biblical texts. The School of Antioch, by contrast, opted for a single sense, the literal-historical. Literal interpretation, however, may make one aware of a type which will require typological interpretation, but not every text contains a type.

John Breck elucidates the position of Antioch, "Diodore [the found-

---

92. Woollcombe, *Essays on Typology*, 40. Cf. Lampe in the same volume, p. 31, "Allegory differs radically from the kind of typology which rests upon the perception of actual historical fulfillment. The reason for this great difference is simply that allegory takes no account of history." Cf. Goppelt, *Typos*, 50, "We have not been able to find any trace of a typological interpretation of Scripture in Philo. This is not accidental. . . . Scripture for him is not at all a record of redemptive history. Instead, he views it as a manual for a philosophy of life."

er of the school] and his disciple Theodore began with a hermeneutic presupposition which was the opposite of Origen's: not every passage of
Scripture has a spiritual meaning, but every passage does have its own
historical and literal meaning. According to Diodore, the task of the exegete is to discern within the historical event both its literal and its spiritual sense."[93] For this combination they used the term *theoria*, which is
the spiritual perception of the exegete to discern an "eschatological and
soteriological reality" in the past events.[94] This starting point shifts the
focus of the interpreter/preacher from the text to the redemptive history
recorded by the text. The major accomplishment of this shift is that the
"spiritual sense" is located within the "literal sense." "Within the historical event itself, *theoria* discovers not two different senses, but rather what
we may call a 'double sense,' of which the spiritual dimension is firmly
grounded in the literal, historical dimension. . . . This relationship expresses a double meaning: the one intended by the author (the literal
sense) and the one which points forward to and finds its fulfillment in the
messianic age."[95] "*Theoria* thus provided Diodore with a middle road between the excesses of allegory and of what he called 'Judaism,' meaning a
concern for the literal sense of Scripture alone."[96]

The main teachers in the School of Antioch were Theodore of
Mopsuestia and Theodoret. Though not a teacher at this school, John
Chrysostom is usually associated with it because of his views on inter-
preting Scripture. We shall now examine more closely the teaching of
Theodore and the preaching of Chrysostom.

Theodore of Mopsuestia (350-428)

Theodore lived in Antioch and became Bishop of Mopsuestia. "He wrote
a treatise against allegorism called *Concerning Allegory and History
Against Origen* in which he argued that Origen's approach deprived biblical history of its reality."[97] He also attacked Origen's appeal to Paul's "allegory" in Galatians 4 for justifying allegorical interpretation. In his commentary on Galatians 4:24a, Theodore "begins by strongly denouncing
those who 'have great enthusiasm for falsifying the sense of divine Scripture,' and who make up 'some senseless fables [*fabulae*] from their own
understanding. . . . The apostle did not do away with history, nor did he

93. Breck, *Power*, 74-75.
94. Ibid., 75.
95. Ibid., 76. Cf. Kaiser and Silva, *Introduction*, 221.
96. Ibid., 78.
97. McCartney and Clayton, *Let the Reader*, 90.

strip away actions which had occurred long ago.' Rather, Paul used the account of past events to elucidate his own words."[98] In other words, Paul used these past historical events merely as illustrations for his own message, not as a model interpretation of these events.

In his own approach, Theodore uses grammatical-historical interpretation. He focusses on the natural, literal sense; like Irenaeus before him, he seeks to determine the original, historical meaning of a passage. For example, "in his work on the Psalms he tries to reconstruct from historical evidence the likeliest occasion for each Psalm's composition."[99] He searches for the meaning originally intended by the author.[100] Only if the author intended to use a word or phrase as a figure of speech will Theodore interpret it figuratively.

In contrast to allegorical interpretation, Theodore's method of interpretation severely limits the number of Old Testament texts that speak of Christ. "From his commentary on the minor prophets, his principle appears to be: unless the New Testament actually cites the text it is not messianic. . . . Even when the New Testament does cite an Old Testament text, it may only be illustrative rather than an indication of a messianic meaning; Hosea 11:1 itself, says Theodore, makes no reference to Christ in spite of Matthew 2:15."[101] Regarding his interpretation of the Psalms, a Synod of Constantinople judged: "He [Theodore] linked all the Psalms in a Jewish way to Zerubbabel and Hezekiah, except for three which he related to the Lord."[102] Blackman informs us that "Theodore was called a 'Judaiser' (as was Calvin later) because he understood the Old Testament in its historic sense and refused to read Christian doctrines into it, as was increasingly being done in his day."[103] He did allow that "some Old Testament passages were fulfilled in Christ, Psalm 22 for example, which although originally written with reference to David and Absalom (thought Theodore) was taken by the

98. Robert Kepple, *WTJ* 39 (1976-77) 241, quoting Theodore from Swete's *Theodori*, 1.73-74. For the complete text of Theodore, see Froelich, *Biblical Interpretation*, 95-103.

99. Enid Mellor, "Old Testament," 191. Cf. Maurice Wiles, "Theodore of Mopsuestia," 497.

100. Cf. Blackman, *Biblical Interpretation*, 104, "He took pains to ascertain the aim and method of each writer and his characteristic usage (*idioma*). He was painstaking and acute on points of grammar and punctuation and even doubtful readings."

101. McCartney and Clayton, *Let the Reader,* 90.

102. My translation of the quotation in S. Greijdanus, *Schriftbeginselen ter Schriftverklaring* (Kampen: Kok, 1946), 168: "Omnes psalmos iudaice ad Zorobabelem et Ezechiam retulit, tribus ad Dominus reiectis."

103. Blackman, *Biblical Interpretation*, 103.

Evangelists quite justifiably to refer to Christ's passion. Similarly Joel 1:28 was appropriately claimed by Peter as illuminating the first Christian Pentecost, although that cannot have been the conscious intention of the old prophet."[104]

Theodore also uses typological interpretation, but given the excesses of Justin Martyr, Irenaeus, and others, he seems to restrict the number of types discovered to those cited in the New Testament.[105] He "developed Irenaeus' idea of typology, but kept it limited to a historical correspondence. The meaning of a text was its historical meaning. Later in redemptive history, one might notice historical correspondences (types), which stem from patterns in God's plan. Thus Psalm 22 is in itself historical only and only tangentially applies to Christ as it would apply to any sufferer. It only applies to Christ par excellence because He is the ultimate sufferer."[106]

From Theodore's writings, John Breck distills three interrelated criteria for discerning an authentic type: "First, a resemblance (mimesis) must exist between the two poles or images, type and antitype. Second, the relationship between these two images (persons or events) must be in the order of promise and fulfillment, so that the type is realized and actualized in the antitype. . . . And third, the transcendent reality of the antitype must actually participate in the type, thereby transforming the historical event into a vehicle of revelation."[107]

Chrysostom (347-407)

John Chrysostom ("the Golden Mouth") was an outstanding preacher in Antioch and later (398) became Archbishop of Constantinople. His "seven hundred or more recorded sermons take the line of sober, historical exegesis."[108] Like Theodore, he warns against allegorical interpretation: "The practice of importing into Holy Scripture alien ideas of one's own imagination instead of accepting what stands written in the text, in

---

104. Ibid.

105. See p. 93 above.

106. McCartney and Clayton, Let the Reader, 90. According to Breck, Power, 54, Theodore "held that the most exalted sense of Scripture was the sense revealed by typology" — with references to Joel (PG 66.232) and Ionam Praef. (PG 66.317ff.).

107. Breck, Power, 82. On the third point, Breck may be reading his own Eastern Orthodox presuppositions back into Theodore. Cf. ibid., "Thus the spiritual sense is seen to be embedded within the literal sense, and the historical event itself becomes the visible expression of a celestial reality or truth." On Theodore's historical and typological interpretation, see also Greer, "Christian Bible," 181-83.

108. Mellor, "Old Testament," 191.

my opinion, carries great danger for those who have the hardihood to follow it."[109] And like Theodore, he attacks Origen's appeal to Galatians 4 for his allegorical method. Chrysostom suggests that Paul "by a misuse of language . . . called the type allegory."[110]

In his own interpretation, Chrysostom, too, seeks to zero in on the intention of the original author. He asserts, "We must not examine the words as bare words . . . nor examine the language by itself, but we must mark the mind of the writer."[111] In addition, he is concerned about understanding the words in their literary context. Anthony Thiselton sums up Chrysostom's approach: "The interpreter is to seek the 'literal' meaning in this contextual and purposive sense. The 'literal' may include the use of metaphor or other figures of speech, if this is the meaning which the purpose of the author and the linguistic context suggest."[112]

But there is more. The Old Testament also functions in the context of the New Testament. Chrysostom, therefore, allows "his understanding of the central, saving message of the whole of Scripture to govern his interpretation of any part."[113] The context of the New Testament allows for interpreting the Old Testament in terms of future fulfillment. In preaching Christ from the Old Testament, Chrysostom uses "prophecy" in two senses: prophecies consisting of words (promise/prediction), and prophecies consisting of historical events (types). He says, "I will give you an example of prophecy by means of things, and of prophecy in words, regarding the same object: 'He was led like a lamb to the slaughter and as a sheep before his shearer' (Is 53:7); that is prophecy in words. But when Abraham took Isaac and saw a ram caught by his horns in a thicket, and actually offered the sacrifice (Gen 22:3-13), then he really proclaimed unto us, in a type, the salutary Passion."[114]

---

109. Chrysostom, *Homily in Genesis* (PG 53.109), as quoted in Jack Rogers and Donald McKim, *Authority*, 20. Cf. Chrysostom, *Interpretatio in Isaiam* 5.3, quoted in Dockery, *Biblical Interpretation*, 117: "We are not the lords over the rules of interpretation, but must pursue scripture's interpretation of itself and in that way make use of the allegorical method. . . . This is everywhere a rule in scripture: when it wants to allegorize, it tells the interpretation of the allegory, so that the passage will not be interpreted superficially or be met by the undisciplined desire of those who enjoy allegorization to wander about and be carried in every direction." He then refers to Ezekiel 17 as an example of biblical allegory.

110. Chrysostom, *Epistle to the Galatians*, 4 (PG 61.662), as quoted in Rogers and McKim, *Authority*, 21.

111. Chrysostom, *Galatians*, 10.675A, as quoted in Thiselton, *New Horizons*, 172.

112. Thiselton, ibid., 173.

113. Rogers and McKim, *Authority*, 21.

114. Chrysostom, *De Poenitentia hom.* 6 (PG 49.320), quoted in Georges Barrois, *Face of Christ*, 43.

Expanding on the idea of typology, Chrysostom states elsewhere, "The type is given the name of the truth until the truth is about to come; but when the truth has come, the name is no longer used. Similarly in painting: an artist sketches a king, but until the colours are applied he is not called a king; and when they are put on the type is hidden by the truth and is not visible; and then we say 'Behold the King!'"[115] In this connection, Chrysostom also shows awareness of progression in God's revelation. The Jewish feasts, he says, need no longer be observed. The reason: "Since the Truth is come, the Types have no longer any place."[116]

Evaluation of Typological Interpretation

Valuable Contributions

In evaluating typological interpretation as refined by the School of Antioch, we begin by acknowledging the positive accomplishments. First, in contrast to allegorical interpretation, typological interpretation continued a form of biblical interpretation which had its roots in the Old Testament (second exodus, second temple) and came to full bloom in the New Testament (especially Hebrews).[117]

Second, over against allegorical interpretation, this school eliminated arbitrary, subjective interpretations. John Broadus judges, "It is among the greatest distinctions of Chrysostom, that his interpretation is almost entirely free from the wild allegorizing which had been nearly universal since Origen."[118]

Third, this school promoted sound historical interpretation. Even in their typological interpretation, they insisted "on strict adherence to the historical form in biblical exposition, even in the discernment and unfolding of the type."[119] According to Leonhard Goppelt, "they advocated typology as a suitable middle ground between the wooden literalness of Jewish exposition and allegorical fictions."[120]

Fourth, in preaching Christ from the Old Testament, "the historical

115. Chrysostom, *Sermons in the Epistle to the Philippians,* no. 10, MPG 62.257, as quoted in Leslie Barnard, *Studia Theologica* 36 (1982) 2.

116. Chrysostom, Homily 14.8, as quoted in Paul Wilson, *Concise History,* 43.

117. See Chapters 5 and 6 below.

118. John A. Broadus, *Lectures on the History of Preaching,* 74.

119. Geoffrey Bromiley, "Church Fathers," 215, with a reference to Diodore, Preface in *Psalms.*

120. Goppelt, *Typos,* 6.

and the Messianic were blended together like woof and warp. The Messianic did not float above the historical, but was implicit in it."[121]

Finally, this school acknowledged that there is progression in God's revelation. "An allegorist might find something far richer about Jesus Christ and salvation in Genesis than in Luke. But if progressive revelation is correctly understood such a maneuver by an exegete is impossible."[122]

Shortcomings in Typological Interpretation

Negatively, typological interpretation faces the danger of degenerating into typologizing, that is, overextending the use of typology by searching for types in rather incidental details in the text. In Justin Martyr, Irenaeus, and others, typologizing resulted in the proliferation of random types. Later, in the Middle Ages, preachers saw the following types: the creation of Eve from Adam's side is a type of Christ on the cross having his side pierced; the bread and wine of Melchizedek are types of the bread and wine in the Eucharist; Isaac carrying the wood up the mountain is a type of Christ carrying his cross; Joseph in the well is a type of Christ in the grave.[123] Even modern preachers are not immune to typologizing. Some samples from recent sermons may sound familiar: Joseph's obedience in looking for his brothers is a prophetic type of Christ's obedience; his sale to the Ishmaelites prefigures Christ being sold by Judas; Jacob's wrestling at Peniel prefigures Christ's wrestling at Calvary; Naomi's care for Ruth foreshadows Christ's care for his people; the homage the women paid David prefigures the homage baby Jesus received in Bethlehem.[124]

Typologizing, in turn, can slip into allegorizing. When the preacher strings some "types" together into an extended metaphor, "types come to be created rather than discovered, and the drift into allegorism comes all too easily."[125] Clearly, the challenge for typological interpretation is to find some measure of control so that it does not spin off into typologizing and even allegorizing. Theodore must have recognized this challenge, for he seems to work with the rule, "Unless the New Testament actually cites

121. Ramm, *Protestant*, 50.
122. Ibid.
123. These examples are taken from M. B. Van 't Veer, "Christologische," 139. Note that Joseph in his humiliation and exaltation is indeed a type of Christ, who in his humiliation and exaltation would also bring blessings on the nations. The objection here is to drawing an analogy between the detail of the well and Christ's grave.
124. Ibid., 142-45.
125. Stanley N. Gundry, "Typology," 235.

the text it is not messianic."[126] But this rule is too restrictive, for there is no reason to think that the New Testament was exhaustive in citing Old Testament texts which found their fulfillment in Jesus. If typological interpretation is a sound method, it should be able to discover types of Christ which the New Testament writers did not mention.

Another danger in typological interpretation is that preachers in their sermons will simply draw a line from the type to the Antitype. But drawing lines to Christ is not preaching Christ. How does a line to Christ edify the hearers? A preacher's task is not just to draw lines to Christ but to preach Christ in such a way that people will be attracted to him and put their faith, trust, and hope in him. We will need to explore typology further in Chapters 5 and 6, but now we must continue our survey and see how the preaching of Christ develops in the Middle Ages.

FOURFOLD INTERPRETATION

Background

After the Schools of Alexandria and Antioch, allegorical and typological interpretation continued to exist side by side in the church. Hilary of Poitiers (ca. 300-367) is said to be "the first Western Father to have absorbed and profited from the influence of Origen."[127] Ambrose (339-97), Archbishop of Milan, also used allegorical interpretation.

The major hermeneutical principle that guided biblical interpretation from Augustine through the Middle Ages was the four senses of Scripture. Origen had already taught the three senses of Scripture analogous to a human person: the body is the literal sense of the text, the soul is the moral sense, and the spirit is the spiritual sense. Like Origen, Ambrose also taught a threefold meaning of Scripture: literal-historical, moral, and mystical.[128] Augustine, who was influenced by Ambrose, added a fourth sense which looks for the eschatological meaning.

The Four Senses of Scripture

In this section we shall examine the work of three key figures: Augustine, John Cassian, and Thomas Aquinas.

126. See McCartney and Clayton, *Let the Reader*, 90.
127. See R. P. C. Hanson, "Biblical Exegesis," 446.
128. See Gunneweg, *Understanding*, 41.

Augustine (354-430)

Augustine's work has been called "the transition from the early Church to the Middle Ages: it is the culmination of several centuries of Christian thought and forms the foundation of theology in the West for the following centuries."[129] Although Augustine is known mainly for his battles against Pelagius and Donatus, he is also a major player in biblical hermeneutics.

Before he became a Christian, Augustine belonged to the Manicheans, a sect which, like Marcion, rejected the Old Testament because of its crudity and immorality. But when he moved to Milan, Augustine was attracted to the allegorical interpretation and preaching of Ambrose, for allegorical interpretation was able to solve the problem passages of the Old Testament. As Augustine himself recalled: "I listened with delight to Ambrose, in his sermons to the people, often recommending this text most diligently as a rule: 'The letter kills, but the spirit gives life' (2 Cor 3:6), while at the same time he drew aside the mystic veil and opened to view the spiritual meaning of what seemed to teach perverse doctrine if it were taken according to the letter."[130]

Augustine eventually became Bishop of Hippo, North Africa. He has the honor of writing the first "handbook of hermeneutics and homiletics,"[131] entitled *On Christian Doctrine*. In book 6 of this handbook "he lays down the principle that all preaching is to be founded on the Word of God."[132] Ironically, Augustine, the former Manichean, became one of "that line of Christian apologists attempting to defend the divine authority of the whole Bible, and particularly of the Old Testament."[133]

In *The City of God* (15-22) Augustine sets forth the relationship between the Old and New Testaments with a view of redemptive history "that would shape the life of the church. Augustine perceived in Scripture a progressive line of divine history and prophecy moving through a series of ages and culminating in that of Christ, the sixth age of the church. Throughout this time there existed two groups of people constituting two cities — one devoted to the love of this world, the other to God. The last age, that of the church, would continue until the day of judgment."[134]

129. Baker, *Two Testaments*, 47.
130. Augustine, *Confessions*, 6.4.6, as quoted in Rogers and McKim, *Authority*, 32.
131. Ramm, *Protestant*, 34.
132. Leroy Nixon, *John Calvin*, 20.
133. James Preus, *From Shadow*, 10.
134. Rodney Petersen, "Continuity," 23.

With respect to preaching Christ from the Old Testament, Augustine is probably best remembered for his maxim: "In the Old Testament the New is concealed; in the New, the Old is revealed."[135] He writes, "These hidden meanings of inspired Scripture we track down as best we can, with varying degrees of success; and yet we all hold confidently to the firm belief that these historical events and the narrative of them have always some foreshadowing of things to come, and are always to be interpreted with reference to Christ and his Church, which is the City of God."[136] In a sermon on 1 John 2:12-17, Augustine reminds the congregation of Jesus' words on the road to Emmaus (Luke 24:25-26), "He opened unto them the Scripture, and showed them that it behoved the Christ to suffer, and all things to be fulfilled that were written concerning him in the law of Moses and the prophets and the psalms — so embracing the whole of the Old Testament. Everything in those Scriptures speaks of Christ, but only to him that has ears. He opened their minds to understand the Scriptures; and so let us pray that he will open our own."[137] Christ is the key for understanding the Old Testament: "Before the intellect arrives at Christ, it cannot presume to have understood it."[138] Especially in his work against Faustus, who denied that the Old Testament witnesses to Christ, Augustine quotes the New Testament time and again to show that the Old Testament speaks of Christ. Everything witnesses to Christ.[139]

Augustine has various means for preaching Christ from the Old Testament. The Old Testament not only contains clear promises of Christ, but it also reveals types of Christ. For example, Joshua is a type of Christ: as Joshua led Israel into earthly Canaan, so Christ leads his church into the heavenly Canaan; Solomon as the king of a kingdom of peace is also a type of Christ who will bring the true kingdom of peace.[140] In addition to promise-fulfillment and typological interpretation, however, Augustine also uses allegorical interpretation.

Although Augustine seeks to discover the intention of the human author,[141] he relativizes historical interpretation in the broader context of

---

135. Augustine as quoted in Rogers and McKim, *Authority*, 33 (PL 34.623).

136. Augustine, *City of God*, 16.2.

137. Augustine, *Homilies of 1 John*, Second Homily, 2.

138. Augustine, *Enarratio in Ps* 96:2, as quoted in B. J. Oosterhoff, *Om de Schriften*, 78 (my translation).

139. Augustine, *Contra Faustum*, 12.3-6, as summarized by Oosterhoff, ibid., 77-78.

140. See Oosterhoff, ibid., 85-86.

141. Augustine, *De Doctrina*, 2.5.6, "The aim of its readers is simply to find out the thoughts and wishes of those by whom it was written down and, through them, the will of God, which we believe these men followed as they spoke." See ibid., 2.9.14

Scripture and the "rule of faith." He writes, "Sometimes not just one meaning but two or more meanings are perceived in the same words of scripture. Even if the writer's meaning is obscure, there is no danger here, provided that it can be shown from other passages of the holy scriptures that each of these interpretations is consistent with the truth."[142] For Augustine, allegorical interpretation is acceptable as long as it does not deny the historicity of the account, and the resultant teaching does not contradict the "rule of faith."[143]

In fact, Augustine notes that mere literal interpretation will lead preachers astray with many biblical passages. So how does one decide when a passage should be interpreted literally and when figuratively? Augustine takes his cue from the New Testament, the threefold norm of faith, hope, and love. He writes, "Generally speaking . . . anything in the divine discourse that cannot be related either to good morals or to the true faith should be taken as figurative. Good morals have to do with our *love* of God and our neighbour, the true *faith* with our understanding of God and our neighbour. The *hope* that each person has within his own conscience is directly related to the progress that he feels himself to be making towards the love and understanding of God and his neighbour."[144]

Some of Augustine's allegorical interpretations serve to overcome problems in the Old Testament. Take the problem passage, "Happy shall they be who take your [Babylonian] little ones and dash them against the rock" (Ps 137:9). Much like Origen before him, Augustine comments that the little ones are "the evil desires that are born in the corrupt human

---

for the important role of literal interpretation: "In clearly expressed passages of scripture one can find all the things that concern faith and the moral life (namely hope and love . . .). Then . . . one should proceed to explore and analyse the obscure passages, by taking examples from the more obvious parts to illuminate obscure expressions and by using the evidence of indisputable passages to remove the uncertainty of ambiguous ones." Cf. ibid., 2.6.8, "Virtually nothing is unearthed from these obscurities which cannot be found quite plainly expressed somewhere else."

142. Ibid., 3.27.38. Augustine continues: "The person examining the divine utterances must of course do his best to arrive at the intention of the writer through whom the Holy Spirit produced that part of scripture; he may reach that meaning or carve out from the words another meaning which does not run counter to the faith, using the evidence of any other passage of the divine utterances."

143. Augustine, *City of God*, 13.21, "There is no prohibition against such exegesis, provided that we also believe in the truth of the story as a faithful record of historical fact." Cf. ibid., 15.26, "But my critic must suggest some other interpretation which is not at variance with the Rule of Faith."

144. Ibid., *De Doctrina*, 3.10.14 (my emphases). Cf. 1.36.40; 1.40.44.

soul. People should eradicate these desires while they are still small, before they acquire strength."[145]

Other allegorical interpretations, however, serve to preach Christ from the Old Testament. For example, Augustine writes, "We can also interpret the details of paradise with reference to the Church. . . . Thus paradise stands for the Church itself . . . , the four rivers represent the four Gospels; the fruit trees, the saints; and the fruit, their achievements; the tree of life, the Holy of Holies, must be Christ himself; while the tree of knowledge of good and evil symbolizes the personal decision of man's free will."[146] With respect to Noah's ark, Augustine claims, "Without a doubt this is a symbol of the City of God on pilgrimage in this world, of the Church which is saved through the wood on which was suspended 'the mediator between God and men, the man Christ Jesus'. . . . The door which it was given in its side surely represents the wound made when the side of the crucified was pierced with the spear. This . . . is the way of entrance for those who come to him, because from that wound flowed the sacraments with which believers are initiated. . . . All the other details mentioned in the construction of the ark are symbols of realities found in the Church."[147]

Gerald Bonner claims that Augustine "diminished the allegorical element in his scriptural exegesis with the passage of the years . . ."[148] and

145. Augustine, *Enarratio in Ps 136,* 21 (*PL* 37.1773-4), as paraphrased in Arthur Wainwright, *Beyond,* 60. For Origen, see p. 87, n. 81 above.

146. Augustine, *City of God,* 13.21.

147. Augustine, ibid., 15.26. See Farrar, *History of Interpretation,* 238, for other examples. For example, "If the Psalmist [3:5] says, 'I laid me down, and slept, and rose again,' Augustine asks whether any one can be so senseless . . . as to suppose that 'the prophet' would have made so trivial a statement, unless the sleep intended had been the Death, and the awakening the Resurrection of Christ!" Cf. Oosterhoff, *Om de Schriften,* 85-86.

148. Bonner, "Augustine," 552. Yet in the very book Bonner cites, *The City of God,* 16.2, Augustine states about the sons of Noah: "Shem, of whom Christ was born in the flesh, means 'named.' And what is of greater name than Christ. . . . Is it not also in the houses of Christ, that is, in the churches, that the 'enlargement' of the nations dwells? For Japheth means 'enlargement.' And Ham (*i.e.,* hot) . . . what does he signify but the tribe of heretics, hot with the spirit, not of patience, but of impatience. . . ." When Shem and Japheth cover their father's nakedness, "the garment signifies the sacrament, their backs the memories of things past: for the church celebrates the passion of Christ as already accomplished." Augustine admits readily, "All will not accept our interpretation with equal confidence, but all hold it certain that these things were neither done nor recorded without some foreshadowing of future events, and that they are to be referred only to Christ and His church, which is the city of God, proclaimed from the very beginning of human history by figures which we now see everywhere accomplished." See also the quotation in n. 147 above.

instead placed more emphasis on the function of redemptive history in interpreting Scripture. He shows a "deepened sense of scripture as the history of God's saving work for man in the past, the present, and the future, until the Second Coming of Christ."[149] Writes Augustine, "The object of the writer of these sacred books, or rather the Spirit of God in him, is not only to record the past, but to depict the future, so far as it regards the City of God; for whatever is said of those who are not its citizens, is given either for her instruction, or as a foil to enhance her glory."[150]

Although Augustine works primarily with two senses of Scripture, the literal-historical and the figurative, he officially teaches that Scripture has four senses: historical, allegorical, analogical, and etiological.[151] He states: "In every sacred book one should note the things of eternity which are communicated, the facts of history which are recounted, future events which are foretold, moral precepts which are enjoined or counseled."[152]

John Cassian (ca. 360-435)

John Cassian was a deacon of Chrysostom and a contemporary of Augustine. Although not a major player in our story, he is credited with naming the four senses of Scripture which became standard in the Middle Ages. Cassian maintains that there are two primary senses of Scripture: a historical sense *(historica interpretatio)* and a spiritual sense *(intelligentia spiritalis)*, but the spiritual sense can be further divided into three different senses. He states, "There are three genera of spiritual *scientia: tropologia, allegoria, anagoge,* of which it is said in the book of Proverbs

149. Ibid., 553.

150. Augustine, *City of God,* 16.2. Interestingly, Augustine continues, "Yet we are not to suppose that all that is recorded has some signification; but those things which have no signification of their own are interwoven for the sake of the things which are significant. . . . It is only the strings in harps and other musical instruments which produce melodious sounds; but that they may do so, there are other parts of the instrument which are not indeed struck by those who sing, but are connected with the strings which are struck, and produce musical notes. So in this prophetic history some things are narrated which have no significance, but are, as it were, the framework to which the significant things are attached."

151. Augustine, "On the Profit of Believing," *Seventeen Treatises,* 582, "Allegory designates the understanding of things said figuratively. . . . Analogy demonstrates the *congruentia* of the Old and New Testaments, and etiology accounts for the causes of things said and done." See James Preus, *From Shadow,* 21, n. 26, for Augustine's explanation of the four senses: historia, allegoria, analogia, and aetiologia.

152. Augustine, *Genesis according to the Literal Sense,* 1.1, as quoted in Rogers and McKim, *Authority,* 33.

[22:20]: 'But you, write those things for yourself *tripliciter* upon the breadth of your heart.'"[153] The tropological and allegorical senses were later reversed so that the three spiritual senses would fit Augustine's hermeneutical rule that Scripture intends to teach faith, love, and hope.[154] The four senses, then, are:

1. the literal sense, which teaches historical facts;
2. the allegorical sense, which shows that the facts of history "prefigured the form of another mystery" [faith];
3. the tropological or moral sense, which provides "moral explanation pertaining to the cleansing of life" [love]; and
4. the anagogical sense, which has to do with "spiritual mysteries arising to more sublime and sacred secrets of heaven [hope]."[155]

Cassian himself provides the famous example of the four senses applied to Jerusalem. I shall incorporate it in the following table:

1. Literal — historical facts   Jerusalem = the city in Israel
2. Allegorical — faith   Jerusalem = the church of Christ
3. Moral (tropological) — love   Jerusalem = the soul of a person
4. Anagogical — hope   Jerusalem = the heavenly city of God

Later in the Middle Ages, manna serves as another clarifying illustration: "Manna may be taken *literally*, for the food miraculously given to the Israelites in the wilderness; *allegorically*, for the Blessed Sacrament in the Eucharist; *tropologically*, for the spiritual sustenance of the soul day by day through the power of the indwelling Spirit of God; and *anagogically*, for the food of blessed souls in heaven — the Beatific Vision and perfected union with Christ."[156]

In general, the Middle Ages show little new initiative in preaching

153. Cassian, *Conlationes*, 14.c.8, as quoted in Preus, *From Shadow*, 21.
154. See Preus, *From Shadow*, 21.
155. Quotations from Cassian, provided by Preus, ibid., 21-22. Later, Rabanus Maurus (d. 856) affirmed this fourfold sense as authoritative.
156. Hebert, *Authority*, 269. In the Middle Ages the four senses were put into Latin poetry in several versions. Dockery, *Biblical Interpretation*, 159, notes that Nicholas of Lyra (1265-1349) "summarized this medieval hermeneutical theory in a much quoted rhyme":

Littera gesta docet,	The letter teaches facts,
Quid credas allegoria,	Allegory what one should believe,
Moralis quid agas,	Tropology what one should do,
Quo tendas anagogia.	Anagogy where one should aspire.

Christ from the Old Testament.[157] This fact is understandable in the light of several considerations. After the collapse of the Roman Empire, the training of priests was in disarray, and often they would simply recycle the sermons of the church fathers.[158] Further, the increasing centralization of celebrating Christ in the Mass decreased the proclamation of Christ in the sermon. Moreover, the unofficial shift to a semi-Pelagian position shifted the emphasis in preaching from the grace of God in Christ for salvation to the good works that Christians needed to perform. In other words, of the four senses, the moral sense gained the upper hand in preaching.

In the year 1054 the Eastern and the Western church separated. To this day the Eastern Orthodox Church relies heavily on the interpretation of the church fathers. In its current writings one can find excellent expositions on the role of redemptive history in biblical exposition and on the typological interpretation of the Old Testament.[159]

Meanwhile, in the Western church, "The theory of the four senses was used without restraint by the scholastics, and its artificiality provoked a demand for a more realistic attitude."[160] During the Middle Ages, several voices called out for restraint in using fourfold interpretation; some even, much like the School of Antioch, called for literal interpretation alone.[161] But it took the influence of the great scholar and churchman Thomas Aquinas to gain a measure of control over the multiplicity of meanings that could be derived from biblical texts.

157. Broadus, *History of Preaching*, 91, "The Christian preaching of these early centuries culminated in Chrysostom and Augustine, and then suddenly and entirely ceased to show any remarkable power."

158. Cf. Edwards, "History," 195, "The only new homiletical materials created during the period were not new sermons but collections of patristic sermons called homiliaries by later scholars. . . . While some clergy might read one of these homilies to their congregations on the appropriate day, others would use them as sources of materials for sermons of their own composition."

159. See, e.g., Georges Florovsky, "Revelation and Interpretation" (1951), and *Bible, Church, Tradition: An Eastern Orthodox View* (1972); Georges A. Barrois, *The Face of Christ in the Old Testament* (1974); and John Breck, *The Power of the Word* (1986).

160. Barrois, *Face of Christ*, 42. Cf. A. Berkeley Mickelsen, *Interpreting*, 36, "From AD 600 to 1200 allegory had a real hold upon the minds of medieval theologians. Collections of allegorical interpretations circulated. These showed how many meanings one word could have. For example, the word 'sea' could mean a gathering of water, Scripture, the present age, the human heart, the active life, heathen, or baptism."

161. For example, Hugo of St. Victor (1096-1141), Andrew of St. Victor (ca. 1110-41), and, after Thomas Aquinas, Nicholas of Lyra (1270-1340).

Thomas Aquinas (ca. 1225-74)

Thomas Aquinas stands at the summit of late medieval thought. He is best known for his accomplishments in systematic theology, but his work in homiletics should not be overlooked. Against his parents' wishes he joined the Order of Preachers (Dominicans), and later he taught homiletics as well as theology.

In his influential work *Summa Theologica*, Thomas tackles the subject of the four senses and seeks to bring some order into the chaos of multiple interpretations. In line with his Aristotelian philosophy, he stresses the importance of the literal sense of the text. The literal (or historical) sense brings a measure of hermeneutical control over the possible meanings of a passage, for it is foundational to all interpretation. The literal sense is the meaning intended by the author.

Thomas distinguishes between the words of the author, the "things" these words signify (for example, historical facts), and what these "things" (for example, historical facts) in turn signify. The literal sense encompasses the words and the "things" they signify. The spiritual sense encompasses what these "things" (for example, historical facts) in turn signify. In his own words:

> The author of Holy Scripture is God, in whose power it lies not only to fit words to a meaning, which man also can do, but also [to fit meaning to] the things themselves. Therefore, while in all sciences words have meanings, the property of this science (theology) is that the things signified by the words receive a meaning. The first mode in which words show the meaning of things belongs to the first sense, which is the *historical* or *literal* sense. The mode by which the things signified by the words further signify other things is called the *spiritual* sense, which is founded upon the literal sense and presupposes it; and this spiritual sense has a three-fold division. . . . Hence, in so far as the things of the ancient law signify those of the new, we have the *allegorical* sense; in so far as the things done in Christ, or the things which signify Christ, signify the things which we ought to do, we have the *moral* sense; while according as they signify the things which belong to eternal glory, we have the *anagogical* sense. . . . Thus there is no confusion in Holy Scripture, since all the senses are founded upon one, the literal sense, from which alone an argument can be drawn, and not from those which are spoken allegorically.[162]

Thomas, as can be seen, still maintains four senses, but he grounds the three spiritual senses firmly in the historical sense. Moreover, although

---

162. Aquinas, *Summa*, 1.1.10, as quoted in Hebert, *Authority*, 268-69.

he himself uses allegorical interpretation, he also warns against it. He argues that "(1) it is susceptible to deception; (2) without a clear method it leads to confusion; and (3) it lacks a sense of the proper integration of Scripture."[163]

We noted that Thomas defines the literal sense in terms of the intention of the author. But he also recognizes that Scripture has both human authors and a divine Author. Later, Nicholas of Lyra (1270-1340) uses this dual authorship and dual intentionality as a foundation for his christological interpretation of Old Testament passages. "For the Old Testament, this theory meant that a christological interpretation, intended by the Spirit, was as much or more so a literal meaning as that which the text had in its original setting."[164]

Evaluation of Fourfold Interpretation

Valuable Contributions

Positively, we can acknowledge that fourfold interpretation at least maintained room for literal-historical interpretation as the first of its four senses of Scripture. We can also appreciate that Augustine as well as Thomas Aquinas identified literal interpretation as the intention of the author and made it the foundation of all interpretation. Moreover, in interpreting the Old Testament, fourfold interpretation looked for a biblical message beyond so-called objective facts. It could suggest several ways of preaching Christ from the Old Testament: the literal sense might have a promise or type of the coming Messiah; the allegorical sense might reveal Christ by way of allegory; and the anagogical sense might reveal Christ by way of eschatology.

Shortcomings in Fourfold Interpretation

We should also note the weaknesses of fourfold interpretation. Although it maintained room for literal-historical interpretation, in actual fact it tended to decrease the significance of literal interpretation, for literal interpretation was only one of four possible interpretations, and it functioned at the lowest level.[165] Moreover, fourfold interpretation lacked the

---

163. Aquinas as summarized by Rodney Petersen, "Continuity," 26.

164. Scott Hendrix, *Int* 37 (1983) 232.

165. Cf. Childs, "Sensus Literalis," 82: "Augustine's emphasis on the content of a Scriptural passage in the context of the love commandment determining the level of

singular focus on preaching Christ because the interpreter could divert the message of a passage into several different directions, and in the context of semi-Pelagianism especially in the direction of the moral sense of doing good works.

Furthermore, fourfold interpretation lacked a sound method for controlling the meanings derived from a passage. If each word can have four different meanings, different combinations of words and senses will result in numerous different meanings. This kind of interpretation leaves itself wide open to all kinds of fantasy and speculation. Thomas Aquinas did seek to provide a firmer footing for the spiritual meaning in the literal sense, but in retaining four different senses he failed to gain the kind of control that enables preachers to say with conviction, "Thus saith the Lord."

Finally, and most importantly, fourfold interpretation forced the text to speak in ways the author may not have intended — allegorical, moral, and eschatological — and thus the message tended to lose its biblical authority.[166] For, as John Bright says, "The Old Testament cannot be appealed to as authoritative in the church, or proclaimed with authority, unless its plain meaning is adhered to, and adhered to plainly."[167]

After many centuries of allegorical, typological, and fourfold inter-

---

interpretation, whether literal or figurative, was replaced by a static concept of three loosely related levels of meaning to be found in all of Scripture, the allegorical, tropological, and anagogical. When this understanding was then joined with earlier elements from Origen, the implicit denigration of the literal sense of Scripture became inevitable."

166. Earlier we noted that allegorical interpretation was not necessarily unbiblical because it was practiced within the framework of the "rule of faith," that is, allegorical interpretations were often used to disseminate biblical truths even while misinterpreting the texts (see p. 88, n. 83 above). Concerning Augustine, Hebert, *Authority*, 278, says "that the authority of these allegorical interpretations does not rest on the texts themselves, but on the truths which they illustrate. . . . It was these truths, depending on the tradition of the Faith, and thus on the general sense of Scripture, that the Fathers were seeking to convey to their readers, in what was to them an attractive form." Although this observation is worthwhile, it does not alleviate but confirms the serious flaw of allegorical interpretation, namely, that it turns the message of the text into something other than what the author meant to convey. As such, allegorical interpretation lacks integrity and at least *textual* authority. And, homiletically, one wonders why a preacher would not select a preaching text that would make his point directly rather than allegorically.

167. Bright, *Authority*, 91. Cf. p. 95, "But if the Old Testament can be preached in the church only by disregarding its plain meaning and rushing on to preach some 'more Christian' meaning, what reason is there to preach from it at all? The game has been forfeited to Marcion."

pretation, the church desperately needed to settle the question of proper biblical interpretation, especially as it pertained to the preaching of Christ from the Old Testament. This discussion ensued particularly in the Reformation.[168]

168. Although we will follow unfolding developments in Protestantism in the next chapter, discussions on biblical interpretation continued, of course, in Eastern Orthodoxy (see n. 159 above) and in Roman Catholicism. The Roman Catholic Church speaks today of two senses: the literal sense and the spiritual. The Encyclical *Divino Afflante*, October 10, 1943, declared, "It is . . . the duty of the exegete to discover and expound not only the proper or 'literal' meaning of the words which the sacred writer intended and expressed, but also their spiritual significance, on condition of its being established that such meaning has been given to them by God. . . . This spiritual sense . . . intended and ordained by God himself, must be shown forth and explained by Catholic commentators with the diligence which the dignity of the word of God demands; but they must be scrupulously careful not to propound other metaphorical meanings as though they were the genuine sense of Holy Scripture." Quoted in Hebert, *Authority*, 264. The latest official document, *The Interpretation of the Bible in the Church*, produced by the Pontifical Biblical Commission in 1993, not only cautions against allegorical interpretations but firmly establishes the priority of the literal sense: "While there is a distinction between the two senses, the spiritual sense can never be stripped of its connection with the literal sense. The latter remains the indispensable foundation. Otherwise one could not speak of the 'fulfilment' of scripture. . . . The spiritual sense is not to be confused with subjective interpretations stemming from the imagination or intellectual speculation. The spiritual sense results from setting the text in relation to real facts which are not foreign to it: the paschal event, in all its inexhaustible richness, which constitutes the summit of the divine intervention in the history of Israel, to the benefit of all mankind." J. L. Houlden, *The Interpretation of the Bible in the Church*, 55. The whole document may be found in Houlden's book.

CHAPTER 4

The History of Preaching Christ from the Old Testament (II)

"The whole Scripture is about Christ alone everywhere, if we look to its inner meaning, though superficially it may sound different."

Martin Luther, *Römerbrief*

IN THIS CHAPTER we shall continue our discussion on the history of preaching Christ from the Old Testament by focussing first on the christological interpretation of Martin Luther, next the theocentric interpretation of John Calvin, and finally the christological interpretation of Charles Spurgeon and Wilhelm Vischer.

CHRISTOLOGICAL INTERPRETATION

The Young Luther

Martin Luther (1483-1546) continued the search for the key to preaching Christ from the Old Testament. His christological interpretation influences preachers to the present day.

The Start of the Reformation

A. S. Wood contends that the Reformation began not in 1510 when Luther visited Rome and was shocked by the crass commercialism promoted by the Vatican, nor in 1517 when Luther tacked his ninety-five theses to the door of the Castle Church in Wittenberg, but in 1514 "in the tower room of the Augustinian cloister where Luther sat before an open Bible and allowed Almighty God to address him face to face."[1] Luther was intensely troubled by Paul's statement that in the gospel "the righteousness of God is revealed" (Rom 1:17). He writes,

> The concept of "God's righteousness" was repulsive to me, as I was accustomed to interpret it according to scholastic philosophy, namely, as the "formal or active" righteousness in which God proves himself righteous in that He punishes the sinner as an unrighteous person. . . . After days and nights of wrestling with the problem, God finally took pity on me, so that I was able to comprehend the inner connection between the two expressions "the righteousness of God revealed in the Gospel" and "the just shall live by faith." Then I began to comprehend "the righteousness of God" through which the righteous are saved by God's grace, namely through faith; that the "righteousness of God" which is revealed through the Gospel was to be understood in a passive sense in which God through mercy justifies man by faith, as it is written, "the just shall live by faith." Now I felt exactly as though I had been born again. . . . I then went through the Holy Scriptures as far as I could recall them from memory, and I found in other parts the same sense: the "work of God" is that which He works in us, the "strength of God" is that through which He makes us strong, the "wisdom of God" is that through which He makes us wise. . . . As violently as I had formerly hated the expression "righteousness of God," so I was now as violently compelled to embrace the new conception of grace, and thus, for me, the expression really opened the gates of Paradise.[2]

This was the beginning of the Reformation's *sola gratia* and *sola fide:* salvation by God's grace alone and by faith alone. This starting point was bound to have an impact on Luther's view of preaching; it had to be a preaching of Christ. But how?

Allegorical Interpretation

Luther was trained in the fourfold interpretation of the Middle Ages, as is evident in his early writings. But, according to James S. Preus, he abandoned it in 1517, when he opted for a single, literal sense.[3] Yet he strug-

---

1. Wood, *Luther's Principles*, 7.
2. Luther, *WA* 54.185-87, as translated in Wood, ibid., 7-8.
3. Preus, *Shadow*, 227.

gled throughout his life to overcome the temptation of allegorical interpretation. He confesses, "When I was a monk I allegorized everything.
But after lecturing on the epistle to the Romans I came to have some
knowledge of Christ. For therein I saw that Christ is not an allegory, and I
learned to know what Christ actually was."[4] Elsewhere he admits, "It
was very difficult for me to break away from my habitual zeal for allegory. And yet I was aware that allegories were empty speculations and
the froth, as it were, of the Holy Scriptures. It is the historical sense alone
which supplies the true and sound doctrine."[5] Luther angrily dismisses
allegorical interpretation: "Origen's allegories are not worth so much
dirt." "Allegories are awkward, absurd, invented, obsolete, loose rags."
"Allegory is a sort of beautiful harlot, who proves herself specially seduc-
tive to idle men."[6]

Of his own development, Luther writes, "Ever since I started to
stick to the historical sense, I have always had a horror of allegories
and did not employ them unless the text itself indicated them or the
interpretation were there in the New Testament."[7] And in discussing
the book which has probably suffered more from allegorical interpretation than any other, the Song of Songs, Luther says, "I leave allegories alone. A young theologian should avoid them as much as he can. I
think that in a thousand years there was no more economical allegorist than myself. . . . Become a text critic and learn about the grammatical sense, whatever grammar intends, which is about faith, patience,
death, and life. The Word of God does not deal with frivolous
things."[8]

Luther's Hermeneutical Method

Sola Scriptura

The foundation of Luther's hermeneutical method is the principle of *sola
Scriptura*. He writes, "The teachings of the Fathers are useful only to lead

4. Luther, *WA* 42.173, as translated in McCartney and Clayton, *Let the Reader*, 93.

5. Luther as quoted in Rogers and McKim, *Authority*, 85, with a reference to *LW*
1.283.

6. Luther, *LW* 1-3, *Lectures on Genesis*, comments on Gen 3:15-20, as cited in Kaiser and Silva, *Introduction*, 224-25.

7. Luther, *WA* 47.173.25, as translated in F. Baue, *LuthQ* 9 (1995) 414. Cf. *LW*
1.232-33.

8. Luther, *WA* 31.592.16, *A Brief, Yet Clear Exposition of the Song of Songs*, as translated in Bornkamm, *Luther and the Old Testament*, 92.

us to the Scriptures as they were led, and then we must hold to the Scriptures alone."[9] The principle of *sola Scriptura* involves a break with the medieval pattern of understanding Scripture in the overall normative context of church "tradition" (a development of the earlier "rule of faith"). *Sola Scriptura* frees Scripture from subjection to church "tradition" and declares that Scripture is the final authority in interpretation. According to Luther's famous phrase, *"Scriptura sui ipsius interpres*, Scripture interprets itself."[10] "That is the true method of interpretation," he says, "which puts Scripture alongside of Scripture in a right and proper way."[11]

Luther can refer to the practice of the church fathers themselves for this move: "The holy Fathers explained Scripture by taking the clear, lucid passages and with them shed light on obscure and doubtful passages."[12] He asserts, "Such is the way of the whole of Scripture: it wants to be interpreted by a comparison of passages from everywhere, and understood under its own direction. The safest of all methods for discerning the meaning of Scripture is to work for it by drawing together and scrutinizing passages."[13]

For Luther, however, the principle that Scripture interprets itself also functions at another level: over against Rome, which held that only the church can understand Scripture, he contends that Scripture possesses clarity in itself.[14] Lay people, too, can read and understand the Scriptures, especially when allegorical interpretation gives way to literal interpretation.[15] Translating the Bible into German, Luther gave the Bible back to the people (the priesthood of believers).

Literal-Prophetic Interpretation

Although Luther struggled with his background in fourfold interpretation, he clearly settled for the single sense of literal interpretation. In developing his own hermeneutical method, he was able to draw on the church fathers, and particularly on Nicholas of Lyra (d. 1340) and Lefèvre

9. Luther, *WA* 18.1588, as translated in McCartney and Clayton, *Let the Reader,* 93.

10. Luther, *WA* 7.97, as translated in Wood, *Luther's Principles,* 21.

11. Luther, *Works,* Holman Edition, 3.334, as cited in Wood, ibid.

12. Luther, *Martin Luthers sämmtliche Schriften* (St. Louis), 20.856, as translated in Wood, ibid.

13. Luther, *LW* 9.21.

14. Klaas Runia, *CTJ* 19/2 (1984) 134.

15. Cf. McCartney and Clayton, *Let the Reader,* 93, "Because the esoterism of allegorical interpretation was no longer primary, the Bible became accessible to ordinary thought and so Luther saw the meaning of the Bible as simple and clear."

(d. 1536), who had emphasized the literal sense.[16] Luther claimed that the literal sense alone "holds the ground in trouble and trial, conquers the gates of hell [Matt 16:18] along with sin and death, and triumphs for the praise and glory of God. Allegory, however, is too often uncertain, unreliable, and by no means safe for supporting faith. Too frequently it depends upon human guesswork and opinion. . . ."[17] Luther's literal interpretation, however, is not wooden literalism; he is quite ready to interpret figures of speech figuratively. But the burden of proof is on the figures of speech. He writes, "Let us rather take the view that neither an inference nor a trope is admissible in any passage of Scripture, unless it is forced upon us by the evident nature of the context and the absurdity of the literal sense as conflicting with one or another of the articles of faith. Instead, we must everywhere stick to the simple, pure, and natural sense of the words that accords with the rules of grammar and the normal use of language as God has created it in man."[18]

While aiming at literal interpretation, however, Luther's concern to preach Christ from the Old Testament forces him to expand the literal sense to a "prophetic sense." In his Preface to the Psalter, entitled significantly "Preface of Jesus Christ," Luther explains that "by 'literal' he does not mean 'historical' (that is, the 'Jewish' misunderstanding) but 'prophetic.' The true, the only *sensus* of the Psalter is the *sensus Christi*."[19] A. S. Wood argues that Luther's christological approach to Scripture "supplies the clue to the paradox involved in his insistence on the primacy of the literal sense whilst conceding that there is a further, inner, spiritual meaning. . . . It is not supplementary to the literal sense but communicated by it."[20] In making this move, Luther can build on the work of Lefèvre: "Following Lefèvre, who had insisted on a twofold literal sense,

16. Luther says, "Here in all simplicity . . . we expound the historical sense, which is genuine and true. For this especially must be done in interpreting Holy Scripture, in order to bring forth from it a certain and simple meaning." Luther, *WA* 47.172.40, as translated in Baue, *LuthQ* 9 (1995) 414. Cf. *LW* 1.230. For elements of continuity between medieval and Reformation exegesis, see Richard Muller, "Biblical Interpretation," 8-13.

17. Luther, *WA* 14.560.14 as translated in Heinrich Bornkamm, *Luther and the Old Testament*, 91. Cf. *LW* 9.24.

18. Luther, *On the Bondage of the Will*, 221, as quoted by Runia, *CTJ* 19/2 (1984) 135. Cf. Bornkamm, *Luther and the Old Testament*, 95.

19. James S. Preus, *Harvard Theological Review* 60 (1967) 146-47. Cf. Preus, *Shadow*, 144, "Luther does not apply the term 'spiritual' to the christological sense; in fact, he avoids the terms 'literal' and 'spiritual' when dealing with the description of the several scriptural senses. Letter-and-spirit are seen by him as a different problem. The terms Luther uses, in a somewhat peculiar fashion, are *historicus* and *propheticus*."

20. Wood, *Luther's Principles*, 34.

a literal historic and a literal prophetic, Luther held to the historical sense in two ways, first as an account of the history of what God has done, and second as having a history which pointed to what God was going to do."[21]

The Unity and Contrast of the Old and New Testaments

Luther emphasizes both the unity of the Old and New Testaments and their differences. He sees the unity of Scripture in its center, Jesus Christ. He states, "There is no word in the New Testament which does not look back on the Old, where it has already been proclaimed in advance. . . . For the New Testament is nothing more than a revelation of the Old."[22] Consequently, Luther feels free to interpret "the New Testament in the light of the Old, and the Old Testament in the light of the New. For him the two sections of Scripture constitute a single entity."[23]

Law and Gospel

While Luther holds to the unity of the Old and New Testaments, he emphasizes their differences even more with his distinction between law and gospel. Brevard Childs states that Luther "began with the prevailing mediaeval view which correlated law and gospel with the two different testaments. However, somewhere in his second series on the Psalter he discovered 'the faithful synagogue' which caused him to recognize the truly theological and spiritual dimension of the Old Testament."[24] Yet Lu-

---

21. McCartney and Clayton, *Let the Reader*, 94. Cf. Muller, *Post-Reformation*, 2.489-90, "The problem encountered by Lefèvre — which is, simply stated, the problem of finding the churchly and doctrinal significance of an ancient Israelite text while at the same time affirming a single literal meaning — was not confined to late medieval and humanist exegesis. It is a problem at the heart of the exegesis of the Reformers." Cf. Bright, *Authority*, 83, "Both Luther and Calvin . . . insisted in principle that Scripture has but one sense, the plain or literal sense. But by this they did not mean precisely what most modern exegetes (who insist on the same thing) would mean. . . . Is not the true author of Scripture the Holy Spirit? The plain sense of a text, then, includes the sense intended by the Holy Spirit, the prophetic sense (*sensus literalis propheticus*), its sense in the light of Scripture as a whole (i.e., Scripture is its own interpreter)."

22. Luther, *WA* 10.1a, 181-82, as translated by Runia, *CTJ* 19/2 (1984) 128. Cf. Luther, *LW* 30.19 (*WA* 12.275.5), as cited in Bornkamm, *Luther in Mid-Career*, 231, "The books of Moses and the prophets are also gospel, since they proclaimed and described in advance what the apostles preached or wrote later about Christ."

23. Wood, *Luther's Principles*, 23.

24. Childs, *Biblical Theology*, 45.

ther continues to accentuate the differences in terms of law and gospel. He grants that the Old Testament has some gospel and the New Testament some law, but the Old Testament is primarily a book of law and the New Testament is gospel. In his "Preface to the Old Testament" (1523) he writes, "The Old Testament is a book of laws, which teaches what men are to do and not to do . . . just as the New Testament is gospel or book of grace, and teaches where one is to get the power to fulfil the law. Now in the New Testament there are also given . . . many other teachings that are laws and commandments. . . . Similarly in the Old Testament too there are . . . certain promises and words of grace. . . . Nevertheless just as the chief teaching of the New Testament is really the proclamation of grace and peace through the forgiveness of sins in Christ, so the chief teaching of the Old Testament is really the teaching of laws, the showing up of sin, and the demanding of good."[25]

For Luther, then, the major role of the Old Testament for Christians is negative: it makes people aware of their total inability to obey God's laws perfectly for earning their salvation. Still the Old Testament also has some positive aspects: "There are three things in the Old Testament of abiding significance for Christians. For the Christian the external laws are dead, unless he adopt them of his own free will because they seem to him suitable for outward conduct, or because, like the Ten Commandments, they correspond to the law of Nature implanted by God in all our hearts. . . . The second thing that the Old Testament gives us is not to be found in Nature . . . , namely the promises of Christ's coming and God's pledges with regard to Him — the best things in the Old Testament. . . . Thirdly we read the Pentateuch because of the fine examples of faith, love and suffering in the beloved forefathers. . . ."[26]

Accordingly, Luther does not wish to ignore the Old Testament in

25. Luther, "Preface to the Old Testament," par. 4, *LW* 35.236-37, quoted in Baker, *Two Testaments,* 51. Cf. Luther's debate with Emser, who interpreted Paul's words in 2 Cor 3:6, "The letter kills, but the Spirit gives life," as the literal sense kills but the spiritual sense gives life. Luther observes, "In that passage St. Paul does not write one iota about these two senses, but declares that there are two kinds of preaching or ministries. One is that of the Old Testament, the other that of the New Testament. The Old Testament preaches the letter, the New Testament the spirit. . . . These, then, are the two ministries. The priests, preachers, and ministries of the Old Testament deal with naught else but the law of God; they have as yet no open proclamation of the spirit and of grace. But in the New Testament all the preaching is of grace and the spirit given to us through Christ. For the preaching of the New Testament is naught else but an offering and presentation of Christ to all men out of the pure mercy of God. . . ." Luther, "Answer to the Superchristian," 156-57.

26. Luther, *WA* 18.80; 24.10; and 24.15, as translated in Kurt Aland, *ExpT* 69 (1957-58) 69.

preaching. In fact, he vehemently opposes those who would reject the Old Testament. He scolds them: "What a fine lot of tender and pious children we are! In order that we might not have to study in the Scriptures and learn Christ there, we simply regard the entire Old Testament as of no account, as done for and no longer valid."[27] But we ought to preach from the Old Testament because Christ is there. The Gospels and Epistles of the apostles "want themselves to be our guides to direct us to the writings of the prophets and of Moses in the Old Testament so that we might there read and see for ourselves how Christ is wrapped in swaddling cloths and laid in the manger, that is, how he is comprehended in the writings of the prophets. It is there that people like us should read and study . . . and see what Christ is, for what purpose he has been given, how he was promised, and how all Scripture tends toward him."[28]

Law and Gospel in Every Sermon

A. S. Wood observes, "Law and Gospel are always set side by side in Luther. They are both works of Christ. Law is His *opus alienum* [strange work]; Gospel is His *opus proprium* [proper work]. 'The Law revealeth the disease: the Gospel ministereth the medicine.'"[29] In Luther's "Against the Heavenly Prophets," he lists in order five "articles of the Christian faith" as priorities for preaching. "The first is the law of God, which is to be preached so that one thereby reveals and teaches how to recognize sin (Rom 3[:20] and 7[:7]). . . . Secondly, when now sin is recognized and the law is so preached that the conscience is alarmed and humbled before God's wrath, we are then to preach the comforting word of the Gospel and the forgiveness of sins, so that the conscience again may be comforted and established in the grace of God. . . ."[30]

Fred Meuser alerts us to the fact that "in his preaching, Luther's concern over law and gospel was not the theological definition of their relationship, but a very pastoral one, namely, Where is your trust? . . . Where is the focus of your life — on your own efforts, or on God's promises in Christ?"[31] In a *Church Postil* to Duke Albrecht, we get a clear idea

---

27. Luther, *A Brief Instruction*, 99.

28. Ibid., 98.

29. Wood, *EvQ* 21 (1949), 119, quoting from *Sermons of Martin Luther*, ed. Kerr, p. 219.

30. The other three are: third, "the work of putting to death the old man, as in Romans 5, 6, and 7"; fourth, "works of love toward the neighbor"; and "in the fifth and last place, we ought to proclaim the law and its works, not for the Christians, but for the crude and unbelieving." Luther, *LW* 40.82-83.

31. Meuser, *Luther*, 23.

of how Luther views preaching the gospel in contrast to preaching law. He writes,

> It is an evil custom to treat the gospels and epistles as books of law, from which we should teach what men ought to do and present the works of Christ as nothing more than examples or illustrations. . . . Beware of turning Christ into a Moses, as if He had nothing more for us than precept and example, like the other saints. . . . You must rise much higher than that, although this best sort of preaching has been practiced but little these many years. The chief and fundamental thing in the Gospel is this, that before you take Christ as your example, you recognize and accept Him as God's gift to you; so that when you see or hear Him in any of His work or suffering, you do not doubt but believe that He, Christ Himself, with such work or suffering of His, is most truly your very own, whereon you may rely as confidently as if you had done that work. . . . See, this is to understand aright the Gospel, that is, the infinite grace of God. . . . This is the mighty fire of God's love toward us whereby He makes the conscience confident, joyful, and content. This is to preach the Christian faith. This it is that makes our preaching a Gospel, viz., glad, good, comfortable tidings.[32]

Luther's Christological Interpretation of the Old Testament

"Whether They Treat of Christ or Not"

In his Preface to the letter of James, Luther sets forth his standard for evaluating biblical books. He writes, "The office of a true apostle is to preach the passion and resurrection and the ministry of Christ, and to lay the foundation for this faith. . . . And therein all honest sacred books agree, they all preach Christ. And that is the proper touchstone for judging all books, that one should see whether they treat of Christ or not. Since all Scripture witnesses to Christ (Rom 3:22ff.) and Paul is determined not to know anything save Christ (1 Cor 2:2), that which does not teach Christ is not apostolic, even though Peter and Paul should teach it."[33]

The witness to Christ is Luther's criterion not just for good preaching but first of all for evaluating biblical books. Hence he questions the place in the Old Testament canon of the book of Esther. Luther says, "Although

---

32. Luther, *Church Postil*, cited in Reu, *Homiletics*, 61-62.
33. Luther, "Preface," *WA*, *Deutsche Bibel*, 7.384, as translated in Kurt Aland, *ExpT* 69 (1957-58) 48.

they have it in the canon, it is in my opinion less worthy of being held canonical than all the others."[34] Conversely, Luther's acceptance of all the other canonical books means that he views them all as witnesses to Christ.

Christological Interpretation of the Old Testament

Luther begins with the premise that Christ is the heart of the Bible. In countless works he states his conviction that the Old Testament, too, is about Christ: "In the whole Scripture there is nothing but Christ, either in plain words or involved words." "The whole Scripture is about Christ alone everywhere, if we look to its inner meaning, though superficially it may sound different." Christ is "the sun and truth in Scripture." "It is beyond question that all the Scriptures point to Christ alone." "The entire Old Testament refers to Christ and agrees with Him."[35]

In an illuminating image, Luther clarifies how the Old Testament must be read. He says, "The New Testament is not more than a revelation of the Old, just as when a man had first a closed letter and afterwards broke it open. So the Old Testament is an epistle of Christ, which after His death He opened and caused to be read through the Gospel and proclaimed everywhere. . . ."[36] In other words, Luther seeks to read the Old Testament in the light of the New.

Given this starting point, the prophetic sense "is understood most emphatically as the christological one."[37] Luther himself exhorts, "Every prophecy and every prophet ought to be understood as *de Christo domino* [about Christ the Lord], except where it is apparent by clear words that they are speaking about something else."[38] According to Bornkamm, Luther's lectures on the Psalms "often bore a New Testament character thanks to the prophetic-christological method Luther employed." "Prophetic-christological interpretation . . . was for him the indispensable bridge to the Old Testament."[39]

---

34. Luther, *On the Bondage of the Will*, WA 18.666.23. Cf. Luther, *Table Talk*, 1534, *Martin Luthers Werke*, Tischreden (Weimar, 1912-21), 3.302.12 (no. 3391a): "I dislike the Book of Esther and that of II Maccabees, for they Judaize too much and contain much pagan naughtiness."

35. Luther, respectively WA 11.223; *Römerbrief*, ed. J. Ficker, 240; WA 3.643; *Works*, Holman Edition, 2.432; and WA 10.576, as translated and cited in Wood, *Luther's Principles*, 33.

36. Luther, *Kirchen Post.*, John 1:1-2, WA 10/2.181.15, as translated in Barth, *Church Dogmatics*, 1/2.14.77.

37. Preus, *Shadow*, 145.

38. Luther, WA 55/1.6.25f., as translated in Preus, ibid.

39. Bornkamm, *Luther in Mid-Career*, 229 and 232.

Luther's Preaching of Christ

Luther's Testimony

Fred Meuser writes, "Luther deeply loved Jesus — the beautiful, caring, human Jesus of the Gospels. Any sermon that failed somehow to hold up that Lord — whose love reached its pinnacle in his self-giving on the cross — so that others could be amazed, as he had been, and then be drawn to trust in the promises and find peace with God and with self, could not be described as preaching Christ."[40] Meuser calls attention to a distinction between Luther's emphases in theology and in preaching: "Justification permeated Luther's theology, but the living, breathing, loving, serving, and suffering Christ permeated his preaching."[41]

Luther begins a Palm Sunday sermon (1521) as follows: "A preacher in the Christian churches should be judged by this — that he preaches Christ alone, so that the people may know in what they may trust and on what to base their conscience."[42] In his Easter sermon the following Sunday he says, "The priests have no other office than to preach the clear sun, Christ. Therefore preaching is a dangerous thing. Let the preachers take care that they preach thus or let them be silent. A bad preacher is more dangerous than a thousand Turks. . . . Whoever does not preach about God's kingdom has not been sent by Christ. . . . Now to preach God's kingdom is nothing else than to preach the gospel which teaches faith in Christ — through which alone God dwells in us."[43]

---

40. Meuser, *Luther*, 24.

41. Ibid., 18-19.

42. Luther, cited by Meuser, ibid., 17. Cf. Luther's statement quoted in Reu, *Homiletics*, 61, "All our sermons have this purpose, that you and we may believe Christ is the only Saviour and hope of the world, the shepherd and bishop of our souls; for the whole Gospel points to Christ, as did the witness of St. John (John 1:8, 29). Hence we do not draw men to ourselves, but lead them to Christ, who is the way, the truth and the life."

43. Luther, cited by Meuser, ibid., also referring to *WA* 10/3.361. Cf. ibid., 24-25, for an Ascension Day sermon of 1534: "Faith in Christ should be preached, no matter what happens. I would much rather hear people say of me that I preach too sweetly . . . than not preach faith in Christ at all, for then there would be no help for timid, frightened consciences. . . . Therefore I should like to have the message of faith in Christ not forgotten but generally known. It is so sweet a message, full of sheer joy, comfort, mercy, and grace."

Luther's Preaching of Christ from the Old Testament

Luther proclaims that "the law and the prophets are not rightly preached or known, save we see Christ wrapped up in them."[44] So how does Luther find Christ in the Old Testament? McCurley suggests that Luther works out his christological exegesis in two ways: "(1) direct predictions of Christ and (2) indirect permeation of the gospel." He finds direct predictions of Christ not only in the so-called "messianic texts" such as Genesis 3:15; 4:1; 28:18; 49:10, and Deuteronomy 18:15, 18.[45] "Beyond these 'messianic' texts," Luther also finds "christological promises in Exodus 33:18-19 ('I will let all my goodness pass before your eyes, and I will preach in the Lord's name before you.') as well as in Exodus 34:5ff. and 8ff. (the appearance of God and the covenant of God), which point to the promise of Christ." Direct predictions of Christ also include the prophecies about David such as "2 Samuel 23:1ff. (where the 'one who rules justly over men' is not David but Christ) and 2 Samuel 7:16 (where 'your house and your kingdom shall be made sure for ever before me' must apply to the king who will replace the earthly house of David)."[46]

Luther's second way of finding Christ in the Old Testament, the indirect permeation of the gospel, is harder to explain. Foster McCurley seeks to unwrap this notion: "The gospel can be said to be present and indeed flood the whole Old Testament land and thus go beyond individual prophetic passages." More specifically, because Luther knows what the gospel is on the basis of the New Testament witness to Christ, he can look back "to see the *gospel as promise* witnessed throughout the Old Testament as well. In God's faithful relationship to his people Israel, pointing them again and again to the establishment of his reign, God acts in terms of the *gospel* 'preached . . . beforehand to Abraham, saying, "In you shall all the nations be blessed."' (Gal. 3:8)."[47]

Of all the Old Testament books, Luther seems to have favored the Psalms. He writes, "The Psalter ought to be a precious and beloved book, if for no other reason than this: it promises Christ's death and resurrection so clearly — and pictures his kingdom and the condition and nature of all Christendom — that it might well be called a little Bible."[48] In his early lectures on the Psalms he "takes the unprecedented step of having

44. Luther, Sermon on Luke 2:1-2, *WA* 10/2.81.8, as cited in Barth, *Church Dogmatics*, 1/2.14.77.

45. Foster McCurley, "Confessional," 234. Cf. Bornkamm, *Luther and the Old Testament*, 101-14.

46. McCurley, "Confessional," 234.

47. Ibid., 234-35.

48. Luther, "Preface to the Psalms," *LW* 35.254.

Christ himself step forward to identify himself, via his New Testament self-witness, as the subject-matter and speaker of the whole Psalter."[49] Note Luther's christological method in the first three Psalms:

> Psalm 1: "The letter is that the Lord Jesus did not yield to the favorite pursuits of the Jews and of the perverse and adulterous generation which were current in his time."
> Psalm 2: "The letter concerns the fury of the Jews and Gentiles against Christ in his passion."
> Psalm 3: "'Lord, how they [my enemies] are multiplied' is *ad literam* a complaint of Christ about his enemies the Jews."[50]

A year later Luther changed his hermeneutical approach. This change came about because of "Luther's discovery of the Old Testament as religiously and theologically relevant — . . . it stands as still-authentic testimony and promise, arousing the *expectatio* and *petitio* of those who live *before* the advent of Christ and long for his coming."[51] In other words, instead of reading the New Testament Christ back into the Psalms, Luther has become more aware of the need for understanding the Psalms in their own historical context as addressed to Israel. The Old Testament words, as "old," "promise, pray for, point to the Christ who is not yet here." Christ now becomes the goal, "the *telos* of the whole exegesis. And the *applicatio* now springs not from our likeness to Christ, but from our likeness to the Old Testament speaker, with whom we share the anticipation of the Coming One."[52]

In his last sermon, preached February 14, 1546, Luther reiterates one more time: "The right sort of preacher should faithfully and diligently preach nothing but the Word of God and seek His glory and honor alone. The hearer likewise should say, 'I do not believe in my pastor, but he tells me of another Lord whose name is Christ; Him he declares unto me, and I will listen to his words so far as he leads me to this true master and preceptor, God's own Son.'"[53]

---

49. James Preus, "Old Testament *Promissio*," 146.
50. Ibid., n. 5.
51. Ibid., 148.
52. Ibid., respectively 156 and 153.
53. Luther, cited in Reu, *Homiletics*, 46-47.

Evaluation of Luther's Christological Interpretation

Valuable Contributions

Luther's christological interpretation and preaching contain many valuable elements. As no one else in his time, Luther preaches the gospel of God's grace, that is, Jesus Christ is God's gift *(sola gratia)*, a gift we can receive only by faith *(sola fide)*. He also insists on *sola Scriptura*, that is, the Scriptures are the only (or ultimate) norm for living and preaching, and thus he sets the Scriptures free from the domination of church "tradition" so that they can interpret themselves.

Luther further stresses that preachers should not merely preach truth objectively but must show the relevance of the Scriptures for us *(pro nobis)*. He asserts, "This is the second part of our understanding and justification, to know that Christ suffered and was cursed and killed, but FOR US. It is not enough to know the matter, the suffering, but it is necessary to know its function."[54] Elsewhere he writes: "It is not enough nor is it Christian, to preach the works, life, and words of Christ as historical facts, as if the knowledge of these would suffice for the conduct of life, although this is the fashion of those who must today be regarded as our best preachers. . . . Rather ought Christ to be preached to the end that faith in him may be established, that he may not only be Christ, but be Christ for you and me, and that what his name denotes may be effectual in us. Such faith is produced and preserved in us by preaching why Christ came, what he brought and bestowed, what benefit it is to us to accept him."[55]

Luther can also be credited for what we today would call expository or textual-thematic preaching. According to Meuser, "With Luther, especially after 1521, came what many interpreters call a totally new form of the sermon: *die schriftauslegende Predigt* [the Scripture-expositing sermon]. . . . The aim of the sermon is . . . to help hearers understand the *text*, not just a religious truth. . . . Its method is to take a given segment of Scripture, find the key thought within it, and make that unmistakably clear. The text is to control the sermon."[56]

---

54. Luther, *LW* 17.220-21, as cited in John L. Thompson, *Studia Biblica et Theologica* 12 (1982) 62. Cf. Meuser, *Luther*, 73, "The resurrection is as much *pro nobis*, for us, as the crucifixion. . . . He takes our death on himself and gives us life."

55. Luther, *Tractatus de libertate christiana*, as quoted in Schubert Ogden, *Point*, xiii.

56. Meuser, *Luther*, 46-47. Cf. ibid., 47, "Luther insisted on finding the *Sinnmitte*, the heart of the text. That heart, that *Kern* or kernel, is to save the preacher from getting lost in details. . . . The main point of a sermon is to be so clear in the preacher's mind that it controls everything that is said."

Shortcomings in Luther's Method

Besides our praise of Luther's method, we also need to consider some shortcomings. First, Luther's christological method may lead to reading Christ back into the Old Testament text. Although we noted this especially in his early phase of interpreting the Psalms, it is not absent later.[57] Heinrich Bornkamm asserts that "the christological-prophetic interpretation is forced to carry the concepts of the New Testament revelation into the Old Testament and put them in the mouths of the patriarchs and writers." And he concludes, "Any research which thinks historically will have to give up, without hesitation or reservation, Luther's scheme of christological prediction in the Old Testament."[58]

A further concern is that Luther's concentration on preaching Christ may lead to a slighting of other fundamental revelations in the Old Testament: What about God's *good* creation, human stewardship of God's earth, redemptive history, the coming kingdom of God in the Old Testament, God's covenant, the value of God's law for Christian living?

Another shortcoming is the distinction between law and gospel as the boundary between the Old Testament and the New. As we have seen, Luther acknowledges some slippage either way, but he doggedly hangs on to the Old Testament as law and the New Testament as gospel. This law-gospel dialectic leads to a lack of appreciation for God's law. Luther even argues at one point that "the Ten commandments did not apply to Christians, being addressed only to the Jews who had come out of Egypt."[59] Although Paul in his battle against works righteousness sets up a radical contrast between "law" and "gospel," these terms, as contrasted, refer not to the Old Testament and the New Testament but to two ways of salvation: works and grace.[60] Moreover, "according to the Gospel

---

57. For example, Luther, *WA* 2, 120.8–121.14, interprets Ps 3:5, "I wake again, for the Lord sustains me," just like Augustine as referring to the resurrection of Christ. As to his later years, Muller, *Post-Reformation*, 2.490, states that "Luther retained this emphasis on a christological reading of the Old Testament . . . as witnessed throughout his lectures on Genesis."

58. Bornkamm, *Luther and the Old Testament*, 263 and 262. Cf. Farrar, *History*, 333, "When Luther reads the doctrines of the Trinity, and the Incarnation, and Justification by Faith . . . into passages written more than a thousand years before the Christian era . . . , he is adopting an unreal method which had been rejected a millennium earlier by the clearer insight and more unbiased wisdom of the School of Antioch."

59. Luther, *WA* 16.363-93, as summarized by McCartney and Clayton, *Let the Reader*, 95-96.

60. For various senses of Paul's usage of "law" and "gospel," see Andrew Bandstra, "Law and Gospel," 18-21.

of Matthew, the law is indeed fulfilled in Jesus Christ, but the effect of that fulfillment creates no dichotomy between law and gospel. Authentic discipleship necessarily entails doing the righteousness expressed in the law, a righteousness rooted in creation itself."[61]

Luther also uses the law-gospel distinction homiletically by teaching that ideally every sermon should proclaim first our need, with the law, and next the solution, with the gospel. Even today one hears the injunction that preachers must ask every text two questions: What is law here? And what is gospel? Richard Lischer points out the danger in this approach, namely, "that we lay the same stencil over every text, asking, Where is the law and gospel? rather than, What is God saying to his people? This rigid approach assures the congregation of an explication of judgment and grace whether this particular text offers it or not."[62]

Finally, in spite of his warnings against allegorical interpretation, Luther continued using this arbitrary method of interpretation himself when the text did not yield "any other useful sense."[63] Ironically, while Luther left some limited room for allegorical interpretation, he apparently had no use for typological interpretation, for, as David Dockery puts it, typology with its foreshadowing "annulled the historical presence of Christ in the Old Testament." The Antioch School "saw shadowy anticipation of what was to come. This meant nothing to Luther. To him, the Old Testament was not a figure of what would be, but a testimony to what always holds true between humankind and God."[64]

---

61. David Holwerda, *Jesus and Israel*, 145. Note that Luther also suggests that we should keep the moral law, not because it is in the Old Testament but because it is a law of creation (see p. 117 above). Cf. W. Eichrodt, *Theology of the Old Testament*, 1.94, "Long before there was any human action in response, this [God's] love chose the people for God's own possession and gave them the law as a token of their special position of favour. To obey the law thus becomes man's response of love to the divine act of election."

62. Lischer, *Theology of Preaching*, 61.

63. Bornkamm, *Luther and the Old Testament*, 95. See pp. 92-95 for many dated examples and the comment (p. 94): "These dates show that Luther used allegory at all periods of his life. Of course he became more cautious in his use of it as time went on. There is a sharp and definite break after 1525."

64. Dockery, *GTJ* 4/2 (1983) 193. Luther's rejection of typology may well be connected with his ideas about history and the presence of Christ in the Old Testament as eternal God. See Bornkamm, *Luther and the Old Testament*, 200-207 and 258-60.

THEOCENTRIC INTERPRETATION

Calvin

Calvin and Luther

John Calvin (1509-64), who was twenty-six years younger than Luther, had quite a different approach to preaching Christ from the Old Testament.[65] Of course, Calvin learned much from Luther, and the two Reformers agreed on many fundamentals. They agreed on *sola gratia, sola fide,* and *sola Scriptura.* They also agreed that Scripture is its own interpreter and that Christ is the center of Scripture.

In spite of broad agreement, however, Calvin's hermeneutical approach is quite different from Luther's. Luther was concerned mainly about the issue of salvation and focussed on justification by faith in Christ. Consequently, finding Christ in the Old Testament became Luther's priority. Calvin, though affirming justification by faith in Christ, has a broader viewpoint, namely, the sovereignty and glory of God.[66] This broader perspective enables Calvin to be satisfied with biblical messages about God, God's redemptive history, and God's covenant without necessarily focussing these messages on Jesus Christ.

In contrast to Luther as well, Calvin appreciates the School of Antioch, especially Chrysostom. "Chrysostom had attained two goals to which Calvin dedicated himself. One was that Chrysostom never strayed from a clear elaboration and explanation of the biblical text. The second was that Chrysostom spoke with the common people in mind."[67] In introducing a French translation of Chrysostom's homilies, Calvin writes, "The outstanding merit of our author, Chrysostom, is that it was his supreme concern always not to turn aside even to the slightest degree from the genuine, simple sense of Scripture and to allow himself no liberties by twisting the plain meaning of the words."[68]

65. According to the calculations of Parker, *Calvin's Old Testament Commentaries,* 9-10, between 1549 and 1564 Calvin preached over two thousand sermons from the Old Testament.

66. Cf. Leroy Nixon, *John Calvin,* 76, "The primary truth in Calvin's preaching is the sovereignty of God." Cf. McCartney and Clayton, *Let the Reader,* 97, "Instead of focussing on the rather narrow matter of justification by faith, Calvin took the much larger rubric of the glory of God as his interpretive viewpoint and was able to hold together the array of biblical teaching much more easily."

67. Rogers and McKim, *Authority,* 114-15. Cf. David Puckett, *Calvin's Exegesis,* 105, "Calvin agreed with Theodore. In so doing, he placed himself in opposition to much of the Christian exegetical tradition."

68. Calvin, *CR* 9.835, as quoted in Rogers and McKim, *Authority,* 114.

Opposition to Allegorical Interpretation

Calvin's introduction to Chrysostom discloses his aversion to "twisting the plain meaning of the words" by way of allegorical interpretation. Commenting on "The letter kills, but the spirit gives life" (2 Cor 3:6), he writes, "This passage has been distorted and wrongly interpreted first by Origen and then by others. . . . This error has been the source of many evils. Not only did it open the way for the adulteration of the natural meaning of Scripture but also set up boldness in allegorizing as the chief exegetical virtue. Thus many of the ancients without any restraint played all sorts of games with the sacred Word of God, as if they were tossing a ball to and fro. It also gave heretics a chance to throw the Church into turmoil, for when it was an accepted practice for anybody to interpret any passage in any way he desired, any mad idea, however absurd or monstrous, could be introduced under the pretext of allegory."[69] In fact, Calvin considers allegorizing a ploy of Satan to undermine biblical teaching. He asserts, "We must . . . entirely reject the allegories of Origen, and of others like him, which Satan, with the deepest subtlety, has endeavored to introduce into the Church, for the purpose of rendering the doctrine of Scripture ambiguous and destitute of all certainty and firmness."[70]

Calvin's Hermeneutical Method

To start our discussion of Calvin's hermeneutical method, we shall follow the eight exegetical principles which Hans Kraus gleaned from Calvin's work.[71]

Clarity and Brevity

In a letter concerning his commentary on Romans, Calvin remarks that the best virtues of commentators are "clarity and brevity."[72] These virtues require the interpreter to aim for both transparency of exposition and focus (an excellent standard for sermons as well!). Kraus elaborates, "An explanation must be clear and concise in order to be clearly understood.

69. Calvin, *Comm.* 2 Cor 3:6, as translated in Puckett, *Calvin's Exegesis,* 107. Cf. *CO* 50.40-41.

70. Calvin, *Comm.* Gen 2:8 (*CO* 23.37), as quoted in Puckett, ibid. See also *Comm.* Gen 6:14.

71. Kraus, *Int* 31 (1977) 8-18.

72. Calvin, *CR* 38.403, as quoted in Kraus, ibid., 13. Cf. Richard Gamble, *CTJ* 23 (1988) 189.

Allegory, which Luther in his Genesis commentary thought could serve to ornament and illustrate . . . , is to be strictly excluded. When the purpose is to let the matter itself speak out in the exposition, there is no time for luxuriating in the wealth of problems that so many exegetes love, not for the sake of the text, but to draw attention to themselves."[73]

The Intention of the Author

"The constant search for the intention of the author is characteristic of Calvin's commentaries."[74] Calvin writes, "Since it is almost the interpreter's only task to unfold the mind of the writer whom he has undertaken to expound, he misses his mark, or at least strays outside his limits, by the extent to which he leads his readers away from the meaning of his author." He underscores the seriousness of biblical exposition: "It is presumptuous and almost blasphemous to turn the meaning of scripture around without due care, as though it were some game that we were playing."[75] David Puckett confirms with many examples that Calvin "throughout his Old Testament commentaries . . . affirms that the role of an interpreter is to expound the intention of the prophet."[76]

The Historical Context

In his *Institutes*, Calvin states, "There are many statements in Scripture the meaning of which depends upon their context."[77] T. H. L. Parker claims that "one of the outstanding features of Calvin's exposition of the Prophets is his historical treatment."[78] In his commentaries, Calvin often sets forth the historical context of a passage before giving an exposition of the text. For example, in dealing with the Psalms, Calvin speaks of "the

---

73. Kraus, ibid., with references to Luther, *WA* 44.93, and Calvin, *CR* 59.33. In his Ph.D. dissertation "L'École de Dieu: Pedagogy and Method in Calvin's Interpretation of Deuteronomy" (Grand Rapids: Calvin Seminary [photocopy], 1998), 89, Raymond Blacketer makes a good case for considering brevity as "a rhetorical style and a method of exposition; it is not a mode of exegesis."

74. Kraus, ibid.

75. Calvin, *The Epistles of Paul the Apostle to the Romans and to the Thessalonians*, 1.4, as cited in Dockery, "New Testament Interpretation," 48.

76. Puckett, *Calvin's Exegesis*, 33-35. Cf. T. H. L. Parker, *Calvin's Old Testament Commentaries*, 81.

77. Calvin, *Institutes*, 4.16.23, in making the point that texts concerning the baptism of adults cannot be used to reject the baptism of infants.

78. Parker, *Calvin's Old Testament Commentaries*, 205-6. Cf. Puckett, *Calvin's Exegesis*, 67-72.

'solemn assembly' at which songs of praise were sung; of a 'public occasion of thanksgiving' in which the psalms of thanks had their setting; and . . . of a 'festival of renewal of the covenant' in which there was a solemn service of renewal and promises were signed and sealed and made binding by a covenant sacrifice."[79]

Original, Grammatical Meaning

In opposing Origen and allegorical interpretation, Calvin asserts, "Let us know that the true meaning of Scripture is the genuine and simple one [*germanus et simplex*], and let us embrace and hold it tightly. Let us . . . boldly set aside as deadly corruptions, those fictitious expositions which lead us away from the literal sense."[80] Brevard Childs suggests that "Calvin does not . . . need to add a secondary or spiritual meaning to the text because the literal sense is its own witness to God's divine plan."[81]

Literary Context

A passage should be understood not only in its historical context but also in its literary context. One place where Calvin refers to this principle is in dealing with the many protestations of innocence in the Psalms: "If you try my heart, if you visit me by night, if you test me, you will find no wickedness in me" (Ps 17:3). After listing about a dozen such passages, Calvin writes, "As for the testimonies [passages] we have adduced at this point, they will not hinder us much if they are understood according to their context, or, in common parlance, circumstances." And he comes to the conclusion that, although the godly may "defend their innocence against the hypocrisy of the ungodly, still, when they are dealing with God alone, all cry out with one voice: 'If thou, O Lord, shouldst mark iniquity, Lord, who shall stand?'"[82]

---

79. Kraus, *Int* 31 (1977) 14, with references respectively to *CR* 59.466 *et passim*; *CR* 59.231; 60.206; and *CR* 59.497 on Ps 50:5; *CR* 59.760 on Ps 81:2ff. See Puckett, *Calvin's Exegesis*, 67-72, for other examples.

80. Calvin, *CO* 50.237, as cited in Richard Gamble, *WTJ* 49 (1987) 163. Cf. Calvin, *Institutes*, 4.17.22. Because of Calvin's historical focus, Philip Schaff designated him the "founder of modern historical-grammatical exegesis." Puckett, *Calvin's Exegesis*, 56.

81. Childs, "Sensus Literalis," 87.

82. Calvin, *Institutes*, 3.17.14. For other examples, see Puckett, *Calvin's Exegesis*, 64-66, and Parker, *Calvin's Old Testament Commentaries*, 80-81.

Meaning beyond the Literal Biblical Wording

In dealing with the Decalogue, Calvin raises the issue of extending the meaning of a law beyond its literal meaning. He states as a general principle, "The commandments and prohibitions always contain more than is expressed in words." But he seeks "to temper this principle" so that it may not lead us "to twist Scripture." He says, "We must if possible, therefore, find some way to lead us with straight, firm steps to the will of God. We must, I say, inquire how far interpretation ought to overstep the limits of the words themselves so that it may be seen to be . . . the Lawgiver's pure and authentic meaning, faithfully rendered. . . . Now I think this would be the best rule, if attention be directed to the reason of the commandment; that is, in each commandment to ponder why it was given to us." In other words, Calvin looks beyond the literal meaning of a passage to the author's goal. He uses as an example the fifth commandment, "Honor your father and your mother": "The purpose of the Fifth Commandment is that honor ought to be paid to those to whom God has assigned it. This, then, is the substance of the commandment: that it is right and pleasing to God for us to honor those on whom he has bestowed some excellence; and that he abhors contempt and stubbornness against them."[83]

Figures of Speech

For Calvin literal interpretation does not mean a wooden literalism. He discusses at length the necessity of interpreting figures of speech as figures. Calvin observes, "Where Scripture calls God 'a man of war' (Exod 15:3), because I see that this saying would be too harsh without interpretation, I do not doubt that it is a comparison drawn from men." He draws attention to such statements in Scripture as: "God's eyes see," "It came up to his ears," and "His hand extended." These statements are anthropomorphic and must be so interpreted. Failure to do so, says Calvin, leads to "a boundless barbarism." "For what monstrous absurdities will these fanatical men not draw forth from Scripture if they be allowed . . . to establish what they please!"[84]

83. Calvin, *Institutes*, 2.8.8. Cf. ibid., on the first commandment: "The intent of the First Commandment is that God alone be worshipped. Therefore the substance of the precept will be that true piety — namely, the worship of his divinity — is pleasing to God; and that he abominates impiety." Calvin clarifies his move to the last clause as follows: "If this pleases God, the opposite displeases him; if this displeases, the opposite pleases him."

84. Ibid., 4.17.23. For a discussion on metonymy, "a figure of speech commonly used in Scripture when mysteries are under discussion," see ibid., 4.17.21.

The Scope of Christ

Commenting on Jesus' words, "These are the Scriptures that testify about me" (John 5:39, NIV), Calvin writes, "We ought to read the Scriptures with the express design of finding Christ in them. Whoever shall turn aside from this object, though he may weary himself throughout his whole life in learning, will never attain the knowledge of the truth; for what wisdom can we have without the wisdom of God?"[85] Since this principle is our particular focus, we need to consider it at length. But before we do this, we need to discuss, beyond the eight categories suggested by Kraus, at least two more principles which are fundamental for Calvin's method of interpretation: the unity of the Old and New Testaments, and understanding a passage in the context of the whole Bible.

The Relation between the Old and New Testaments

In our historical survey we have seen from the beginning the crucial importance of the way the interpreter understands the relation between the Old and New Testaments. This significance obtains here as well, for the relation between the Testaments turns out to be the hermeneutical fork in the road where Calvin and Luther proceed in different directions. Luther, we have seen, saw the relationship mainly as a contrast between law and gospel. Calvin, on the other hand, emphasizes the unity of the Old and the New Testaments. Whereas Luther looked for unity only in the witness to Christ, Calvin sees the unity across a broad front: one God, one Savior, one redemptive history, one covenant of grace, and even one law.[86]

The Unity of Old and New Testaments

In his *Institutes*, Calvin begins his chapter "The Similarity of the Old and New Testaments" as follows: "Now we can clearly see from what has already been said that all men adopted by God into the company of his people since the beginning of the world were covenanted to him by the same law and by the bond of the same doctrine as obtains among us. It is

---

85. Calvin, *Comm.* John 5:39. Kraus, *Int* 31 (1977) 17, quotes this passage in a different translation from *CR* 47.125.

86. For example, Calvin comments on Matt 5:17, "With respect to doctrine we must not imagine that the coming of Christ has freed us from the authority of the law; for it is the eternal rule of a devout and holy life, and must, therefore, be as unchangeable as the justice of God, which it embraced, is constant and uniform." *Comm.* Matt 5:17, as cited in Bandstra, "Law and Gospel," 11.

very important to make this point."[87] There is but *one* covenant underlying the Old and the New Testaments. Calvin continues, "The covenant made with all the patriarchs is so much like ours in substance and reality that the two are actually one and the same. Yet they differ in the mode of dispensation."[88] The only difference Calvin here acknowledges between Old and New is in the form of its administration, but the substance is "one and the same." This one covenant is a covenant of *grace*.

Calvin, therefore, moves the Reformation's *sola gratia* and *sola fide* back to the beginning of the Old Testament. He states, "the Old Testament was established upon the free mercy of God, and was confirmed by Christ's intercession. . . . Who, then, dares to separate the Jews from Christ, since with them . . . was made the covenant of the gospel, the sole foundation of which is Christ?"[89] He clinches his point with a reference to the teaching of Jesus: "Christ the Lord promises to his followers today no other 'kingdom of Heaven' than that in which they may 'sit at table with Abraham, Isaac, and Jacob' (Matt 8:11)."[90]

Even as Calvin finds God's grace and redemption in Christ in the Old Testament, so he tones down the idea that the gospel brought something radically new. "The gospel," he writes, "did not so supplant the entire law as to bring forward a different way of salvation. Rather, it confirmed and satisfied whatever the law had promised, and gave substance to the shadows."[91] In commenting on Matthew 5:21, Calvin declares, "We must not imagine Christ to be a new legislator, who adds anything to the eternal righteousness of his Father. We must listen to him as a faithful expounder that we may know what is the nature of the law, what is its object, and what is its extent."[92]

The "Third Use" of the Law

Because of his emphasis on the unity of the Old and New Testaments, Calvin, in distinction from Luther, recognizes a "third use" for Old Testament law: the law not only discloses our sinfulness and serves to restrain

87. Calvin, *Institutes*, 2.10.1. Cf. "God has never made any other covenant than that which he made formerly with Abraham, and at length confirmed by the hand of Moses." Calvin, *Comm*. Jer 31:31, as cited in Bandstra, "Law and Gospel," 22.

88. Ibid., 2.10.2.

89. Ibid., 2.10.4.

90. Ibid., 2.10.23.

91. Ibid., 2.9.4.

92. Calvin, *CR* 45.175, as cited in John Leith, *Int* 25 (1971) 339. See ibid. for Calvin's assertion that "the God who spoke in the law is also the God who speaks in the gospel." *CR* 55.8.

sinful acts in society, but also has a positive function for believers. Writes Calvin, "The third and principal use, which pertains more closely to the proper purpose of the law, finds its place among believers in whose hearts the Spirit of God already lives and reigns. . . . They still profit by the law in two ways. Here is the best instrument for them to learn more thoroughly each day the nature of the Lord's will to which they aspire, and to confirm them in the understanding of it. . . . Again, because we need not only teaching but also exhortation, the servant of God will also avail himself of this benefit of the law: by frequent meditation upon it to be aroused to obedience, be strengthened in it, and be drawn back from the slippery path of transgression."[93]

Differences between the Old and New Testaments

Calvin is aware of differences between the Old and the New Testament, of course, but they pale in the light of his emphasis on the unity. He writes, "I freely admit the differences in Scripture, to which attention is called, but in such a way as not to detract from its established unity." For the differences "pertain to the manner of dispensation rather than to the substance. . . . In this way there will be nothing to hinder the promises of the Old and New Testaments from remaining the same, nor from having the same foundation of these very promises, Christ!"[94]

Calvin goes on to discuss at length five differences, which I shall only list here. The Old Testament stresses earthly benefits in contrast to the heavenly; it speaks in images and shadows in contrast to "the substance"; it has the character of the outward letter in contrast to the spirit (Jer 31:31-34); it is characterized as bondage in contrast to freedom; and it was restricted to one nation in contrast to all nations.[95] For Calvin, however, these differences between Old and New are only differences in the form of administrating the covenant, not in the substance of the covenant of grace. For example, in discussing the ceremonial law, Calvin argues that the ceremonies "have been abrogated not in effect but only in use. Christ by his coming has terminated them, but has not deprived them of anything of their sanctity. . . . Just as the ceremonies would have provided

93. Calvin, *Institutes,* 2.7.12. Cf. ibid., 2.7.6-17.

94. Ibid., 2.11.1.

95. See ibid., 2.11.1-12. In his commentaries more so than in his *Institutes,* Calvin elucidates the contrast between letter and spirit and between bondage and freedom. In his commentaries he speaks even of the "antithesis between law and gospel" and "the law insofar as it is opposed to the gospel." But by "law" Calvin does not mean the Old Testament but "the bare law with its precepts and rewards." See Bandstra, "Law and Gospel in Calvin and in Paul," 11-39.

the people of the Old Covenant with an empty show if the power of Christ's death and resurrection had not been displayed therein; so, if they had not ceased, we would be unable today to discern for what purpose they were established."[96]

The major difference for Calvin between the Old Testament and the New is the degree of clarity regarding Jesus Christ and the kingdom of God. As he says in one of his commentaries, "Under the Law was shadowed forth only in rude and imperfect lines what is under the Gospel set forth in living colours and graphically distinct." Yet to believers in the old covenant and believers in the new covenant, "the same Christ is exhibited, the same righteousness, sanctification, and salvation; and the difference only is in the manner of painting."[97]

Christ in the Old Testament

In the 1559 edition of his *Institutes,* Calvin adds a new chapter entitled "Christ, although he was known to the Jews under the Law, was at length clearly revealed only in the Gospel."[98] In fact, the title of his second book in the *Institutes* is, "On the knowledge of God the Redeemer in Christ, first disclosed to the fathers under the Law, and then to us in the Gospel." The decisive question here is how, according to Calvin, was Christ "known to the Jews under the Law"?

Calvin asserts, "If the Lord, in manifesting his Christ, discharged his ancient oath, one cannot but say that the Old Testament always had its end in Christ."[99] He also declares that "apart from the Mediator, God never showed favor toward the ancient people, nor ever gave hope of grace to them."[100] And again, the Jews "had and knew Christ as Mediator, through whom they were joined to God and were to share his promises."[101]

But let us push this crucial question further: How did the Israelites in the Old Testament know Christ long before he was born? Calvin seeks

---

96. Ibid., 2.7.16.

97. Calvin, *Comm.* on Heb 10:1, quoted in Runia, *CTJ* 19/2 (1984) 143. Cf. Calvin, *Institutes,* 1.11.10, on "the clarity of the gospel and the obscurer dispensation of the Word that had preceded it."

98. Calvin, *Institutes,* 2.9.

99. Ibid., 2.10.4. Cf. 2.6.2, "Since God cannot without the Mediator be propitious toward the human race, under the law Christ was always set before the holy fathers as the end to which they should direct their faith."

100. Ibid., 2.6.2.

101. Ibid., 2.10.2. Cf. 2.10.23, "The Old Testament fathers (1) had Christ as pledge of their covenant, and (2) put in him all trust for future blessedness."

to answer this question as follows: "It may be objected, 'Why is Christ appointed to a covenant which was ratified long before? for, more than two thousand years before, God had adopted Abraham, and thus the origin of the distinction was long previous to the coming of Christ.' I reply, the covenant which was made with Abraham and his posterity had its foundation in Christ; for the words of the covenant are these, 'In thy seed shall all nations be blessed' (Gen 22:18). And the covenant was ratified in no other manner than in the seed of Abraham, that is, in Christ, by whose coming, though it had been previously made, it was confirmed and actually sanctioned."[102]

Calvin's most helpful comment on this issue occurs in his commentary on 1 Peter 1:12, where he says that the Old Testament believers "possessed Christ as one hidden and as it were absent . . . absent not in power or grace, but because he was not yet manifested in the flesh."[103] The power and grace of Christ's redemption are present in the Old Testament long before he is born. At the same time, Old Testament believers look forward to the coming of Christ, when they will receive "far more light."[104] In the meantime, God gave many promises of the coming Messiah and raised up types that prefigured him. As Calvin puts it, "The gospel points out with the finger what the law foreshadowed under types."[105]

Understanding in the Context of the Whole Bible

Because of his view of the unity of Scripture, Calvin seeks to understand a passage within the overall thrust of Scripture. Today we speak of the hermeneutical circle (or spiral): one cannot understand a part without understanding the whole, and one cannot understand the whole without understanding the parts. The key question for preachers is how to enter this hermeneutical circle in the right way. How does one gain a view of the whole of Scripture so as to understand and preach the parts correctly? Interestingly, in his Preface to his *Institutes* Calvin declares that he wrote

102. Calvin, *Comm.* Isa 42:6 (*CO* 37.64).
103. Calvin, *CO* 55.218, as cited in I. John Hesselink, "Calvin," 170.
104. Cf. Calvin, *Institutes*, 2.9.1, "'The sun of righteousness shall rise' [Mal 4:2]. By these words he teaches that while the law serves to hold the godly in expectation of Christ's coming, at his advent they should hope for far more light."
105. Ibid., 2.9.3. Cf. Gordon Bates, *Hartford Quarterly* 5/2 (1965) 47, "His [Calvin's] typology was centered in Christ. It was those events and persons of the Old Testament which were clearly relatable to the Person and Work of the Redeemer which drew his attention, a fact which stemmed directly from his conviction of the unity of the Bible."

this work precisely to help his students gain an overall view of Scripture: "It has been my purpose in this labor to prepare and instruct candidates in sacred theology for the reading of the divine Word, in order that they may be able both to have easy access to it and to advance in it without stumbling. For I believe I have so embraced the sum of religion in all its parts, and have arranged it in such an order, that if anyone rightly grasps it, it will not be difficult for him to determine what he ought especially to seek in Scripture, and to what end he ought to relate its contents."[106] Brevard Childs remarks on the radical nature of this proposal in contrast to "the entire mediaeval tradition": "Thomas Aquinas wrote a *Summa* to encompass the whole of Christian teaching into which structure the Bible provided the building blocks. In striking contrast Calvin reversed the process! The role of theology was to aid in interpreting the Bible. His move was in the direction of dogmatics to exegesis."[107]

Calvin's Theocentric Interpretation of the Old Testament

In order to distinguish Calvin's method of interpreting the Old Testament from Luther's christological method, we shall call it theocentric interpretation. In focussing on the sovereignty and glory of God,[108] theocentric interpretation is broader than christological interpretation but does not necessarily exclude christocentric interpretation. Calvin seeks to combine God-centered, historical interpretation of the Old Testament with the Bible's Christ-centered focus. First we shall discuss his theocentric interpretation and then his christocentric interpretation.

Theocentric Interpretation

Calvin is frequently satisfied to bring just a message about God. For example, Isaiah 63:1 raises the question, "Who is this that comes from Edom, from Bozrah in garments stained crimson?" Traditional Christian interpretation tended to identify this person with Christ. But Calvin objects, "They have imagined that here Christ is red, because he was wet

---

106. Calvin, *Institutes*, 1559 ed., Preface. This statement is found already in the Preface to the 1536 edition. The words "the sum of religion in all its parts" remind one of Irenaeus's "rule of faith," but the *Institutes* also provides hermeneutical principles and countless examples of interpretation.

107. Childs, *Biblical Theology*, 49.

108. See p. 127 above.

with his own blood which he shed on the cross." This identification, he thinks, can be made only by violently distorting the text, for "the Prophet meant nothing of that sort." Instead, the prophet pictures God as the avenger "returning from the slaughter of the Edomites, as if he were drenched with their blood."[109] The main reason for Calvin's opposition to excessive christological interpretation is his concern for historical interpretation.

Historical Interpretation

Calvin insists on historical interpretation, that is, to seek the meaning of a passage as intended by its author in its original historical context.[110] For example, Psalm 2:7, "You are my son; today I have begotten you," was usually applied directly to Christ. But Calvin comments: "David, indeed, could with propriety be called the son of God on account of his royal dignity. . . . David was begotten by God when the choice of him to be king was clearly manifested. The words *this day*, therefore, denote the time of this manifestation; for as soon as it became known that he was made king by divine appointment, he came forth as one who had been lately begotten of God, since so great an honour could not belong to a private person." Only after this historical explanation does Calvin continue, "The same explanation is to be given of the words as applied to Christ. He is not said to be begotten in any other sense than as the Father bore testimony to him as being his own Son."[111] Similarly, in his Preface to the "christological" Psalm 72, Calvin warns, "Those who would interpret it simply as a prophecy of the kingdom of Christ, seem to put a construction upon the words which does violence to them; and then we must always beware of giving the Jews occasion of making an outcry, as if it were our purpose, sophistically, to apply to Christ those things which do not directly refer to him." Having said this, however, Calvin freely acknowledges that the kingdom of David is "only a type or shadow" of the kingdom of Christ.[112]

---

109. Calvin, *Comm.* Isa. 63:1 (*CO* 37.392). For more examples, see Puckett, *Calvin's Exegesis*, 65-66. Pieter Verhoef, *NGTT* 31 (1990) 113-14, offers a list of texts which church and synagogue traditionally understood as "messianic" but which Calvin in his commentaries views as "nonmessianic": Gen 3:15 (!); 5:29; 9:25-27; 27:29; Num 23:21; Psalms 46, 61, 76, 80, 89, 93, 99; Isa 41:2-4; 42:5-9; 45:1-7; 50:4-9; Jer 16:13; 30:4-6; Joel 2:23; Amos 5:15, 18; 8:11-12; 9:8-10; Hag 2:6-8, 18; Mal 2:17; 4:4-6.

110. For examples of Calvin's emphasis on the intention of the author, see Puckett, *Calvin's Exegesis*, 33-34.

111. Calvin, *Comm.* Ps 2:7.

112. Calvin, *Comm.* Psalm 72, Preface. Note, e.g., Calvin's comments on v 7, "This prediction receives its highest fulfilment in Christ." Regarding the Jews, see also

Calvin is critical of Luther's christological exegesis. He writes, "The speculation of Luther here, as in other places, has no solidity."[113] Elsewhere he asserts, "Subtle speculations please at first sight, but afterwards vanish. Let every one, then, who desires to be proficient in the Scriptures always keep to this rule — to gather from the Prophets and Apostles only what is solid."[114]

Lutheran Critique

Lutheran theologians were quick to charge Calvin with undercutting the genuine sense of Scripture with his historical method. In 1593 Hunnius attacked Calvin in a work with the main title *Calvin the Judaizer*. He saw Calvin's interpretation as nothing more than Jewish interpretation. Richard Muller observes that "angry Lutheran exegetes and theologians . . . would refer to . . . judaizing Calvin, precisely because Calvin adamantly refused the wholesale christologizing of the Old Testament and the trinitarian reading of the plural form of *Elohim*."[115]

Calvin, however, is at odds not only with excessive christological interpretation but also with Jewish interpretation. David Puckett observes, "Although Calvin often makes use of Jewish linguistic expertise and sometimes approves of Jewish interpretations in other matters, most of his comments about Jewish exegesis are negative."[116] Take, for example, the familiar passage about Immanuel in Isaiah 7:14. Calvin argues that the Jews "are hard pressed by this passage, for it contains an illustrious prediction concerning the Messiah, who is here called *Immanuel*, and therefore they have laboured, by all possible means, to twist the

---

Calvin's statement on Psalm 16, "It is better to adhere to the natural simplicity of the interpretation which I have given, that we may not make ourselves objects of ridicule to the Jews." Cited in Puckett, *Calvin's Exegesis*, 53.

113. Calvin, *Comm.* Gen 13:14 (*CO* 23.193), as cited in Puckett, *Calvin's Exegesis*, 55. See also *Comm.* Gen 11:27 (*CO* 23.170) and *Comm.* Dan 8:22-23 (*CO* 41.114).

114. Calvin, *Comm.* Hos 6:2 (*CO* 42.320), as cited in Puckett, *Calvin's Exegesis*, 17. Richard Muller, "Hermeneutic," 77, notes, "Calvin's complaint against excessively christological interpretation ought probably to be seen against the background of the famous psalm commentary of Faber Stapulensis where, in the name of a single, literal meaning, Christ is taken to be the sole reference of the text, and David disappears entirely as a focus of meaning. Calvin's caveat is not an objection to a christological promise-fulfillment hermeneutics but a demand that the historical figure of David be allowed its rightful place in the scheme of promise and fulfillment and that the literal meaning of the text be lodged in the promise as first given to the historical David."

115. Muller, *Post-Reformation*, 2.218.

116. Puckett, *Calvin's Exegesis*, 83.

Prophet's meaning to another sense."[117] Obviously, there is more to Calvin's interpretation than merely historical interpretation.

Christocentric Interpretation

Where he considers this appropriate, Calvin will move beyond literal-historical interpretation to christocentric interpretation. This move is supported by his views of the unity of the Old and New Testaments and the necessity of understanding a passage in the context of the whole of Scripture.

The Intention of the Holy Spirit

We have heard Calvin speak frequently of the intention of the author. He also speaks often of the "intention of the Holy Spirit" or the "intention of God."[118] For example, in rejecting a particular interpretation, Calvin says, "I think the Holy Spirit has a different intention here."[119] By referring to the intention of the Holy Spirit, Calvin seems to be moving beyond the intention of the human author. Yet the two are intimately related. David Puckett lists half a dozen instances where Calvin seems to correct himself, "Now, therefore, we understand the intention of the prophet, or rather of the Holy Spirit"; "We now understand the intention of the prophet, or rather of the Holy Spirit." But these "corrections" are quite deliberate. Puckett concludes, "It is apparent that Calvin is unwilling to divorce the intention of the human writer from the meaning of the Holy Spirit. It is difficult to escape the conclusion that for him, the intention, thoughts, and words of the prophet and of the Holy Spirit in the production of scripture are so closely related there is no practical way to distinguish them."[120]

The Goal of Finding Christ in the Old Testament

Jesus says to the Jews, "You diligently study the Scriptures, because you think that by them you possess eternal life. These are the Scriptures that testify about me" (John 5:39, NIV). Calvin comments, "We ought to read the Scriptures with the express design of finding Christ in them. . . . By *the Scriptures*, it is well known, is here meant the Old Testament; for it was not in the Gospel that Christ first began to be manifested, but, having re-

117. Calvin, *Comm.* Isa 7:14 (*CO* 36.154), as cited in Puckett, *Calvin's Exegesis*, 85.
118. See Puckett, *Calvin's Exegesis*, 32-33, for both phrases in Calvin: *consilium spiritus sancti* and *Dei consilium*.
119. Calvin, *Comm.* Dan 12:4, as quoted in Puckett, *Calvin's Exegesis*, 32.
120. Puckett, *Calvin's Exegesis*, 36-37.

ceived testimony from the Law and the Prophets, he was openly exhib-ited in the Gospel."[121] Elsewhere he writes, "This is what we should in short seek in the whole of Scripture: truly to know Jesus Christ, and the infinite riches that are comprised in him and are offered to us by him from God the Father."[122]

Progressive Revelation

In searching for Christ in the Old Testament, Calvin is aware that God's revelation concerning Christ is not as clear in the Old Testament as it is in the New. But even in the Old Testament, it becomes ever clearer. Calvin seeks to convey this progression in revelation with images which move from shadow to reality and from a spark to the sun. He writes in his *Institutes*, "The Lord held to this orderly plan in administering the covenant of his mercy: as the day of full revelation approached with the passing of time, the more he increased each day the brightness of its manifestation. Accordingly, at the beginning when the first promise of salvation was given to Adam (Gen 3:15) it glowed like a feeble spark. Then, as it was added to, the light grew in fullness, breaking forth increasingly and shed-ding its radiance more widely. At last — when all the clouds were dis-persed — Christ, the Sun of Righteousness, fully illumined the whole earth."[123] Progressive revelation, therefore, does not mean that God's people in the Old Testament were without any light. The patriarchs, says Calvin, were not "without the preaching that contains the hope of salva-tion and of eternal life, but . . . they only glimpsed from afar and in shad-owy outline what we see today in full daylight."[124]

How, then, is Christ present in the Old Testament? From the evi-dence we can gather that Calvin would answer in at least three ways: Christ is present in the Old Testament as the eternal Logos, as promise, and as type. We shall discuss each in turn.

The Eternal Logos

Calvin has such an exalted view of God that he questions whether any-one can know God without Christ. He says, "We must first ponder the

---

121. Calvin, *Comm.* John 5:39.

122. Calvin, Preface to the French translation of the New Testament, as cited in Leith, *Int* 25 (1971) 341. Cf. *Institutes*, 3.2.1.

123. Calvin, *Institutes*, 2.10.20. Cf. Parker, *Calvin's Old Testament Commentaries*, 56-62.

124. Ibid., 2.7.16. Cf. 2.9.1; and *Comm.* Gal 3:23.

vastness of the divine glory and at the same time the slenderness of our understanding. Far from certain is it that our keenness could climb so high as to apprehend God. Therefore all thinking about God, apart from Christ, is a bottomless abyss which utterly swallows up all our senses."[125]

This inability to know God without Christ held in Old Testament times as well. Calvin writes, "Holy men of old knew God only by beholding him in his Son as in a mirror (cf. 2 Cor 3:18). When I say this, I mean that God has never manifested himself to men in any other way than through the Son, that is, his sole wisdom, light, and truth. From this fountain Adam, Noah, Abraham, Isaac, Jacob, and others drank all that they had of heavenly teaching. From the same fountain, all the prophets have also drawn every heavenly oracle that they have given forth."[126]

In view of this presence of Christ in Old Testament times, it is not surprising that Calvin follows tradition in identifying the Angel of Yahweh with Christ. Concerning the Angel at the burning bush (Exod 3:2) he agrees, "The ancient doctors of the Church rightly felt that the eternal Son of God was so called in respect of his person of Mediator. Granted he only truly undertook it at his Incarnation, yet he performed the figure of it from the beginning."[127] Notice, however, that Calvin is not satisfied with merely identifying the Angel as Christ. He is interested in Christ incarnate. He makes this abundantly clear in a later comment: "I willingly accept what the old writers teach, that when Christ appeared in those early times in the form of a man, it was the prelude of the mystery which was revealed when God was manifested in the flesh. But we must beware of imagining that Christ then was incarnate; for we do not read that God sent his Son in the flesh before the fullness of times. . . ."[128]

Promise and Fulfillment

The major category under which Calvin sees Christ incarnate in the Old Testament is that of promise. But before he focusses the Old Testament promise on its fulfillment in Christ, Calvin's historical bent looks for fulfillment in Old Testament times. He frequently finds this fulfillment of prophecy in the exile of Israel or in its return to the promised land. For ex-

125. Calvin, *Comm.* 1 Pet 1:20. Calvin continues, "Hence it is clear that we cannot trust in God save through Christ. In Christ God so to speak makes himself little, in order to lower himself to our capacity; and Christ alone calms our consciences that they may dare intimately approach God."

126. Calvin, *Institutes*, 4.8.5.

127. Calvin, *CO* 24.35, as quoted in Parker, *Calvin's Old Testament Commentaries*, 120.

128. Ibid., 25.464, as quoted in Parker, ibid., 119.

ample, in Isaiah 52:10 we read, "The LORD has bared his holy arm before the eyes of all the nations; and all the ends of the earth shall see the salvation of our God." Although Calvin extends this salvation to the salvation we have in Christ, he begins with the fulfillment in Old Testament times: "This prophecy is maliciously restricted by the Jews to the deliverance from Babylon, and is improperly restricted by Christians to the spiritual redemption which we obtain through Christ; for we must begin with the deliverance which was wrought under Cyrus (2 Chr 36:22-23), and bring it down to our own time."[129]

Calvin, therefore, looks for progressive fulfillment of prophecy. The main possibilities of fulfillment are: first, fulfillment in Old Testament times; second, in the coming of Christ; third, in the contemporary church; and finally, in Christ's second coming.[130] This does not mean that every prophecy has multiple fulfillments. "When the discourse is concerning Christ's kingdom, they [the prophets] sometimes refer to its commencement only, and sometimes they speak of its termination. But they often designate with one connection in discourse the whole course of the kingdom of Christ, from its beginning to its end. . . ."[131] In commenting on Daniel 7:27, Calvin explains his method of interpreting prophecy: "I may here remark again, and impress upon the memory what I have frequently touched upon, namely, the custom of the Prophets, in treating of Christ's kingdom, to extend their meaning further than its first beginnings; and they do this while they dwell upon its commencement."[132] The prophets, Calvin says, "include the whole progress of Christ's kingdom when they speak of the future redemption of the people. . . . These prophecies are not accomplished in one day, or in one year, no, not even in one age, but ought to be understood as referring to the beginning and the end of Christ's kingdom."[133] Fulfillment of a promise, therefore, is not a static entity but continues the process to ever greater fulfillments.

Richard Muller provides us with a good summary of Calvin's meth-

129. Calvin, *Comm.* Isa 52:10, as cited in Willem A. VanGemeren, *WTJ* 46 (1984) 276-77. See also W. McKane, *NGTT* 25/3 (1984) 256-59.

130. Cf. Muller, *Post-Reformation*, 2.490.

131. Calvin, *CO* 42.573-74, as quoted in Muller, "Hermeneutic," 73.

132. Calvin, *Comm.* Dan 7:27, as cited in Holwerda, "Eschatology," 328-29.

133. Calvin, *Comm.* Jer 31:24 (*CO* 38.682), as cited in Puckett, *Calvin's Exegesis*, 130. Cf. Puckett, ibid., 126-32. Calvin also sees the promises of the land broaden from the land of Canaan to the whole earth: "This was not, in every respect, fulfilled in the Jews; but a beginning was made with them, when they were restored to their native country, that, by their agency, the possession of the whole earth might afterwards be given to them, that is, to the children of God." Calvin, *Comm.* Gal 4:28, as quoted in VanGemeren, *WTJ* 46 (1984) 277.

od: "The strict promise/fulfillment model, in which the Old Testament is fulfilled in the New Testament, coupled with the idea of an extended meaning of the text which encompasses the entire kingdom of God, provided Calvin with a structure of interpretation within which both a grammatical-historical reading of the text and a strong drive toward contemporary application can function."[134]

Typology

Calvin's conviction of the unity of the Old and New Testaments in one covenant of grace and the unity of redemptive history also paves the way for discovering types of Christ in the Old Testament. In his typological interpretation, as in his historical interpretation, he follows the trail cleared initially by the School of Antioch. T. H. L. Parker states that for Calvin "the history of the Jews was not only a preparation for the coming of Christ; it was also a deliberate pre-enactment of him and his work. Certain persons and institutions were types or figures or images (he uses the words interchangeably)." He further observes that "a type is not for Calvin an accidental resemblance between the two Covenants, but something deliberately set up by God's providence to pre-enact the Incarnate Christ, and thus to stand for Christ and stand for him effectually."[135]

Consequently, Calvin finds types of Christ not only in Old Testament ceremonies such as the sabbath and the paschal lamb, but especially in many Old Testament figures: Joseph, Aaron and the Levitical priesthood, Samson, and King David and his successors.[136] Calvin explains, "Now we know that in David was promised a spiritual kingdom, for what was David but a type of Christ? As God then gave in David a living image of his only-begotten Son, we ought ever to pass from the temporal kingdom to the eternal, from the visible to the spiritual, from the earthly to the celestial. The same thing ought to be said of the

134. Muller, "Hermeneutic," 71. A good overview is provided in this article, pp. 68-82, and in David Holwerda, "Eschatology and History: A Look at Calvin's Eschatological Vision," 311-42.

135. Parker, *Calvin's Old Testament Commentaries*, 74-75. In view of contemporary discussions regarding typology at the literary level, it is important to notice that Calvin looks for types at the historical level in the confidence that God's providence guides the course of history. Cf. *Institutes*, 1.11.3, "He [God] willed that, for the time during which he gave his covenant to the people of Israel in a veiled form, the grace of future and eternal happiness be signified and figured under earthly benefits, the gravity of spiritual death under physical punishments."

136. See Puckett, *Calvin's Exegesis*, 114-17. See also S. H. Russell, "Calvin and the Messianic Interpretation of the Psalms," *SJT* 21 (1968) 38-43.

priesthood; for no mortal can reconcile God to men, and make an atonement for sins; and further, the blood of bulls and of goats could not pacify the wrath of God, nor incense, nor the sprinkling of water, nor any of the things which belonged to the ceremonial laws; they could not give the hope of salvation, so as to quiet trembling consciences. It then follows that that priesthood was shadowy, and that the Levites represented Christ until he came."[137]

Calvin is aware of the danger of typological interpretation sliding into typologizing minute details of the text. "Nothing is better," he asserts, "than to contain ourselves within the limits of edification; and it would be puerile [childish] to make a collection of the *minutiae* wherewith some philosophize, since it was by no means the intention of God to include mysteries in every hook and loop. . . ."[138]

Calvin's Theocentric Preaching

Commenting on Jesus' words in John 14:1, "Believe in God, believe also in me," Calvin says, "The Son of God, then, who is Jesus Christ, holds out himself as the object to which our faith ought to be directed. . . . It is one of the leading articles of our faith, that our faith ought to be directed to Christ alone. . . ."[139] In the light of this comment as well as others we have heard from Calvin so far, it is surprising that his sermons on the Old Testament can, in general, best be described as God-centered rather than

137. Calvin, *Comm.* Jer 33:17, quoted in Puckett, *Calvin's Exegesis,* 116-17. Cf. Calvin, *Comm.* Ps 2:2, "As David's temporal kingdom was a kind of earnest to God's ancient people of the eternal kingdom, which at length was truly established in the person of Christ, those things which David declares concerning himself are not violently, or even allegorically, applied to Christ, but were truly predicted concerning him. If we attentively consider the nature of the kingdom, we will perceive that it would be absurd to overlook the end or scope, and to rest in the mere shadow."

138. Calvin, *Comm.* Exod 26:1, as cited in Puckett, *Calvin's Exegesis,* 116. The unity of the Old and New Testaments also enables Calvin to use the concept of analogy or similarity for application in the sermon. He states, "We must hold that between us and the Israelites there is anagogē, or similarity." *Comm.* Exod 6:7 (*CO* 24.80), as cited in Parker, *Calvin's Old Testament Commentaries,* 72. Calvin is not using *anagogē* as in medieval fourfold interpretation but in the sense of "the act of transference or application." Parker, ibid., 73. Analogy is different from typology. "The distinction Calvin makes between application by anagogy and typology is that typology is truly prophetic — that is, the prophet knows he is speaking to a future age as well as his own." Analogy, by contrast, serves to transfer the message to today when the prophet seemingly addresses only Israel. See Puckett, *Calvin's Exegesis,* 68-69.

139. Calvin, *Comm.* John 14:1 (*CO* 47.321-22).

Christ-centered. This is not to say that he did not deliver any Christ-centered sermons from the Old Testament. Calvin's printer, Badius, reports, "It pleased God to let us hear the most excellent preaching that could be heard or uttered, on the end of Isaiah 52 and the whole of chapter 53, where the mystery of the death and passion of our Lord Jesus Christ and the causes thereof are described and depicted in so living a way that it seems as if the Holy Spirit wanted to set before our eyes Jesus Christ condemned in our name and nailed to the cross for our sins. . . ."[140]

Besides using promise-fulfillment to preach Christ from the Old Testament,[141] Calvin employs typology where he thinks this appropriate. For example, in his sermons on Second Samuel, not only does King David function as a type of Christ but so also do the high priest, the sacrifices, and the temple.[142]

But on the whole, Calvin's sermons on the Old Testament are best described as theocentric. In introducing Calvin's *Sermons from Job*, Harold Dekker writes, "One of the most noticeable features of Calvin's preaching is its utter theocentricity. . . . Very significantly, most of the Old Testament sermons [159 on Job] make no specific mention at all of Christ."[143] Not even the words of Job, "I know my redeemer lives," warrant a reference to Christ.[144] The same holds true for many of Calvin's sermons on Deuteronomy.[145]

---

140. Badius as quoted by Parker, in John Calvin, *Sermons on Isaiah's Prophecy of the Death and Passion of Christ*, trans. and ed. T. H. L. Parker (London: James Clarke, 1956), 16.

141. See also, e.g., Calvin's *Sermons on 2 Samuel*, Sermon 22 on 2 Sam 7:12-15, and Sermon 26 on 2 Sam 7:25-29.

142. Ibid. For example, David functions as a type in Sermon 12 on 2 Sam 5:1-5 and in Sermon 23 on 2 Sam 7:12-17, but also in references in Sermons 21 and 22; the high priest and sacrifices in Sermon 17 on 2 Sam 6:6-12; and the temple in Sermon 21 on 2 Sam 7:4-13 and in Sermon 22 on 2 Sam 7:12-15.

143. Dekker, "Introduction," *Sermons from Job*, xxviii. Cf. ibid., "Not only is God the authority and motive for the preacher, the source and object of every preachment, and the abiding center of reference for every sermon, but very conspicuously He is that in His Triune fullness."

144. Calvin, *Sermons from Job*, Sermon 8 on Job 19:17-25, pp. 117-18: "Now in the end Job adds, *that he knows that his Redeemer lives*. It is true that this could not be understood as fully then as now; so we must discuss the intention of Job in speaking thus. He intends, then, that he was not acting the part of a hypocrite by pleading his cause before men, and by justifying himself; he knew that he had to do with God. . . . Now Job . . . says, 'I know that my God is living, and that He shall stand in the end upon the dust.'"

145. Cf. John Leith, *Int* 25 (1971) 341, "It is very difficult to square this intention ['truly to know Jesus Christ'] with many of his sermons on Deuteronomy: Certainly Christ is not a canon within Scripture for Calvin, as he was for Luther."

There is no doubt that Calvin deeply believes in Christ's presence in the Old Testament. He speaks of Christ as the "fundamentum," "anima," "vita," "spiritus," "scopus," "finis," and "perfectio" of the law.[146] But for some reason he does not feel obliged to bring this out explicitly in every sermon.[147] To my knowledge Calvin nowhere accounts for this lack of explicitly preaching Christ from the Old Testament, but several reasons come to mind. The first is Calvin's understanding of the triune God. Calvin himself says, "Under the name of God is understood a single, simple essence, in which we comprehend three persons. . . . Therefore, whenever the name of God is mentioned without particularization, there are designated no less the Son and the Spirit than the Father. . . ."[148] When Calvin, therefore, preaches a God-centered sermon, it is implicitly Christ-centered. Another reason for Calvin's lack of Christ-centered preaching is his emphasis on historical interpretation and his disdain for allegorical interpretation.[149] Still another reason is probably Calvin's view of expository preaching as limiting the sermon to the text for the day: "For what ought sermons and all teaching to be but exposition of what is contained there? It is certain that if we add anything to it, however little, it is only a corruption."[150] Finally, we must remember that in Geneva Calvin preached from the Old Testament in the homily style on consecutive verses *(lectio continua)* and usually on consecutive weekdays when com-

---

146. Calvin, *Comm.* 2 Cor 3:16-17 *(CO* 50.45-46); *Comm.* Rom. 10:4 *(CO* 49.196); *Comm.* Exod 24:29 *(CO* 25.118); *Comm.* Ezek 16:61 *(CO* 40.395); *Comm.* Acts 28:17 *(CO* 48.567), as found in Hesselink, "Calvin," 166.

147. In fact, it has been suggested that "Christ is for Calvin so radically and totally the scopus of Scripture that this need not be repeated over and over again." C. Veenhof, "Calvijn en Prediking," in *Zicht op Calvijn,* ed. J. Stellingwerff (Amsterdam: Buijten & Schipperheijn, 1965), 80.

148. Calvin, *Institutes,* 1.13.20. Cf. Johann Le Roux, "Betekenis," 191, to the effect that the highest goal of preaching for Calvin is the motif of honoring the triune God *(soli Deo gloria)* rather than the soteriological motif. Cf. Dekker, "Introduction," xxviii, "Whereas preaching for Luther found its purpose in pointing to Christ, for Calvin it was realized in showing forth more comprehensively the Triune Redeemer God."

149. According to Parker, *Calvin's Preaching,* 92, in his sermons on the Old Testament, Calvin "keeps to the historical context in the interpretation and exegesis of passages. For this reason there may be little or no mention of Jesus Christ or the Gospel in a sermon. When, however, he comes to the application of passages, the situation is at once different. 'We,' to whom he is speaking, do not live before the Incarnation and the witness of the New Testament and it would be artificial and foolish to try to carry over the superseded historical conditions. So now he is free to speak in a Christian way to Christian people."

150. Calvin, *Supplementa Calvinalia,* 5.89.41–90.4, quoted in Parker, *Calvin's Preaching,* 24.

mitted Christians were in attendance.[151] Thus he may not have thought it necessary to preach Christ explicitly each time.

However that may be, after reviewing many of Calvin's sermons, Parker concludes, "through all the variety occasioned by the variety of the texts there runs the Biblical point of view — the hidden God reveals himself for man's eternal and temporal good. It is this that governs Calvin's interpretation and application of his texts. In each of our examples we saw God in his gracious activity."[152] And it is understood throughout that God's grace comes to us only in and through Jesus Christ.[153]

Evaluation of Calvin's Theocentric Interpretation

Valuable Contributions

From our contemporary perspective, we should be able to appreciate many of Calvin's contributions to the interpretation and preaching of the Old Testament. Most modern scholars single out for approval Calvin's emphasis on historical interpretation, that is, his emphasis on the intention of the author, the historical context, and the original, grammatical meaning in its literary context.[154] In addition, we should be able to appreciate Calvin's emphasis on the unity of the Old and New Testaments in the one covenant of grace. Historical interpretation in the context of the unity of the Old and New Testaments provides Calvin with a rather bal-

---

151. Calvin had the custom of preaching from the New Testament on Sundays when all citizens of Geneva were required to attend; sometimes he would use a Psalm for the Sunday afternoon service. On weekdays he would preach from the Old Testament. For example, Calvin preached 159 sermons on Job from February 26, 1554, to March 1555, which was followed by 200 sermons on Deuteronomy from March 20, 1555, to July 15, 1556. See John Leith, "Calvin, John," in *Concise Encyclopedia of Preaching*, ed. William H. Willimon and Richard Lischer (Louisville: Westminster/John Knox, 1995), 62. For a more detailed schedule of Calvin's preaching texts from 1549 to 1563, see Parker, *Calvin's Preaching*, 63-64, 90-92. On Calvin's homily style in distinction from the scholastic thematic style, see Ellen Borger Monsma, "The Preaching Style of Jean Calvin: An Analysis of the Psalm Sermons of the Supplementa Calvinia" (Ph.D. thesis, Rutgers University, 1986), esp. pp. 90-110.

152. Parker, *Calvin's Preaching*, 107.

153. See ibid., 93-107. Cf. Calvin, *Institutes*, 2.12.2, The task of Christ the Mediator "was so to restore us to God's grace as to make of the children of men, children of God; of the heirs of Gehenna, heirs of the Heavenly Kingdom."

154. See, e.g., F. W. Farrar, *History*, 345-48. According to John Broadus, *History of Preaching*, 115, "Calvin gave the ablest, soundest, clearest expositions of Scripture that had been seen for a thousand years. . . ."

anced approach to preaching from the Old Testament. As David Puckett graphically puts it, Calvin "has not uprooted the Old Testament from its historical soil nor has he been content to look at the roots once the full flowering has taken place in Jesus Christ. He uses the New Testament interpretation of the Old to establish the meaning of the Old Testament text."[155] Moreover, with his theocentric emphasis, Calvin is a good corrective to allegorical interpretation and excessive christological interpretation. Finally, Calvin carries into modern times the ancient legitimate ways of preaching Christ from the Old Testament: the ways of promise-fulfillment and typology.

Shortcomings in Calvin's Method

According to John Leith, "Calvin's purpose in preaching was to render transparent the *text* of scripture itself."[156] Although this goal is admirable in itself, from our perspective Calvin did not sufficiently focus on producing explicitly Christ-centered sermons in the context of the whole of Scripture. For Calvin, as we have seen, is frequently satisfied with a God-centered sermon. Of course, Calvin preached in Christian Geneva, where he may have assumed that his hearers would make the connections to Christ, but this still leaves us with an inadequate model for preaching in our post-Christian culture.

Ironically, another shortcoming in Calvin's interpretation is that he still succumbs once in a while to the lure of the allegorical interpretation of the church fathers. For example, commenting on clean and unclean meat in Leviticus 11, Calvin says, "Although, I am afraid, there is little solidity in allegories, I neither attack nor reject one that has been handed down from the early writers, that by parting the hoof is meant wisdom in understanding ('distinguishing') the mysteries of Scripture and by chewing the cud, serious meditation on the heavenly teaching."[157]

155. Puckett, *Calvin's Exegesis*, 132. Cf. Nixon, *John Calvin*, 129-30, "Calvin's force . . . comes almost exclusively from the fact that he was saturated in the Word. . . . Calvin saw Scripture as a whole. He knew how to relate each specific passage to the whole round of Christian truth."

156. Leith, in *Concise Encyclopedia of Preaching*, 62 (my emphasis).

157. Calvin, CO 24, 347, quoted in Parker, *Calvin's Old Testament Commentaries*, 76-77. Cf. Parker, ibid., 74, on Gen 15:11, "And the fowls came down upon the carcasses, and Abraham drove them away." Calvin comments, "Although the sacrifice had been dedicated to God, it was not immune from the attack and violence of the birds. For after believers have been received into the care of God they are not so covered by his hand as to cease to be assailed on every side. Satan and the world do not give up molesting them. Therefore, that the sacrifice we have once offered to God may

Still another shortcoming in Calvin's sermons is occasioned by a combination of his pastoral concern for relevance and his employment of the homily style. Although this patristic method of explaining and applying sentence by sentence and clause by clause keeps him close to the text, in narrative texts it leads to moralistic applications of dos and don'ts being attached to mere elements of the preaching-text. Frequently Calvin attaches these applications to the actions or words of biblical characters. For instance, in his first sermon in the series on Second Samuel, he exhorts the congregation to learn from the example of David at the defeat of Israel "to accept any trial which he [God] chooses to test us," and like David at learning of the death of Saul not to "hate the evil in him (and our enemies) without at the same time honouring the favours God had bestowed on him." Moreover, in the same sermon the death of Saul teaches us that "we should always be examining ourselves. We are given this example of Saul as an admonition, especially when God punishes us in some strange and unusual way which we cannot understand." And, still in the same sermon, there is "this Amalekite [who] pretended to grieve, and yet was nothing but an insincere flatterer. . . . Thus, let us learn not to put ourselves forward, hoping to please men, for when we do this, God will cast us down all the more quickly."[158]

In this character-imitation preaching, Calvin carries forward the tropological or moral sense of the Middle Ages and, more broadly, the moralistic preaching tradition that stretches from the ancient Greeks to the

---

remain pure and unharmed and not be violated, attacks against it must be driven away, but this will be with trouble and striving." *CO* 23, 217. Blacketer, "L'École de Dieu," chap. 6, seeks to make the case "that Calvin does reserve some very limited place for allegory in his exposition of Scripture, at least in his sermons, and under highly circumscribed conditions" (p. 33).

158. Calvin, *Sermons on 2 Samuel,* Sermon 1 on 2 Sam 1:1-16. Sermon 2 continues with applications of what we should "learn from David's example." In Sermon 3 on 2 Sam 1:21-27 Calvin judges that "David's mourning over Saul was excessive. Let that instruct us to keep ourselves under control when we feel inclined to anger and despair over something." Further, "there is still another principle to be taken from this passage. . . ." In the *Sermons from Job,* we find the same trend of attaching dos and don'ts to elements in the text. In Sermon 1 on Job 1:1, e.g., Calvin states that "it is good that we have examples who show us that there are men frail like us, who nevertheless have resisted temptations, and have persevered constantly in obeying God, although He afflicted them to the limit. Now we have here an excellent example of it." Next we read that Job was "upright." "Now by this we are admonished to have a conformity between the heart and the outward senses." Next, " 'He had fear of God'. . . . Now by this we are admonished that to rule our life well we must regard God and then our neighbours. . . ." Next, "He kept himself from evil." "We must withdraw from evil; that is to say, we must fight against such assaults after the example of Job. . . ."

present day.[159] In following this tradition, Calvin clearly operates at the historical level of the biblical characters — David, Saul, the Amalekite — and seeks to draw practical lessons for his congregation from these characters' actions and words. Unfortunately, Calvin failed to evaluate this traditional tropological/moral sense in the light of the intention of the author, as he did the allegorical sense. Was this moral sense the author's intention for Israel? Although Calvin's historical emphasis on the author's intention gave him the key to break out of this character-imitation mold, he often fails to connect this intention with the message for ancient Israel. Thus in his sermons on narrative texts, his homily style of explaining and applying every sentence and clause leads to the loss of the central message of the biblical author for Israel. This loss of focus, in turn, leads to a lack of unity in his sermons, and, ultimately, blurs the Christ-centered focus.

MODERN CHRISTOLOGICAL INTERPRETATIONS

We have now covered the major historical options of preaching Christ from the Old Testament: Alexandria's allegorical interpretation, Antioch's typological interpretation, the Middle Ages' fourfold interpretation, Luther's christological interpretation, and Calvin's theocentric interpretation. To continue this historical overview to the present time, we shall briefly review the work of two Protestant preachers known for their christological approach to preaching, Charles Haddon Spurgeon and Wilhelm Vischer.

Spurgeon

Background

Charles Haddon Spurgeon (1834-1892) is considered one of the most influential Baptist preachers. From 1854 to 1892 he was pastor in London, England, of a church which grew into the then "largest regular congregation in the world."[160] His influence spread throughout the world by way

---

159. See my *Sola Scriptura: Problems and Principles in Preaching Historical Texts*, 8-18. Cf. Reu, *Homiletics*, 280, "Zwingli's and especially Calvin's sermons on the Old Testament have the following features in common with those of Luther. They present the Old Testament saints as patterns and warning examples. . . ." For Luther, see p. 117 above.

160. Craig Skinner, "Spurgeon, Charles Haddon," in *Concise Encyclopedia of Preaching*, (see n. 151 above), 450. According to Edwin C. Dargan, *History of Preaching*,

of his sermons, which were translated into thirty-three foreign languages, and his *Lectures to My Students*.[161] No one less than Helmut Thielicke recommended Spurgeon to modern preachers in admitted hyperbole: "Sell all that you have (not least of all some of your stock of current sermonic literature) and buy Spurgeon. . . ."[162] John Talbert suggests, "Perhaps the one factor that has had more impact on the contemporary pulpit than any other is Spurgeon's christological approach to the sermon."[163] This probably overstates the case, but it may well be true for many Evangelical pulpits.

Spurgeon has been called "Heir of the Puritans."[164] He was raised in his grandfather's Puritan parsonage. According to Talbert, "The appreciation that Spurgeon acquired as a youth for the Puritans laid the foundation for his 'christocentric' focus in theology. In addition, he learned his interpretative approach to the Scriptures from the theological works he read as a boy."[165] "Puritan interpreters were staunch advocates of interpreting a passage in its literal sense, but at the same time, they made allowances for spiritual senses which were 'ancillary and derivative' to the literal meaning. Spurgeon followed this practice in his interpretation of Old Testament passages."[166]

2.537, "Within ten years from the commencement of his London pastorate, 3,569 persons had been baptized into the fellowship of the church."

161. See John Talbert, "Charles Haddon Spurgeon's Christological Homiletics," 17-18.

162. Thielicke, *Encounter with Spurgeon*, 45.

163. Talbert, "Spurgeon's Christological Homiletics," 18-19.

164. A subtitle and chapter in Richard Ellsworth Day's *The Shadow of the Broad Rim: The Life Story of Charles Haddon Spurgeon, Heir of the Puritans* (Judson Press, 1934); cf. E. W. Bacon, *Spurgeon: Heir of the Puritans* (London: Allen and Unwin, 1967). Spurgeon called himself a Calvinist who subscribed to the "five points" of Calvinism. See Talbert, "Spurgeon's Christological Homiletics," 43, n. 39, "Spurgeon believed that the minister must proclaim the 'five points' of Calvinism. . . . At the opening of the Metropolitan Tabernacle, he chaired a meeting in which visiting preachers discussed these five essential 'doctrines of grace': 'election,' 'human depravity,' 'particular redemption,' 'effectual calling,' and 'the final perseverance of believers in Christ Jesus.'" In spite of his doctrinal affinity with Calvinism, Spurgeon's christological method of preaching the Old Testament has more affinity with Luther's method than with that of Calvin.

165. Talbert, "Spurgeon's Christological Homiletics," 31-32. Cf. ibid., "He also utilized Puritan categories of religious experience in his appeals to the unregenerate from the pulpit."

166. Ibid., 66-67.

Preaching Christ

Spurgeon's *Lectures to My Students* is filled with sound advice for beginning preachers, but the main burden is that they preach Christ. He starts his lectures as follows: "The grand object of the Christian ministry is the glory of God. Whether souls are converted or not, if Jesus Christ be faithfully preached, the minister has not laboured in vain, for he is a sweet savour unto God as well in them that perish as in them that are saved. Yet as a rule, God has sent us to preach in order that through the gospel of Jesus Christ the sons of men may be reconciled to him."[167]

This is Spurgeon's main concern, the conversion of sinners. He asks, Apart from dependence on the Holy Spirit, "what else should be done if we hope to see conversions? . . . I answer, we should first and foremost preach *Christ and him crucified.* . . . The Christian minister should preach all the truths which cluster around the person and work of the Lord Jesus. . . ."[168] Spurgeon continues by enumerating some of these truths: "the evil of sin, which created the need of a Saviour," the righteousness of God, the judgment to come, "the great soul-saving doctrine of the atonement; we must preach a real bona fide substitutionary sacrifice, and proclaim pardon as its result"; justification by faith, the love of God in Christ Jesus. "The best way to preach sinners to Christ is to preach Christ to sinners."[169] Toward the end of his lectures, Spurgeon returns to this dominant theme: "Of all I would wish to say this is the sum: my brethren, preach CHRIST, always and evermore. He is the whole gospel. His person, offices, and work must be our one great, all-comprehending theme."[170]

Spurgeon puts the challenge for textual preachers most graphically in instructing a young preacher: "Don't you know, young man, that from every town and every village and every hamlet in England, wherever it may be, there is a road to London? So from every text of Scripture there is

167. Spurgeon, *Lectures to My Students,* 49.
168. Ibid., 50.
169. Ibid., 51-55.
170. Ibid., 194. Cf. Richard E. Day, *The Shadow of the Broad Rim* (Grand Rapids: Baker, 1976), 218, citing Spurgeon's first words in the Metropolitan Tabernacle, March 25, 1861, "In the days of Paul, the sum and substance of theology was JESUS CHRIST. I would propose that the subject of the ministry of this house, as long as this platform shall stand, shall be the person of JESUS CHRIST. I am not ashamed to vow myself a Calvinist. . . . I do not hesitate to take the name of Baptist. . . . But if I am asked what is my creed, I must reply, 'It is Jesus Christ' . . . Christ Jesus, who is the sum and substance of the gospel, the incarnation of every precious truth, the all glorious embodiment of the way, the truth, and the life!"

a road to Christ. And my dear brother, your business is, when you get to a text, to say, now, what is the road to Christ? I have never found a text that had not got a road to Christ in it, and if ever I do find one, I will go over hedge and ditch but I would get at my Master, for the sermon cannot do any good unless there is a savor of Christ in it."[171]

Spurgeon's Method of Interpretation

Spurgeon works with two basic senses of Scripture: the literal sense or "the plain meaning," and the spiritual sense, which covers a broad spectrum.

The Literal Sense

Spurgeon advises his students: "In no case allow your audience to forget that the narratives which you spiritualize are facts, and not mere myths or parables. The first sense of the passage must never be drowned in the overflow of your imagination; it must be distinctly declared and allowed to hold the first rank; your accommodation of it must never thrust out the original and native meaning, or even push it into the background."[172]

The Spiritual Sense

Spurgeon has much more to say about the spiritual sense than the literal one. "Within limits, my brethren, be not afraid to spiritualize, or to take singular texts. Continue to look out [sic] passages of Scripture, and not only give their plain meaning, as you are bound to do, but also draw from them meanings which may not lie upon their surface." In this connection Spurgeon warns against straining the text "by illegitimate spiritualizing," spiritualizing "upon indelicate subjects," or "for the sake of showing what an uncommonly clever fellow you are," or novel spiritual meanings that "pervert Scripture."[173]

Among the legitimate uses of the spiritual sense, Spurgeon lists first "the types": "You have frequently been shown that *the types* yield ample scope for the exercise of a sanctified ingenuity." As examples of types he

---

171. Spurgeon, "Christ Precious to Believers," as quoted in David L. Larsen, *The Anatomy of Preaching*, 168. A different version from a different source, *The Soul Winner*, 106-7, is quoted by Talbert, "Spurgeon's Christological Homiletics," 19.

172. Spurgeon, *Lectures to My Students*, 109-10. For more references, see Talbert, "Spurgeon's Christological Homiletics," 56.

173. Ibid., 107-9.

mentions "the tabernacle in the wilderness, with all its sacred furniture, the burnt-offering, the peace offering, and all the various sacrifices which were offered before God." Also "the temple with all its glories." "The largest capacity for typical interpretation will find abundant employment in the undoubted symbols of the Word of God, and it will be safe to enter upon such an exercise, because the symbols are of divine appointment."[174]

Next Spurgeon mentions metaphors. "When you have exhausted all the Old Testament types, you have left to you an heirloom of a thousand *metaphors*."[175]

Finally, and surprisingly, Spurgeon names as a legitimate form of "spiritualizing," allegorical interpretation. He writes, "When the apostle Paul finds a mystery in Melchizedek, and speaking of Hagar and Sarah says, 'Which things are an allegory,' he gives us a precedent for discovering scriptural *allegories* in other places besides the two mentioned. Indeed, the historical books not only yield us here and there an allegory, but seem as a whole to be arranged with a view to symbolic teaching."[176] Even though Spurgeon has just warned his students not "to emulate Origen in wild, daring interpretations,"[177] here he uses the very argument of Origen in support of allegorical interpretation.

Spurgeon's Preaching of Christ from the Old Testament

Spurgeon uses many "roads" to preach Christ from the Old Testament — so many, in fact, that it is difficult to systematize his approach.[178] In reading his sermons from the Old Testament, however, it soon becomes evident that he often has another agenda than passing on the message revealed by the literal sense.

174. Ibid., 110.
175. Ibid.
176. Ibid.
177. Ibid., 109. Cf. Spurgeon, *Commenting*, 31, as cited in Talbert, "Spurgeon's Christological Homiletics," 57, "To allegorize with Origen may make men stare at you, but your work is to fill men's mouths with truth, not to open them with wonder."
178. See the Ph.D. thesis of John Talbert, "Charles Haddon Spurgeon's Christological Homiletics." In addition to the ways we set forth here, Talbert discusses "Spurgeon's interpretation of the text as an illustration of Christ" with three subheadings: illustrations of Christ, illustrations of man in need of Christ, and illustrations of grace" (pp. 86-97) and "rhetorical approaches to preaching Christ" with three subheadings: Spurgeon's use of the text for instruction about Christ, for consolation in Christ, and for consecration in Christ (pp. 111-51).

Beyond the Literal Sense

Frequently Spurgeon does not ask about the author's message for Israel but hurries on to a spiritual sense. For example, in a sermon on the fruit of Canaan which the spies brought back (Deut 1:25), Spurgeon says in his third sentence, "I shall not say much, at this time, concerning the Israelites; but I want to show you that, as they learned something of what Canaan was like by the fruit of the land brought to them by the spies, so you and I, even whilst we are on earth, if we are the Lord's chosen people, may learn something of what heaven is — the state to which we are to attain hereafter — by certain blessings which are brought to us even while we are here." In the sermon he goes on to "present to you a series of views of heaven in order to give you some idea how it is that the Christian on earth enjoys a foretaste of the blessings that are yet to be revealed."[179] Another sermon in the same volume is on Genesis 19:23, "The sun was risen upon the earth when Lot entered Zoar." Spurgeon begins the sermon as follows, "The destruction of Sodom was, undoubtedly, a literal fact; and the record of it in Genesis is as true a piece of history as any event that is recorded by Tacitus or Josephus. But it was also intended to be a great parabolic lesson to us, — a lesson in the shape of a parable, by which we might receive both instruction and blessing."[180]

Promise-Fulfillment

Preaching Christ from Old Testament promises places Spurgeon on firmer, historical ground. For example, in a sermon on God's promises to David (2 Sam 7:21), Spurgeon naturally moves from Solomon to Christ: "Nathan was sent to David, to reveal to him God's great purposes of grace towards him, and his son Solomon, and the whole of his dynasty, and to give the promise that one descended from him should sit upon his

---

179. Spurgeon, *Metropolitan Tabernacle Pulpit*, 45.49.

180. Ibid., 469. Another sermon in the same volume is on Prov 27:10, "Thine own friend, and thy father's friend, forsake not." After a one-paragraph introduction on friendship, Spurgeon says, "I do not think that I should waste your time if I were to give you a lecture upon friendship . . . ; but it is not my intention to do so. There is one Friend to whom these words of Solomon are specially applicable, there is a Friend who is the chief and highest of all friends; and when I speak of him, I feel that I am not spiritualizing the text in the least." Ibid., 289-90. Cf. p. 482, a sermon on Prov 27:18, "He that waiteth on his master shall be honoured." Spurgeon says, "I am sorry that they [these words] are not always true in that sense now, but I am going to leave that literal meaning of the words, and apply the text to those who wait upon the Lord Jesus, having made him to be their Master."

throne forever, as he does and will, for the King of kings and Lord of lords, whom we greet with cries of 'Hosannah!' is the Son of David; and still he reigns. . . ."[181] Spurgeon is also able to see multiple fulfillments, first in the history of Israel and then in the coming of Christ and the history of the church.[182]

Typology

Spurgeon also utilizes typology for proclaiming Christ from the Old Testament. For example, in a sermon on Abraham offering the ram instead of his son Isaac (Gen 22), Spurgeon exclaims, "When he took the ram from the thicket, and so saved the life of his son, how clearly he must have understood that blessed doctrine of substitution, which is the very center of the gospel! I have no other hope than this. Nor can I conceive anything else that would be good news to me but the fact 'that Christ died according to the Scriptures'; that there was offered another life instead of mine, through which I live."[183] Or, preaching on Solomon's prayer at the dedication of the temple (2 Chron 6:28-30), Spurgeon asserts, "Our Temple is the person of the Lord Jesus Christ: 'In him dwelleth all the fulness of the Godhead bodily.' When we pray, we turn our faces toward him. . . . Though he is to us of the same use as the temple was to Israel, yet he is infinitely more precious and far greater than the temple; and whosoever, whatsoever his trouble shall be, shall pray unto God with his face toward Jesus . . . , he shall be forgiven, whatever his trouble or whatever his sin."[184]

Typologizing

Spurgeon often pushes typological interpretation into the details and ends up with a form of typologizing which blends into allegorizing. For example, in another sermon on Abraham offering Isaac (Gen 22), Spurgeon states after a brief introduction, "Without detaining you with any lengthened preface, for which we have neither time nor inclination, we shall, first, draw the parallel between the offering of Christ and the offering of Isaac. . . ." The first parallel is that the servants stayed behind and "Abraham and Isaac were alone." Similarly, when Jesus' disciples

---

181. Ibid., 458.

182. See Talbert, "Spurgeon's Christological Homiletics," 76-77.

183. Spurgeon, *Metropolitan Tabernacle Pulpit*, 37.500.

184. Ibid., 45.410. For more examples of Spurgeon's typology and questions about his approach, see Talbert, "Spurgeon's Christological Homiletics," 78-86.

fled in Gethsemane, "the Father and the Son were equally alone. . . ." "Do you observe also that Isaac carried the wood! — a true picture of Jesus carrying his cross." "A point worthy of notice is, that it is said, as you will find if you read the chapter of Abraham and Isaac, 'that they went both of them together'. . . . It is to me delightful to reflect that Christ Jesus and his Father went both together in the work of redeeming love." "They proceeded together, and at last, Isaac was bound, bound by his father. So Christ was bound. . . ." "The parallel goes still further, for while the father binds the victim, the victim is willing to be bound. . . . Even so with Jesus. . . ." "Yet the parallel runs a little further, . . . Isaac was restored again. . . . Isaac was for three days looked upon by Abraham as dead, on the third day the father rejoiced to descend the mountain with his son. Jesus was dead, but on the third day he rose again." "But I must pass on. . . . God provided a ram instead of Isaac. This was sufficient for the occasion as a type; but that which was typified by the ram is infinitely more glorious. In order to save us God provided *God*."[185]

Allegorizing

Spurgeon follows his own advice and frequently uses allegorical interpretation to preach Christ from the Old Testament. In his sermons we meet the traditional allegorical interpretations: the Song of Solomon (and its parts) is an allegory of Christ and the church;[186] the wood Moses threw into the bitter water at Marah is an allegory of Jesus' cross and the human soul: "I do know a tree which, if put into the soul, will sweeten all its thoughts and desires; and Jesus knew that tree, that tree whereon he died. . . ."[187] Israel's wanderings from Egypt to Canaan are an allegory of

185. Spurgeon, *Christ in the Old Testament*, 47.52-53 and 64. Cf. ibid., pp. 93-97, a sermon on Gen 14:1-5. "I need not say to you, beloved, who are conversant with Scripture, that there is scarcely any personal type in the Old Testament which is more clearly and fully a portrait of our Lord Jesus Christ than is the type of Joseph. You may run the parallel between Joseph and Jesus in very many directions. . . . In making himself known to his brethren, he was a type of our Lord revealing himself to us." The sermon has three points: "I. Notice, first, that the Lord Jesus Christ, like Joseph, reveals himself in private for the most part." "II. The second remark I have to make is this, — when the Lord Jesus Christ reveals himself to any man for the first time, it is usually in the midst of terror, and that first revelation often creates much sadness." "III. Now, thirdly, though the first appearance of Jesus, like that of Joseph, may cause sadness, the further revelation of the Lord Jesus Christ to his brethren, brings them the greatest possible joy."

186. For details, see Talbert, "Spurgeon's Christological Homiletics," 105-7.

187. Spurgeon, *Metropolitan Tabernacle Pulpit*, 28.333, as cited in Talbert, "Spurgeon's Christological Homiletics," 104.

our Christian pilgrimage from bondage to sin (Egypt), to deliverance through Christ (Passover) and conversion (going through the Red Sea), to trials, temptations, and triumphs (wilderness), to the victorious Christian life or heaven (Canaan).[188] Without apology, Spurgeon uses his rich imagination to preach Christ from the Old Testament by way of the allegorical method.[189]

Evaluation of Spurgeon's Christological Interpretation

Valuable Contributions

The most valuable contribution of Spurgeon is his clear preaching of Jesus Christ. He follows his own advice: "My brethren, preach CHRIST, always and evermore."[190] Everyone who listened to Spurgeon preach would learn something about Jesus Christ. Another valuable contribution is that his preaching is personal, focussed, and urgent. Even on the printed page, he communicates a genuine concern for his hearers, especially unbelievers, and he asks pointedly for their commitment to Jesus. A small sample will here have to suffice. This is the final paragraph of a sermon on "The ungodly are not so: but are like the chaff which the wind driveth away" (Ps 1:4): "I exhort you, sinners, lay hold on Christ. Touch the hem of his garments now. Behold, he hangs before you on the cross. As Moses lifted up the serpent in the wilderness, even so is Jesus lifted up. Look, I beseech you, look and live. Believe on the Lord Jesus Christ and you shall be saved. As though God did beseech you by me, I pray you in Christ's stead, be ye reconciled to God. And O may the Spirit make my appeal effectual! May angels rejoice this day over sinners saved and brought to know the Lord! Amen."[191]

Another contribution of Spurgeon to the preaching of Christ from

---

188. For details, see Talbert, "Spurgeon's Christological Homiletics," 101-5.

189. For example, a sermon on Lot fleeing Sodom for Zoar (Gen 19:23) has three allegorical points: I. "Lot running in the dark is just the picture of a poor sinner, when he comes out of Sodom." II. "Lot, when he reached Zoar, had the sunlight; and when the sinner gets to Christ, then he gets sunlight too." III. "Now, thirdly, we have to consider a sadder fact. God can do two things at a time. . . . with one hand he lights the sun, and with the other hand he darkens Sodom with the smoke of devouring flames (judgment)." Spurgeon, *Metropolitan Tabernacle Pulpit*, 45.469-77. Cf. ibid., 218-22, for an allegorical sermon on the cities of refuge (Num 35:11). Cf. ibid., 37.73-81, for an allegorical sermon on Exod 14:3, "Entangled in the Land," and pp. 589-93, for an allegorical sermon on Eliezer seeking a wife for Isaac (Gen 24:49).

190. See p. 153, n.170 above.

191. Spurgeon, sermon in Thielicke, *Encounter*, 283.

the Old Testament is his use of some other "roads" to Christ than the traditional promise-fulfillment and type-antitype. Sometimes he selects Old
Testament passages that suggest "a dominant theological motif of Scripture," for example, "some attribute or redemptive activity of God."[192]
This theme, then, can function as a road leading to the New Testament
and Jesus Christ. He also discovers a road to Christ which at first appears
to be a dead end because it does not allude to Christ as promise, type, or
theme; instead it presents a problem. For example, the text may speak of
human sin, or God's justice, or the Day of the Lord, but these problems
for sinners need a solution, and the solution is Christ. So in the sermon,
Spurgeon moves naturally from the human predicament to the New Testament answer in Christ.[193]

Shortcomings in Spurgeon's Method

There are also obvious shortcomings in Spurgeon's method. Even the
most generous reviewers will admit that Spurgeon makes many errors
in his interpretation of Scripture. They will usually attribute these errors to his lack of formal theological education and/or lack of time. But
it is also clear that his single-minded concern to preach Jesus Christ often leads him to reading Christ back into the Old Testament text. He
generally uses the life of Jesus as a grid for interpreting the Old Testament.[194] In other words, he frequently fails to do justice to the literal
sense and the historical context of the Old Testament passages.[195] He
does not ask about the intention of the original author;[196] he does not
inquire about the message for Israel. Instead, he tends to use the Old
Testament text as a "springboard" for his message about Jesus Christ.[197]
He can do so all the more readily because he usually selects extremely
brief texts ("singular texts"), a fragment instead of a literary (message)

192. Talbert, "Spurgeon's Christological Homiletics," 191-92. For examples, see
ibid., 192-97.

193. For examples, see ibid., 92-94.

194. See ibid., 107-10, 165, 189.

195. For examples, see ibid., 160-70. Cf. Craig Loscalzo, "Preaching Themes
from Amos," *RevExp* 92 (1995) 198, "Spurgeon focused on the vision of fruit of Amos
8. . . . A careful reading of it [his sermon] reveals little exposition of the Amos text. Instead, Spurgeon picked up on the idea of a basket of ripe fruit and used it as the controlling metaphor for the sermon. He never described the situation to which Amos
wrote or preached, crucial information needed to understand the thrust and reason for
the passage."

196. For examples, see ibid., 131-33, 170-79.

197. Ibid., 154-55.

unit. For example, in one sermon he selects as a text only the first verse of the narrative of God asking Abraham to sacrifice Isaac, Genesis 22:1. "Let us look at our text. It is a kind of preface to this unique, this unparalleled story of Abraham's test. First, 'It came to pass after these things, that God did tempt (or "prove") Abraham' — here we see the Lord's way with believers. And, secondly, when God 'said unto him, Abraham,' the patriarch instantly answered, 'Behold, here I am,' — here we learn the believer's way with the Lord. These two heads will not be difficult to remember: the Lord's way with believers, and the believer's way with the Lord."[198] Of the 532 sermons examined by Talbert, "Spurgeon used only one verse or a part of one verse of Scripture in almost 70 percent of the messages. In eleven sermons he utilized subordinate clauses or brief phrases from the Old Testament."[199] Although these brief texts will send people home with a clear idea of the point(s) of the sermon, a textual fragment is usually an open invitation to twist the meaning intended by the inspired author.

In addition to faulty text selection and interpretation, Spurgeon also makes errors in application. In his lectures to his students he says, "The faculty which turns to spiritualizing will be well employed in generalizing the great universal principles evolved by minute and separate facts. This is an ingenious, instructive, and legitimate pursuit. . . . In hundreds of scriptural incidents you may find great general principles which may nowhere be expressed in so many words."[200] This move is today known as the fallacy of generalizing. Spurgeon's generalizing, in turn, leads to moralizing, especially where he looks for "lessons" we can learn from the lives of Old Testament characters: for instance, we can identify with the sadness of Job; we ought to imitate Ruth's commitment to the Lord; on the other hand, we ought to avoid the doubting of Jacob.[201]

Spurgeon vowed that if he would ever find a text "that had not got a road to Christ in it," he would "go over hedge and ditch but I would get at my Master. . . ." Frequently Spurgeon fails to see the right road to his Master and, instead, travels through the swamp of typologizing and allegorizing. He may warn his students about Origen, but Spurgeon's own method is arbitrary and lacks any form of control. He not only teaches that allegorical interpretation is a legitimate form of "spiritualiz-

198. Spurgeon, *Metropolitan Tabernacle Pulpit,* 37.494.

199. Talbert, "Spurgeon's Christological Homiletics," 156.

200. Spurgeon, *Lectures,* 112. Cf. Talbert, "Spurgeon's Christological Homiletics," 183-84.

201. Talbert, "Spurgeon's Christological Homiletics," respectively 136, 146, 182. See esp. 181-85.

ing," but he also preaches numerous historical narratives as if they were allegories.[202] Today we would call this a genre mistake.

Another shortcoming in some of Spurgeon's sermons is that his single-minded desire to preach Jesus Christ isolates the person and work of Christ from the person and work of God the Father.[203] As we shall see in Chapter 5, however, Christ-centered preaching should always be God-centered.

A final shortcoming we should consider is Spurgeon's sole focus on individual salvation. In one of his sermons Spurgeon says, "I aim not at fine language, but only to get at poor sinners' hearts. Oh that I could bring the sinner to his Saviour. . . . To point the sinner to Christ must be our sole desire."[204] And in his lectures he writes, "We are not called to proclaim philosophy and metaphysics, but the simple gospel. Man's fall, his need of a new birth, forgiveness through an atonement, and salvation as the result of faith — these are our battle-axe and weapons of war. . . . More and more am I jealous lest any views upon prophecy, church government, politics, or even systematic theology should withdraw one of us from glorying in the cross of Christ."[205] In introducing Spurgeon's work, Thielicke acknowledges that "Spurgeon did have his eye primarily upon the individual; he gave little or no thought to the theology of social and political order and to Christ as the Lord of the cosmos."[206] Although his Metropolitan Tabernacle did start many different philanthropic organizations — from an orphanage to a Pastors' College and from almshouses to mission halls[207] — it cannot be denied that in his preaching Spurgeon considerably narrowed the scope of the gospel from the immense view of the coming kingdom of God to the salvation of the individual through the substitutionary atonement of Christ.[208]

202. For examples, see ibid., 97-107; cf. p. 153, n. 2.

203. See Le Roux, "Betekenis," 145-49.

204. Spurgeon, *Metropolitan Tabernacle Pulpit,* 29.343-44, as cited in Talbert, "Spurgeon's Christological Homiletics," 50.

205. Spurgeon, *Lectures,* 194-95.

206. Thielicke, *Encounter,* 43. Thielicke acknowledges that Spurgeon "at the beginning of the Civil War . . . vehemently and without regard for personal loss advocated the liberation of the slaves, and thus took a stand on a social problem."

207. See Craig Skinner, "Spurgeon," in *Concise Encyclopedia of Preaching* (see n. 151 above), 451-52.

208. "Substitution is the very marrow of the whole Bible, the soul of salvation, the essence of the gospel; we ought to saturate all our sermons with it, for it is the life-blood of a gospel ministry." Spurgeon, *Metropolitan Tabernacle Pulpit,* 17.544, as cited in Talbert, "Spurgeon's Christological Homiletics," 48. Cf. ibid., n. 53.

Wilhelm Vischer

Wilhelm Vischer (1895-1988) brings us almost to the present time. In contrast to Spurgeon who was self-educated, Vischer received an outstanding formal theological education. He was born in a parsonage in Germany, but he grew up in Basel, where his father accepted an appointment as Professor of New Testament in 1902. Vischer studied theology in Lausanne, Basel, and Marburg, after which he served as pastor in several churches. In 1928 he accepted an appointment as lecturer in Old Testament in Bethel, Germany, but in 1933 the Nazis banned him from teaching and preaching. Thereupon he served a church in Lugano, Switzerland, and in 1936 became pastor in Basel, where Karl Barth was one of his parishioners. He also became an adjunct faculty member at the University of Basel, where he taught Old Testament alongside Walter Baumgartner and Walther Eichrodt. In 1946 he accepted an appointment as Professor of Old Testament to the "Faculté Reformée" in Pontpellier, France, where he lived until his death at age 93.[209]

Vischer is best known for his two-volume work, *Das Christuszeugnis des Alten Testaments,* 1 (1934), 2 (1942), of which the first volume was translated into English as *The Witness of the Old Testament to Christ* (1949). David Baker judges this work to be "a turning-point in the history of the interpretation of the Old Testament."[210] To understand Vischer and this "turning-point," we must know a little of the complex situation in which he wrote.

Background

Rejection of the Old Testament

In Chapter 1 we noted the rejection of the Old Testament by several influential German theologians: Schleiermacher, von Harnack, and Bultmann. In 1921 Harnack claimed, "To keep it [the Old Testament] after the nineteenth century as a canonical document within Protestantism results from a religious and ecclesiastical paralysis."[211] According to Rolf Rendtorff, at that time "not a single Old Testament scholar, as far as I know,

209. These statistics are gleaned from A. J. Bronkhorst, *Kerk en Theologie* 40/2 (1989) 142-53.

210. Baker, *Two Testaments, One Bible,* 211. Cf. Brevard Childs, "On Reclaiming," 2, "Wilhelm Vischer's famous — for many, infamous — book *The Witness of the Old Testament to Christ* (1934) was a lightning rod."

211. Quoted by Vischer, *The Witness of the Old Testament to Christ,* 26.

made any public declaration in response to Adolf von Harnack's un-equivocal rejection of the Old Testament. . . ."[212]

An even more vicious assault against the Old Testament was launched by Friedrich Delitzsch, son of the famous commentator Franz Delitzsch. In 1921 he published *The Great Deception*, which he summa-rized as follows: "That the Old Testament is full of deceptions of all kinds: a veritable hodge-podge of erroneous, incredible, undependable figures, including those of biblical chronology; a veritable labyrinth of false portrayals, misleading reworkings, revisions and transpositions, therefore also of anachronisms, a constant intermixture of contradictory particulars and whole stories, unhistorical inventions, legends and folk-tales — in short, a book full of intentional and unintentional deceptions, in part self-deceptions, a very dangerous book, in the use of which the greatest care is necessary."[213]

Rising Anti-Semitism

The viciousness of the last quotation already indicates that more is going on here than scholarship. This was the time of rising anti-Semitism in Germany, and the Old Testament was equated with the religion of the Jews. In 1933 a notorious assembly of "German Christians" demanded "that our regional church, as a German folk church, should liberate itself from everything that is un-German in its worship and creed, especially from the Old Testament, with its Jewish 'recompense' morality."[214]

In that setting, Wilhelm Vischer courageously defended the value of the Old Testament. Here are a few of his titles: 1931, "The Old Testament and Preaching"; 1932, "Does the Old Testament Still Belong in the Bible of Today's German Christians?"; 1933, "On the Jewish Question: A Brief Discussion of the Jewish Question in Connection with a Presentation on the Meaning of the Old Testament";[215] 1934, *The Witness of the Old Testa-ment to Christ*.

Vischer defends the Old Testament against all takers. Quoting Harnack's counsel to reject the Old Testament, Vischer challenges Harnack's position and that of others. He writes, "By this step we aban-don the Christian confession — the confession that Jesus of Nazareth is the Christ. . . . For Christianity means precisely the confession that Jesus

---

212. Rendtorff, *Canon*, 77.

213. Quoted in Kraeling, *Old Testament*, 158.

214. Cited by Rendtorff, *Canon*, 77.

215. My translations of the German titles given in Bronkhorst, *Kerk en Theologie* 40/2 (1989) 144-45.

is the Christ in the sense in which the Old Testament defines Israel's Messiah. The New Testament understands it in this way. . . . With complete consistency the early Church took over Israel's Scripture."[216] Rendtorff, who disagrees with Vischer's method, frankly acknowledges that "his book at the time was understood and perceived as a deliverance of the Old Testament from the attacks of the Nazis."[217]

Fruitless Old Testament Scholarship

Vischer not only had to face the rejection of the Old Testament and anti-Semitism, but he also had to work in a climate in which a large segment of Old Testament scholarship had become theologically sterile. Higher criticism ruled the day: source criticism (known as literary criticism), form criticism, and history of religion. Gerhard von Rad writes of that time, "When National Socialism came, with its repellent and gross 'no' to the Old Testament, . . . the situation became critical, for this challenge found Old Testament scholarship almost completely unprepared. With an almost religious earnestness, it had trained people to the ethic of an incorruptible historical discernment; but it had not trained them to acknowledge the Old Testament publicly, indeed in the political sector, in a crucial situation. . . ."[218]

In his 1935 review of Vischer's *Christuszeugnis*, von Rad acknowledges, "The links of the churches with Old Testament scholarship have been almost completely broken for more than a generation, and the churches are not prepared to accept the teachings of Old Testament scholars." In this review von Rad is extremely critical of Vischer's method and argues that there is no going back on the results of scholarly research in "history, history of religion, and literary history."[219]

Vischer, however, is much more critical of modern scholarship than is von Rad. He acknowledges the value of some of the research, for example, "Albrecht Alt's territorial-historical investigations and Johannes

---

216. Vischer, *Witness*, 26. In a later work Vischer also tackles Rudolf Bultmann. See Vischer, "Everywhere the Scripture Is about Christ Alone," 90-101.

217. Rendtorff, "Towards a New Christian Reading of the Hebrew Bible," *Immanuel* 15 (Winter 1982-83) 13-21.

218. Von Rad, "Gerhard von Rad über von Rad," in *Probleme biblischer Theologie*, ed. H. W. Wolff (Munich, 1971), 660, as cited in Rendtorff, *Canon*, 76. Cf. Herbert F. Hahn, *The Old Testament in Modern Research* (Philadelphia: Fortress, 1966), 10: "By the beginning of the twentieth century, theological exegesis as the paramount concern of biblical scholarship had been supplanted by the scientific-historical conception of the scholar's task."

219. Von Rad, *Theologische Blätter*, 249 and 251 (my translation).

Pedersen's researches in Hebrew psychology and sociology."[220] But in his opinion much of Old Testament scholarship is counterproductive. He bristles at the charge that "the modern study of the Bible . . . is imbued with the conviction that the Christological interpretation of Old Testament texts can be substantiated only by an artificial exegesis." He counters, "But the question is whether the methods and results of this [modern] kind of research do not arouse legitimate doubts concerning its validity. Is it not influenced by modern philosophy to an extent which is not permissible when we are seeking to understand ancient texts? Does it not introduce points of view alien to the text? Does it not work with ideas and categories which were unknown to ancient authors?"[221]

Vischer wishes to uphold the unity of the Bible. But, he writes, "it is characteristic of this 'scientific study' of the Bible to interpret the Old Testament texts, not by reading what is there, but by reconstructing an 'original' context and meaning. It interprets the testimony backwards, in order to discover records of something which has happened, instead of being ready to look forward to that which should come as the records indicate. Since it is characteristic of the Old Testament to look forwards and not backwards, that can be done only by a violent dissolution and reconstruction of the text."[222]

Dialectic Theology

Besides the obstacles Vischer faced, he found a supporter and friend in Karl Barth and his neoorthodox theology. Vischer writes, "The new orientation which Karl Barth has brought into Protestant theology constrains and helps us today to interpret the Bible once again as the Bible in its own characteristic sense, however strange this may seem to our modern ways of thought."[223] In a letter written in 1965, Barth, in turn, credits Vischer: "You have called our attention to the reality of the Old Testament witnesses to Christ."[224]

---

220. Vischer, *Witness*, 29.

221. Ibid., 28-29.

222. Ibid., 29-30. Vischer continues, "The Church has never maintained that documents of the religious history of Israel-Judah so reconstructed testify that Jesus is the Christ. It is not surprising if such a procedure leads to other conclusions."

223. Ibid., 29. For Barth's view of the unity of the two Testaments and what this means for preaching the Old Testament, see, e.g., Karl Barth, *The Preaching of the Gospel* (Philadelphia: Westminster, 1963), 48-49; and his *Homiletics* (Louisville: Westminster/ John Knox, 1991), 80-81.

224. Bronkhorst, *Kerk en Theologie* 40/2 (1989) 143 (my translation).

Vischer's Presuppositions

Vischer had specific, Barthian, presuppositions concerning God, Christ, revelation, the Bible, history, and other concepts. We shall not touch on all of these, but briefly note three presuppositions which are directly related to our topic.

Theology Is Christology

Vischer's most basic presupposition is that theology is Christology. In the introduction to his *Witness of the Old Testament to Christ*, he writes, "The hallmark of Christian theology is that it is Christology, a theology that can affirm nothing of God except in and through Jesus Christ, because no man has seen God at any time; the only begotten Son, which is in the bosom of the Father, He hath declared Him — *exegesato* (John 1:18). . . . From this it is clear that all the knowledge of God which resides in the Old Testament scriptures is mediated through Jesus Christ. Consequently, the theological exposition of these writings within the Church can be nothing other than Christology."[225]

The Unity of Old and New Testaments

On the basis of Christ, Vischer argues for the unity of the Old and New Testaments. He writes, "The two main words of the Christian confession 'Jesus is the Christ' — the personal name 'Jesus' and the vocational name 'Christ' — correspond to the two parts of the Holy Scriptures: the New and the Old Testament. The Old Testament tells us *what* the Christ is; the New, *who* he is."[226] He likens the witnesses of the Old and New Testaments to "the two sections of an antiphonal choir looking towards a central point, then at this point stands as an historical event Immanuel, God-with-us, the Mediator between God and man. . . ."[227]

Vischer insists, "The Christian Church stands and falls with the recognition of the unity of the two Testaments. A 'Church' which disparages the value of the Old Testament in face of the New disbelieves the decisive element in the apostolic teaching, and ceases to be 'Christian.' For the dis-

---

225. Vischer, *Witness*, 28, n. 1. Note that Vischer's conclusion does not follow, for he switches from Christ as the subject (the mediator) of revelation to Christ as the object (the content) of this revelation.

226. Ibid., 7.

227. Ibid., 25.

tinctive doctrine of apostolic preaching is that Jesus is the Christ of the Old Testament."[228]

The Old Testament Witnesses to Christ

A third presupposition of Vischer is that the Old Testament witnesses to Christ. He writes, "According to Biblical testimony, Jesus the Christ is the 'corner stone' of the edifice of God's revelation; and the controversy of the exegetes, whether the corner stone should be understood as the keystone of the arch or as the foundation stone, can only be settled by the realization that Jesus Christ is both the foundation stone [the eternal Logos] and the keystone [the incarnate Christ] — and therefore the stone of stumbling, the 'skandalon' in the eyes of reason."[229]

Vischer realizes, of course, that not every person discovers this witness to Jesus Christ in the Old Testament, for the Holy Spirit must open our eyes to see this witness. "The writings of the Old Testament no less than those of the New are for all who seek Him signs and tokens of the Son of God who was born in a manger; crib and swaddling clothes they are, not the Child Himself; testimonies are dead characters, not the living Christ. Unless the Holy Spirit breathe through them, they remain dead."[230]

Vischer's Christological Interpretation of the Old Testament

Unfortunately, christological interpretation can easily slide into eisegesis. Vischer is aware of this pitfall: "There is always a great danger that we should read our own ideas into Biblical writings. We shall therefore be ready to be instructed by anyone who reads more correctly. Above all, to keep on the highroad of exposition, we shall follow the footprints of Luther and Calvin."[231]

Because Vischer's interpretations are creative and vary widely, it is difficult to discern a particular methodology. According to Leonhard Goppelt, "Vischer follows no definite method in his interpretation because 'the discovery is the gift of God.' He usually proceeds typologically

---

228. Ibid., 27.

229. Ibid., 18. Cf. the title of Vischer's 1964 article, "Everywhere the Scripture Is about Christ Alone." The title is a quotation from Luther's *Vorlesung über den Römerbrief*, 1515/1516, on Rom 15:15-16.

230. Ibid., 17. Vischer concludes his introduction to *The Witness of the Old Testament to Christ* with words of Augustine: "Read the prophetic books without reference to Christ — what couldst thou find more tasteless and insipid? Find therein Christ, and what thou readest will not only prove agreeable, but will intoxicate thee." Ibid., 34.

231. Ibid., 32.

and sometimes allegorically, but always with a claim to general evidence. Frequently he supplies the meaning of a particular passage directly from the New Testament interpretation. Vischer speaks of the faith of Abraham, Joseph, and Moses as is done in Hebrews 11. Genesis 14 is interpreted on the basis of Hebrews 7, and the story of the crossing of the Red Sea is interpreted on the basis of 1 Corinthians 10. Vischer goes far beyond anything indicated in the New Testament in his discovery of prefigurations of Christ."[232] In spite of this diversity of moves, it will be helpful to note some common patterns.

Typology

Goppelt judges that Vischer "usually proceeds typologically" (above). Although Vischer does not use the terms type-antitype,[233] he does use typology rather frequently. His heavy reliance on the letter to the Hebrews would already indicate as much. For example, "'Melchisedek,' which means in English 'a king of righteousness' and also 'king of Salem,' i.e. 'king of peace,' who is without father, without mother, without descent, having neither beginning of days nor end of life, is compared with the Son of God and abides priest in eternity, when every priesthood ordained for time has been dissolved."[234] Moses is also portrayed as a type of Christ: "As Moses was a 'faithful servant appointed to witness to that which should later be declared,' so Jesus as the faithful Son is the Word itself which God finally speaks, the heir whom He has set over all, by whom also He made the worlds, and who, being the express image of His person, upholdeth all things by the word of His power (Heb 1:1-3)."[235] When Moses asks for a successor, the Lord says, "Take Joshua . . ." (Num 27:16-21). Vischer comments, "From the gospel we know that the Lord by this answer gave exceeding abundantly above all that Moses could ask or think. For with these words He promised to send the conquering hero of His Kingdom, whose name shall be Jehoshua, Jesus, because He was so named of the angel before He was conceived in the womb (Luke 2:21)."[236] Concerning Old Testament sacrifices, Vischer

232. Goppelt, *Typos*, 2 (the page references in this quotation to Vischer's *Witness* are, respectively, 32, 28, 146, 164, 167-68, 132-33, 177, 146-47, 157, 167).

233. In fact, James White, "A Critical Examination of Wilhelm Vischer's Hermeneutic of the Old Testament," 50, contends, "Vischer also rejects the typological approach to the Old Testament."

234. Vischer, *Witness*, 132.

235. Ibid., 229.

236. Ibid., 231. Cf. Vischer's comments on Joshua conquering Jericho, "It is undeniable that the capture of Jericho after a seven-day procession, with the sound of the

writes, "Vicarious life is perpetually slain so that the Israelites may be granted new life. The vital elements in the laws governing sacrifice are those of mediation and substitution. . . . It is clear that every sacrifice points beyond itself to the Day of Atonement, and beyond that to the sacrifice which once for all shall cover all sin."[237]

Link to a New Testament Text

Vischer frequently moves from his passage in the Old Testament to a text in the New Testament. Rendtorff dubs this move "Vischer's expository method": "He interprets a central concept in the Old Testament text by way of a New Testament quotation in which the same word appears, related to Christ; and he then expands the christological aspect, a detailed quotation [of Luther or Calvin] playing a central role. . . ."[238] For example, concerning the story of God demanding Abraham to sacrifice Isaac (Gen 22), Vischer comments, "He [Abraham] accounted, as Heb. 11:19 says, that God can raise from the dead and make alive. Thus Abraham well understood the article of the resurrection of the dead, and by it resolved the contradiction which otherwise cannot be resolved. . . . Can we not see how this path of sacrifice is overhung with the darkness of Good Friday, and how this dark cloud itself is tinged with the radiance of the Easter sun?"[239] Or, dealing with the burning bush (Exod 3:1-12), Vischer comments, "The burning bush, 'Sené,' is a parable and symbol of God's revelation at Sinai where the whole mountain 'was wrapped in smoke, because the Lord had descended upon it in fire' (Exod 19:18). . . ." After tracing the idea of divine fire further through Exodus and Isaiah, Vischer finally lands at the words of Jesus in Luke 12:49, "I am come to send fire on the earth. . . ."[240]

Year of Jubilee trumpets, prophetically foreshadows the cosmic Sabbath when, at the end of days, with the sound of the last trump the kingdoms of this world shall become the kingdoms of the Lord and of his Christ." *Christuszeugnis*, 2.30 (my translation). Cf. ibid., 209, David the shepherd boy who slays Goliath "becomes a royal witness to the true Shepherd, through whom God saves his flock. This Shepherd does not flee like the hired hand when the wolf comes, and as David's Son and Lord he does what David could not do: he offers his life for his people and gives them eternal life (John 10)" (my translation).

237. Ibid., 217-18. Cf. ibid., 211, a quotation of Kohlbrügge regarding the building of the tabernacle: "In the picture of that age it was shown to the people until Christ should come and put the shadows to flight. The import of the exalted words, 'Thou shalt make a house' is therefore: 'thus and thus shalt thou foreshadow Christ.'"

238. Rendtorff, *Canon*, 80.

239. Vischer, *Witness*, 142.

240. Ibid., 168-69.

Link to the Story of Jesus

In addition to linking the Old Testament passage to a New Testament text, Vischer will often move from the Old Testament passage to a parallel event in the life of Christ. In discussing the joy at the birth of Isaac, Vischer wonders, "Is there not hidden in the depths of these ancient accounts the paternal joy of God, the joy of the Father in heaven over the birth of His own Son as Son of man and Son of Abraham? . . . And under the oaks of Hebron and in the tent of Sarah do we not breathe that singular blend of odours of earth and the air of heaven which meets us in the fields of the shepherds and in the manger at Bethlehem?"[241] Or, concerning baby Moses in the Nile, Vischer remarks, "The story of this little child in the ark whom He had chosen to be the saviour of Israel is a symbol of the childhood of the Saviour of the world, who, because there was otherwise no room for Him on the earth, was born in a manger, and whom neither Herod could murder nor the seven-headed dragon . . . could devour (Matt 2; Rev 12)."[242]

Christ the Eternal Logos

In his introduction to *The Witness of the Old Testament to Christ*, Vischer reminds us of the New Testament passages which speak of Christ as eternal God, such as John 1:1, "In the beginning was the Word, and the Word was with God, and the Word was God," and Revelation 22:13, "I am the Alpha and the Omega, the first and the last, the beginning and the end." Vischer continues, "He [Jesus] is the finisher and author of faith, who sets His seal upon all the faithful from Noah to the last generation. It is not merely that His faith is greater than theirs, but rather that their faith is directed to Him."[243]

Consequently, the work of the eternal Logos in the Old Testament becomes another witness to Christ. For example, Vischer comments on Joseph's death (Gen 50): "Jesus is the guarantee that this whole race is no prancing of fools. He is the Finisher who guides the race to its goal. But He is also the Beginner . . . , the primal leader of the whole race. All the time He is there; as He was with the first, so shall He be with the last, invisibly present with every generation."[244] Vischer also states that the covenant with Noah and later with Abraham were "sealed in Christ." "The

241. Ibid., 139-40.
242. Ibid., 167.
243. Ibid., 18-19.
244. Ibid., 165.

covenants of the Bible are so to speak circles of revelation of varying radii, but all have *one* centre. Moreover we do well to reflect that this one centre — Jesus, the Saviour of the World — is the fountain-head of all these circles of revelation and not simply their product."[245]

Evaluation of Vischer's Christological Method

Vischer's books hit a raw nerve in the scholarly world, and he became the target of severe criticism. But the critics were not always fair and frequently failed to agree with each other.[246] This lack of agreement demonstrates the difficulty of trying to "peg" Vischer's free, creative approach. Nevertheless, we can note some positive values and some general problems in his approach.

Valuable Contributions

The outstanding contribution of Vischer is that he reclaimed the Old Testament for the Christian church and pulpit. This was no mean accomplishment in the face of the rejection of the Old Testament by leading theologians and the Nazi movement. In 1937 R. Abramowski wrote, "Vischer's book has become *the* Old Testament book of our day, because it is necessary and right. It is *necessary* because the theological and political situation required a Christian testimony in the light of the Old Testament, not merely an opinion about the Old Testament. . . . It is *right* . . . because the New Testament and the Reformation proclaim to us with a single voice that the Old Testament witnesses to Christ."[247] Vischer's work gave many pastors "the courage to preach from the Old Testament."[248]

In addition, Vischer's work started a discussion concerning the relationship between biblical scholarship and the church.[249] At this time Old

---

245. Ibid., 102, 138. See also James White, "Critical Examination," 108, to the effect that Vischer "calls preachers to take seriously the depiction of 'Wisdom' given in the eighth chapter of Proverbs as the key to understanding how to preach Christ from that book."

246. See the various evaluations listed by Baker, *Two Testaments*, 222-26. Cf. Bright, *Authority*, 86, "Vischer has been the target of a great deal of criticism, even scornful criticism, not a little of which one feels to be unjust."

247. Cited in Rendtorff, *Canon*, 78.

248. Martin Kuske, *Old Testament*, 76. See also Horst Preuss, *Alte Testament*, 86.

249. Cf. Kuske, ibid., "It even motivated Old Testament science to ask itself, What is the task of theological science?" Cf. ibid., 16, "With daring abandon breaking through to the Reformation message, Vischer achieved the new orientation of Old Testament science."

Testament scholarship was off on a mission of its own and had largely abandoned the church and its preachers. A. H. J. Gunneweg, an opponent of Vischer's methodology, cautions: "It was easy for biblical critics to show that his approach was illegitimate. . . . But his attempt should not be dismissed too lightly. The Old Testament was being repudiated in increasingly drastic terms and scholars were dissociating themselves more and more from the burning questions of its significance, validity and character: were these the only possible alternatives? Vischer offered an answer in a book which announced its intention of rescuing the Old Testament from its exile in the realm of alien religious documents, paying attention to its claims and promises, and expressing once again the significance of the biblical testimony for the present. This reaction to the negative approach of scholars and non-scholars alike, and the neutral, quasi-objective perspective adopted by historians was a necessary one."[250]

Another contribution of Vischer is his insistence that the Old Testament cannot be understood in isolation but must be understood in the context of the New Testament. This was a good corrective to the direction in which Old Testament scholarship was moving and is moving today. John Bright states, "Vischer certainly deserves thanks for being among the first to remind us that we cannot rest content with a purely historical understanding of the Old Testament but must press on to see it in its Christian significance."[251]

A final contribution of Vischer we should highlight is his presupposition that the Old Testament witnesses to Christ. In his books he demonstrates various ways in which one can preach Christ from the Old Testament, the most convincing way being his use of typology.

Shortcomings in Vischer's Method

A major shortcoming in Vischer's work is the speculation in which he engages. Some of this speculation is due to his creative, almost playful, approach, which allows him intuitively to posit connections and move to parallels between the Old Testament and the New. But speculation is not

---

250. Gunneweg, *Understanding the Old Testament*, 160-61. Cf. Karl Barth, *Church Dogmatics*, 1/2, 79-80, who laments "the parlous [shocking] result of the unconcern shown by Old Testament experts for the last 200 years or so to their main theological task." Barth then acknowledges his dependence on the work of Eichrodt, and "above all" that of Vischer, adding, "In reading this [*Christuszeugnis*], one should add the review by G. v. Rad . . . as not unprofitable (a fruitful criticism of Vischer can, of course, be delivered only by one who is in a position to perform the same task better)."

251. Bright, *Authority*, 88.

proper interpretation, nor is it a sound foundation for preaching the sure Word of God.

Another form of speculation flows from his hermeneutical use of Christ being the eternal Logos.[252] For example, commenting on God's command, "Let there be light" (Gen 1:4), Vischer asserts that this refers to the light of Jesus Christ: "This light is — the expression can no longer be avoided if we are to expound our text faithfully and guard it against every kind of speculative misinterpretation — 'the glory of God in the face of Jesus Christ' (2 Cor 4:6)."[253] Vischer also follows Luther in identifying the man with whom Jacob wrestled as Jesus Christ. "Fantastic though the interpretation may appear, it is in fact conclusive. That is the central miracle attested by all the stories and words of the Bible, that Jesus Christ appeared as a man upon earth to wrestle with men, and to be overcome of them. In Jesus, and only in Him, does the inconceivable happen, that the Almighty gives Himself into the power of men. However fiercely reason may revolt against this, this and nothing else is the message of Jesus, the Crucified."[254]

Another problem area is Vischer's view of the relationship of the Old and New Testaments. He sees it as a "relationship not only involving 'unity' but 'identity.'"[255] He asserts, "the two parts of the primitive Biblical documents have really the same purport"; and, as we have seen, he likens the two Testaments to "the two sections of an antiphonal choir looking towards a central point, . . . Immanuel."[256] This assumption fails to do justice to the progression in redemptive history and the progression in God's revelation from the Old Testament to the New.[257] G. C. Berkouwer observes, "Vischer presents parallels without making plain the redemptive-historical perspective and, for that reason, his exegesis strikes us as arbitrary. He is not sufficiently aware that the Old Testament witness to Christ is imbedded in

252. Vischer, *Witness*, 21, even argues that "the doctrine of the unity of the Bible establishes the genuine historicity of the incarnation, the fact that it happened once for all in space and time, and equally assures the recognition that the events which happened in the life of Christ as temporal history form an eternal *now*. . . . In every generation every true Christian is contemporaneous with Christ."

253. Ibid., 44.

254. Ibid., 153.

255. Baker, *Two Testaments*, 228.

256. Vischer, *Witness*, 25.

257. Cf. White, "Critical Examination," 81, "Vischer's expositions very often show a certain disregard for history. Consequently . . . [they] lack any strong feeling for historical progression which would seem to be one of the essential characteristics of a sound biblical theology."

a long history in which the witness concerning redemption is related to God's guidance of Israel."[258]

Vischer's rather static view of God's revelation, in turn, allows him to move back and forth freely between the two Testaments without taking into account different historical settings and different stages in God's revelation. This procedure can result in simply reading the New Testament back into the Old. In many cases, says Norman Porteous, "he interprets the Old Testament simply by placing a New Testament passage which refers to it side by side with it. The New Testament meaning is read into the Old Testament passage and so Vischer knows beforehand what the latter must mean."[259]

From time to time Vischer also resorts to typologizing and allegorizing. In the section on Vischer's "link to the story of Jesus" (above) we see typologizing when he uses textual details for establishing parallels with the life of Christ. Another example of this is his interpretation of Genesis 14, "In Melchisedek's bringing of bread and wine we have a clear allusion to the sacrament of the New Covenant which Jesus instituted for the completion and dissolution of the old."[260] A form of allegorizing can be seen in Vischer's claim that the sign of Cain (Gen 4:15) points to the cross of Christ,[261] as do the gallows of Haman.[262] A more elaborate form of allegorizing is found in Vischer's interpretation of the sacrifice of the red heifer (Num 19). He comments, "This chapter in fact presents a remarkable allusion to Christ Jesus. We read that an unblemished heifer which had never been placed under the yoke should be slain outside the camp. . . . The allusion to Christ is manifest. He who is with-

258. Berkouwer, *Person of Christ*, 128. Cf. Norman W. Porteous, *The Old Testament and Modern Study* (Oxford: Clarendon, 1951), 337, "Vischer fails to see that the New Testament does not only tell us who Christ is; it also tells us more fully than the Old Testament what He is. Jesus transcended all the expectations and hopes of the Old Testament."

259. Porteous, *Old Testament*, 338. Cf. T. C. Vriezen, *Outline*, 86, "We must not attempt to find or project Jesus Christ in the O.T. retrospectively. Behind this view lies the theology of Karl Barth, who places Christology so much in the foreground, on account of the Logos-doctrine, that this theology as a whole is made dependent on this, not only systematically but also with respect to the course of revelation in *history* itself. The 'once and for all' character of the appearance of Jesus Christ in history does not receive justice here. . . ."

260. Vischer, *Witness*, 132.

261. Ibid., 74-76. In approving this interpretation, Donald Bloesch, "Christological Hermeneutic," 88, calls Cain's sign "a type of the sign of the cross."

262. Vischer, "The Book of Esther," *EvQ* 11 (1939) 14, "The two crosses, that reared before the gates of the holy city, and the fifty cubit high scaffold at Susa, greet one another across the continents and the centuries."

out spot and is the only one who never came under the yoke of sin, offers Himself to God without the gate on the accursed tree. . . . Nothing but being sprinkled with the blood of Christ can absolve us, and nothing but the transfer of the merit of His obedience to us can open the door of God's service. . . . That is the gospel which is proclaimed in the passage concerning the red heifer and confirmed in the sacraments of baptism and communion."[263]

A final concern about Vischer's method is that his sole focus on the witness to *Christ* leads to Christomonism, that is, an exclusive concentration on Jesus Christ. This exclusive focus slights the triune God who, ever since the fall into sin, has been working out his plan to redeem his people and restore his creation.

*   *   *

This completes our survey of the history of preaching Christ from the Old Testament. Vischer's efforts in the 1930s were followed by much criticism of his method and a half century of virtual silence on the topic of preaching Christ from the Old Testament. The biblical theology movement did step into the gap for a few decades, starting with Vischer's colleague Walther Eichrodt,[264] but in tracing longitudinal themes from the Old Testament to the New, its concern was not specifically with preaching Christ from the Old Testament.

This historical survey discloses that the church in all stages of its history has endeavored to preach Christ from the Old Testament as well as the New. It has also made us aware of the difficulties of this endeavor, the various hermeneutical approaches as well as their pros and cons. The major question that emerges at the end of this survey is, What constitutes a legitimate method of interpreting the Old Testament with an eye to preaching Jesus Christ? In the next chapter we shall investigate whether the New Testament can offer us some viable principles for preaching Christ from the Old Testament.

---

263. Vischer, *Witness,* 226-27.

264. According the Goppelt, *Typos,* 3, "Although he [Eichrodt] has a very positive attitude toward the results of previous research, he wants to break the tyranny of historicism and publish — for the first time in 25 years — an OT theology that interprets the OT as a structural unity and not as the result of successive phases of religion (pp. 27f.). Moreover, Eichrodt wants to take seriously the conviction that the OT points beyond itself and only comes to rest in the NT, and that the NT leads back to the main contents of the OT. . . ."

CHAPTER 5

New Testament Principles
for Preaching Christ
from the Old Testament

"Preach CHRIST, always and evermore. He is the whole gospel. His person, offices, and work must be our one great, all-comprehending theme."

Spurgeon, *Lectures to My Students*, 194

THE OLD TESTAMENT is clearly theocentric. Its concern is to reveal God, Yahweh. A crucial teaching for Israel concerning God is the Shema, which was recited daily, "Hear, O Israel: The LORD [Yahweh] our God, the LORD [Yahweh] is one" (Deut 6:4, NIV). In the midst of the worship of many gods, the Old Testament teaches Israel the unity of God. Preaching from the Old Testament, therefore, is naturally theocentric, and the church's struggle has been how to preach christocentric sermons from texts that are theocentric. Before we move further to arrive at some New Testament guidelines for preaching Christ from the Old Testament, we need to consider the New Testament principle that Christ-centered sermons ought to be God-centered.

CHRIST-CENTERED PREACHING
IS TO BE GOD-CENTERED

In the historical chapters we noted a tendency in "christological preaching" to slide at times into Christomonism, that is, the preaching of Christ in isolation from God.[1] We observed this especially in the work of the neoorthodox Wilhelm Vischer, who held that "the theological exposition of the [Old Testament] writings within the church can be nothing other than Christology."[2] Vischer's method easily leads to the preaching of Christ to the neglect of God.

The Danger of Christomonism

The pitfall of Christomonism is a temptation not only for Vischer but also for other faith communities. Edmund Steimle warns particularly his own Lutheran community against this danger. He asserts that "the Christocentric emphasis in Lutheran preaching . . . has been twisted so out of proportion, even though unintentionally, that for the people in the pew the essential Gospel, the revelation and redemptive act of *God* in Christ, has been all but lost. To 'accept Christ as my personal Saviour' apparently has little or nothing to do with God."[3]

The tendency toward Christomonism is also noticeable in other Christian communities where the Psalms are no longer sung and "gospel songs" as well as sermons focus primarily on Jesus in isolation from God the Father. Fred Craddock observes that today many "who sit before pulpits have been given a steady diet of Jesus Christ without a context in theology. A listener might get the impression that faith in Christ had replaced faith in God or that faith in Christ had been added to faith in God as though an increase in the number of items in one's faith meant an increase in salvific effect."[4]

---

1. Cf. the concern of Johann Le Roux, "Betekenis," 147, "When the 'center' or 'midpoint' idea included in Christocentric means something other than 'Mediator,' the divine economy is skewed. Preaching then degenerates into Christomonism. . . . Christ is preached as if he alone is God" (my translation).

2. Vischer, *Witness*, 28, n. 1.

3. Steimle, *LuthQ* 6 (1954) 14. Cf. p. 13 regarding "its emphasis upon Christocentric preaching to the neglect of theocentric preaching. Which is to say that a perfectly proper and necessary emphasis upon Christ has been so heightened as to result in an improper de-emphasis upon God."

4. Craddock, "The Gospel of God," in *Preaching as Theological Task: World, Gospel, Scripture,* ed. Thomas G. Long and Edward Farley (Louisville: Westminster/John Knox, 1996), 74.

Preaching Christ to the Glory of God

In contrast to Christomonistic tendencies, the first New Testament principle to remember is that Christ is not to be separated from God but was sent by God, accomplished the work of God, and sought the glory of God. What may have escaped many in their proper concern to preach "Christ and him crucified" is that Paul links these very references to God.

Paul Preaches Christ to the Glory of God

Paul's Christ-centered preaching is never isolated from God. A few quotations from Paul speak for themselves. Notice Paul's emphasis in the classic passage: "We proclaim Christ crucified, a stumbling block to Jews and foolishness to Gentiles, but to those who are called, both Jews and Greeks, Christ the power of *God* and the wisdom of *God*" (1 Cor 1:23, my emphases; cf. 2:2-5). Or again, "We do not proclaim ourselves; we proclaim Jesus Christ as Lord. . . . the light of the knowledge of the glory of *God* in the face of Jesus Christ" (2 Cor 4:5-6). Or again, "All this is from *God*, who reconciled us to himself through Christ . . . , in Christ *God* was reconciling the world to himself. . . . So we are ambassadors for Christ, since *God* is making his appeal through us; we entreat you on behalf of Christ, be reconciled to *God*" (2 Cor 5:18-20; cf. Eph 3:8-12). It is Paul who quotes the early Christian hymn about Jesus' humiliation and exaltation: "Therefore *God* also highly exalted him and gave him the name that is above every name, so that . . . every tongue should confess that Jesus Christ is Lord, to the glory of *God the Father*."[5]

Although the New Testament phrase "God the Father" usually refers to the first person of the Trinity, it can also refer to God, that is, the triune God.[6] Moreover, Paul teaches that Christ, on the last day, will hand over "the kingdom to God the Father, after he has destroyed every ruler and every authority and power. . . . When all things are subjected to him [the Son], then the Son himself will also be subjected to the one who put all things in subjection under him, so that God may be all in all" (1 Cor 15:24, 28; cf. Eph 4:6).

---

5. Phil 2:9-11. Peter writes similarly, "Whoever speaks must do so as one speaking the very words of God . . . , so that God may be glorified in all things through Jesus Christ" (1 Pet 4:11).

6. In 1 Cor 8:6, Paul reflects the Shema ("Hear, O Israel: The LORD our God, the LORD is one"): "For us there is one God, the Father, from whom are all things and for whom we exist." Cf. Eph 3:14; 4:6; Heb 12:9; James 1:17.

Jesus' Preaching Aims at the Glory of His Father

According to Mark, Jesus proclaimed "the good news of *God*, and saying, 'The time is fulfilled, and the kingdom of *God* has come near'" (1:14). Jesus taught his disciples to pray for God's glory and kingdom: "Our Father in heaven, hallowed be your name. Your kingdom come. Your will be done, on earth as it is in heaven" (Matt 6:9-10).

In his Gospel, John especially highlights Jesus' mission to reveal his Father. He begins with, "No one has ever seen God. It is God the only Son, who is close to the Father's heart, who has made him known" (John 1:18). Then we hear Jesus say, "No one can come to me unless drawn by the Father who sent me . . ." (John 6:44). Later Jesus asserts, "Whoever believes in me believes not in me but in him who sent me. And whoever sees me sees him who sent me" (John 12:44-45; cf. 12:49; 14:10). Then Jesus announces, "I am the way, and the truth, and the life. No one comes to the Father except through me" (John 14:6). In that context Jesus says, "Whoever has seen me has seen the Father. How can you say, 'Show us the Father'? Do you not believe that I am in the Father and the Father is in me?"[7] Jesus continues to assure his disciples, "I will do whatever you ask in my name, so that the Father may be glorified in the Son" (John 14:13). At the end of his life on earth, Jesus prays, "Father, the hour has come; glorify your Son so that the Son may glorify you" (John 17:1). And Jesus concludes, "This is eternal life, that they may know you, the only true God, and Jesus Christ whom you have sent. I glorified you on earth by finishing the work that you gave me to do" (John 17:3-4; cf. 7:16-18; 8:49-50).

After examining many New Testament passages "which are normally understood to present a 'high' Christology," James Dunn comes to the conclusion that "the Christian gospel has to do first and last and foremost with God. . . . Christian faith is primarily faith in the one God, Creator, Savior, Judge. . . . The writers [of the New Testament] had no thought to present Christ as an alternative to God, as an object sufficient in himself of Christian worship. . . . Worship which stops at him and does not pass through him to God, the all in all, at the end of the day falls short of Christian worship."[8]

---

7. John 14:9; cf. 10:30; 10:38; 14:10-11; 17:21; 1 John 2:23.

8. Dunn, "Christology as an Aspect of Theology," 212. Cf. Craddock, *Pre-Existence*, 156-57, "With all the rich variety in the New Testament Christological affirmations, there is through it all a common factor: the message about Jesus was presented in such a way as to permit the Essence, the Ultimate, God, to be seen in and through the account of a saying or an event. After all, the interest in Jesus was precisely this: What was *God* saying or doing here?"

Our Christ-Centered Preaching
Must Aim at the Glory of God

The New Testament indisputably teaches the principle that Christ-centered preaching must converge on God. In Romans Paul asks the well-known series of questions about preaching: "But how are they to call on one in whom they have not believed? And how are they to believe in one of whom they have never heard? And how are they to hear without someone to proclaim him? And how are they to proclaim him unless they are sent? As it is written, 'How beautiful are the feet of those who bring good news!'" (10:14-15). What is that good news? The quotation is from Isaiah, and the good news is, "Your God reigns" (Isa 52:7). Your God reigns! John Piper quotes Cotton Mather, who said three hundred years ago, "The great design and intention of the office of a Christian preacher [is] to restore the throne and dominion of God in the souls of men." And Piper asks, "Is this what people take away from worship nowadays — a sense of God, a note of sovereign grace, a theme of panoramic glory, the grand object of God's infinite Being? Do they enter for one hour in the week . . . into an atmosphere of the holiness of God which leaves its aroma upon their lives all week long?"[9] New Testament writers as well as Jesus himself clearly teach us that Christ-centered preaching must aim at the glory of God.

Concern about Preaching the Holy Spirit

With the focus on preaching Christ to the glory of the Father, some have raised the concern that we may not be doing justice to the third person of the Trinity, the Holy Spirit. They advocate not Christ-centered preaching or God-centered preaching but "trinitarian preaching." For example, Johann Le Roux contends that "every sermon should bear witness to the Father and the Son and the Holy Spirit as the one singular God, who while being one, is at the same time three distinguishable Persons."[10]

We should acknowledge, of course, the crucial role of the Holy

9. Piper, *Supremacy of God in Preaching*, 22. Cf. 20, "My burden is to plead for the supremacy of God in preaching — that the dominant note of preaching be the freedom of God's sovereign grace, the unifying theme be the zeal that God has for his own glory, the grand object of preaching be the infinite and inexhaustible being of God, and the pervasive atmosphere of preaching be the holiness of God." Cf. Ridderbos, *Coming of the Kingdom*, 22.

10. Le Roux, "Betekenis," 257; see esp. 183-204. See also K. Dijk, *De Dienst der Prediking* (Kampen: Kok, 1955), 83-87.

Spirit in inspiring the biblical authors and in illumining contemporary preachers and hearers; we should further acknowledge the vital role of the Holy Spirit in our salvation: regeneration, conversion, faith, sanctification. However, neither the important role of the Holy Spirit nor our faith in the triune God requires that every sermon give more or less equal time to each person in the Godhead. Not systematic theology but the preaching-text determines the focus of the sermon. Systematic theology functions as the "rule of faith" which sets the boundaries of valid interpretation; but only the text — understood in its biblical and redemptive historical contexts — provides the focus of the sermon. Accordingly, if a congregation needs to hear more about the work of the Holy Spirit, one should select a preaching-text that focusses primarily on the Holy Spirit.[11] But one places unnecessary burdens on preachers by requiring that "every sermon should bear witness to the Father and the Son and the Holy Spirit." The New Testament letters do not even do this in their opening greetings and concluding benedictions.[12] Moreover, the New Testament teaches that the Spirit does not call attention to himself but desires to glorify Christ and the Father. Jesus says, "The Spirit of truth . . . will glorify me, because he will take what is mine and declare it to you. All that the Father has is mine. For this reason I said that he will take what is mine and declare it to you" (John 16:13-15).

INTERPRET THE OLD TESTAMENT
FROM THE REALITY OF CHRIST

Over against the extreme of Christomonism in preaching, we have observed the New Testament principle that Christ-centered preaching must be God-centered. The opposite extreme, which may be even more prevalent today, is that of preaching the Old Testament in a God-centered way without relating it to God's ultimate revelation of himself in Jesus Christ. Over against this extreme, the New Testament offers the corrective that Christian preaching must be Christ-centered. Some have argued that God-centered preaching meets this requirement because Christ is God.

---

11. The focus on the Holy Spirit, of course, is connected with the Father as well as the Son. See, e.g., John 14:26 and Rom 8:9-10.

12. None of the twelve letters has an opening greeting using the words "the Holy Spirit": eleven open with the greeting, "Grace to you and peace from God our Father and the Lord Jesus Christ," and Colossians opens with, "Grace to you and peace from God our Father." Out of the twelve possibilities, the closing benediction mentions the Holy Spirit only once: "The grace of the Lord Jesus Christ, the love of God, and the communion of the Holy Spirit be with all of you" (2 Cor 13:13).

But, as we saw earlier, this position sidesteps the New Testament principle that preaching Christ is preaching Christ incarnate. Moreover, this
general God-centered preaching feeds into the contemporary inclination
of making the Christian faith less distinctive than it is in order to connect
with other people who also believe in God. Raymond Brown, for one, objects: "We Christians are a people whose definition comes, not simply in
terms of what we say about God, but in terms of what we say about Jesus,
precisely because we think that we cannot understand God unless we understand who Jesus was and is."[13] What is more, Jesus himself claimed,
"No one comes to the Father except through me. . . . Whoever has seen
me has seen the Father" (John 14:6, 9). God's redemptive activity and
self-revelation reach a climax in the death and resurrection of Jesus. "It is
here that God's Self-disclosure bursts forth with unexcelled and unprecedented clarity."[14] The issue we need to resolve, therefore, is how to
preach Christ incarnate from the Old Testament.

Richard Lischer asserts, "Christian preaching was born in the resurrection of Jesus."[15] Although we may agree with this statement, when we
think of preaching Christ from the *Old* Testament, we tend to move automatically from the past to the present:

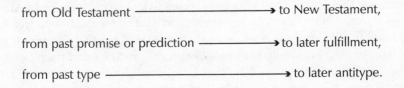

from Old Testament ⎯⎯⎯⎯⎯⎯⎯→ to New Testament,

from past promise or prediction ⎯⎯⎯⎯→ to later fulfillment,

from past type ⎯⎯⎯⎯⎯⎯⎯⎯⎯→ to later antitype.

Some time ago, while reflecting on the various ways in which we can
preach Christ from the Old Testament, I asked myself, What if we reversed directions? What if we moved from Christ as we know him from
the New Testament to the Old Testament? At the time it seemed like a
revolutionary paradigm shift. An obvious danger is that we would simply be reading the Christ of the New Testament back into the Old Testament. But I soon realized that I was in good company because this is precisely the way the apostles and Gospel writers preached Christ from the
Old Testament: they started from the reality of Jesus Christ.

---

13. Brown, *Biblical Exegesis and Church Doctrine*, 140.
14. Robert Mounce, *Essential Nature*, 152.
15. Lischer, *Theology of Preaching*, 30.

Understanding the Old Testament
from the Reality of Christ

Most of the writers of the New Testament had lived with Jesus for three years, had heard his preaching, had marveled at his miracles, had been devastated by his crucifixion, and then had been stunned at meeting the living Lord in person. Luke records that at first they still did not catch on to what had really happened. Two of Jesus' disciples were sad and hopeless when he met them on the road to Emmaus. Jesus chided them, "Oh, how foolish you are, and how slow of heart to believe all that the prophets have declared! Was it not necessary that the Messiah should suffer these things and then enter into his glory?" (Luke 24:25-26). Still they did not catch on. But then, as Jesus was breaking bread with them, just as he had done three days earlier, "their eyes were opened and they recognized him" (Luke 24:31). That same evening Jesus met his disciples and "opened their minds to understand the scriptures, and he said to them, 'Thus it is written, that the Messiah is to suffer and to rise from the dead on the third day, and that repentance and forgiveness of sins is to be proclaimed in his name to all nations. . . . And they worshiped him . . ." (Luke 24:45-47, 52). Jesus' disciples finally fathomed the incredible truth that the crucified Jesus was God's promised Messiah and the living Lord. From that faith perspective the disciples looked back at the Old Testament and saw numerous references to the Jesus they knew. In other words, they now read the Old Testament in the light of their knowledge of Jesus Christ, the crucified and risen Lord.

A few days after my pondering of the paradigm shift — from past to present, to present to past — I witnessed a perfect illustration of this shift. At the time I was doing research in South Africa, and a relative offered to show us some of the gorgeous scenery. He drove us to a "dam" (man-made lake) which supplies water to Cape Town. As we drove to the dam through a scenic valley, everything looked green. To my surprise, on our return trip a half hour later the whole valley looked white, for it was covered with white flowers. Astonished, I wondered why I had missed seeing these flowers on our way up. I turned around and amazingly saw mostly green scenery, just a hint of a flower here and there; I looked ahead and again was surprised to see the whole valley white with flowers. Why was it that the valley appeared green when we traveled west, and white when we traveled east? The valley, I learned, was covered with flowers that turn toward the sun. When we drove west into the sun we saw the green backside of the flowers, but when we reversed course and had the sun behind us, we saw all the flowers pointing at the sun.

That is the way it was for Jesus' disciples. When they used to read the Old Testament, from past to present or future, they saw some indications of the coming Messiah but not the complete picture. But after Jesus' resurrection, when they read the Old Testament in the light of their crucified and risen Lord, the whole Old Testament lit up like the White House Christmas tree, "a thousand points of light" pointing to Jesus the Messiah. That is how they preached Christ from the Old Testament: they read it from the perspective of their risen Lord and found it filled with promises of Christ, types of Christ, references and allusions to Jesus Christ.[16] As Peter said to the Gentiles in the house of Cornelius, "All the prophets testify about him [Jesus Christ]" (Acts 10:43). Given this spontaneous, Christ-centered use of the Old Testament, we should not expect the writers of the New Testament to provide us with a carefully worked out hermeneutical method for interpreting the Old Testament.

New Testament Use of the Old Testament

The New Testament writers frequently quote or allude to the Old Testament. Henry Shires has calculated that "there are at least 1,604 N.T. citations of 1,276 different O.T. passages. To this total could be added several thousand more N.T. passages that clearly allude to or reflect O.T. verses."[17] An even more telling statistic is that 229 of the 260 chapters in the New Testament have each "at least two citations of or specific references to the O.T.," and another 19 chapters have one instance, leaving only 12 chapters in the entire New Testament without a specific reference to the Old Testament.[18] From another angle, it has been calculated that "32 percent . . . of the New Testament is composed of Old Testament quotations and allusions."[19]

What puzzles scholars is not that New Testament writers frequently use the Old Testament but *how* they use it. Hundreds of books and articles have been written on this topic, with no agreement in sight. Some argue that the New Testament writers used a rabbinic form of interpretation which is not normative for today. Others contend that since the New

16. Cf. von Rad, *Old Testament Theology*, 2.328-29, "The New Testament . . . is absolutely permeated with a sense of wonder at the advent of a tremendous new event, an overwhelming awareness of standing at a new beginning from which entirely new horizons of God's saving activity have become visible: the kingdom of God is here. . . . The Old Testament was now read as a divine revelation which was the precursor of Christ's advent, and was full of pointers towards the coming of the Lord; and this led to a completely new interpretation of the Old Testament."

17. Shires, *Finding the Old Testament in the New*, 15.

18. Ibid., 122.

19. Andrew E. Hill, *A Survey of the Old Testament* (Grand Rapids: Zondervan, 1991), 435. For other calculations and references, see pp. 50-51 above.

Testament writers were inspired, they offer the definitive interpretation of Old Testament passages and their method is normative for Christians today. Still others hold that the New Testament writers used the Old Testament in an impromptu way.[20] We shall first examine the influence of Jewish methods of interpretation.

Influence of Jewish Methods of Interpretation

Most New Testament scholars today hold that the New Testament writers were influenced by the methods of interpretation current in Jewish circles.[21] The influence of Jewish methods is not surprising, of course, since most of the New Testament writers were Jews.[22] Awareness of Jewish methods of interpretation can help us better understand the way the New Testament sometimes cites or alludes to Old Testament passages and interprets them.

Scholars have identified several methods of Jewish interpretation:

1. *Peshat* — "a literalist type of exegesis. . . . The natural meaning of the text is applied to the lives of the people — particularly in applying deuteronomic legislation."[23]
2. *Targum* — "a paraphrase or explanatory translation."[24]
3. *Midrash* — an exposition of a passage "whose aim is to bring out the relevance of the sacred text to the present."[25]
4. *Pesher* — a more focussed interpretation than *midrash;* "it refers to exposition of texts that sees in them eschatological fulfillment in the current era."[26]

20. For example, Barnabas Lindars, "The Place of the Old Testament in the Formation of New Testament Theology," *NTS* 23 (1977) 64, writes, "Believing that Christ is the fulfillment of the promises of God, and that they are living in the age to which all the scriptures refer, they employ the Old Testament in an *ad hoc* way, making recourse to it just when and how they find it helpful for their purposes." Cf. von Rad, *Old Testament Theology,* 2.230-32.

21. G. C. Berkouwer, *Heilige Schrift,* 2 (Kampen: Kok, 1967), 172, states, "This insight has become practically a *communis opinio.*"

22. "The Jewish roots of Christianity make it *a priori* likely that the exegetical procedures of the NT would resemble to some extent those of then contemporary Judaism." Richard Longenecker, *Themelios* 13 (1987) 7.

23. Ibid., 6.

24. James Dunn, "The Use of the Old Testament," 83.

25. Ibid., 84. Cf. Longenecker, *Biblical Exegesis in the Apostolic Period,* 114-26; David Dockery, *Biblical Interpretation,* 29-30.

26. Darrell Bock, "Use of the OT in the New," 101. Cf. Longenecker, *Biblical Exegesis,* 129-32.

5. Typology — interpretation which sees "a correspondence between people and events of the past and of the future (or present)."[27]
6. Allegory — "a more extreme form of midrash" which "regards the text as a sort of code or cipher" which must be decoded to get at the deeper meaning.[28]

Some scholars detect all of the above methods of interpretation in the New Testament,[29] while others argue that "one would be hard-pressed to find an exegetical example in Paul's writings that is distinctively rabbinic, that is, some technique that could not be paralleled elsewhere."[30]

Another major point of contention among scholars is whether New Testament writers ever use allegorical interpretation. The general consensus is that they do so minimally, if at all. James Dunn claims that in the New Testament, "the only really clear examples are 1 Cor 10:1-4, Gal 4:22-31 and probably 2 Cor 3:7-18," but the latter belongs "more closely" to midrash.[31] Richard Longenecker sees 1 Corinthians 10:1-4 ("the rock was Christ") as midrash, possibly recalling "the rabbinic legend of a following rock."[32] He agrees that Galatians 4:22-31 (Paul's "allegory" of Hagar and Sarah being two covenants) is allegorical interpretation, and adds 1 Corinthians 9:9 ("You shall not muzzle an ox while it is treading out the grain").[33] Others argue that Galatians 4:22-31 involves typological interpretation[34] and that in 1 Corinthians 9:9-10 Paul employs a "*qal vahomer* argument (argument from the lighter to the heavier)," which would make it midrash.[35]

27. Dunn, "The Use of the Old Testament," 86.

28. Ibid., 86-97, 90-91.

29. See, e.g., the scholars mentioned by Childs, *Biblical Theology*, 237-43, concerning Paul's use of the Old Testament.

30. Moisés Silva, "Old Testament in Paul," in *Dictionary of Paul and His Letters*, ed. G. F. Hawthorne and R. P. Martin (Downers Grove, IL: InterVarsity, 1993), 637. But Silva also states (p. 638), "Increased familiarity with first-century Jewish interpretation is of inestimable help, at least in a general way, as we seek to appreciate Paul's use of Scripture."

31. Dunn, "The Use of the Old Testament," 90-91.

32. Longenecker, *Biblical Exegesis*, 119-20. For contrary opinions, see Goppelt, *Typos*, 145-46, and Kaiser and Silva, *Introduction*, 217-18.

33. Ibid., 126-27.

34. See, e.g., Leonhard Goppelt, *Typos*, 139-40; and Donald Hagner, "The Old Testament in the New Testament," in *Interpreting the Word of God*, ed. S. J. Schultz and M. A. Inch (Chicago: Moody, 1976), 101.

35. Donald Juel, *Messianic Exegesis*, 56. See also Walter C. Kaiser, "The Current Crisis in Exegesis and the Apostolic Use of Deuteronomy 25:4 in 1 Corinthians 9:8-10,"

Of course, even if Paul used allegorical interpretation to convince those who put stock in it, that would be no license (let alone requirement) for contemporary preachers to do so, as Origen argued. Suppose one illustrates a sermon on the presence of the kingdom of God (e.g., Luke 11:20) with an "allegory" of the Second World War: D-day is Christ's first coming to establish the kingdom of God as a beachhead on planet earth (the allies landing in Normandy = Christ's first coming), but the kingdom will not be complete till V-day (Victory day = Christ's second coming). This is only an illustration of the already and not yet of the kingdom of God. It is not intended as an interpretation of the meaning of D-day in World War II. Similarly, Paul's illustration of Hagar and Sarah, even if allegorical, offers no warrant for interpreting Genesis 21 allegorically. As Theodore of Mopsuestia said 1600 years ago, it is only an illustration.[36]

Unfortunately, some interpreters have exploited the use of Jewish methods of interpretation in the New Testament to undermine its reliability. New Testament interpretations of the Old Testament are then characterized as "rabbinic" in the sense of fanciful and forced exegesis. But this creates a false impression. I. Howard Marshall points out that the New Testament usually interprets the Old Testament in a "straightforward 'literal' manner when reference is being made to events described in it," when dealing with Old Testament commands, and when asserting fulfillment of Old Testament promises. But, he observes, "this use is so 'obvious' that it is often passed over without comment."[37] Naturally, "passing over" the many literal interpretations in the New Testament would skew the overall picture. Henry Shires states, "The great bulk of the quotations are careful reproductions or translations of the original Scripture. In most instances the historical sense is carefully preserved, and often the source of the quotation is accurately acknowledged even though such reference was not the normal practice at that time."[38]

Although awareness of contemporary Jewish methods of interpretation may be helpful at times in understanding the argument of the New

---

JETS 21/1 (1978) 3-18. On p. 14 Kaiser quotes F. Godet: "Paul does not in the least allegorize. . . . From the literal and natural meaning of the precept he disentangles a profound truth, a law of humanity and equity."

36. See pp. 92-93.

37. Marshall, "Assessment of Recent Developments," 10.

38. Shires, Finding the Old Testament, 38. Cf. Jack Weir, Perspectives in Religious Studies 9 (1982) 67, with references to Fitzmyer, NTS 7 (1961) 305, 330-31, "In general, according to Joseph A. Fitzmyer, the Old Testament quotations in the New Testament have exactly the same meanings as they did in their original contexts." Cf. Kaiser, Uses of the Old Testament in the New, 228-30.

Testament authors, we need to be aware of the danger of focussing so much on rabbinic methods that we overlook the uniqueness of the interpretation of New Testament writers. Richard Hays points out, "Even when Paul does occasionally use such tropes in ways that bear a certain formal affinity to rabbinic practice, as, for example, in Romans 4, the material uses to which he puts Scripture differ fundamentally from those of the rabbis; his hermeneutic is materially informed by his Christian convictions much more than by some list of approved hermeneutical procedures. The message that Paul finds in the Old Testament is the gospel of Jesus Christ. . . ."[39] After a lengthy study of Jewish methods of interpretation, Richard Longenecker comes to a similar conclusion: "There is little indication in the New Testament that the authors themselves were conscious of varieties of exegetical genre or of following particular modes of interpretation. . . . What the New Testament writers are conscious of, however, is interpreting the Old Testament (1) from a Christocentric perspective, (2) in conformity with a Christian tradition, and (3) along Christological lines."[40] It is this christocentric approach that makes New Testament interpretation unique.

The New Testament Not a Textbook on Biblical Hermeneutics

As we noted earlier, the New Testament writers did not set out to produce a textbook on biblical hermeneutics. Simply to copy their methods of interpretation in preaching on specific Old Testament passages is to go beyond their intent.[41] Their concern clearly was to preach Christ from the Old Tes-

---

39. Hays, *Echoes*, 13.

40. Longenecker, *Biblical Exegesis*, 206. Cf. p. 207, "The Jewish context in which the NT came to birth, significant though it was, is not what was distinctive or formative in the exegesis of the earliest believers. At the heart of their biblical interpretation is a Christology and Christocentric perspective." Cf. E. Earle Ellis, "Biblical Interpretation in the New Testament Church," 724, "In one fundamental respect it [the New Testament church] differed from other religious parties and theologies in Judaism, that is, in the christological exposition of the OT totally focused upon Jesus as the Messiah. This decisively influences both the perspective from which they expound the OT and the way in which their presuppositions are brought to bear upon the specific biblical texts."

41. See my *Sola Scriptura*, 107-13. Cf. Andrew Bandstra, *CTJ* 6 (1971) 20, "Neither the Bible as a whole nor the New Testament in particular was meant to be a textbook on the science of hermeneutics. It is meant to be proclamation which centers in creation, fall, and redemption. To proclaim their message the authors of the NT use and interpret the Old, but in so doing they do not intend to lay down hermeneutical rules. To use the NT in such a fashion would be putting it to a use for which it was not intended." Cf. Norman Ericson, *JETS* 30 (1987) 338, "The apostolic purposes were imme-

tament, and they did so in ways that were current at that time. Many of these ways still work today, but others do not. This became clear to us already in Paul's use of Sarah and Hagar as "an allegory" (Gal 4). If we were to preach the story of Sarah and Hagar (Gen 21) guided by Paul's use in Galatians 4, we would miss the point of the Old Testament story.

Already the first chapter of the New Testament demonstrates the impossibility of indiscriminately copying New Testament interpretation. Here Matthew preaches Christ with a striking genealogy of Jesus: "So all the generations from Abraham to David are fourteen generations; and from David to the deportation to Babylon, fourteen generations; and from the deportation to Babylon to the Messiah, fourteen generations" (1:17). We should know that fourteen is the numerical value in Hebrew of the name "David," that is, DVD. Matthew starts tracing the line of redemptive history with Abraham, and number fourteen in the line of generations is the great king David himself. But then things go downhill: the next number fourteen ("Jeconiah, the captive," 1 Chron 3:17) finds himself in exile in Babylon. The kingdom may be gone, but at least the house of David is still alive. More generations come and go, and again we arrive at a number fourteen, another David, Jesus, "who is called the Messiah" (1:16). Clearly, Matthew is trying to persuade the Jews that Jesus of Nazareth is the great son of David, the Messiah. Although the device of three times fourteen is not persuasive today as it was in Matthew's time,[42] we can still use Matthew 1 to preach the message that Jesus is the promised son of David. But suppose we would take as our preaching-text 1 Chronicles 3:1-17, the second string of fourteen mentioned by Matthew. Although we can still preach God's faithfulness in keeping the house of David alive, even through severe judgment, we cannot use Matthew's number fourteen — David. For the text lists not fourteen names from David to Jeconiah but eighteen.

Longenecker advises, "We should not attempt to reproduce their midrashic handling of the text, their allegorical explications, or much of their Jewish manner of argumentation. All of this is strictly part of the cultural context through which the transcultural and eternal gospel was expressed."[43] But he does not totally reject New Testament interpretation of the Old Testament as a guide for our interpretation. He asks, "Can we reproduce the exegesis of the New Testament?" He answers both No and

---

diate and pragmatic rather than an historical-grammatical interpretation of the Hebrew canon for academic purposes." Cf. H. C. Van Zyl, *Fax Theologica* 6/1 (1986) 65-74.

42. Some commentators argue that because 3 × 14 = 6 × 7, therefore Jesus ushers in the 7th period of 7, which leads to the full sabbath rest.

43. Longenecker, *Biblical Exegesis*, 218.

Yes. "Where that exegesis is based upon a revelatory stance, where it evidences itself to be merely cultural, or where it shows itself to be circumstantial or *ad hominem* in nature 'No.' Where, however, it treats the Old Testament in more literal fashion, following the course of what we speak of today as historico-grammatical exegesis 'Yes.' Our commitment as Christians is to the reproduction of the apostolic faith and doctrine, and not necessarily to the specific apostolic exegetical practices."[44]

Although Matthew 1 and Galatians 4 make clear that today we cannot copy the New Testament writers in all of their "exegetical" moves, this does not mean that the New Testament cannot guide us in developing a method for preaching Christ from the Old Testament. It just means that we have to dig a little deeper than the surface features and inquire first into New Testament presuppositions that support its christocentric use of the Old Testament.

New Testament Presuppositions for Interpreting the Old Testament

The New Testament reveals several foundational presuppositions for interpreting the Old Testament christocentrically. The first and most encompassing presupposition concerns redemptive history.

God Progressively Works Out His Redemptive Plan in History

A major New Testament presupposition for interpreting the Old Testament is that God acts uniformly but progressively in redemptive history.

---

44. Ibid., 219. In *Themelios* 13 (1987) 8, Longenecker gives some examples of the "more circumstantial and *ad hominem*" interpretations: "Paul's catena of polemically motivated passages in Gal. 3:10-13, or his argument on the generic 'seed' in Gal. 3:16, or his allegorical treatment of Hagar and Sarah and their sons in Gal. 4:21-31." Already in 1938, J. L. Koole, *De Overname*, 11-14, warned against viewing New Testament interpretations of the Old Testament as normative for our interpretation of the Old Testament. He wrote, "One may highly value the NT exegesis of the OT, but one may certainly not consider it entirely normative for our present-day exegesis." He gave two reasons: First, the New Testament use of the Old Testament is a child of its time; second, our belief in the inspiration of the New Testament writers forbids our usurpation of their methods as if we could discover profound truths in the Old Testament the way they did. In 1960 he refined his viewpoint by saying, "I would rather no longer speak here [e.g., Matt 2:15] of an exegesis of the OT by the NT (as I did in my dissertation) but of a *usus*, a use of the OT by the NT." See my *Sola Scriptura*, 109-10.

According to C. H. Dodd, "the New Testament writers . . . interpret and apply the prophecies of the Old Testament upon the basis of a certain understanding of history, which is substantially that of the prophets themselves." According to this understanding, "history . . . is built upon a certain pattern corresponding to God's design for man His creature. It is . . . a kind of master-plan imposed upon the order of human life in this world by the Creator Himself, a plan which man is not at liberty to alter, but within which his freedom works. It is this pattern, disclosed 'in divers parts and divers manners' in the past history of Israel, that the New Testament writers conceive to have been brought into full light in the events of the gospel story, which they interpret accordingly."[45]

The New Testament writers initially had learned about God's master-plan from the Old Testament itself.[46] In broad strokes, it began "in the beginning" when God created a peaceful and righteous world where he would be honored and obeyed as the sovereign King (Gen 1–2). But the fall into sin changed all that: evil, enmity, and violence spread across the world (Gen 3–6). Ever since that time, God has been working to restore his peaceable kingdom on earth with his acts of redemption and judgment and by making covenant with various individuals and their offspring: Noah, Abraham, Israel, David. Annually, when they offered God their firstfruits, the Israelites were required to confess God's mighty acts of redemption. They were to say:

> A wandering Aramean was my ancestor; he went down into Egypt and lived there as an alien, few in number, and there became a great nation, mighty and populous. When the Egyptians treated us harshly and afflicted us, by imposing hard labor on us, we cried to the Lord, the God of our ancestors; the Lord heard our voice and saw our affliction, our toil, and our oppression. The Lord brought us out of Egypt with a mighty hand and an outstretched arm, with a terrifying display of power, and with signs and wonders; and he brought us to this place and gave us this land, a land flowing with milk and honey. (Deut 26:5-9)

45. Dodd, *According to the Scriptures*, 128. Cf. Floyd Filson, *Int* 5 (1951) 148, "In one way or another we are forced to a view which sees in the Bible the unity of a connected and divinely directed history in which 'the purpose of God,' as Suzanne de Dietrich has called it, is being worked out. It is all one history; it is all God's working; it all finds its center in Christ."

46. John Bright, *Authority*, 130, "The genius of the Old Testament faith . . . lies in its understanding of history, specifically of Israel's history, as the theater of God's purposive activity."

In Psalms 78, 105, and 106 Israel continued to recite God's mighty deeds of deliverance. "Psalm 78 is noteworthy not merely for the amplification of the story of the Exodus, the wilderness and the settlement but also because it carries the recital on to the establishment of David and his dynasty on Mount Zion: in this the psalmist sees the climax of God's mighty acts on His people's behalf."[47]

Other Psalms expanded this vision by picking up ancient themes of God's sovereignty not only over Israel but over the *whole earth*. Moses had said to Pharaoh, "There will be no more hail, so that you may know that the earth is the Lord's [Yahweh's]" (Exod 9:29; cf. 19:5). And after the Lord defeated Pharaoh and his army, Moses sang, "The Lord will reign *forever and ever*" (Exod 15:18). The Psalms picked up these themes of Yahweh's rule extending across both space and time. For example, Psalm 96:13 declared that Yahweh "is coming to judge the *earth*. He will judge the world with righteousness, and the peoples with his truth."[48] And Psalm 145:13 proclaimed, "Your kingdom is an *everlasting* kingdom, and your dominion endures throughout all generations."

The prophets continued the proclamation of these messages about Yahweh's rule. Isaiah prophesied that "all nations shall stream . . . to the mountain of the Lord . . . ; that he may teach us his ways and that we may walk in his paths" (2:2-3). Micah proclaimed the same message, but he soon focussed it on Bethlehem, from which will come forth "one who is to rule in Israel, whose origin is from of old, from ancient days. . . . And he shall stand and feed his flock in the strength of the Lord. . . . And they shall live secure, for now he shall be great to the ends of the earth; and he shall be the one of peace" (4:2-5; 5:2-5; cf. Zech 9:10). Subsequently God's prophets began to announce a complete restoration of creation:

> I am about to create new heavens and a new earth. . . .
> They shall not labor in vain, or bear children for calamity. . . .
> The wolf and the lamb shall feed together,
>   the lion shall eat straw like the ox. . . .
> They shall not hurt or destroy on all my holy mountain.
>
> (Isa 65:17-25)

---

47. F. F. Bruce, *New Testament Development*, 37.

48. Christopher Wright, *Knowing Jesus*, 249, suggests that "'putting things right' is probably the best way to catch what the Hebrew means by 'he comes to judge.' It does not just mean 'to condemn'. . . . Since the coming of God is made the subject of universal rejoicing, it must also include the idea of God re-establishing his original desire and design for his world, in which the liberation of the peoples will spell joy for nature also (cf. Rom 8:19-25)."

The blueprint of all of redemptive history is found in the Old Testament: Creation–Fall–Redemption–New Creation.

Finally, Jesus came and claimed to be the one who fulfilled the prophecy of Isaiah 61, "The Spirit of the Lord is upon me, because he has anointed me . . . to proclaim the year of the Lord's favor. . . . Today this scripture has been fulfilled in your hearing" (Luke 4:18-21). Jesus would restore peace and harmony in the world; he would bring in the Year of Jubilee. And he did inaugurate this new age with his preaching, his miracles, and his death and resurrection. He invited people to enter the kingdom of God by submitting themselves "to the rule of God."[49] But Jesus' coming was only the beginning. When he comes again, the prophecy of Isaiah 65 about the new creation will be completely filled up, paradise will be restored on earth, the way God intended it from the beginning (see Rev 21–22).

Some scholars have rightly claimed that "Jesus and the apostles had an unparalleled redemptive-historical perspective on the Old Testament in relation to their own situation. . . ."[50] The early Christians did not search the Old Testament for some fanciful prooftexts concerning Jesus, says Donald Miller. "They believed that the God who had acted in him was the same God who acted in the Exodus recorded in the Old Testament and in all the events which flowed from it in the history of Israel. They believed that this God had the end in view from the beginning." He likens God's design in redemptive history to a play. "As a playwright works into the earlier scenes of his play certain ideas which are only perplexing at the time they are introduced, but which are made clear as one looks back to them from the standpoint of the climax, God was working into the earlier acts of the drama of redemption elements which, when recapitulated in a higher key in Jesus, received a clarity which they did not have in their original setting."[51]

We can picture God's master-plan of redemptive history as follows:[52]

---

49. See ibid., 247-48, "To enter the Kingdom of God means to submit oneself to the rule of God and that means a fundamental reorientation of one's ethical commitments and values into line with the priorities and character of the God revealed in the scriptures." Cf. Isa 2:3 above, "that we may walk in his paths."

50. G. K. Beale, *Themelios* 14 (1989) 90. Cf. A. T. Hanson, *Living Utterances*, 183, "What all the New Testament writers have in common as far as concerns the interpretation of scripture is a belief in salvation history and a christocentric approach."

51. Miller, *Way to Biblical Preaching*, 134.

52. See Oscar Cullmann, *Christ and Time*, 116-17: "Thus down to Jesus Christ the redemptive history unfolds in the . . . sense of a progressive reduction: mankind–people of Israel–remnant of Israel–the One, Christ. . . . From the center reached in the res-

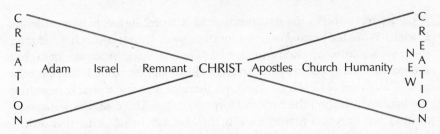

Because God progressively works out his redemptive plan in human history, the New Testament writers can preach Christ from the Old Testament as the culmination of a long series of redemptive acts. Moreover, because God works out his redemptive plan in regular patterns, the New Testament writers can detect correspondences between God's act in Jesus and God's redemptive acts in the past. Thus God acting in redemptive history also becomes the foundation for New Testament typological interpretation.

Jesus Inaugurated the Messianic Age

A second presupposition of the New Testament writers is the conviction that Jesus ushered in the messianic or kingdom age. Earle Ellis explains: "Jesus and his disciples conceive of history within the framework of two ages, this age and the age to come. This perspective appears to have its background in the Old Testament prophets, who prophesied of 'the last days' and 'the day of the Lord' as the time of an ultimate redemption."[53] The New Testament writers were convinced that Jesus' coming signaled the beginning of "the last days." At Pentecost, Peter proclaimed, "This is what was spoken through the prophet Joel: 'In the last days it will be. . . .'"[54] The fact that Peter changed Joel's "afterward" (Joel 2:28) to "in the last days" makes the point even more deliberate: Jesus ushered in the last days.

The disciples had learned this conviction of having entered "the last days" from Jesus himself. Mark relates that Jesus began his ministry preaching, "The time is fulfilled, and the kingdom of God has come near" (1:15). This was sensational news. The messianic kingdom, for which

---

urrection of Christ the way . . . leads . . . from the One, in progressive advance, to the many."

53. Ellis, "How the New Testament Uses the Old," 209.

54. Acts 2:16-17. Later Peter writes about Christ, "He was destined before the foundation of the world, but was revealed at the end of the ages for your sake" (1 Pet 1:20). Cf. 1 Cor 10:11; Heb 9:26; and 1 John 2:18.

people had longed for generations, had arrived in the person of Jesus Christ. "What they knew as a matter of hope in worship was now among them as a matter of reality in person. The eschatological was breaking into history. God had come to reign."[55] Jesus demonstrated the presence of the kingdom of God by casting out demons, healing the sick, restoring the maimed, feeding the hungry, forgiving sins. The disciples witnessed all this and believed that Jesus was the Messiah — until he died on the cross and all their hopes were shattered. But then Jesus rose from the dead and explained to them from the prophets that it was "necessary that the Messiah should suffer these things and then enter into his glory" (Luke 24:26). Jesus' resurrection was more than the astounding miracle of a dead person returning to life; Jesus' resurrection confirmed that God had indeed brought in the new age.[56]

The conviction that Jesus inaugurated the messianic age enables the New Testament writers to preach Christ from the Old Testament, for this presupposition means that God's redemptive history reaches its climax in Jesus. In him all the Old Testament promises come to fulfillment. As R. T. France puts it, "The earthly life and future glory of Jesus of Nazareth is presented as the fulfillment of the Old Testament hopes of the day of Yahweh. . . . The coming of Jesus is that decisive act of God to which the Old Testament looked forward, and in his coming all the hopes of the Old Testament are fulfilled; the last days have come."[57]

Jesus Is Eternal God

A third presupposition of the New Testament writers is that Jesus is truly God and as Son of God has existed with God the Father from all eternity. John begins his Gospel with the familiar allusion to Genesis 1:1, "In the beginning was the Word [*logos*], and the Word was with God, and the Word was God. . . . All things came into being through him, and without him not one thing came into being" (John 1:1, 3; cf. 3:13; 17:5). Thus John sees Christ at work in the beginning, present and active in God's work of

---

55. Christopher Wright, *Knowing Jesus,* 250. Cf. W. D. Davies, *Invitation to the New Testament,* 149-60; John Bright, *The Kingdom of God,* 187-243; N. T. Wright, *Jesus and the Victory of God,* 198-229.

56. Ralph P. Martin, *The Worship of God* (Grand Rapids: Eerdmans, 1982), 105. Cf. Robert H. Mounce, *Essential Nature,* 39: "The uniqueness of the Kingdom lay not only in that it had become a present reality, but also in that it was redemptive action. In and through Jesus Christ, God's timeless sovereignty was invading history and victoriously waging redemptive warfare against the evil powers. The kingdom of God had come."

57. France, *Jesus and the Old Testament,* 161.

creation. In John 8:56-58, we hear Jesus tell the Jews that he was present at the time of Abraham: "'Your ancestor Abraham rejoiced that he would see my day; he saw it and was glad.' Then the Jews said to him, 'You are not yet fifty years old, and have you seen Abraham?' Jesus said to them, 'Very truly, I tell you, before Abraham was, I am.'" In the "I am" we sense the allusion to the great "I AM" of the Old Testament, Yahweh. In fact, in John 10:30 we hear Jesus say, "The Father and I are one" (cf. 14:9-10). Paul also writes, "For in him all things in heaven and on earth were created . . . — all things have been created through him and for him" (Col 1:16; cf. 1 Cor 8:6; Heb 1:2).

Today some would use the divinity of Christ as a way of preaching him from the Old Testament.[58] Some speak of "Christophanies,"[59] appearances of Christ in the Old Testament. Figures like the Angel of Yahweh, the Commander of the Lord's army, and the Wisdom of God are then identified with Christ. Some even substitute the name *Christ* wherever the name *Yahweh* is mentioned because the Septuagint translates *Yahweh* as *Kyrios*, which is what the disciples called Jesus.[60] But nothing is gained by these shortcuts to preaching Christ. Not only does the speculation involved put the sermon on a shaky footing, but this identification of Christ with Old Testament figures short-circuits the task of preaching Christ as the fullness of God's self-revelation in his incarnate Son, Jesus. Moreover, when the New Testament authors speak of Christ as God, their intent is not to suggest that Christ can be identified with a number of figures in the Old Testament, but to witness to the divinity of Jesus. This doctrine of the divinity of Jesus functions as a presupposition in interpreting the Old Testament rather than a specific way of preaching Christ from the Old Testament.

Corporate Personality

A fourth presupposition guiding New Testament understanding of the Old is that of corporate personality. Especially in our individualistic age, we need to be mindful of this corporate way of thinking which the New Testament writers learned from the Old Testament. Earle Ellis claims that "for Jesus and the New Testament writers this perception of man as a corporate being is determinative for the proper understanding of Scripture."[61]

---

58. See my *Sola Scriptura*, 142-45, on Klaas Schilder, B. Holwerda, and others.

59. A. T. Hanson, *Living Utterances*, 107. Cf. his *Jesus Christ in the Old Testament* (London: SPCK, 1965). For a critique of Hanson's approach, see G. W. Grogan, *TynBul* 18 (1967) 65-66.

60. For references, see p. 3, n. 8.

61. Ellis, "Biblical Interpretation," 716-18.

In 1935 H. Wheeler Robinson wrote his influential "The Hebrew Conception of Corporate Personality." The 1964 introduction to this classic succinctly describes corporate personality as "that important Semitic complex of thought in which there is a constant oscillation between the individual and the group — family, tribe, or nation — to which he belongs, so that the king or some other representative figure may be said to embody the group, or the group may be said to sum up the host of individuals."[62] Think of the Servant songs in Isaiah and the endless debate whether the Servant is the nation of Israel or an individual person. Robinson writes, "The Hebrew conception of corporate personality can reconcile both, and pass without explanation or explicit indication from one to the other, in a fluidity of transition which seems to us unnatural."[63] The notion of corporate personality explains how the meaning of the Servant can oscillate between corporate Israel and an individual representing Israel. This concept also made it possible for Jesus to identify himself with the suffering Servant: Jesus is the individual suffering Servant, and he represents faithful Israel.

The New Testament writers also use the concept of corporate personality to preach Christ from the Old Testament. For example, Paul assumes it as he teaches, "As all die in Adam, so all will be made alive in Christ" (1 Cor 15:22). Earle Ellis writes, "The corporate extension of the person of the leader to include individuals who belong to him illumines the use of a number of Old Testament passages. It explains how the promise given to [David about] Solomon (2 Sam 7:12-16) can be regarded as fulfilled not only in the Messiah (Heb 1:5) but also in his followers (2 Cor 6:18) and, similarly, how the eschatological temple can be identified both with the individual (Mark 14:58; John 2:19ff.) and corporate (1 Cor 3:16; 1 Pet 2:5) Christ. It very probably underlies the conviction of the early Christians that those who belong to Christ, Israel's messianic king, constitute *the true Israel*."[64]

---

62. John Reumann, "Introduction to the First Edition" to H. Wheeler Robinson's *Corporate Personality in Ancient Israel* (Philadelphia: Fortress, 1964), 15. Robinson himself (p. 27) speaks of "the fluidity of reference, facilitating rapid and unmarked transitions from the one to the many, and from the many to the one."

63. Robinson, *Corporate Personality*, 40.

64. Ellis, "How the New Testament Uses the Old," 213. See also Dockery, *Biblical Interpretation*, 25: "Because Jesus saw himself as the representative of Israel, words originally spoken of the nation could rightly be applied to him, and because Jesus is the representative of humankind, words spoken originally by the psalmist can be fulfilled by him (cf. John 13:18; 15:25; 19:28)."

Reading the Old Testament from the Reality of Christ

All the foregoing presuppositions support the final principal presupposition of the New Testament writers in preaching Christ from the Old Testament, and that is to read the Old Testament from the perspective of the reality of Christ.[65] To reinterpret the Old Testament from a later perspective is not entirely new, for it is found already in the Old Testament.[66] The New Testament continues this process of reinterpretation, but now from the reality of Christ incarnate.

The Book of Testimonies

An early indication of Christ-centered interpretation of the Old Testament may be found in the so-called "Book of Testimonies." New Testament scholars have long been puzzled by the way different New Testament writers cite the same Old Testament texts (and sometimes sequences of texts) in wording that is different from the Septuagint and other known texts.[67] To account for these phenomena, Rendel Harris offered the hypothesis in 1916 that these writers were quoting a collection of "messianic proof-texts."[68] In 1950, C. H. Dodd rejected the idea that the phenomena could be explained by "the postulate of a primitive anthology of isolated proof-texts." Instead, he suggested the existence at a very early date of a "*selection* of certain large sections of the Old Testament scriptures, especially from Isaiah, Jeremiah and certain minor prophets, and from the Psalms. These sections were understood as *wholes*, and particular verses or sentences were quoted from them rather as pointers to the whole context than as constituting testimonies in and for themselves."[69]

Both of these hypotheses point to a very early Christian use of the Old Testament for preaching Christ. Harris thinks of an early collection of

---

65. While the New Testament uses the Old Testament to teach about God, the church, and Christian morality, its main focus is Jesus Christ. "Few would disagree that the major focus of early scriptural interpretation was 'christological,' meaning that it had Jesus in view." Juel, *Messianic Exegesis*, 1. Note, however, that Hays, *Echoes*, 86, argues that "Paul operates with an *ecclesiocentric* hermeneutic."

66. See von Rad, *Old Testament Theology*, 2.319-35.

67. "The best example of these interesting phenomena is the agreement between 1 Peter 2 and Romans 9. First Peter 2:6-10 uses Isaiah 28:16; Psalm 118:22; Isaiah 8:14; parts of several other texts and Hosea 2:23. Romans 9:25-33 uses Hosea 2:23, other texts from Isaiah, and then a conflation of Isaiah 28:16 and 8:14 in the same non-Septuagintal form that 1 Peter has." Klyne Snodgrass, "Use of the Old Testament," 422.

68. See C. H. Dodd, *According to the Scriptures*, 23-27.

69. Ibid., 126. The subsequent discovery of two pre-Christian, Jewish collections in Cave 4 of Qumran makes the existence of an early Christian collection quite plausible.

"messianic proof-texts." Dodd thinks of large sections of the Old Testament and suggests four groups illustrating "themes of the *kerygma*": "apocalyptic-eschatological Scriptures," "Scriptures of the New Israel," "Scriptures of the Servant of the Lord and the Righteous Sufferer," and "unclassified Scriptures" consisting of other passages applied to Jesus as Messiah.[70] As can be seen from the four themes, most of the Old Testament passages are understood to focus on Jesus as the fulfillment of God's promises to Israel, the suffering and risen Messiah.

New Testament Christ-Centered Interpretation of the Old Testament

More certain than a hypothetical "Book of Testimonies" are the actual "testimonies" we find in the New Testament. Sometimes the Old Testament texts are strung together like beads on a string (e.g., Heb 1).[71] Ellis defines these "testimonies" as "citations 'testifying' to the messiahship of Jesus," and suggests that they "presuppose a worked-out christological understanding of the particular passages and are not simply proof texts randomly selected."[72]

James Dunn confirms that the New Testament writers did not randomly select proof texts from the Old Testament. In discussing the principles which governed the interpretation of the first Christians, he writes, "The first thing that needs to be said is that the choice of Old Testament text as a rule was not arbitrary. . . . The passages they quote . . . are for the most part passages which had already been accepted as messianic (like Ps 110:1), or which in the light of Jesus' actual life have a *prima facie* claim to be messianic (like Ps 22 and Isa 53)." Next Dunn confirms the principle that the New Testament writers interpret the Old Testament from the reality of Christ: "Second, the interpretation was achieved again and again by reading the Old Testament passage or incident quoted *in the light of the event of Christ*, by viewing it from the standpoint of the new situation brought about by Jesus and of the redemption effected by Jesus."[73]

---

70. Ibid., 61-108.

71. See also n. 67 above on 1 Peter 2 and Romans 9.

72. Ellis, "How the New Testament Uses the Old," 201.

73. Dunn, "The Use of the Old Testament," 94. Dunn continues, "The technique is best illustrated in Gal 3:8, 4:22-31; 2 Cor 3:1-18 and Matt 2:23." Cf. p. 101, "The event of Jesus, the Jesus-tradition, the belief in Jesus exalted, the new experience of the Spirit — these were the determinative elements in the process of interpretation." For example, Cullmann, *Christ and Time*, 131, observes, "The New Testament authors wrote no new story of the Creation; they only showed its relation to the mid-point (especially John 1:1ff.; Col 1:16; Heb 1:2, 10)."

In fact, Paul declares that a strictly Jewish, that is, historical, interpretation of the Old Testament is inadequate. He writes about non-Christian Jews, "Indeed, to this very day whenever Moses is read a veil lies over their minds; but when one turns to the Lord, the veil is removed" (2 Cor 3:15-16). Accordingly, even though historically Isaiah 8:13 speaks of "the LORD of hosts" as a "rock one stumbles over," Paul applies this word to Christ (Rom 9:33). Psalm 2:7 historically speaks of the king, "You are my son; today I have begotten you," but Paul applies these words to Jesus (Acts 13:33; cf. Ps 2:1-2 and Acts 4:25-7).[74] Psalm 118 also speaks historically of the king, but Matthew 21:9 applies it to Christ, "Blessed is the one who comes in the name of the Lord."

A Christian reading of the Old Testament, however, is not only one-way traffic, that is, reading the Old Testament in the light of Christ. The traffic also moves from the Old Testament to Christ. Oscar Cullmann writes perceptively, "The Christ-event at the mid-point . . . is on its part illuminated by the Old Testament preparation, after this preparation has first received its light from that very mid-point." He acknowledges, "We have to do here with a circle. The death and resurrection of Christ enable the believer to see in the history of Adam and in the history of Israel the preparation for Jesus, the Crucified and Risen One. But only the thus understood history of Adam and the thus understood history of Israel enable the believer to grasp the work of Jesus Christ, the Crucified and Risen One, in connection with the divine plan of salvation."[75] Again we meet up with a form of the hermeneutic circle: we can only understand Christ in the light of the Old Testament, and we can only understand the Old Testament in the light of Christ.

---

74. Brevard Childs, *Biblical Theology*, 241, comments, "For Paul genuine interpretation depends on its bearing witness to its true subject matter, who is Christ. In this sense, Paul is not interested in the OT 'for its own sake,' if what is understood thereby is the biblical text separated from its true christological referent."

75. Cullmann, *Christ and Time*, 137. For example, Childs, *Biblical Theology*, 229, points out "the central role of the OT in the early church's understanding and interpreting the death and resurrection of Christ. . . . Psalm 110 provided the imagery for seeing Jesus exalted at God's right hand and reigning sovereign over the powers of death (Mark 12:35-37 par.; Acts 2:34; Heb 7:17, 21). Psalm 89 formed the link to Christ's humiliation (Luke 1:51; Acts 2:30), and Psalm 22 spoke of his righteous suffering (Mark 15:34 par.). Psalm 2 and 2 Samuel 7 provided the language for the royal messianic office as Son of God (Acts 13:33f.; Heb 1:5) and Daniel 7 spoke of the eschatological hope of his kingdom (Mark 13:26; 14:62)."

Christ-Centered Interpretation
Originated with Jesus

The question has often been raised where the New Testament writers, in contrast to their non-Christian Jewish counterparts, got the idea of interpreting the Old Testament from the reality of Christ. An obvious answer is that most had been disciples of Jesus and/or met the risen Lord. But a more complete answer is that Jesus himself taught them to read the Old Testament this way.[76] For three years the disciples heard Jesus preach and teach, heard him speak of himself as the Son of Man, that is, the person who receives a kingship "that shall never pass away" (Dan 7:14), heard him say over and over that he fulfilled Old Testament promises, heard him apply to himself the role of the figure of the Servant of Yahweh who "was wounded for our transgressions, crushed for our iniquities" (Isa 53:5). After his resurrection, Luke reports, Jesus found it necessary to continue teaching his disciples that the Old Testament spoke of him. Jesus said, " 'Was it not necessary that the Messiah should suffer these things and then enter into his glory.' Then beginning with Moses and all the prophets, he interpreted to them the things about himself in all the scriptures."[77]

There is no doubt that Jesus interpreted the Old Testament with an

---

76. Cf. Shires, *Finding the Old Testament*, 92, "There is abundant evidence to support the belief that it is Jesus who begins the Christological interpretation of the O.T. that permeates early Christian writings. Undoubtedly, he was much influenced by the picture of the Son of man that is drawn in Dan 7 and . . . the image of the Suffering Servant of Isa 52:13 to 53:12. . . ." Regarding the current debate whether the New Testament writers present Jesus' own use of the Old Testament or put words into his mouth, Longenecker, *TynBul* 21 (1970) 25, argues that "it can also be postulated — more plausibly I believe — that Jesus Himself was both the source and the pattern for early Christian interpretation: that certain selected verses which He interpreted continued to be interpreted in the same way by the earliest Christians (e.g., Isa 53:12 in Mark 15:28 and Isa 53:7-8 in Acts 8:32-33, and less directly elsewhere: the 'stone' citations in Acts 4:11 and 1 Pet 2:6-8; and Ps 110:1 in Acts 2:34-36 and a number of times in Hebrews) and that His treatment of them furnished the paradigm for further exegetical endeavour within the early apostolic community." Cf. Charles A. Kimball, *Jesus' Exposition of the Old Testament in Luke's Gospel* (Sheffield: Sheffield Academic Press, 1994), 202: "I conclude that Jesus' biblical expositions and his choice of biblical texts furnished the foundation for the theology of the New Testament, and that Jesus' exegetical methods influenced the exegetical procedures of his followers and the NT writers." Cf. France, *Jesus and the Old Testament*, 225.

77. Luke 24:26-27; cf. Luke 24:44-47. Dodd, *According to the Scriptures*, 110, judges that "the NT itself avers that it was Jesus Christ Himself who first directed the minds of His followers to certain parts of the scriptures as those in which they might find illumination upon the meaning of His mission and destiny."

authority that impressed his hearers and even his opponents.[78] There is equally no doubt that Jesus interpreted the Old Testament in a christocentric way. He saw his mission in terms of the Old Testament figures of the Servant of the Lord (especially Isa 52:13–53:12) and of the Son of Man (Dan 7:13-14).[79] France summarizes the evidence from the synoptic Gospels: "He [Jesus] uses persons in the Old Testament as types of himself (David, Solomon, Elijah, Elisha, Isaiah, Jonah) . . . ; he refers to Old Testament institutions as types of himself and his work (the priesthood and the covenant); he sees in the experiences of Israel foreshadowings of his own; he finds the hopes of Israel fulfilled in himself. . . ."[80]

MANY ROADS LEAD FROM THE OLD TESTAMENT TO CHRIST

The New Testament presuppositions for interpreting the Old Testament led to various ways of preaching Christ from the Old Testament. Although these ways are not scientifically precise and overlap considerably, it will be valuable for us to try to sort out the different ways the New Testament writers use to preach Christ from the Old Testament and thus gain some clarity on what is distinctive about each way. In the following chapter we can then examine these ways of preaching Christ in the light of contemporary discussions. Here we shall seek to distinguish six major ways of preaching Christ from the Old Testament: the ways of redemptive-historical progression, promise-fulfillment, typology, analogy, longitudinal themes, and contrast.

The Way of Redemptive-Historical Progression

Redemptive history is not only a New Testament presupposition for interpreting the Old Testament, it is also one of the major ways of preaching Christ from the Old Testament. Redemptive-historical progression links

78. "The crowds were astounded at his teaching, for he taught them as one having authority, and not as their scribes." Matt 7:28-29. Cf. Luke 20:39.

79. See France, *TynBul* 19 (1968) 51, "We conclude . . . that Jesus saw His mission as that of the Servant of Yahweh, that He predicted that in fulfillment of that role He must suffer and die, and that He regarded His suffering and death as, like that of the Servant, vicarious and redemptive." Cf. p. 52, "Isaiah 53 is the blueprint for His earthly ministry, Daniel 7:13-14 for His future exaltation." Cf. Jensen, *God's Word to Israel*, 206.

80. France, *Jesus and the Old Testament*, 75.

Christ to Old Testament redemptive events which find their climax in him. As we have seen, Matthew begins his Gospel with a "genealogy of Jesus the Messiah" which reaches all the way back in redemptive history to the great king David and to the patriarch Abraham. David had received God's promise, "Your throne shall be established forever" (2 Sam 7:16), and Abraham had received God's promise, "In you all the families of the earth shall be blessed" (Gen 12:3). Matthew uses redemptive-historical progression to preach Christ as the successor of a royal line which had received God's wondrous promises of eternal rule over the entire earth.

Luke, similarly, includes in his Gospel a genealogy of Jesus which traces his roots through redemptive history all the way back to "Adam, son of God" (Luke 3). Adam is the person who fell for the devil's lie and brought death into the world. Like Adam, Jesus will now be tempted by the devil (Luke 4), but Jesus, the Son of God, conquers the devil. In Jesus, God provides humanity with a second chance at eternal life.

Luke is probably best known for presenting Jesus as the midpoint of redemptive history.[81] There are two stages in redemptive history, the "time of Israel" which lasted till John the Baptizer (Luke 16:16) and the "time of fulfillment."[82] Jesus ushers in the "time of fulfillment," the kingdom of God. In Acts, Luke recounts several early Christian sermons, most of which make use of redemptive-historical progression to proclaim Christ. At Pentecost Peter quotes from the prophet Joel and from Psalm 16. In his sermon he asserts that Jesus' death and resurrection were in God's master-plan: "Jesus of Nazareth, a man attested to you by God with deeds of power, wonders, and signs that God did through him among you, as you yourselves know — this man, handed over to you *according to the definite plan and foreknowledge of God,* you crucified . . ." (Acts 2:22-23). Later, Luke records how Stephen traces in detail the history of redemption from Abraham to Christ, "the Righteous One" (Acts 7:2-52). Then Luke reports on Paul's sermon in Antioch of Pisidia, which begins with God making Israel great in Egypt, giving them the promised land and granting their request for a king, first Saul, and next the great king David — reminiscent of Psalm 78, where King David is the climax. But

---

81. Cf. Hans Conzelmann's commentary on Luke, *Die Mitte der Zeit.* Cullmann, *Salvation in History,* 270, also claims this honor for John: "If we can speak and must speak anywhere of a 'mid-point of time,' the centre and climax which gives history a meaning, it is in the Gospel of John, and not just in Luke. All revelation, all God's acting is disclosed from this mid-point. If the subject of this action at the decisive climax in history is the incarnate Lord, Jesus of Nazareth, if in him God has revealed his inmost essence, his *doxa* (John 1:14), then *he* must be the vehicle of all God's acting in relation to the world."

82. Jack Kingsbury, *Jesus Christ,* 97.

Paul moves beyond King David to the decisive climax in redemptive history, "Of this man's posterity God has brought to Israel a Savior, Jesus, as he promised." Paul then recounts the story of Jesus, urging the people to believe in him (Acts 13:16-41).[83]

In his letters, Paul also uses redemptive-historical progression as a way of preaching Christ. Paul begins his letter to the Romans, "Paul, a servant of Jesus Christ, called to be an apostle, set apart for the gospel of God, which he promised beforehand through his prophets in the holy scriptures, the gospel concerning his Son, who was descended from David according to the flesh . . ." (Rom 1:1-3). Later Paul goes all the way back to Adam, who brought sin and death into the world, and contrasts him with Jesus Christ, whose "act of righteousness leads to justification and life for all" (Rom 5:18). In Galatians, Paul writes about God's promises to Abraham and about the law which came 430 years later and which served as "our disciplinarian until Christ came, so that we might be justified by faith" (3:24). He speaks of Jesus' life on earth as the climax of redemptive history: "When the fullness of time had come, God sent his Son, born of a woman, born under the law, in order to redeem those who were under the law . . ." (4:4-5). In Colossians, Paul writes about "the mystery that has been hidden throughout the ages and generations but has now been revealed to his saints" (1:26).[84] And in 2 Corinthians he speaks of the *now* of salvation: "See, now is the acceptable time; see, now is the day of salvation!" (6:2).

Paul not only uses past redemptive history to preach Christ; he also, from the midpoint of Christ, speaks of future redemptive history. In Ephesians, he writes about God's plan, "With all wisdom and insight he has made known to us the mystery of his will, according to his good pleasure that he set forth in Christ, as a *plan* for the fullness of time, to gather up all things in him . . ." (1:8-10).[85] In 1 Corinthians 15, Paul speaks of the

83. N. T. Wright, *New Testament and the People,* 396, states that "all three synoptic gospels . . . share a common pattern behind their wide divergences. All tell the story of Jesus . . . as the end of a much longer story, the story of Israel, which in turn is the focal point of the story of the creator and the world." Regarding the Gospel of John, see ibid., 410-17.

84. Cf. Domenico Grasso, *Proclaiming,* 12, "According to the Apostle [Paul] all history is a complex of facts, a warp of happenings, foreordained by God and following in order, so that the Revelation and the communication of Christ may be realized. Before the Incarnation, history is directed towards Him, while after the Incarnation it streams from Him. Christ is the center and the meaning of history."

85. Cf. Eph 3:3-5, "The mystery was made known to me by revelation, as I wrote above in a few words, a reading of which will enable you to perceive my understanding of the mystery of Christ. In former generations this mystery was not made known to humankind, as it has now been revealed to his holy apostles and prophets by the Spirit." Cf. Rom 16:25-27.

resurrected Christ as "the first fruits of those who have died" and speaks in great detail about the rest of the harvest which will be brought in at his Second Coming. And in Romans, he expands our vision of redemption: it is not only for God's people, but "the creation itself will be set free from its bondage to decay and will obtain the freedom of the glory of the children of God" (8:21).

The Way of Promise-Fulfillment

Another way the New Testament writers preach Christ from the Old Testament is that of promise-fulfillment. The way of promise-fulfillment is embedded in redemptive history, for God gives his promises at one stage of redemptive history and brings them to fulfillment in subsequent stages.[86]

Complexity in Promise-Fulfillment

In the New Testament, fulfillment is a much broader category than fulfillment of specific promises.[87] For example, Matthew is known for his "formula quotations." Ten times he repeats, "All this took place to fulfill what had been spoken by the Lord through the prophet," followed by a quotation. But not all of these quotations are prophecies about the future. In Matthew 2:15 we read about Jesus' escape to Egypt, "This was to fulfill what had been spoken by the Lord through the prophet, 'Out of Egypt I have called my son.'" The quotation is from Hosea 11:1 and is as such not a promise or prediction about the future but a statement about the past that God called Israel, "my son," out of Egypt (Exod 4:22-23). Matthew here uses the word "fulfill" not for a promise of Christ but at best for a type of Christ.[88] We must be aware, therefore, that New Testament writers employ "fulfillment" for both promises and types.[89]

---

86. Dwight Moody Smith, "Use of the Old Testament," 36-65, contends that every New Testament writer sees fulfillment in Christ in terms of redemptive history.

87. This is evident already from the two Greek roots used for "fulfill." The first words *teleioō/teleō* "point to the accomplishment of God's will, even if they do not always cite a particular promise." The second root is *plēroō*, "used exclusively in the Gospels and in Acts to refer to the whole event of Christ." McCurley, *Wrestling*, 22 and 24. Cf. Moo, "Problem of *Sensus Plenior*," 191.

88. The larger context of Hosea 11, specifically vv 8-11, does promise a return from Egypt/Assyria. See David Holwerda, *Jesus and Israel*, 38-40.

89. Luke similarly posits fulfillments of a combination of promises and types. "What God did in one era to move covenant promises along, He can and will do in

But matters are still more complicated, for New Testament writers speak of fulfillment when the Old Testament referent is neither promise nor type. For example, after noting that Jesus told the crowd parables, Matthew 13:35 states, "This was to fulfill what had been spoken through the prophet, 'I will open my mouth in parables. . . .'" The quotation is from Psalm 78:2. Although the Psalms are not prophecy, they can contain types (think of the Psalms about the victorious king and about righteous sufferers). But this quotation is neither prediction, promise, nor type; yet Matthew includes it in his formula quotations about fulfillment. Some scholars classify this use of the Old Testament as "a pesher type of interpretation."[90] Whatever the classification, it is clear that Matthew looks back at the Old Testament from the reality of Christ, and from this perspective the sacred book is like a valley with white flowers, all pointing to the sun. "Matthew sees the whole Old Testament as the embodiment of promise — in the sense of presenting to us a God of gracious and saving purpose, liberating action, and covenant faithfulness to his people. That generates a tremendous sense of expectation and hope, reflected in all parts of the Hebrew canon. Hence, all kinds of Old Testament writing (not just prophecies) can be drawn on in relating that promise to Jesus. The dynamic reality of Jesus was plugged into the no less dynamic potential of the Old Testament's future hope."[91]

While the New Testament term "fulfillment" thus covers a broad range, we are specifically interested in the narrower channel, also evidenced in the New Testament, of the fulfillment of specific Old Testament promises or predictions.

Promise-Fulfillment in the Old Testament

The Old Testament itself demonstrated this way of promise-fulfillment. For example, God repeated his promise to Abraham and Sarah that they would receive a son (Gen 18:10), and a year later God fulfilled this promise with the birth of Isaac (Gen 21:2). God promised Abraham and his offspring the land of Canaan (Gen 17:8), and five centuries later God ful-

---

those times when He again actively becomes involved in directing and completing His program. This is a major theological supposition to Luke's use of the OT, which allows him to appeal to the variety of texts which he does. . . . Thus while many texts Luke uses are not exclusively prophetic, they are 'typological-prophetic' in that the pattern of God's activity is reactivated in ways that mirror and enhance His acts of old. . . . In the repetition is the presence of design and thus of prophecy." Darrell Bock, "Use of the Old Testament," 495.

90. See, e.g., Longenecker, *Biblical Exegesis*, 70-75.
91. Christopher Wright, *Knowing Jesus*, 63-64.

filled this promise (Josh 21:43-45). God promised/forewarned the people of Judah that he would send them into exile, and in 587 B.C. he fulfilled this threat.

In addition to promises that were fulfilled in the Old Testament, other promises still awaited fulfillment. God's promise to Abraham, "In you all the families of the earth shall be blessed" (Gen 12:3), did not come to final fulfillment in Old Testament times. God's promise to "set up a kingdom that shall never be destroyed. . . . It shall stand forever" (Dan 2:44; cf. 7:13-14) did not come to fulfillment in Old Testament times. God's promise of a glorious new creation (Isa 65) did not come to fulfillment in Old Testament times. Because of these unfulfilled promises, the Old Testament "always points forward, beyond itself and its own experience."[92]

Even fulfilled promises can still point forward toward the future. The Old Testament acquaints us with the concept of multiple fulfillments or progressive fulfillment, that is, the initial fulfillment may hold the promise of further fulfillment. For example, God had promised Abraham, "I will make of you a great nation" (Gen 12:2). This promise started to be fulfilled with the birth of Isaac but obviously required further filling. Exodus 1:5 records that God's covenant people had grown to seventy when they went to Egypt, but the promise to Abraham awaited further fulfillment. Exodus 1:7 reports that "the Israelites were fruitful and prolific; they multiplied and grew exceedingly strong, so that the land was filled with them." They were now many people but not yet "a great nation." So the promise awaited still further fulfillments: the gift of the land of Canaan and later the gift of the great king David. Finally, Israel was a great nation; it seemed that the promise was full. But at that very apex, God made another promise to David: "Your house and your kingdom shall be made sure forever before me; your throne shall be established forever" (2 Sam 7:16). And the promise again reached out for the future. Christopher Wright likens progressive fulfillment to a "time-traveling rocket, the promise is launched, returning to earth at some later point of history in a partial fulfillment, only to be relaunched with a fresh load of fuel and cargo for yet another historical destination and so on."[93] The progressive fulfillment of God's promise to Abraham about becoming a great nation can be pictured as follows:

Abraham   Isaac   Jacob   Egypt   Canaan   David   Exile   Remnant   Future

92. Foster McCurley, *Wrestling*, 27.
93. Wright, *Knowing Jesus*, 72.

Promise-Fulfillment in the New Testament

The New Testament writers learned the way of promise-fulfillment not only from the Old Testament but especially from Jesus. In one of his first sermons, in the synagogue of Nazareth, Jesus read Isaiah 61:1-2a about the Lord's anointed Servant ushering in the year of the Lord's favor and proclaimed, "Today this scripture has been fulfilled in your hearing" (Luke 4:21). Fulfillment of Old Testament types and promises was Jesus' theme.[94] Jesus' favored self-designation was "Son of Man," as in, "'You will see the Son of Man seated at the right hand of the Power,' and 'coming with the clouds of heaven'" (Mark 14:62). The Son of Man, of course, is the person Daniel saw "coming with the clouds of heaven. . . . To him was given dominion and glory and kingship, that all peoples, nations, and languages should serve him. His dominion is an everlasting dominion that shall not pass away, and his kingship is one that shall never be destroyed" (Dan 7:13-14). Jesus, however, saw himself not only as the eternal King but also as the Servant of Yahweh pictured in Isaiah (42:1-9; 49:1-13; 50:4-11; 52:13–53:12). In fact, Jesus merged these two figures into one. He said, "The Son of Man came not to be served but to serve, and to give his life a ransom for many" (Mark 10:45). When he celebrated his final Passover with his disciples, Jesus reminded them of the suffering Servant of Yahweh (Isa 53:12), "I tell you, this scripture must be fulfilled in me, 'And he was counted among the lawless'; and indeed what is written about me is being fulfilled" (Luke 22:37; cf. 18:31-33). Not once but twice Jesus here mentioned that he was *fulfilling* the role of the suffering Servant. When Jesus was arrested in Gethsemane, he told the crowds, "All this has taken place, so that the scriptures of the prophets may be fulfilled" (Matt 26:56). Later, when the Ethiopian eunuch asked Philip about the identity of the suffering Servant of Isaiah 53, "Like a sheep he was led to the slaughter," Philip had a ready answer: "Starting with this scripture, he proclaimed to him the good news about Jesus" (Acts 8:32-35). There was no doubt that Jesus fulfilled the role of the Servant of Yahweh (cf. Matt 12:15-21).

In fact, as far as the Gospel writers are concerned, Jesus fulfilled the promises of all the prophets. Mark begins his Gospel, "The beginning of the good news of Jesus Christ, the Son of God. As it is written in the prophet Isaiah, 'See, I am sending my messenger ahead of you, who will prepare your way; the voice of one crying out in the wilderness: 'Prepare the way of the Lord, make his paths straight'" (1:1-3). Mark begins his

---

94. Cf. The Sermon on the Mount (Matt 5:17), "Do not think that I have come to abolish the law or the prophets; I have come not to abolish but to fulfill."

Gospel by noting that even the forerunner of Jesus, John the Baptizer, was promised by the prophets (Mal 3:1 and Isa 40:3).[95] Next he reports that Jesus' preaching focussed on the fulfillment of time itself: "The time is fulfilled and the kingdom of God has come near; repent, and believe in the good news" (1:15).

In contrast with Mark, Matthew, writing primarily to Jews, focusses much more on the fulfillment of Old Testament promises. In Matthew 1:22 we find the first of the quotation formulas, "All this took place to fulfill what had been spoken by the Lord through the prophet, 'Look, the virgin shall conceive and bear a son, and they shall name him Emmanuel,' . . ." In its original context, this promise concerns a sign for King Ahaz, who was threatened with an invasion of the combined armies of Syria and Ephraim. Isaiah says to Ahaz, "The Lord himself will give you a sign. Look, the young woman is with child and shall bear a son, and shall name him Immanuel. . . . Before the child knows how to refuse the evil and choose the good, the land before whose two kings you are in dread will be deserted" (Isa 7:14, 16). A few years after this prophecy, God fulfilled his promise: Assyria destroyed Syria in 732 B.C., defeated Ephraim, and ten years later took her into captivity. But Matthew sees further fulfillment of this prophecy in the virgin (LXX, *parthenos*) birth of Jesus, who is truly Immanuel, God with us. Through him God will not just deliver his people from their enemies, but "from their sins" (Matt 1:21).

Next Matthew reports that even the chief priests and scribes could deduce from the Old Testament "where the Messiah was to be born." They told Herod, "In Bethlehem of Judea; for so it has been written by the prophet: 'And you, Bethlehem, in the land of Judah, are by no means least among the rulers of Judah; for from you shall come a ruler who is to shepherd my people Israel'" (Matt 2:4-6). The quotation is from Micah 5:2, but Matthew has made a few changes to focus his point. First, Micah 5:2 spoke of Bethlehem as "one of the little clans of Judah." Because Christ was born in Bethlehem, Matthew upgrades Bethlehem's status to "by no means least among the rulers of Judah." Second, Matthew has added to Micah's prophecy a line from 2 Samuel 5:2 which describes David's role in Israel, "who is to shepherd my people Israel." As in his first chapter, Matthew again makes the point that Jesus fulfills Old Testament promises as the son and successor of the great king David.

Luke also uses promise-fulfillment, but in his own unique manner. He does not use formula quotations but "simply lays the text out by the

---

95. All four Gospels see the fulfillment of Isa 40:3-5 in John the Baptizer: in addition to Mark 1:3, see Matt 3:3; Luke 3:4-6, and John 1:23.

event. . . . He lets the event speak for itself and declare its fulfillment."[96] Luke begins his Gospel with a reminder "of the events that have been fulfilled among us" (1:1). Then the angel recalls God's promise to David (2 Sam 7:16) when he says to Mary that her son will receive "the throne of his ancestor David. He will reign over the house of Jacob forever, and of his kingdom there will be no end" (1:32-33). This is followed by Mary's song, which speaks of "the promise he made to our ancestors, to Abraham and to his descendants" (1:55). Next Zechariah proclaims that the Lord God of Israel "has raised up a mighty savior for us in the house of his servant David, as he spoke through the mouth of his holy prophets from of old . . ." (1:69-70). Luke ends his Gospel with Jesus' words, "Everything written about me in the law of Moses, the prophets, and the psalms must be fulfilled" (24:44).

In Acts, similarly, Luke uses the speeches of others to proclaim fulfillment of God's promises. At Pentecost Peter begins his sermon, "This is what was spoken through the prophet Joel: In the last days it will be, God declares, that I will pour out my Spirit upon all flesh . . ." (2:16-17). In a later sermon, Peter alludes to Isaiah's suffering Servant when he calls Jesus God's "servant" (3:13, 26) and says, "In this way God fulfilled what he had foretold through all the prophets, that his Messiah would suffer" (3:18).[97] Later Philip uses the prophecy of the suffering Servant (Isa 53:7-8) to preach to the Ethiopian Eunuch "the good news about Jesus" (8:32-35). In the sermon in Antioch of Pisidia, Paul recounts the history of Israel to the great king David and says, "Of this man's posterity God has brought to Israel a Savior, Jesus, as he promised." Paul goes on to speak of Jesus' suffering as fulfillment of "the words of the prophets" and to argue that "everything that was written about him" had to be carried out (13:23, 27, 29). Paul strikes the same note before Agrippa when he explains his preaching as "saying nothing but what the prophets and Moses said would take place: that the Messiah must suffer, and that, by being the first to rise from the dead, he would proclaim light both to our people and to the Gentiles" (26:22-23).

In his letters, too, Paul uses the way of promise-fulfillment to preach Christ. He begins his letter to the Romans, for example, by speaking of "the gospel of God, which he promised beforehand through his prophets in the holy scriptures, the gospel concerning his Son, who was descended from David . . ." (1:1-3). And in the key chapter on the resurrection, Paul emphasizes "that Christ died for our sins in accordance with the scriptures, and that he was buried, and that he was raised on the third day in accordance with the scriptures . . ." (1 Cor 15:3-4).

96. Bock, "Use of the Old Testament," 502.
97. Cf. 1 Pet 2:22-25.

Before we move to typology, we ought to note one final point about promise-fulfillment. We became aware of progressive fulfillment in the Old Testament, that is, a promise is fulfilled and yet remains open to further fulfillment. The same is true with respect to Christ: in fulfilling Old Testament promises Christ turns them into new promises of even larger scope. In Galatians 3:29 Paul writes, "If you belong to Christ, then you are Abraham's offspring, heirs according to the promise." The ramifications of these promises for us are staggering. As God promised Abraham to be his God, so God promises us to be our God in Christ. As God promised Abraham's descendants redemption, so God promises us redemption, but not merely temporary redemption from physical slavery, from Egypt or Babylonia, but redemption from the slavery of sin and eternal life. God also promises to give us "the land," but it now extends far beyond the land of Canaan to the entire earth. Jesus says, "Blessed are the meek, for they will inherit the earth" (Matt 5:5). In a vision, John sees the fulfillment of Isaiah 65, "a new heaven and a new earth" (Rev 21:1).[98] God still promises to make us "a great nation," but now it goes far beyond the kingdom of David and encompasses all nations of the world. Jesus gave his church the mandate, "Go . . . and make disciples of all nations. . . . And remember, I am with you always, to the end of the age" (Matt 28:19-20). And so at last will be fulfilled God's promise to Abraham, "In you all the families of the earth shall be blessed" (Gen 12:3; Acts 3:25).[99]

The Way of Typology

As promise-fulfillment functions within redemptive history because God makes and fulfills his promises in redemptive history, so typology functions within redemptive history because God acts in redemptive history in regular patterns.[100] God accomplishes his redemptive plan not only progressively from promise to fulfillment but also uniformly through similarity of redemptive acts. The New Testament writers are able, therefore, to discern analogies between God's present acts in Christ and his redemptive acts in the Old Testament. "New Testament typology is thus es-

98. See Rom 4:13, where Paul changes the promise to Abraham from "the land" to "the world." Cf. Eph 6:3.

99. On the universalizing of particular promises, see David Holwerda, *Jesus and Israel*, 177-84.

100. Cf. Cullmann, *Salvation in History*, 133, "All typology . . . presupposes a salvation-historical background, namely, the relationship between the Old and New Testaments understood from a salvation-historical point of view."

sentially the tracing of the constant principles of God's working in history, revealing 'a recurrent rhythm in past history which is taken up more fully and perfectly in Gospel events.'"[101] Especially because the New Testament writers believe that Jesus has ushered in the messianic age, they see God's past acts of redemption as shadows, prefigurations, and types of the new age that has dawned in Christ.[102] Typology, therefore, is characterized by analogy and escalation.[103]

The major presupposition underlying typological interpretation is that God as Lord of history works out his redemptive plan in history. "The rationale of New Testament typological exegesis is not only 'the continuity of God's purpose throughout the history of His Covenant,' but also His Lordship in moulding and using history to reveal and illumine His purpose. God writes His parables in the sands of time. . . . Things which were hidden or only partially revealed are now revealed to the Church — the Messianic Community — in whom the fulfillment is realized."[104] Faith in God's providence is the indispensable foundation of typological interpretation.

Complexity in Typology

The New Testament writers generally do not use the word *"typos"* in a technical sense. The word occurs fifteen times in the New Testament but with different meanings such as "the *mark* of the nails in his hands" (John 20:25), "the *form* of teaching" (Rom 6:17), "the *images* that you made to worship" (Acts 7:43), "the *pattern* that was shown you on the mountain" (Heb 8:5). David Baker comes to the conclusion that *typos* is never used in a technical sense and that it can best be translated "example" or "pattern."[105] Leonhard Goppelt, on the other hand, argues, "So far as we can

101. France, *Jesus and the Old Testament*, 39, with a quotation from Lampe, *Essays*, 27.

102. See Goppelt, *TDNT* 8.259, Typology's "true root is the idea of consummation in salvation history."

103. Cf. Cullmann, *Salvation in History*, 132, "Typology at the same time stresses analogy and heightening, repetition and consummation, with respect to the two points in contrast."

104. Ellis, *Paul's Use*, 127-28, with a quotation from Lampe, *Theology* 51 (1953) 202. Cf. France, *Jesus and the Old Testament*, 76, New Testament "typology is essentially the expression of a conviction of the unchanging principles of the working of God, and of the continuity between his acts in the past and in the present." Cf. Mickelsen, *Interpreting*, 237, "The correspondence is present because God controls history, and this control of God over history is axiomatic with the New Testament writers."

105. Baker, *Two Testaments*, 253.

tell, Paul was the first to use the Greek word *typos* (adj. *typikos*) as a term for the prefiguring of the future in prior history. God dealt in a typical way *(typikōs)* with Israel in the wilderness, in a manner that is a pattern for his dealing with the church in the last days. The fortunes of Israel are types *(typoi)* of the experiences of the church (1 Cor 10:11)."[106] Elsewhere Goppelt refers to Romans 5:14, where Paul speaks of Adam as "a type of the one who was to come." He comments, "In the universal havoc he caused, Adam is for Paul a *typos*, an advance presentation, through which God intimates the future Adam, namely, Christ in His universal work of salvation. . . . [The term] *typos* can be the 'hollow form' which makes an opposite impression on some other material. Paul can adopt the term, which was familiar to him already in the sense of a moulding original, for a technical use consonant with this basic meaning."[107] I agree with Goppelt that Paul begins to use the word *typos* in a technical sense,[108] but even if Baker is right, New Testament writers can still use the method we call typology without using the word *typos* in a technical sense.

A further complexity is that writers like Matthew are very creative in suggesting parallel patterns between Jesus' life and that of Old Testament figures such as Moses, Elijah, and Israel and that some scholars call these parallels "types" or "typological interpretation." Earle Ellis writes, "The picture of Christ in Matthew is particularly suggestive of the rabbinical parallels between Moses and Messiah: Like Moses, he is saved from Herod's slaughter, comes forth out of Egypt, calls out the 'twelve sons of Israel,' gives the law from the mount, performs ten miracles (like Moses, ten plagues), provides 'manna' from heaven." Ellis admits that "the picture is not certain," and that "at least as good a case can be made out that Matthew has in mind Christ as the 'embodiment' of Israel."[109] Richard Longenecker makes the case for "parallels between Jesus and the nation: a child of promise . . . , delivered from Herod's slaughter . . . , coming out of Egypt . . . , passing through the waters . . . , entering the wilderness for testing . . . , calling out the 'twelve sons of Israel' . . . , giving the Law from the mount . . . , performing ten miracles . . . , sending out the

106. Goppelt, *Typos*, 4-5.

107. Goppelt, *TDNT* 8.252.

108. See pp. 217-18 below on Rom 5:12-19; see also the way 1 Pet 3:21 uses *antitypos* for baptism.

109. Ellis, *Paul's Use*, 126. W. D. Davies, "Jewish Sources," 504-5, sees the Jesus-Moses parallels particularly in Matthew 1–2, the Jesus-Israel parallels in Matthew 3–4, and Jesus as the new Moses in Matthew 5:1–8:1. David Holwerda, *Jesus and Israel*, 37, states that "Matthew is interested not so much in Moses as in the Israel that Moses represents."

Twelve to 'conquer' the land . . . , feeding the multitudes with 'manna' from heaven . . . , and being transfigured before his disciples. . . ."[110] Longenecker concludes that "behind the Evangelist's presentation stand the Jewish concepts of corporate solidarity and typological correspondences in history. . . . Jesus is portrayed in Matthew's Gospel as the embodiment of ancient Israel and the antitype of earlier divine redemption."[111]

I would not call all these parallels and allusions of Matthew "types,"[112] for when every parallel and allusion is typology, nothing is typology. Moreover, it is obvious that today we cannot use every one of these parallels and allusions as a bridge to preaching Christ. Suppose we make a sermon on Moses being saved from Pharaoh's slaughter (Exod 2:1-10). If we were to develop the sermon "typologically" with Moses being a "type" of Christ who was saved from Herod's slaughter, we would miss the message of Exodus 2:1-10. The point is this: not every parallel presented in the New Testament is a type; a type is more than a parallel. We are, however, able to discern in the New Testament a way of typology that is more disciplined and that can also be used today as a bridge from the Old Testament to Christ in the New Testament.

Old Testament Use of Typology

We find the roots of typology in the Old Testament. For example, Isaiah frequently uses pictures of the exodus from Egypt to promise Israel in Babylonian exile a new exodus. Returning to Canaan from Babylon, Israel needed to cross neither sea nor desert, but these are the images Isaiah uses: "Do not fear, for I have redeemed you. . . . When you pass through the waters, I will be with you. . . . Thus says the LORD, who makes a way in the sea, a path in the mighty waters. . . . I will make a way in the wilderness and rivers in the desert."[113] Jeremiah speaks of a new covenant in

110. Longenecker, *Biblical Exegesis*, 141.

111. Ibid., 142.

112. For example, Robert Gundry, *The Use of the Old Testament in St. Matthew's Gospel*, 206-7, speaks of "Moses-Jesus typology," "Elijah-John typology," and "David-Jesus typology."

113. Isa 43:2, 16, 19. See also, e.g., Isa 11:15-16; 48:20-21; 51:9-11; 52:11-12. Cf. Lampe, *Essays*, 27, "In such passages as Isaiah 51:9-11, the prophetic interpretation of the pattern of history assumes a form which may fairly be called typological. The creation struggle finds its antitype in the Exodus and both alike are in turn recapitulated and fulfilled in the future act of deliverance from the Exile." For the escalation of this new exodus over the old one, see von Rad, *Old Testament Theology*, 2.246-49. Cf. Bernhard Anderson, "Exodus Typology," 194-95.

terms of the old; it is still the covenant of grace, but in the new covenant God promises, "I will put my law within them, and I will write it on their hearts" (Jer 31:33). In this prophecy we see clearly the two elements that characterize typology: correspondence between the old and the new and escalation. The prophets also promise another King David. God says, "I will set up over them one shepherd, my servant David, and he shall feed them. . . . And I, the LORD, will be their God, and my servant David shall be prince among them; I, the LORD, have spoken."[114] Here the original King David functions as a type for a later shepherd king. Isaiah (65:17-25) prophesies that God is "about to create new heavens and a new earth." Again we notice the two elements that characterize typology: correspondence between this earth and the new earth as well as escalation — no more weeping, no more infant mortality, "not labor in vain, or bear children for calamity. . . . The wolf and lamb shall feed together. . . . They shall not hurt or destroy. . . ."

Jesus' Use of Typology

Jesus uses typology both to set forth the correspondence between past redemptive events and his own work and to show the escalation. He says, "For just as Jonah was three days and three nights in the belly of the sea monster, so for three days and three nights the Son of man will be in the heart of the earth. The people of Nineveh will rise up at the judgment with this generation and condemn it, because they repented at the proclamation of Jonah, and see, something greater than Jonah is here!" Then Jesus refers again to the final judgment, "The queen of the South will rise up at the judgment with this generation and condemn it, because she came from the ends of the earth to listen to the wisdom of Solomon, and see, something greater than Solomon is here!" (Matt 12:40-42). That Jesus uses the disobedient prophet Jonah as a type of himself may come as a surprise, but the parallels are restricted to "three days and three nights in the belly of the sea monster" and the subsequent preaching of Jonah which led to repentance in Nineveh. R. T. France comments, "The theological correspondence, the repeated principle of God's working, lies in the sending of a preacher of repentance, whose mission is attested by a miraculous act of deliverance. As God sent Jonah to the Ninevites, so Jesus is sent to the Jews of his day. The typology thus places Jesus in the succession of God's prophetic messengers to men. Now, in the sending of a 'greater than Jonah' (verse 41), this long-continued method of God's working has reached its climax,

114. Ezek 34:23-24; cf. 37:24-28; Jer 23:5-6; 30:9; Hos 3:5.

and in a greater act of deliverance God will accredit this supreme call to repentance."[115]

In John 3:14-15, Jesus compares himself with the bronze serpent that was lifted up by Moses (Num 21:9): "Just as Moses lifted up the serpent in the wilderness, so must the Son of man be lifted up, that whoever believes in him may have eternal life." Again, it seems strange that Jesus would compare himself to a serpent, which usually functions in Scripture as a symbol of evil. But the parallel is restricted to the lifting up, the faith required, and the resultant life. Again the escalation of this type is astonishing since it moves from those who looked at the serpent and lived, only to die later, to those who believe in the Son of Man and live forever.[116]

We find other examples of Jesus' use of typology in Mark 14:24, "This is my blood of the [new] covenant, which is poured out for many," and in John 6:49-51, where Jesus sees the manna in the wilderness as a type of himself: "Your ancestors ate the manna in the wilderness, and they died. This is the bread that comes down from heaven, so that one may eat of it and not die. I am the living bread which came down from heaven. Whoever eats of this bread will live forever. . . ." Again we notice the analogy and the escalation.[117]

New Testament Use of Typology

Paul's use of typology is most explicit in Romans 5:12-19 with his use of the word *"typos"* in verse 14, "Adam, who is a type of the one who was to come." In this passage Paul exposes the analogy between Christ and Adam: each is head of a new creation; each represents "all" (v 18). Paul underscores the analogy by twice using the conjunctions "just as . . . so"

---

115. France, *Jesus and the Old Testament,* 45. Cf. John Stek, "The Message of the Book of Jonah," *CTJ* 4/1 (1969) 43-46. Jesus' comparison to Solomon is similar to that of Jonah. France, ibid., 45-46, observes, "There seem to be two points: (a) the response of the Gentiles to God's OT messengers must put to shame the impenitence of Jewish hearers, and (b) the presence of something greater than Jonah or Solomon renders their guilt yet greater."

116. Cf. A. Berkeley Mickelsen, *Interpreting,* 237. Notice the difference between this typological interpretation and the allegorical interpretation of Philo: "If the mind (= Israel) when bitten by pleasure, the serpent of Eve, shall have succeeded in beholding in soul the beauty of self-mastery, the serpent of Moses, and through beholding this, beholds God Himself, he shall live." *Legum Allegoriae* 2.81, as cited in Goppelt, *Typos,* 218, n. 37.

117. According to Dockery, "Typological Exegesis," 174, "Jesus became the direct and primary source of the church's understanding of the Old Testament."

(vv 18-19). Adam is a type of Christ, yet Paul shows that Christ is the opposite of Adam. This antithetic typology[118] enables Paul to highlight the escalation even more. Twice he uses "not like": "But the free gift is not like the trespass. . . . And the free gift is not like the effect of the one man's sin" (vv 15-16). And twice he describes the work of Christ as being much more effective ("much more surely"): "For if the many died through the one man's trespass, much more surely have the grace of God and the free gift in the grace of the one man, Jesus Christ, abounded for the many." And again, "If, because of the one man's trespass, death exercised dominion through that one, much more surely will those who receive the abundance of grace and the free gift of righteousness exercise dominion in life through the one man, Jesus Christ" (vv 15, 17).[119]

In contrast to this detailed presentation of analogy and escalation, Paul also uses simpler forms of typology. In 1 Corinthians 5:7, for example, he writes, "Our paschal lamb, Christ, has been sacrificed." That is all that is needed to establish the typological relationship between the annual sacrifices of paschal lambs (types) and the antitype, Christ.

Goppelt makes the important point that "Paul does not seek the correspondence between type and antitype in superficial similarities but in the theological essence of the events. Israel's experience at the Red Sea, for example, is not a type of baptism because both involve passing through water, but only because each is a fundamental saving act of God."[120] After analyzing 1 Corinthians 10:1-13, Romans 5:12-19, and Romans 4, Walter Roehrs also reaches this conclusion: "In these pericopes Paul establishes an analogy of correlation between man's relationship to God, as it is portrayed in the three Old Testament accounts, and the relationship to God as it pertains to the New Testament. . . . The analogy has as its common and unifying element the dynamic Word and sovereign doing of God in all instances."[121] In view of this theocentric link between type and antitype and to prevent the misuse of typology, we need to add a third criterion: valid typology is characterized not only by analogy and

118. Just as parallelism can be synonymous or antithetic, so typology can be synonymous or antithetic.

119. See Goppelt, *Typos*, 220-23. For more Adam-Christ typology, see 1 Cor 15:21-22, 45-49.

120. Ibid., 222. Cf. Goppelt's definition of Paul's typology: "A type is something that happens between God and man and that points to the salvation which has come in Christ. It is testified to by the Scripture and it prefigures a corresponding event in the last days" (p. 220).

121. Roehrs, *Concordia Journal* 10 (1984) 205-6. On 1 Cor 10:1-11, see Andrew Bandstra, *CTJ* 6 (1971) 5-21, and Walter Kaiser, *The Uses of the Old Testament in the New*, 103-21.

escalation between type and antitype but also by theocentricity, that is, both type and antitype should reveal a meaningful connection with God's acts in redemptive history.

The Gospel writers often use typology in rather subtle ways. John writes, "And the Word became flesh and lived among us, and we have seen his glory . . ." (1:14). From the English translation, we might never suspect typology, but the Greek clarifies that "lived among us" is literally "tabernacled among us." In the Old Testament "the glory of the LORD filled the tabernacle" (Exod 40:34). Now John proclaims the fulfillment of this type in Jesus, the Word made flesh. Next, John the Baptizer introduces Jesus with the words, "Here is the Lamb of God who takes away the sin of the world!" (John 1:29, 36). In the arrival of Jesus he sees fulfillment of the Old Testament sacrifices of lambs to atone for sin (cf. 1 Pet 1:19; Rev 5:6, etc.). Mark states that Jesus "was in the wilderness forty days" (1:13), probably recalling the forty days Moses fasted (Exod 34:28). With the Sermon on the Mount, Matthew pictures Jesus as the new Moses who "went up the mountain" (Matt 5:1; cf. LXX, Deut 9:9), proclaimed the Torah for the new age, and "had come down from the mountain" (Matt 8:1; cf. LXX, Exod 34:29).[122] John reports that the soldiers did not break the legs of Jesus. John comments, "These things occurred so that the scripture might be fulfilled, 'None of his bones shall be broken'" (19:33, 36). John here pictures Jesus as the antitype of the Passover lamb whose bones were not to be broken (Exod 12:46; Num 9:12).

More than any other New Testament writer, the author of Hebrews is known for his use of typology.[123] Although he uses the word *"typos"* only once,[124] he indicates types with other words such as copy or sketch (*hypodeigma*, 8:5; 9:23; *antitypos*, 9:24), shadow (*skia*, 8:5; 10:1), and symbol (*parabolē*, 9:9). He begins his letter, significantly, by reminding his readers of the progression in redemptive history: "Long ago God spoke to our ancestors in many and various ways by the prophets, but in these last days he has spoken to us by a Son . . ." (1:1-2). Jeffrey Sharp contends that "the key to understanding the author's thought is to realize that he sees all of Scripture fundamentally from the perspective of salvation history. Christ is the ultimate fulfillment of God's age long plan to reconcile mankind to Himself." This perspective means that "for our author the Old Covenant with

---

122. See W. D. Davies, "Jewish Sources," 505.

123. Although New Testament commentators frequently imply his dependence on the Alexandrian school of Jewish Platonists, this is not the case. See Longenecker, *Biblical Exegesis*, 170-74.

124. Heb 8:5, where it refers to the heavenly prototype of the tabernacle.

its events, institutions, and persons historically and metaphysically foreshadowed and 'shadowed' the reality of God's redemptive plan to be realized in Christ and his New Covenant."[125] This viewpoint causes many
types of Christ to light up in the Old Testament. For example, Melchizedek
as "priest of the Most High God" and as "king of righteousness" and "king
of peace" "resembles" the Son of God (7:1-3). Moses is a type of Christ: Moses "was faithful in all God's house. Yet Jesus is worthy of more glory than
Moses. . . . Moses was faithful in all God's house as a servant, to testify to
the things that would be spoken later. Christ, however, was faithful over
God's house as a son . . ." (3:2-6). The high priest also is a type of Christ: the
high priest who makes "a sacrifice of atonement for the sins of the people"
foreshadows the high priest "who is seated at the right hand of the throne
of the Majesty in the heavens" (2:17; 8:1-6). Also, the high priest who sacrifices "the blood of goats and calves" foreshadows the high priest who sacrifices "his own blood, thus obtaining eternal redemption" (9:12-14; 10:1-
10). Moreover, "Christ did not enter a sanctuary made by human hands, a
mere copy of the true one, but he entered into heaven itself, now to appear
in the presence of God on our behalf" (9:24-28). And so the Old Testament
tabernacle foreshadows "the true tent that the Lord, and not any mortal,
has set up" (8:2). The author of Hebrews also speaks of the "first covenant"
and a "second one" which is "better" (8:6-13). And he identifies Christ as
"the mediator of a new covenant, so that those who are called may receive
the promised eternal inheritance" (9:15).

Goppelt concludes from Hebrews that "typology is a comparative
relationship and is arranged qualitatively rather than quantitatively. The
type is not essentially a miniature version of the antitype, but is a prefiguration in a different stage of redemptive history that indicates the outline
or essential features (skia, parabolē — eikōn) of the future reality. . . ."[126]

The Way of Analogy

In addition to redemptive-historical progression, promise-fulfillment,
and typology, another way the New Testament uses to preach Christ from
the Old Testament is analogy. Analogy also finds its roots in the Old Testament, where the narrators frequently highlight the continuities in the
history they relate by casting later events and persons more or less in the
image of earlier events and persons. For example, the narrator of Genesis
"depicts Abraham as in a sense a new Adam, one in whom the destiny of

125. Sharp, *East Asia Journal of Theology* 4/2 (1986) 101.
126. Goppelt, *Typos*, 177.

mankind would be decided." He also sketches Joseph saving "all the world" (Gen 41:57) from a universal famine as analogous to Noah saving humankind from a universal flood.[127] Further, Moses' little "ark" saving him from the waters of the Nile is depicted as analogous to Noah's ark saving him from the waters of the flood. Later Samuel is presented as another Moses, and David is another Joshua.[128] The use of analogies between earlier and later events and persons enabled the Old Testament writers to emphasize both the continuity and progression in God's dealings with his people.

The New Testament writers also use analogy to establish the continuity and progression in God's dealings with Israel and through Christ with the church. Elizabeth Achtemeier rightly stresses that "this correspondence, this analogy between the Old Israel and the new, has as its sole basis the salvation history, in which the church is understood as the realization of that new people of God, created in Christ, which was promised in the Old Testament."[129]

We can describe the way of analogy for preaching Christ from the Old Testament as the move from what God was for Israel to what God through Christ is for the New Testament church.[130] In distinction from the analogy of typology, the analogy here lies between the relationship of God to Israel and that of Christ to the church. This relationship allows for different emphases.

The New Testament writers sometimes stress the analogy between God and Christ (1), at other times between Israel and the church (2), and then again between the relationship between God and Israel and the relation-

---

127. John Stek, *CTJ* 13 (1978) 143 and 145.

128. These examples were suggested to me by John Stek.

129. Achtemeier, *Old Testament and Proclamation*, 122. She is fighting the erroneous idea that "men are the same in every age and that therefore Israel's experience is instructive for the church." For many New Testament analogies between Israel and the church, see ibid., 116-23.

130. John Drane, *EvQ* 50 (1978) 199, describes analogy as "the use of O.T. language and concepts to describe N.T. realities, as, for instance, when Paul refers to the Galatian Christians as 'the Israel of God' (Gal 6:16)."

ship between Christ and his church (3). We shall note some examples in each category.

The New Testament writers can apply to Jesus Old Testament passages that speak of God acting to redeem his people Israel. For example, Malachi proclaims, "See, I am sending my messenger to prepare the way before me [the Lord] . . ." (3:1). According to Matthew, Jesus uses this verse to indicate that John the Baptizer had prepared *his* way (11:10). Ezekiel speaks of God as the good shepherd (34:11-16; cf. Isa 40:11). In John 10:1-16, we hear Jesus say, "I am the good shepherd." In fact, as we noted earlier, Jesus' "I am" sayings in John allude to Yahweh, the great I AM of the Old Testament. In Jesus Christ, Yahweh has again visited his people and tabernacled in their midst to make himself known for their salvation (John 1:14-18).

Not only does analogy show that Jesus in the New Testament continues God's redemptive work in the Old Testament, but the analogy can also emphasize the correspondence between Israel and the church. For example, in the Old Testament Israel is pictured as the bride of Yahweh (Jer 2:2; Hos 2:14-20). In the New Testament Paul speaks of the church as the bride of Christ (2 Cor 11:2; Eph 5:32). And Peter can address the New Testament church with the ancient words first spoken to Israel (Deut 10:15; Exod 19:6), "You are a chosen race, a royal priesthood, a holy nation, God's own people . . ." (1 Pet 2:9).

Frequently the analogy is drawn between the relationship between God and Israel and Christ and the church. Joel says of God, "Everyone who calls on the name of the LORD shall be saved" (2:32). Paul says of Christ, "If you confess with your lips that Jesus is Lord and believe in your heart that God raised him from the dead, you will be saved"; and then goes on to quote Joel, "Everyone who calls on the name of the Lord shall be saved" (Rom 10:9, 13). In Isaiah God says, "To me every knee shall bow, every tongue shall swear" (45:23). In Philippians Paul quotes an early Christian hymn, ". . . so that at the name of Jesus every knee should bend . . . and every tongue should confess that Jesus Christ is Lord, to the glory of God the Father" (2:10-11).

The Way of Longitudinal Themes

The Bible discloses the gradual development of themes because God progressively reveals more of himself and his will as he works out his redemptive plan in history. We see this development of themes already in the Old Testament itself. For example, some of the Psalms celebrate the victories of the present or future kings. But during the exile, when there is no Davidic king, the prophets extend this theme of victory from the royal king to the coming Messiah king.[131]

The New Testament writers also preach Christ by extending Old Testament themes to Christ, reinterpreting them in the light of Christ. They probably learned this from Jesus himself, for he often took Old Testament themes such as kingdom of God or covenant or specific laws and intensified them in the light of his own coming. Matthew provides a good example in the Sermon on the Mount, where Jesus reiterates, expands, and deepens many Old Testament themes. John Bright asserts, "Everywhere the New Testament seizes hold of the key themes of the Old and gives them new meaning in Christ."[132]

For example, the major theme of redemption is found at the beginning of the Old Testament and can be traced straight to Jesus Christ. According to Genesis, redemption is grounded in God's desire to save his creation from the rebellion of his creatures by putting enmity between the seed of the serpent and the seed of the woman (Gen 3:15). It is further grounded in God's promise to Abram, "In you all the families of the earth shall be blessed" (Gen 12:3). The central redemptive event in the Old Testament is God's liberation of Israel from slavery in Egypt. Moses reminds Israel of God keeping his oath, "It was because the LORD loved you and kept the oath that he swore to your ancestors, that the LORD has brought you out with a mighty hand, and redeemed you from the house of slavery . . ." (Deut 7:8). But redemption comes at a price: a "ransom" has to be paid; only the blood of an unblemished lamb will cause the angel of death to pass over the houses of the Israelites (Exod 12:13). Later in redemptive history a ransom has to be paid to free slaves (Lev 25:47-49). In the New Testament Jesus applies the payment of a ransom to his own mission: "the Son of Man came . . . to give his life a ransom for many" (Mark 10:45; cf. 1 Cor 7:23; 1 Tim 2:6). And Paul relates both redemption and ransom to the work of Jesus: "In him we have redemption through his blood, the forgiveness of our trespasses, according to the riches of his [God's] grace" (Eph 1:7).

Another theme that can be traced into the New Testament is the theme of sacrifices. In the Old Testament God carefully stipulated his requirements concerning sacrifices: sin offerings, guilt offerings, burnt of-

---

131. N. H. Ridderbos and P. C. Craigie, "Psalms," in *ISBE* (rev. ed., 1986) 1038. See ibid., 1039, "The Psalms are not so much messianic in any anticipatory or predictive sense as they are ancient Psalms that have come to take on new and deeper meaning within the revelation of God in Jesus Christ." In this example the way of longitudinal themes overlaps with the way of typology.

132. Bright, *Authority*, 140.

ferings. The New Testament proclaims that Christ's sacrifice on the cross fulfilled all these sacrifices (typology). But this fulfillment does not mean that God no longer requires sacrifices. New Testament writers continue the Old Testament theme but apply it in a new way. Peter urges the church "to be a holy priesthood, to offer spiritual sacrifices acceptable to God through Jesus Christ" (1 Pet 2:5). And Paul writes, "I appeal to you . . . to present your bodies as a living sacrifice, holy and acceptable to God . . ." (Rom 12:1; cf. Heb 13:15-16).

Sometimes an Old Testament theme is alluded to with a single word. Mark relates in the story of Jesus stilling the storm that his disciples "were filled with great awe and said to one another, 'Who then is this, that even the wind and the sea obey him?'" (4:41). The disciples may not yet know who Jesus is, but Mark the narrator has given us a clue: "He woke up and *rebuked* the wind" (v 39). "The Greek verb *epitimaō* in the Greek Old Testament is owned by Yahweh. Yahweh 'rebukes' the channels of the sea (Ps 18:15), the primordial Deep (Ps 104:5-9), the sea (Nah 1:3b-5), rivers (Isa 50:2), rider and horse (Ps 76:6), Assyrian armies (Isa 17:13), wicked nations (Ps 9:5), and Satan (Zech 3:1-2)."[133] In his first miracle recorded in Mark, Jesus "rebuked" an unclean spirit (1:25); later he will "rebuke" Satan, "Get behind me, Satan!" (8:33). Therefore, when Jesus here "rebukes" the wind, Mark's point is clear: in Jesus we see Yahweh in action battling chaos and seeking to restore order in his kingdom.[134]

The Way of Contrast

The New Testament also preaches Christ by way of contrast. Whereas the other ways focus on the continuity between the Old Testament and Christ, contrast focusses on the discontinuity Christ brings. For example, we observe a major difference in the manner in which God sought to reestablish his kingdom on earth before Christ and after Christ. To reestablish his holy kingdom in Old Testament times God ordered Israel to "utterly destroy" the seven sinful nations living in the promised land along with their altars, pillars, sacred poles, and idols (Deut 7:1-6). In New Testament times, by contrast, Jesus orders his church to "make disciples of all nations, baptizing them in the name of the Father and of the Son and of the Holy Spirit, and teaching them to obey everything that I have commanded you" (Matt 28:19-20).

133. McCurley, *Wrestling*, 21.
134. In this example the theme of rebuking overlaps with the analogy: as Yahweh rebuked, so Jesus rebukes.

We can also observe a major difference between the manner in which Israel was expected to fulfill the requirements of the old covenant and the manner in which Christians are expected to fulfill the requirements of the new covenant. Jeremiah had already predicted this contrast: "It will not be like the covenant that I made with their ancestors when I took them by the hand to bring them out of the land of Egypt — a covenant that they broke. . . ." The Sinai covenant required obedience to covenant stipulations that were external, written on stone tablets. Not so the new covenant: "I will put my law within them, and I will write it on their hearts" (Jer 31:32-33). Jesus inaugurates this new covenant with his death and resurrection: "This cup is the new covenant in my blood" (1 Cor 11:25). The apostle Paul in particular emphasizes this difference between the law as an external demand and the law the Spirit writes internally on our hearts. He tells the Corinthians, "You show that you are a letter of Christ, prepared by us, written not with ink but with the Spirit of the living God, not on tablets of stone but on tablets of human hearts" (2 Cor 3:3).

As a final exhibit, the Sermon on the Mount contains a whole series of contrasts between Jesus' teaching and the Old Testament torah as interpreted by the rabbis: "You have heard that it was said to those of ancient times, 'You shall not murder. . . .' But I say to you that if you are angry with a brother or sister, you will be liable to judgment. . . . You have heard that it was said, 'You shall not commit adultery.' But I say to you that everyone who looks at a woman with lust has already committed adultery with her in his heart. . . . It was also said, 'Whoever divorces his wife, let him give her a certificate of divorce.' But I say to you. . . . Again, you have heard . . . , 'You shall not swear falsely.' But I say to you. . . . You have heard that it was said, 'An eye for an eye and a tooth for a tooth.' But I say to you. . . . You have heard that it was said, 'You shall love your neighbor and hate your enemy.' But I say to you, Love your enemies and pray for those who persecute you . . ." (Matt 5:21-48).

In the next chapter we shall examine these New Testament ways of preaching Christ from the Old Testament in the light of contemporary hermeneutical discussions.

CHAPTER 6

The Christocentric Method

"We ought to read the Scriptures with the express design of finding Christ in them. Whoever shall turn aside from this object,
though he may weary himself throughout his whole life in learning, will never attain the knowledge of the truth; for what wisdom can we have without the wisdom of God?"

Calvin, *Comm.* John 5:39

SINCE THE METHOD of preaching Christ from the Old Testament I here
propose falls somewhere between Calvin's theocentric method and Luther's christological method, I shall call it the christocentric method, or,
more precisely, the redemptive-historical christocentric method. The
christocentric method complements the theocentric method of interpreting the Old Testament by seeking to do justice to the fact that *God's* story
of bringing his kingdom on earth is centered in *Christ:* Christ the center of
redemptive history, Christ the center of the Scriptures. In preaching any
part of Scripture, one must understand its message in the light of that
center, Jesus Christ.

REDEMPTIVE-HISTORICAL
CHRISTOCENTRIC INTERPRETATION

It should be clear by now that our concern is not to preach Christ to the
exclusion of the "whole counsel of God" but rather to view the whole
counsel of God, with all its teachings, laws, prophecies, and visions, in

227

the light of Jesus Christ. At the same time, it should be evident that we must not read the incarnate Christ back into the Old Testament text, which would be eisegesis, but that we should look for legitimate ways of preaching Christ from the Old Testament in the context of the New.

Redemptive-historical interpretation seeks to understand an Old Testament passage first in its own historical-cultural context. Only after we have heard a passage the way Israel heard it can we move on to understand this message in the broad contexts of the whole canon and the whole of redemptive history. It is at this point that the questions concerning Jesus Christ, the center, emerge. We shall first discuss these two basic interpretive moves and then consider legitimate ways for preaching Christ from the Old Testament.

First, Understand the Passage in Its Own Historical Context

A preacher's first responsibility is to seek to understand the message of the selected passage in its own historical-cultural context. As John Bright puts it, "All biblical preaching must begin with grammatico-historical exegesis of the text, with all that that entails. . . . Whatever message it may legitimately have for hearers today must grow out of, and remain true to, its original meaning."[1]

This original, historical meaning is important for preachers because it offers the only objective point of control against deriving from the text all kinds of subjective and arbitrary messages. "Once the plain meaning has been abandoned, control over interpretation is gone and Scripture may mean anything the spirit (and who shall say if it be the Holy Spirit or the preacher's?) may see in it."[2] In addition to offering an objective point of control for deriving the contemporary significance of a passage, the original meaning can also prevent a Christomonistic reduction of its meaning (as we saw in Vischer), for the original message of the Old Testament is clearly God-centered.

To uncover the original, historical meaning of a passage, preachers need to do justice to three intertwined strands of the text: the literary, the

---

1. Bright, *Int* 20 (1966) 189.
2. Bright, *Authority*, 91. Cf. Gordon Fee and Douglas Stuart, *How to Read the Bible*, 26, "The only proper control for hermeneutics is to be found in the original intent of the biblical text. . . . In contrast to . . . [pure] subjectivity, we insist that the original meaning of the text — as much as it is in our power to discern it — is the objective point of control."

historical, and the theocentric. Although in the actual practice of interpretation one may often work with all three strands at the same time, for the sake of analysis we shall unravel the strands and note the specific questions each raises for interpreting the text.

Literary Interpretation

Under the category of literary interpretation we should ask first, *How* does it mean?[3] That is to say, What genre of literature is this? Narrative? Wisdom? Psalm? Prophecy? Further, what subgenre or form did the author use? Law? Parable? Proverb? Lament? Autobiography? Lawsuit? Finally, moving to the smallest forms, What figures of speech did the author employ? Metaphor? Simile? Hyperbole? Irony? These how-does-it-mean questions need to be answered before we can confidently answer the what-did-it-mean question, for the how question guides the what.

Next we can proceed to the question, *What* did it mean? At this point in the process of interpretation our question should be restricted to, What did it mean in the context of this particular book? Here more literary questions need to be asked: If it is a story, what are the conflict and resolution?[4] If it is an argument, what is the flow of the argument? Further, what rhetorical structures did the author use to make his point? Repetition? Parallelism? Chiasm? Inclusio? Further, the usual grammatical questions need to be posed: forms of nouns, verbs, and clauses as well as syntax. Finally, how does the passage function in the context of this book?

Historical Interpretation

Historical interpretation digs deeper into the question of a text's meaning by raising two basic questions. First, what was the author's intended meaning for his original hearers? To answer this question, we need to ask further questions about the author, the original hearers, the approximate period, the social and geographical setting, and the purpose for writing — in short, who wrote this text? to whom? when? where? and why?

The final "why" question introduces the second basic question that must be answered under historical interpretation: What need of the hearers did the author seek to address? This question is especially significant for preachers, for it seeks to uncover the passage's original relevance, which will form the bridge to present relevance. The author's original

---

3. For the idea of asking the unusual "how" question before the usual "what" question, I am indebted to my colleague John H. Stek.

4. See my *Modern Preacher*, 197-213.

message and the need of his hearers are related as arrow and target. The need of Israel at that time was the target the Old Testament writer aimed at with his message.

Theocentric Interpretation

Scholars usually speak of "theological interpretation," but many agree that it is a term which different people use in different senses. We shall use the term "theocentric interpretation" because it describes exactly the important question that needs to be answered at this point: <u>What does this passage reveal about God and his will?</u> The question concerns God not in the abstract but as he has revealed himself in his relationship with his creation and creatures. This question, therefore, seeks to discover what the passage says about God's acts, God's providence, God's covenant, God's law, God's grace, God's faithfulness, and so on. Gerhard von Rad states that "the primary concern of the Old Testament writings" is Israel's "relationship to God."[5] John Rogers adds perceptively, "While God is the Subject of his own story, he has graciously, and irrevocably, chosen to include us. Herein lies the key to the deepest meaning of human existence as originating in God's intention; of human life received and lived as a trust from God."[6] With sound literary and historical interpretation, theocentric interpretation might not be necessary, but our predilection to slight the God-centered focus of Old Testament literature requires this additional question.[7] Moreover, it will prove to be an important link to Christ-centered preaching.

Next, Understand the Message in the Contexts of Canon and Redemptive History

Christian preachers cannot preach an Old Testament text in isolation, but must always understand the text in the contexts of the whole Bible and redemptive history. Simply to preach the message of an Old Testament text in isolation is to preach an Old Testament sermon, for the histories of revelation and redemption have moved on. Therefore a Christian sermon on an Old Testament text will necessarily move on to the New Testament. This is obvious when the text contains a promise that is fulfilled in Christ: preachers cannot stop with the promise but will naturally move on in the sermon to its fulfillment. The same holds when the text contains a type

---

5. Von Rad, *God at Work*, 14.
6. Rogers, *Int* 45 (1991) 241.
7. See my *Modern Preacher*, 102-6.

that is fulfilled in Christ: one would move in the sermon from the type to the Antitype. And the same holds when the text relates a theme which is further developed in the New Testament: one would move in the sermon from the Old Testament theme to its latest development in the New Testament.

Required for Sound Expository Preaching

Sometimes the classification of "textual preaching" is misunderstood as preaching only the message of the selected text. But the term "textual preaching" was coined to contrast biblical-textual preaching with topical preaching; it was never intended to confine the sermon strictly to the message of the selected text in isolation from its context. We can avoid this misunderstanding by using the term "expository preaching," provided we avoid the confusion of definitions around this term ranging from verse-by-verse explication and application (more precisely homily) to preaching on a Bible passage "longer than two or three verses."[8] Expository preaching, as its name implies, is to expose, to lay open, the meaning of the preaching-text in its contexts. Merrill Unger has provided a fine description of "expository preaching": handling the text "in such a way that its real and essential meaning as it existed in the mind of the particular Biblical writer and as it exists in the light of the over-all context of Scripture is made plain and applied to the present-day needs of the hearers."[9] Sound expository preaching always requires these three basic moves: from (1) determining the original meaning, to (2) the meaning in the context of the whole canon, to (3) the application of this meaning for our hearers today.

Canonical Interpretation

In understanding the meaning of a passage in the contexts of the canon and redemptive history, we can also distinguish the three strands of literary, historical, and theocentric interpretation, but this time the questions in each classification will be much broader.

At this level, literary interpretation is canonical interpretation and asks the question, What does this passage mean (not just in the context of the book, but) in the context of the whole Bible? Old Testament promises gradually fill up until they are fulfilled in Christ's First or Second Coming; biblical themes develop from the Old Testament to the New; biblical laws develop from the Old Testament to the New. Because of progression

8. See my *Modern Preacher*, 10-12.
9. Unger, *Principles*, 33.

in God's redemptive history and revelation, one will discover both continuity and discontinuity in Old Testament promises, themes, and laws.

Redemptive-Historical Interpretation

At this broader level, historical interpretation is redemptive-historical interpretation and asks not, What was the author's intended meaning for
his original hearers? but, How does the redemptive-historical context
from creation to new creation inform the contemporary significance of
this text? The context of redemptive history will reveal continuity as well
as discontinuity. For example, when one preaches on a passage like Genesis 17:9-14, the textual theme is, "Circumcise every male among you as a
sign of God's covenant." But to preach this message today would be to
preach an Old Testament sermon. Christian preachers will need to examine what happens to this Old Testament ordinance in redemptive history.
They will soon discover that the first council of the Christian church
dropped the requirement of circumcision (Acts 15) and that baptism
gradually became the sign of the new covenant (Col 2:11-12). This sign,
moreover, was applied to both males and females (Gal 3:27-29). In the
light of the redemptive-historical context, therefore, the theme of the sermon shifts from "Circumcise every male among you as a sign of God's
covenant" to "Baptize all members of the body of Christ as a sign of
God's covenant." In order to do justice to both the Old Testament textual
theme and its later development, one may wish to settle for a sermon
theme that covers both circumcision and baptism: "Apply the sign of
God's covenant to all God's covenant people." Where the contrast turns
out to be so great, however, one should consider selecting as a preaching-
text one of the New Testament passages and develop this against the
backdrop of the Old Testament ordinance regarding circumcision.

Christocentric Interpretation

At this level theocentric interpretation is Christocentric interpretation
and goes beyond the earlier question, What does this passage reveal
about God and his will? to the questions, What does this passage mean in
the light of Jesus Christ? And what does this passage reveal about Jesus
Christ? Christopher Wright maintains, "We may legitimately see in the
event, or in the record of it, additional levels of significance in the light of
the end of the story — i.e. in the light of Christ."[10] For example, "Looking
back on the event [of the exodus] . . . in the light of the fullness of God's

---

10. Wright, *Knowing Jesus*, 28.

redemptive achievement in Jesus Christ, we can see that even the original exodus was not merely concerned with the political, economic, and social aspects of Israel's predicament. There was also a level of spiritual oppression in Israel's subjection to the gods of Egypt."[11]

Some scholars speak of these additional levels of significance we discover in the broad contexts of canon and redemptive history as the *sensus plenior,* the fuller sense.[12] Others prefer to speak of a "'theological' literal sense," which "means nothing other than the meaning of the scripture read as a whole and in the *analogia fidei* [rule of faith]."[13] Still others prefer to speak of canonical interpretation.[14] I continue to favor the name that refers to the broadest possible context and gives due recognition to God's acts in history, "redemptive-historical interpretation." Whatever name we use, the important point is that a passage understood in the contexts of the whole Bible and redemptive history may reveal more meaning than its author intended originally. For example, it is not likely that the author of Numbers 21 realized that in relating the story of the bronze serpent he was sketching a type of Christ. The type in this passage is discovered only from the New Testament perspective when Jesus makes use of this event to proclaim his own saving work.

The question, What does this passage reveal about Jesus Christ? gives rise to the more specific question: Which of the six ways we discovered in the New Testament lead to the incarnate Christ? Redemptive-historical progression? Promise-fulfillment? Typology? Analogy? Longitudinal themes? Or contrast?

Because of the completion of the New Testament, we can now add to these six ways a seventh way the preacher can employ: New Testament references. This additional way gives rise to another issue, namely, where to place New Testament references in our rather logical order of raising

11. Ibid., 29.

12. Raymond Brown offers the following definition, "The *sensus plenior* is that additional, deeper meaning, intended by God but not clearly intended by the human author, which is seen to exist in the words of a Biblical text (or group of texts, or even a whole book) when they are studied in the light of further revelation or development in the understanding of revelation." *The "Sensus Plenior" of Sacred Scripture,* 92. For further references, see my *Modern Preacher,* 111-12. A fine historical overview is provided by Wilfrid J. Harrington, *The Path of Biblical Theology* (Dublin: Gill and Macmillan, 1973), 293-313.

13. Norbert Lohfink, in *The Christian Meaning of the Old Testament,* 42-43, as cited by Douglas Moo, "The Problem of *Sensus Plenior,*" 205.

14. The method of understanding a text in the context of the Christian canon has been developed especially by Brevard Childs. For references see my *Modern Preacher,* 73-77.

questions about ways that lead from the text to Christ. Because the New Testament writers were inspired, our first inclination might be to place these references first on our list. But we have seen that these writers sometimes refer to Old Testament passages merely to illustrate their own specific messages rather than to proclaim and extend the message of the passage they cite.[15] Moreover, if there is only a single New Testament reference, we might be tempted to read the Old Testament text through this single lens. But this was one of our objections against "pairing" the Old Testament text with one from the New Testament: it might skew the interpretation of the Old Testament passage. It seems best, therefore, to consider any New Testament references either last or at the end of the five ways of continuity, just before the way of contrast. In this position, the New Testament references can confirm our findings, correct our insights and oversights, or provide new angles.

Usually one can make a case for several of these seven ways. This does not mean that preachers should use all the discovered ways in the sermon; in the interest of a unified sermon, they should use only the ways that are in line with the sermon theme. In the light of contemporary discussions, we shall now examine in turn these seven ways in which the modern preacher can preach Christ from the Old Testament.[16] Although there is some overlap between these ways and they can often be used in combination, we shall look at many examples to discover what is distinctive about each way. We shall begin our discussion with the way on which all the other ways depend: redemptive-historical progression.

THE WAY OF
REDEMPTIVE-HISTORICAL PROGRESSION

Redemptive-historical progression is the foundational way of preaching Christ from the Old Testament. Redemptive history, or kingdom history, is the bedrock which supports all the other ways that lead to Christ in the New Testament. Today redemptive history is also called the "metanarrative," or "The Story."

15. For example, preaching on Jericho and Rahab (Josh 6), one finds that Heb 11:31 refers to Rahab as an illustration of faith, while James 2:25 refers to her as an illustration of being "justified by works." But neither of these is the point of Joshua 6.

16. Cf. Gerhard Hasel, *OT Theology*, 157, "It would seem that the only adequate way to come to grips with the multiplex nature of the relationship between the Testaments is to opt for a multiplex approach, which makes a guarded and circumspect use of typology, employs the idea of promise and fulfillment, and also uses in a careful way the approach of *Heilsgeschichte*."

Pivotal Points in Redemptive History

We have seen that the meta-narrative that underlies Scripture has certain pivotal points: Creation–Fall–Redemption–New Creation. From the perspective of God's acts in history in seeking to bring his kingdom on earth, we might better highlight these major points:

1. Creation: God's acts of turning chaos into his structured kingdom (Gen 1–2);
2. Redemption in Old Testament times: God's acts, after the fall into sin, of redeeming his people Israel to be a light to the nations (Gen 3—Mal 4);
3. Redemption through Jesus Christ: God's acts in Jesus to redeem all nations and restore his fallen creation into his kingdom (Matt 1–Rev 20); and
4. New Creation: God's final victory over evil and the establishment of his perfect kingdom on earth (Rev 21–22).

Walther Zimmerli has graphically caught the flow of the Old Testament section of redemptive history with the picture of a river: "When we survey the entire Old Testament, we find ourselves involved in a great history of movement from promise toward fulfillment. It flows like a large brook — here rushing swiftly, there apparently coming to rest in a quiet backwater, and yet moving forward as a whole toward a distant goal which lies beyond itself."[17] That goal is Jesus Messiah and ultimately the rule of God over a restored and transformed creation.[18]

Characteristics of Redemptive History

Redemptive history is the bedrock for preaching Christ from the Old Testament. Donald G. Miller maintains, "In order to confront men with the crucial question of Christ, our *preaching must centre in the history of redemption.* We do not confront men with Christ by preaching theological ideas, nor by ethical exhortations, but by rehearsing the saving events wit-

---

17. Zimmerli, "Promise and Fulfillment," 111.

18. Cf. Domenico Grasso, *Proclaiming,* 116-17, "The history of salvation has Christ as its center and its frame of reference. . . . If everything has its true meaning in Christ, everything discussed in preaching must be seen in the light of Christ: any other light would be false or at least incomplete. Morals, dogma, the liturgy, the Church, Scripture — all have their frame of reference in Christ."

nessed in Scripture."[19] Allegorical interpretation, with its flights of fancy, strayed from the solid foundation of redemptive history and is therefore to be rejected. The deistic/secular form of modern historical-critical interpretation, ironically, ended up in even worse straits: with its presuppositions it eliminated God as sovereign Lord and agent in history and thus altogether lost the vision of a single redemptive history.[20] Even Wilhelm Vischer, with his "witness-concept," "presents parallels without making plain the redemptive-historical perspective and, for that reason, his exegesis strikes us as arbitrary."[21] Whatever ways we use for preaching Christ from the Old Testament, they must be grounded in God's redemptive history and/or God's history of revelation.

Besides acknowledging redemptive history as the foundation for preaching Christ from the Old Testament, we should note two other characteristics of redemptive history. Since it is God's story of redeeming his people and restoring his creation, redemptive history is God-centered. As Georges Florovsky puts it, "The Bible . . . is the story of God's dealings with his chosen people. The Bible records first of all God's acts and mighty deeds, *Magnalia Dei*. The process has been initiated by God."[22] The recognition that redemptive history is God-centered is important because it establishes the connection to God's climactic act in Christ.

Another characteristic of redemptive history is that it is a unified history. In spite of switchbacks, stops, and starts, it progresses steadily to its ultimate goal. "There is a beginning and an end, which is also a goal. . . . There is one composite and yet single story — from Genesis to Revelation. And this story is history. There is a process going on between these two terminal points. . . . Every particular moment is correlated to both terms and has thereby its proper and unique place within the whole. No moment therefore can be understood except in the whole context and perspective."[23] Because redemptive history is a unified history, sound interpretation requires that every part of this history be interpreted in the context of its beginning and end or goal.

---

19. Miller, *SJT* 11 (1958) 396.

20. Specifically the presuppositions of analogy based on the similarity of all events and of correlation based on the assumption that we live in a closed universe of immanent causes and effects. See my *Modern Preacher*, 24-36, 95-96. Cf. Alvin Plantinga, "Two (or More) Kinds of Scripture Scholarship," *Modern Theology* 14 (1998) 243-78. For the disastrous effects of the secular historical-critical method on the Christian pulpit, see Elizabeth Achtemeier, *Preaching from the Old Testament*, 29-32.

21. G. C. Berkouwer, *Person of Christ*, 128.

22. Florovsky, "Revelation," 165.

23. Ibid. Cf. my *Modern Preacher*, 94-101.

The Way of Redemptive-Historical Progression

Accordingly, the way of redemptive-historical progression sees every Old Testament text and its addressees in the context of God's dynamic history, which progresses steadily and reaches its climax in the life, death, and resurrection of Jesus Christ and ultimately in the new creation.[24] The whole Old Testament throbs with a strong eschatological beat. Every passage in some way or in some degree voices or echoes the message: "God is acting! God is coming! God is faithful to his covenant promises! His mercy indeed endures forever! God will not cast off His chosen people! God is preparing salvation."[25] From our position later in redemptive history, we should not only hear this eschatological beat but also recognize its fulfillment in the First and Second Coming of Jesus. Ross Mackenzie writes, "One can therefore preach a Christian sermon from the Old Testament because its whole history leads to Christ and finds fulfillment in him. In a thousand Old Testament passages the Christian preacher sees depths of significance not apparent to old Israel, because he knows where the story came out."[26]

We can picture redemptive-historical progression as follows:

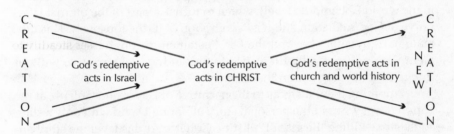

Since Old Testament redemptive history steadily progresses to its center of God's climactic acts in Christ, Christian preachers need only locate

24. Cf. von Rad, *God at Work*, 155, "Old Testament history, in judgment and in salvation, bears witness to *that* action of God that becomes finally revealed in Jesus Christ." Cf. Larsen, *Anatomy*, 167, "God's saving work is everywhere in the Old Testament. In this holistic sense, all of the Old Testament prepares for and is fulfilled in Christ. We can't preach the Old Testament as if the fulfillment had not come."

25. Herbert Mayer, *CTM* 35 (1964) 605. Cf. p. 606, "The preacher is overwhelmed by the magnificent portrayal of the acting, merciful, loving, faithful, and judging God. From this point of view every word in the Old Testament is 'Messianic.'"

26. Mackenzie, *Int* 22 (1968) 24. Cf. Louis Berkhof, *Principles*, 142: "The various lines of the Old Testament revelation converge towards it [the Word made flesh], and those of the New Testament revelation radiate from it. It is only in their binding center, Jesus Christ, that the narratives of Scripture find their explanation."

their preaching-text in the sweep of redemptive history to sense its movement to Christ.

The Way of Redemptive-Historical Progression in Narrative

Redemptive-historical progression works especially well for preaching Christ from historical narrative. For example, if we make a sermon on the narrative of David and Goliath, we may not isolate this narrative from the flow of redemptive history and hold David up to the congregation as a hero whose courage we should imitate in fighting our individual Goliaths. Instead, we should endeavor to discover the meaning of this narrative in the context of the whole of redemptive history. To make this move, it may be helpful to remember an intermediate step. Old Testament narratives can be understood at three levels: the bottom level is seeing the story as personal history, the middle level is viewing it as national history, and the top level is understanding it as redemptive history. Gordon Fee and Douglas Stuart write: "Every individual Old Testament narrative (bottom level) is at least a part of the greater narrative of Israel's history in the world (the middle level), which in turn is a part of the ultimate narrative of God's creation and His redemption of it (the top level). This ultimate narrative goes beyond the Old Testament through the New Testament. You will not fully do justice to any individual narrative without recognizing its part within the other two."[27]

Applying these insights to the narrative of David and Goliath, at the bottom level we read the personal story of young David with only a sling and a stone killing the giant Philistine Goliath. At this level the story appeals to many people, and some preachers are quick to sketch David as our role model of courage. But the biblical author is not interested in this personal story as such; his interest lies at the middle level. He goes to great lengths to show that this story of David and Goliath is an important part of Israel's national/royal history: Samuel had just secretly anointed the young shepherd David as king over Israel (1 Sam 16). Next (1 Sam 17), the young shepherd-king saves Israel from its arch-enemy by killing Goliath. The message is: David, God's anointed king, delivers Israel and secures its safety in the promised land.

Now we are ready to move to the top level: What does this story mean in the totality of God's redemptive history? Notice that David does

27. Fee and Stuart, *How to Read the Bible*, 74-75. Cf. Willem VanGemeren, *Progress*, 32, "The interpreter asks what the text has to do with the coming of Jesus and our hope in the restoration of all things at his return."

not rely on his own strength, or weapons, or skill. David says, "I come to you in the name of the LORD of hosts, the God of the armies of Israel . . . so that all the earth may know that there is a God in Israel, and that all this assembly may know that the LORD does not save by sword and spear; for the battle is the LORD's . . ." (1 Sam 17:45-47). The essence of this story, therefore, is more than Israel's king defeating the enemy; the essence is that the Lord himself defeats the enemy of his people. This theme locates this passage on the highway of God's kingdom history which leads straight to Jesus' victory over Satan. This history of enmity began right after the fall into sin when God said to the serpent (later identified as Satan): "I will put enmity between you and the woman, and between your offspring and hers; he will strike your head, and you will strike his heel" (Gen 3:15). Thus the battle between David and Goliath is more than a personal scrap; it is more than Israel's king defeating a powerful enemy; it is a small chapter in the battle between the seed of the woman and the seed of the serpent — a battle which reaches its climax in Jesus' victory over Satan, first with his death and resurrection, and finally at his Second Coming when Satan will be thrown "into the lake of fire and sulfur" (Rev 20:10). In the sermon, then, one can travel the road of redemptive-historical progression from the battle of David and Goliath to the battle of Christ and Satan. And to apply this passage to God's people today, one can follow redemptive-historical progression to the present day when the church, the body of Christ, is still involved in this universal battle. The precise application will differ according to the church's circumstances. If the church addressed suffers from persecution, one can comfort God's people with the assurance that "the battle is the LORD's": in Christ he has conquered and will conquer. If the church addressed is selfishly enjoying the prosperity of the nation and has lost sight of the universal battle, one can apply this passage to urge God's people to get involved in the battle against the evil one in our day and age. If the church addressed is engaged in the battle but is relying on its own strength, one can urge God's people to allow God to work through them, for God fights the battle by empowering his servants. The point is that redemptive-historical progression can provide not only a Christ-centered focus but also contemporary application.

The Way of Redemptive-Historical Progression in the Psalms and Wisdom Literature

Redemptive-historical progression enables us to preach Christ not only from historical narrative but also from other Old Testament genres of literature. Take, for example, the Psalms. In Psalm 84 the Psalmist expresses his longing to go to the temple, "the courts of the LORD." Frequently preachers apply the Psalmist's longing directly to God's people today, as if redemptive history had not moved on. Preachers tell their congregations, "That longing we must have when we go to church!" In contrast, B. Holwerda notes the progression in redemptive history: "The Psalmist could enter the forecourts only a few times per year; he could not raise his family or have his work within the temple, and this made him jealous of the sparrows and swallows who made their nests in the temple. But this lack is fulfilled in Christ. Through him the place of worship is raised everywhere; family life and work are now permanently linked to the temple. We now have access not only to the forecourts but to the holy of holies. So the application of this passage is: How rich we are after Pentecost! And there is room for the admonition: How shall we escape if we neglect so great a salvation? Unfaithfulness in church attendance can then be much more harshly reprimanded."[28]

Wisdom literature is notoriously difficult for Christ-centered preaching, but here also redemptive-historical progression can at times open up an approach. Suppose we set out to make a sermon on Ecclesiastes 12:1-8. Our theme is "Remember your Creator in your youth!" The author instructs the youth in Israel to remember their Creator "before the days of trouble come." At that point in redemptive history, they knew their Creator through his acts of saving Israel and through his revelation in creation. Today we know our Creator not only through his general revelation and his special revelation to Israel; we know him especially through Jesus Christ. In Christ we see not only the power and might of our Creator but especially his saving love for his people and his creation. How much more, then, ought we to be motivated to remember our Creator, and that not only in our youth but also in the "days of trouble."

THE WAY OF PROMISE-FULFILLMENT

Promise-fulfillment fell upon hard times in the twentieth century. According to Brevard Childs, "the last full-blown, scholarly attempt to defend the traditional Christian understanding of Old Testament messianism as a unified, organic development according to the structure of the Hebrew canon . . . was that of Hengstenberg (*Christology of the Old Testament . . .*)." The two volumes were published almost 150 years ago and translated into English in 1854. Childs claims that "the new literary criticism" of Wellhausen and others, because of their "radical redating of the

---

28. B. Holwerda, *Begonnen*, 111 (my translation).

biblical material broke the back of the traditional understanding of the growth of Old Testament messianism."[29] Breaking "the back of the traditional understanding" overstates the case considerably, for source criticism and its results were not accepted in large segments of Protestantism, Roman Catholicism, and especially Eastern Orthodoxy; moreover, after many attempted revisions, it has been pretty well eclipsed by the new literary criticism (narrative criticism) of the 1980s, which abandoned the scrambled results of source criticism in favor of the final text.[30] What is more, the church has always accepted as the inspired scriptures not hypothetical sources behind the text but the final, canonical text. Nevertheless, it is true that Wellhausen's radical redating took much of the steam out of research seeking to show the gradual development in Old Testament messianic predictions from Genesis 3:15 to Malachi 4:5-6. Childs claims that today "the vast majority of Old Testament scholars connect the origin of a messianic hope with the establishment of the Davidic monarchy which received its divine legitimacy in 2 Samuel 7."[31] Happily, some scholars hold to a broader view of God's promise than simply "messianic hope,"[32] and others seek to trace even "messianic hope" back all the way to Genesis 3:15.[33] In any event, in the canonical Scriptures as the church has received them, the concept of God's promise goes back all the way to God's covenant promises to Abraham (Gen 12:1-3), and even beyond that to Genesis 3:15.

Edmund Clowney writes: "When the Old Testament is interpreted in the light of its own structure of promise and when that promise is seen as fulfilled in Jesus Christ, then the significance of the Old Testament can be preached in theological depth and in practical power. Preaching that does not center on Christ will always miss the dimension of depth in Old Testament revelation."[34] So how should preachers today preach Christ as the fulfillment of Old Testament promises?

29. Childs, *Biblical Theology*, 453.

30. Note, however, that many of the proponents of the new literary criticism wish to "bracket out" the question of historicity. For references, see my *Modern Preacher*, 78-79, and my "The Value of a Literary Approach for Preaching," in *A Literary Guide to the Bible*, ed. Leland Ryken and Tremper Longman III (Grand Rapids: Zondervan, 1993), 509-19.

31. Childs, *Biblical Theology*, 453.

32. For example, Walther Zimmerli, "Promise and Fulfillment."

33. See, e.g., T. Desmond Alexander, "Messianic Ideology in the Book of Genesis," in *The Lord's Anointed: Interpretation of Old Testament Messianic Texts*, 19-39; Walter Kaiser, *The Messiah in the Old Testament*; and Gerard Van Groningen, *Messianic Revelation in the Old Testament*.

34. Clowney, "Preaching Christ from All the Scriptures," 183.

Special Rules for Promise-Fulfillment

As we seek to use promise-fulfillment, we should keep in mind especially two rules for interpreting Old Testament promises. First, take into account that God usually fills up his promises progressively — in installments, as it were. We noticed progressive fulfillment already in the Old Testament. William LaSor contrasts biblical prophecy with mere prediction of a future event. He writes, "Prophecy, in the sense that it reveals some part of God's redemptive purpose, is capable of being filled, of achieving fullness, so that when it is *filled full* it is *fulfilled*. If we understand prophecy in this sense, we no longer ask the question 'Is prophecy capable of more than one fulfillment?' It is capable of more and more filling until it is entirely fulfilled."[35] For example, even though Peter on the day of Pentecost declared, "This is what was spoken through the prophet Joel," several of Joel's predictions still await fulfillment, such as, "The sun shall be turned to darkness, and the moon to blood, before the great and terrible day of the LORD comes" (Joel 2:31).

Second, in interpreting the text, move from the promise of the Old Testament to the fulfillment in Christ and back again to the Old Testament text. Willem VanGemeren explains, "In order not to miss the full impact of the prophetic message as a basis for the hope in the promise of God, the Christian exegete moves from the Old Testament message to the New Testament, explores the progression of the kingdom of Christ, and returns again to the prophetic message in order to determine more clearly how the word was fulfilled, is being fulfilled and will be fulfilled. The danger exists of reading the New Testament into the Old Testament and thereby missing aspects of hope and promise which are in the Old Testament passage, but which were not brought out in the New Testament quotation."[36]

With these two rules in mind, we shall examine some Old Testament promises.

Promises in the Prophets

We shall begin with the most obvious place to look for messianic promises: the prophets. In Isaiah 61:1-4, God gives his people in Babylonian exile the wonderful promise of deliverance: "The spirit of the Lord GOD is upon me. . . . They shall build up the ancient ruins . . . ; they shall repair the ruined cities" (vv 1, 4). This prophecy was originally fulfilled in the years fol-

35. LaSor, *TynBul* 29 (1978) 55.
36. VanGemeren, *WTJ* 46 (1984) 281.

lowing 538 B.C. when the remnant returned from exile. But some 570 years later, when Jesus read this passage in the synagogue of Nazareth, he proclaimed further fulfillment: "Today this scripture has been fulfilled in your hearing" (Luke 4:21). Now, instead of completing our interpretation at this point, we move back to our text and notice, for example, that Jesus did not mention "the day of vengeance of our God." This day still lies in the future. But even the elements of Jubilee Jesus began to fulfill during his years on earth await further fulfillment. We can, therefore, sketch the process of the filling up of this prophecy by focussing on three major points:

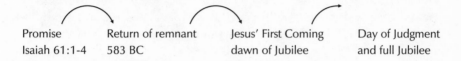

| Promise | Return of remnant | Jesus' First Coming | Day of Judgment |
| Isaiah 61:1-4 | 583 BC | dawn of Jubilee | and full Jubilee |

When we preach on God giving King Ahaz, under threat from Syria and Ephraim, the sign of Immanuel (Isa 7:11-17), we know that it was fulfilled sometime before 732 B.C. when Tiglath-Pileser defeated both countries. But Matthew sees further fulfillment especially in the name of the child, as is evident from his added translation of "Emmanuel": "All this took place to fulfill what had been spoken by the Lord through the prophet: 'Look, the virgin shall conceive and bear a son, and they shall name him Emmanuel,' which means, 'God is with us'" (Matt 1:22-23). In this case, "God is with us," an ancient Old Testament theme, provides the opening for further fulfillments. Before Jesus ascends to the Father, he promises his disciples, "And see, I am sending upon you what my Father promised; so stay here in the city until you have been clothed with power from on high" (Luke 24:49). This promise was fulfilled on the day of Pentecost, when they "were filled with the Holy Spirit" (Acts 2:4): God is with us. But the promise of "God is with us" stretches even beyond the church age to the new creation when, according to the voice John heard, "the home of God is among mortals. He will dwell with them; they will be his peoples, and God himself will be with them" (Rev 21:3). We can, therefore, sketch the filling up of this prophecy at four major points:

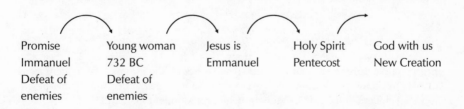

Promise	Young woman	Jesus is	Holy Spirit	God with us
Immanuel	732 BC	Emmanuel	Pentecost	New Creation
Defeat of	Defeat of			
enemies	enemies			

Another instance of promise-fulfillment in the prophets is provided by Zechariah 9:9-10. Matthew sees the fulfillment of verse 9 in Jesus' triumphal entry into Jerusalem: "This took place to fulfill what had been spoken through the prophet, saying, 'Tell the daughter of Zion, Look, your king is coming to you, humble, and mounted on a donkey, and on a colt, the foal of a donkey'" (21:4-5). Having noted the fulfillment in Jesus, we move back to our text and discover elements in the prophecy that Jesus must yet fulfill: "He shall command peace to the nations; his dominion shall be from sea to sea, and from the River to the ends of the earth" (Zech 9:10).

Promises in the Psalms

Messianic promises are found not only in the prophets but also in the Psalms. Although the Psalms are not the literary genre of prophecy, the so-called "royal Psalms" (e.g., Pss 2, 18, 20, 45, 72, 89, and 110) begin to function as prophecy of the coming Messiah. Originally they celebrated the crowning of a king of Judah (e.g., Pss 2, 72, and perhaps 110) or a reigning king (e.g., Ps 45). John Stek notes that these Psalms proclaim the king's "status as God's anointed and declare what God will accomplish through him and his dynasty. Thus they also speak of the sons of David to come — and in the exile and the postexilic era, when there was no reigning king, they spoke to Israel only of the great Son of David whom the prophets had announced as the one in whom God's covenant with David would yet be fulfilled."[37] James Mays suggests that under the influence of later messianic prophecy, "the royal psalms themselves came at a later stage in their history to be read as hope for the one who comes. . . . Once Isaiah had been on the scene, the psalms began to be drawn into the context of prophecy itself, and to move into another genre. Within Old Testament history itself, these psalms began to be read and understood themselves as messianic prophecy. The inauguration they described awaited a candidate; the title 'Son of God' hung in the air because there was no specific human historical person to whom it could be given."[38]

---

37. Stek, "Introduction: Psalms," NIV Study, 786.

38. Mays, "Isaiah's Royal Theology," 48. Cf. Bright, Authority, 223. See also Bruce Waltke's argument that the human subject of all the Psalms is ultimately Jesus Christ. "A Canonical Process Approach to the Psalms," in Tradition and Testament, ed. John S. Feinberg and Paul D. Feinberg (Chicago: Moody, 1981), 3-18.

Promises in Narrative

The Psalms link the messianic promises to King David. According to Claus Westermann, "the 'messianic' promises proper . . . are all based on the prophet Nathan's oracle of promise for the Davidic royal house (2 Sam 7)."[39] This passage is one of the outstanding messianic promises in Old Testament narrative, for God promises David, "Your house and your kingdom shall be made sure before me; your throne shall be established forever" (2 Sam 7:16). This key promise draws the books of Samuel-Kings and Chronicles into the orbit of the messianic promise, for even as the history of its kings is recounted, Israel begins to expect another king like David. These books also repeatedly speak of the king as "the LORD's anointed," the Hebrew *Messiah*, which would also feed into the hope for another righteous king like David.[40] Preaching Christ from Samuel-Kings, therefore, one may be able to use promise-fulfillment, but a more likely road to Christ is typology, for the Davidic king as "the LORD's anointed" functions as a type of Christ. Another possibility for preaching Christ is redemptive-historical progression: "The writer of Kings was concerned to demonstrate the historical reality of God's faithfulness to his promises to David. He presents an unbroken dynasty maintained in Judah through about three and a half centuries. The book ends on this note of hope, that even during the Exile and under foreign domination, divine favor still attended David's descendants."[41] This hope is subsequently fulfilled with the coming of Jesus Christ, the great Son of David.

We have saved for last the hotly contested issue of God's messianic promises in the book of Genesis. The most crucial (and controverted) passage today is Genesis 3:15, "I will put enmity between you and the woman, and between your offspring [or seed] and hers; he will strike [or crush] your head, and you will strike his heel." Traditionally this verse

39. Westermann, "The Way of the Promise," 215.

40. Raymond Dillard and Tremper Longman, *Introduction,* 146, "The idea of a Messiah for Israel grows out of her ideology about a righteous king, one who would be like David."

41. Ibid., 165-66. These authors continue, "The New Testament shows that this same hope was alive in Israel during the days of Roman rule. The gospel writers are concerned to trace the Davidic ancestry of Jesus and his rightful claim to the title 'Son of David,' heir to the kingdom that God would erect as a consequence of his promises to David. . . ." See also Philip E. Satterthwaite, "David in the Books of Samuel: A Messianic Hope?"; Iain W. Provan, "The Messiah in the Books of Kings"; and Brian Kelly, "Messianic Elements in the Chronicler's Work," in *The Lord's Anointed: Interpretation of Old Testament Messianic Texts* (Grand Rapids: Baker, 1995), respectively pp. 41-65, 67-85, and 249-64.

was understood as a promise of God; in fact, the church fathers called it the *protoevangelium*, the first gospel. But today many scholars refuse to see this verse as a promise.[42] Claus Westermann speaks for many modern scholars: "There are two main reasons that do not allow such an interpretation: First, it is beyond doubt that *zera* [seed] is to be understood collectively. The text is speaking of the line of descendants of the woman as well as of the serpent. The second reason is form-critical. The word occurs in the context of a pronouncement of punishment (or of a curse). It is not possible that such a form has either promise or prophecy as its primary or even as its secondary meaning."[43]

To start with the second objection, Westermann himself states that "the two metrical pronouncements in v 14 and v 15 . . . are relatively independent of each other."[44] If verses 14 and 15 are "relatively independent of each other," there is no compelling reason to interpret verse 15 within the confines of the curse of verse 14. Moreover, one should not use the restrictive form-critical definition of "curse" to muzzle the text before listening to it. For in the Old Testament God's judgment and his grace often go together: God judges in order to restore. For example, the flood was both God's judgment on human sin and God's grace in cleansing the earth; hence Peter can use the flood as a type of baptism (1 Pet 3:20-21). Similarly, the judgment God pronounces on the serpent (Satan, according to Rom 16:20 and Rev 12:9) is at the same time good news for God's people, for the enmity God pronounces breaks up the unholy alliance between God's people and Satan.[45]

The first objection, that "seed" is to be understood only collectively, also vanishes when we take into account that Hebrew singular nouns can refer either to an individual or a group of like individuals. We may also think here of the ancient use of corporate personality which, depending on the context, allows the meaning of "seed" to oscillate between a collective entity and an individual. Although Genesis customarily uses "seed" collectively for a group of individuals, as in Genesis 13:16 where God promises Abraham, "I will make your offspring [seed] like the dust of the

42. See the authors mentioned by Alexander, "Messianic Ideology in the Book of Genesis," 28.

43. Westermann, *Genesis 1–11* (London: SPCK, 1984), 260.

44. Ibid., 258; cf. p. 259 regarding v 15, "The sentence is only very loosely joined with the curse formula in v 14; it could be quite independent of it."

45. In countering Westermann's form-critical approach, Alexander, "Messianic Ideology," 37, asserts: "It is methodologically unsound to argue that individual passages are not messianic on the basis of source and/or form critical considerations. Clearly, what needs to be assessed is the picture created by the combination of all the different elements which constitute the book of Genesis as it now stands."

earth," we also find the individual use, for example, in Genesis 4:25, where Eve says, "God has appointed for me another child [seed] instead of Abel" (cf. Gen 21:13). This mixed use would suggest that "seed" in Genesis 3:15 is open-ended and can be understood either collectively or individually, or both. In the context of the *toledoth* structure of Genesis, it is clear that the author regards "the seed of the woman" as the line of descendants which runs from Adam to Noah (number 10, Gen 5:32) and from Noah's son Shem to Abram (number 10, Gen 11:26). With Abram we find renewed emphasis on the "seed": "The LORD appeared to Abram and said, 'To your offspring [seed] I will give this land'" (Gen 12:7). The fact that Abram's wife Sarai was barren (Gen 16:1) heightens the tension about the seed. But God announced, "I will bless her, and she shall give rise to nations; kings of peoples shall come from her" (Gen 17:16). When Isaac is born, God promises Abraham, "Through your offspring [seed] all nations on earth will be blessed" (Gen 22:18, NIV). But Isaac's wife Rebekah is barren, and it looks as if the line of the seed of the woman has come to an end. However, in answer to Isaac's urgent plea, "the LORD granted his prayer, and his wife Rebekah conceived" (Gen 25:21). Later Jacob's wife Rachel is barren (Gen 30:1), but "God remembered Rachel, and God heeded her and opened her womb. She conceived and bore a son . . . and she named him Joseph . . ." (Gen 30:22-24). Clearly the message is that God's power and grace alone keep the seed of the woman alive from generation to generation. Further, the message is that God's purpose is the salvation of all nations. For God repeats his promise to Abraham, "Through your offspring [seed] all nations on earth will be blessed" (Gen 22:18, NIV), to Isaac in Genesis 26:4, and to Jacob in Genesis 28:14. Israel is to be a light to the nations. But when Israel fails to fulfill its mission, God sends *the* seed of the woman, Jesus Christ, the true Israel.

It may readily be granted that the inspired author who penned Genesis 3:15 did not foresee the coming of Jesus the Messiah and his victory over Satan. For we usually cannot comprehend biblical promises in isolation but must understand them in retrospect as the promises fill up in redemptive history, sometimes in surprising ways. However, at a minimum Genesis 3:15 tells Israel that God promised enmity between the seed of the serpent and the seed of the woman. We need not resolve the ambiguity of "seed" at this point but must allow later redemptive history to show us whether the word is to be understood collectively or individually. When Cain kills Abel, the enmity comes to expression between two individuals. But the author of Genesis is also at pains to show that the enmity exists between two kinds of people: people who rebel against God and people who seek to obey God. He contrasts the genealogies of these two kinds of people in his intricate *toledoth* structure. The first listing of descendants runs via Adam and Cain to the ruthless violence of Lamech (Gen 2:4–4:26). But meanwhile God has started another line of descendants which runs from Adam via Seth and Enoch to the righteous Noah (Gen 5:1–6:8). Later the line of the descendants of Ishmael is briefly accounted for (Gen 25:12-18), while the descendant of Isaac, Jacob, receives an extensive review (Gen 25:19–35:29). Finally, the descendants of Esau (Gen 36:1–37:1) are juxtaposed with the descendants of Jacob (Gen 37:2–50:26).

Enmity between two kinds of people works itself out in redemptive history: Israel versus Egypt; Israel versus Edom; Israel versus Canaan; Israel versus Babylonia. But throughout this history we also see that at times the two kinds of people are represented by two individuals: Abel versus Cain; Isaac versus Ishmael; Jacob versus Esau; Moses versus Pharaoh; David versus Goliath. In fact, the Septuagint (third century B.C.) and Jewish targums understand Genesis 3:15 "as referring to a victory over Satan in the days of King Messiah."[46] From a later New Testament redemptive-historical perspective we see that the promise of enmity between the seed of the woman and the seed of the serpent finally results in the confrontation between Jesus and Satan and Jesus' victory in the wilderness (Matt 4:1-11), at Golgotha (Matt 28), and at his Second Coming (Rev 12:9; 20:10).

The Relevance of Using the Way of Promise-Fulfillment

Preaching messianic promises with an eye to further fulfillment is relevant because it enlarges people's vision to the full scope of kingdom history; in fact, it places the hearers right in the dynamic flow of God's promises and fulfillments. In difficult times, such preaching can provide good hope for the future as we wait for God to fulfill his promises to usher in his perfect kingdom. Preaching the prophetic vision of the Messiah can also serve as a corrective to some contemporary views of Jesus. James Mays writes, "Christians are tempted to limit the role of Jesus, messiah, king, to the sphere of the church, to speak and think of a community related to Jesus in isolation from world history, to believe that what God is doing in the church is all that God is doing in the world. The church needs the prophet's vision of a glory of God that fills the whole earth. The church needs Isaiah's vision of a heavenly king with an emphasis on the word *king*. Jesus at the right hand of God does not mean

---

46. Alexander, "Messianic Ideology," 27.

that God has vacated history, or ceased, so to say, to use Assyria as the rod of God's anger."[47] Moreover, God not only guides the history of nations today, he also promised to judge the nations at Jesus' Second Coming and to bring in his kingdom in perfection. God's promises that justice will prevail in the end and that his perfect kingdom will come can give Christians hope and courage, even in the midst of persecution, while they eagerly wait for God to fulfill his promises.

THE WAY OF TYPOLOGY

Typology has also come under severe criticism in modern times. Sometimes scholars will lump typology together with allegorical interpretation and reject both out of hand. This guilt by association is rather unscholarly, for historically the school of Antioch employed typological interpretation precisely in opposition to Alexandria's allegorical interpretation (see pp. 91-92 above). We should realize, however, that scholars who work on the basis of the presuppositions of the secular or deistic form of the historical-critical method have little choice in rejecting typology: their presupposition of living in a closed universe has done it for them.[48] For without the biblical teaching of God working sovereignly in history, typology is sheer nonsense. Once the providence of God is rejected, typology must necessarily follow, for it cannot exist without the foundation of God working out his redemptive plan in history.

Typology, of course, is quite different from allegorical interpretation, which can make a text say whatever the interpreter wants to make of it. Typology, by contrast, is limited to discovering specific analogies along the axis of God's acts in redemptive history as revealed in Scripture. As G. W. H. Lampe says, "Allegory differs radically from the kind of typology which rests upon the perception of actual historical fulfillment. The reason for this great difference is simply that allegory takes no account of history."[49]

47. Mays, "Isaiah's Royal Theology," 50.

48. See p. 236, n. 20 above.

49. Lampe, "The Reasonableness of Typology," 31. Cf. Walther Eichrodt, "Is Typological Exegesis an Appropriate Method?" 227, "For typology, the historical value of the text to be interpreted forms the essential presupposition for the use of it. For allegory, on the contrary, this is indifferent or even offensive, and must be pushed to one side to make room for the 'spiritual' sense which lies behind." Cf. John Breck, *Power of the Word*, 94, "By treating historical events as parabolic symbols, allegory threatens the historical basis of faith. But . . . typological *theoria* does preserve the historical nature of revelation." See ibid., 93-104.

Typology and Exegesis

Some scholars question whether typological interpretation is proper exegesis. John Bright, for one, contends that typology "cannot be used as a tool for the exegesis of Old Testament texts." This does not mean that he rejects typology, but he wishes to keep it outside the confines of exegesis proper, which uses only "the grammatico-historical method." "Exegesis," he says, "has the task of discovering, through careful historical and philological examination of the text, the meaning the author intended to convey, and it can never legitimately go beyond that task. Typology, on the contrary, has to do with the later interpretation of texts — or better, of the events described in them — and is a way of expressing the new significance that is seen in them in the light of later events."[50] David Baker agrees: "Typology is not an exegesis or interpretation of a text but the study of relationships between events, persons and institutions recorded in biblical texts."[51]

If the relationship of typology and exegesis were merely a matter of definitions, we would not need to spend much time on it, but the significant hermeneutical issue behind this discussion is whether a type is *predictive* as prophecy is. Some argue, Yes, types are predictive and therefore typology is exegesis, for typology only brings out of the text what is already in the text.[52] Others argue, No, types are not predictive but are discovered only from a later stage of redemptive history; therefore, typology is not exegesis proper, for typology discovers more meaning than is in the text itself. R. T. France writes, "While strict exegesis is a prerequisite of typology, it is not correct to describe typology itself as a method of exegesis. . . . If every type were originally intended explicitly to point forward to an antitype, it might be correct to classify typology as a style of exegesis. But this is not the case. There is no indication in a type, as such, of any

50. John Bright, *Authority*, 92. Similarly, Geoffrey Grogan, *Scottish Bulletin of Evangelical Theology* 4 (1986) 10.

51. Baker, *SJT* 29 (1976) 149. Note that Bright is open to speaking of "typological *interpretation.*" *Authority*, 92, n. 82.

52. For example, G. K. Beale, *Themelios* 14 (1989) 93: "If typology is classified as partially prophetic, then it can be viewed as an exegetical method since the New Testament correspondence would be drawing out retrospectively the fuller prophetic meaning of the Old Testament type which was originally included by the divine author. . . . In this regard, typology can be called contextual exegesis within the framework of the canon, since it primarily involves the interpretation and elucidation of the meaning of earlier parts of Scripture by later parts." Cf. Bruce Waltke, "Kingdom Promises," 278, "Since God divinely determined the type, it follows that the type is a divine *prediction.*"

forward reference; it is complete and intelligible in itself."[53] The basic issue in this discussion, therefore, is the question: Is an Old Testament type predictive as prophecy is or is it discovered retrospectively?

The answer, I think, is not an either-or but a both-and: some Old Testament types are predictive and others are not. I suspect that most types are not predictive, but specific persons or events are later seen to have typological significance. For example, it is not likely that Israel during David's reign saw King David as a prediction of a greater king. King David only became a type centuries after he lived, when the prophets began to announce the coming of a new shepherd-king.[54] Of course, when the prophets used typology in promising a new King David, the type, now linked to a promise, did become predictive. But this predictive element is not present when the preaching-text is, say, 2 Samuel 5:1-12. When David is anointed king of all Israel and captures Jerusalem as his capital, there is no hint in the text itself that David is a type. But this changes when we look at this event from a New Testament perspective. Now we discover that God's anointed king ruling a united people from Jerusalem, the city of peace, is God's pattern for bringing his kingdom on earth. In the New Testament we see Jesus, the Son of David, anointed with the Holy Spirit, the new Shepherd-King, weeping over the city of God: "Jerusalem, Jerusalem. . . . How often have I desired to gather your children together . . . and you were not willing!" (Matt 23:37). The great King has arrived, but Jerusalem refuses to be united under him in a kingdom of peace. But that day will surely come! John already saw it in a vision: "I saw the holy city, the new Jerusalem, coming

53. France, *Jesus and the Old Testament*, 41-42. Cf. ibid., p. 40, "The idea of fulfillment inherent in New Testament typology derives not from a belief that the events so understood were explicitly predicted, but from the conviction that in the coming and work of Jesus the principles of God's working, already imperfectly embodied in the Old Testament, were more perfectly re-embodied, and thus brought to completion." Cf. Ellis, Foreword to Goppelt's *Typos*, xvi, "Only in the light of the NT fulfillment is the typological significance of an OT personage, event, or institution made clear." Cf. Klein, Blomberg, and Hubbard, *Introduction*, 130, "This need not imply that the OT authors actually intended, in a prophetic kind of way, the type that the NT writers later discovered. Typology is more a technique of a later writer who 'mines' prior Scripture for similarities to God's present activities." Cf. Unger, *Principles*, 202-3.

54. See John Bright, *Authority*, 223, "The kingly ideal (e.g. Ps 72) lay beyond the capabilities of the Davidic dynasty, or any of its representatives. . . . In time there developed (and first with Isaiah himself: 9:1-7; 11:1-9) the expectation of an ideal king of David's line . . . under whose just and beneficent rule all the promises would be fulfilled. But that hope, too, was disappointed. . . . Yet hope was not abandoned. Ever it looked ahead, beyond tragedy, frustration, and despair, for the coming of a King, the Anointed One, the Messiah, who, endowed with God's power, would bring victory and peace to his people and establish God's kingdom on earth."

down out of heaven from God, prepared as a bride adorned for her husband" (Rev 21:2). Consequently, 2 Samuel 5 in isolation is not predictive, but looked at from the perspective of the New Testament, King David is here clearly a type of Christ.

But there are also types which are predictive for Israel in their original historical context — types God set up specifically to teach his people Israel, types such as the sabbath, Passover, the tabernacle, and blood sacrifices. For example, God instructed Moses precisely how to build the tabernacle so that it could be a sign of God's presence in the midst of his people Israel. This sign was significant for its own time, but as a type it also pointed forward to further fulfillment. But to what specifically? The temple in Jerusalem? God present among us in human flesh? Even with a predictive type, we still need the New Testament perspective to fill out the picture: God's presence in the midst of his people through his Son Jesus.

I suspect that the underlying concern about reading typology retrospectively is that we leave ourselves open to the charge of reading meaning back into the Old Testament text that is not there. But one could counter that typological interpretation is not reading meaning back into the event described in the text but simply understanding this event in its full redemptive-historical context. Moreover, even though we *discover* this fuller meaning only retrospectively from a later stage of redemptive history, from God's perspective it was always there in his overall design of redemptive history.

This discussion has helped clarify somewhat the difference between typology and promise-fulfillment. Whereas promises are usually words spoken, types are historical events, persons, and institutions. Further, whereas promises point forward to future fulfillment, typology generally moves in the opposite direction, from New Testament fulfillment to the past type.

Dangers along the Way of Typology

Unfortunately, preachers have often misused typology (see Chapters 3 and 4). John Goldingay speaks of the "built-in danger of turning real people or events that had significance of their own into mere representative symbols or puppets in a cosmic drama." He also mentions the "danger posed by the more pietistic typology that (for instance) sees the blue, purple, and red coloring of the tabernacle hangings as pointing to Christ's heavenliness, kingship, and death."[55] The latter we can call typologizing,

55. Goldingay, *Models*, 65.

that is, interpreting even details as "types." In our survey of the history of interpretation we noticed that the search for "types" in every detail led interpreters straight into the chaos of allegorizing.

Even today, people easily slip from a legitimate use of typology into typologizing.[56] One *Dictionary of Types* states that the story of Abraham sending his servant to find a wife for Isaac (Gen 24) contains the following types: "Abraham is a type of the Father who sent His servant (the Spirit) to obtain a bride (Rebekah) for his son Isaac. . . . Isaac represents the Lord Jesus Christ. . . . Rebekah represents the Church."[57] Even though the word "type" is used, this is not typology but allegorizing. A few samples from different sermons about Joseph may also flesh out the meaning of typologizing: Joseph's obedience in looking for his brothers is a prophetic type of Christ's obedience; his sale to the Ishmaelites prefigures Christ's sale by Judas; his good fortune in Egypt prefigures God's blessing of Jesus who is also led to Egypt; his imprisonment and subsequent crowning show the humiliation and crowning of Christ to save his people.[58] Only the last sermon comes close to presenting a true type; the others have latched onto incidental parallels that have nothing to do with typology.

Because of the dangers of misinterpretation, some have suggested that we play it safe and use typology only where the New Testament reveals an Old Testament person or event as a type. A hundred and fifty years ago the influential Patrick Fairbairn considered this option recommended by a Bishop Marsh and immediately rejected it as "arbitrary and inexplicable." Fairbairn wrote, "What is there to distinguish the characters and events, which Scripture has thus particularized, from a multitude of others, to which the typical element might equally have been supposed to belong? . . . We instinctively feel, if these really possessed a typical character, so also must others, which hold an equally, or perhaps even more prominent place in the history of God's dispensations." Fairbairn then provides some good examples, "What reason can we imagine for Melchizedek and Jonah having been constituted types — persons to whom our attention is comparatively little drawn in Old Testament history — while such leading characters as Joseph, Samson, Joshua, are omitted? Or, for selecting the passage through the Red Sea,

56. Louis Berkhof, *Principles,* 146, mentions that "some interpreters found in the fact that the brazen serpent was made of an inferior metal, a figure of Christ's outer meanness or humble appearance; in its solidity, a sign of his divine strength; and in its dim lustre, a prefiguration of the veil of his human nature."

57. W. L. Wilson, *Wilson's Dictionary of Bible Types* (Grand Rapids: Eerdmans, 1957), 15.

58. For references to these and other sermons, see my *Sola Scriptura,* 83-84.

and the incidents in the wilderness, while no account should be made of the passage through Jordan, and the conquest of the land of Canaan?"[59] But Bishop Marsh's "safe" suggestion is not completely answered. His question remains, "By what means shall we determine, in any given instance, that what is *alleged* as a type was really *designed* for a type?" Fairbairn responds, "It is possible, surely, that in this, as well as in other things, Scripture may indicate certain fundamental views or principles, of which it makes but a few individual applications, and for the rest leaves them in the hand of spiritually enlightened consciences."[60]

Typology Defined

In spite of the dangers of eisegesis, many scholars and communities today accept typology as a valid method, though they may define it quite differently. In the Western world, the influence of scholars like Walther Eichrodt, Gerhard von Rad, and Leonhard Goppelt has returned typological interpretation to a measure of scholarly respectability. Von Rad asserts, "We see everywhere in this history brought to pass by God's Word, in acts of judgment and acts of redemption alike, the prefiguration of the Christ-event of the New Testament. . . . This renewed recognition of types in the Old Testament is no peddling of secret lore, no digging up of miracles, but is simply correspondent to the belief that the same God who revealed himself in Christ has also left his footprints in the history of the Old Testament covenant people. . . ."[61] The Eastern Orthodox Church, in their dependence on the church fathers, never questioned the value of typological interpretation. Georges Barrois contends, "The neglect or rejection of the typological approach results unavoidably in spiritual impoverishment, and it constitutes a serious fault of method."[62]

The dangers of reading things into the Old Testament text, however, indicate that typology must be carefully defined and even then handled with great care. One of the better definitions of types is that of Eichrodt: Types "are persons, institutions, and events of the Old Testament which are regarded as divinely established models or prerepresentations of cor-

59. Fairbairn, *Typology*, 23.
60. Ibid., 24.
61. Von Rad, "Typological Interpretation," 36. Cf. Merrill Unger, *Principles*, 201, "The greatest transgression against this most rewarding field of Bible study [typology] is apparently not committed by those who overdo in the matter, but by those who 'underdo,' who as the result of extreme caution completely bypass many bona fide types." Cf. Poythress, *The Shadow of Christ in the Law of Moses*.
62. Barrois, *Face of Christ*, 44.

responding realities in the New Testament salvation history."[63] But since not even a good definition of typology can prevent misinterpretation, we need to spell out specific characteristics of types as well as special rules for their interpretation.

Characteristics of Types

Merrill Unger states, "A genuine type always contains certain unmistakable elements. Knowledge of these distinguishing features is indispensable not only for recognizing a bona fide type, but is fundamental as well to its correct interpretation."[64] In general we can say that a genuine type is grounded in God's design as we see this develop in typical patterns in redemptive history.[65] As Barrois puts it, "Typology . . . appears to be an integral part of the divine economy, essentially linked with the progression of Sacred History toward its *telos*, its ultimate goal, the kingdom that is to come."[66] Lampe focusses especially on the recurring patterns: "The great events of Israel's past exhibited a certain pattern of God's acts. . . . The prophets from time to time look forward in the future to a repetition or recapitulation of the rhythm of divine action evident in the history of the past."[67] From these general statements about types and typology we shall glean four specific characteristics of types that will help us to distinguish between a genuine type and typologizing.

63. Eichrodt, "Is Typological Exegesis an Appropriate Method?" 225. Cf. I. Howard Marshall, "Assessment," 16, "Typology may be defined as the study which traces parallels or correspondences between incidents recorded in the OT and their counterparts in the NT such that the latter can be seen to resemble the former in notable respects and yet to go beyond them."

64. Unger, *Principles*, 204.

65. Cf. Edmund Clowney, "Preaching Christ," 174, "Typology is grounded in God's design. It flows from the continuity and difference of God's saving work. There is continuity, for it is God who begins His work of salvation long before He gives His Son. Yet there is discontinuity, too."

66. Barrois, *Face of Christ*, 42. Cf. John Breck, *Power*, 41, "'Typology' is not simply a human mode of interpretation. It is first of all a *divine mode of activity within history*. God acts in terms of promise and fulfillment, coordinating historical events in such a way that the future fulfillment is continually being realized throughout the history of Israel and in the subsequent history of the Church." Cf. ibid., p. 55, The justification of typology "lies in the conviction that God Himself, as author of history as well as of Scripture, ordains events in terms of 'promise and fulfillment'. . . . It is truly a . . . salvation-history, the sphere of divine economy in which man and the cosmos progress under the guidance of God towards eternal salvation."

67. Lampe, *Essays*, 26.

First, a genuine type is *historical*. Goppelt states, "Only historical facts — persons, actions, events, and institutions — are material for typological interpretation; words and narratives can be utilized only insofar as they deal with such matters."[68] The School of Antioch used the characteristic of historicity primarily to distinguish typology from allegorical interpretation.

Second, a genuine type is *theocentric*, that is, it has to do with *God's* acts in and through human persons and events. As John Stek puts it, "The biblical types are to be found in specific persons, institutions, and events *as these were used by God* in his dealings with Israel. . . ."[69] The theocentric character of types eliminates the kind of typologizing we noted above regarding Joseph's obedience, his sale to the Ishmaelites, and the blue, purple, and red coloring of the tabernacle hangings.

Third, a genuine type exhibits a *significant analogy* with its antitype. David Baker states, "Typology implies a real correspondence. It is not interested in parallels of detail but only in an agreement of fundamental principles and structure. There must be a correspondence in history and theology or the parallel will be trivial and valueless for understanding the Bible."[70] This characteristic rules out as genuine typology all superficial parallels that might be drawn between the Old and New Testaments, including those about Joseph mentioned above.

Fourth, the relation of a genuine type to its antitype is marked by *escalation*. We noticed this feature already in the New Testament use of

68. Goppelt, *Typos*, 17-18. Later Goppelt broadens the requirement of historicity from simple facticity to God's revelation in history: "The validity of a typology does not depend on the historicity of individual scenes, but on the truth and reality of God's revelation of himself in history and on a standard for the historicity of the historical phenomena that can only be developed from the subject matter." Ibid., 232-33. Cf. Unger, *Principles*, 204, A type "consists of a person, event or an institution that is actual and not fictional, real and not imaginary."

69. Stek, *CTJ* 5 (1970) 157. Note that Fairbairn, *Typology*, 46, adds that a type must be "divinely established." A type is not just *"any* character, action, or institution occurring in OT Scripture, but such only as had their ordination of God, and were designed by Him to foreshadow and prepare for the better things of the Gospel."

70. Baker, *SJT* 29 (1976) 153. Cf. Louis Berkhof, *Principles*, 145, "The type must be designed by divine appointment to bear a likeness to the anti-type. Accidental similarity between an Old and New Testament person or event does not constitute the one a type of the other." Cf. John Stek, *CTJ* 5 (1970) 138, "A superficial similarity in external features is irrelevant. This the older typologists had failed to observe, and so had brought typology into disrepute. The resemblance must be one of an 'internal agreement' [Fairbairn] (p. 66), like that between a symbol and the reality it symbolizes." Cf. Unger, *Principles*, 204-5.

typology: "See, something greater than Jonah is here! . . . See, something greater than Solomon is here!" (Matt 12:41-42).[71]

Rules for Using Typology

With this background, we can now formulate a few specific rules for handling typological interpretation: First, always precede typological interpretation with *literary-historical interpretation* (literary includes grammatical). We must know the author's message for Israel before we look for ways to focus the message on Jesus Christ and apply it to the church. To reverse the process is to court disaster, for literary-historical interpretation is the indispensable foundation for sound typological interpretation.

Second, look for a type not in the details but in the *central message* of the text concerning God's activity to redeem his people. Clowney notes, "The typical aspects of Samson's life are not to be sought in the similarity of details. The gates of Gaza, removed by Samson . . . , cannot be identified directly with the gates of death. . . . The structure that grounds the typology of the Old Testament narratives is the continuity of God's work of redemption as it unfolds through history."[72] Since preachers have often found all kinds of "types" in the details of the tabernacle, Unger pointedly observes, "While Israel's ancient worship was designedly typical and richly instructive of the person and work of the Messiah to come, all the boards, sockets, and curtains are not to be construed as prefiguring redemptive truths."[73] In short, the rule is, Don't wander off the typological trail into the morass of incidental parallels and farfetched analogies.

Third, determine the *symbolic meaning* of the person, institution, or event in Old Testament times. If it has no symbolic meaning in Old Testament times, it cannot be a type. Geerhardus Vos writes, "A type can never be a type independently of its being first a symbol. The gateway to the house of typology is at the farther end of the house of symbolism. . . . Only after having discovered what a thing symbolizes, can we legiti-

71. Goppelt, *Typos,* 18, speaks of "a heightening of the type." On p. 33 he makes the strange comment, "Since there is no typological heightening it would be better not to designate Adam in his fallen condition as a type of present humanity that bears his likeness." Adam, of course, is not a type of humanity in any case, but according to Paul he is a type of Christ (Rom 5:12-21). The escalation, in this case, is found in the antithetic relationship between Adam and Christ. See our discussion on pp. 217-18 above.

72. Clowney, *Unfolding Mystery,* 141.

73. Unger, *Principles,* 205. Cf. Goppelt, *Typos,* 10, "Typology must not become involved in details, but must seek to compare the spirit of the OT historical narrative with the spirit of the NT event. . . ."

mately proceed to put the question what it typifies, for the latter can never be aught else than the former lifted to a higher plane. The bond that holds the type and antitype together must be a bond of vital continuity in the progress of redemption."[74] For example, in Old Testament times the tabernacle was a symbol of God dwelling with his people. "The typical significance of the tabernacle should be sought in close dependence upon its symbolic significance. We must ask: where do these religious principles and realities, which the tabernacle served to teach and communicate, reappear in the subsequent history of redemption, lifted to their consummate stage?"[75]

Clowney has further developed the rule concerning the symbolic meaning. He comments, "An Old Testament event, a ceremony, or a prophetic, priestly, or royal action may . . . symbolize, pointing to a revealed truth at a particular point in the history of redemption. . . . We may be sure that this truth will be carried forward to Jesus Christ. . . . We may therefore connect the event, ceremony, or action directly with that truth as it comes to full expression in Christ. . . . the line of typology." However, Clowney also warns, "If the symbolism of an Old Testament incident or person is not perceived, or does not exist, no line of typology can be drawn. Nor can the event be a type in a sense different from its symbolic function in its Old Testament setting."[76] In terms of logical development in the sermon, we can picture this third rule as three, possibly four, steps:

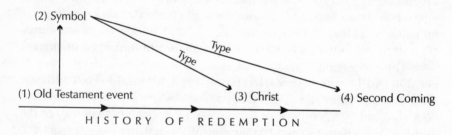

This rule helps weed out illegitimate types. For example, since the scarlet cord Rahab hung out her window in Jericho did not function in the Old Testament as a symbol, this traditional "type" cannot really function as a type of the blood of Christ. On the other hand, the blood of the Passover

74. Vos, *Biblical Theology*, 162. Cf. Louis Berkhof, *Principles*, 145, "It is well to bear in mind . . . that the Old Testament types were at the same time symbols that conveyed spiritual truths to contemporaries, for their symbolical meaning must be understood before their typical meaning can be ascertained."

75. Vos, *Biblical Theology*, 171. Cf. pp. 164-72.

76. Clowney, "Preaching Christ," 180.

lamb did function in Old Testament times as a symbol of God's protection from the angel of death, and so it can legitimately be understood as a type of Christ, our Passover lamb, who protects us from eternal death. Similarly, the exodus from Egypt was a symbol to Israel of God's deliverance from an evil empire, and therefore it can be a type of Christ delivering his people from the power of Satan.

Fourth, note the *points of contrast* between the Old Testament type and the New Testament antitype. The difference is as important as the resemblance, for the difference reveals not only the imperfect nature of Old Testament types but also the escalation entailed in the unfolding of redemptive history: one "greater than Jonah is here."

Fifth, in moving from the Old Testament symbol/type to Christ, carry forward the *meaning of the symbol* even as its meaning escalates.[77] In other words, do not switch to a different sense. For example, an Old Testament passage which speaks of God providing manna in the desert may symbolize God's miraculous provision in keeping his people alive. In carrying this meaning forward to Christ, we should not link it with Jesus' teaching, "Give us this day our daily bread," but rather with Jesus' teaching that he is "the bread of God . . . which comes down from heaven and gives life to the world" (John 6:33) — the same sense plus escalation. Or, if we preach on an Old Testament passage about lambs being sacrificed as sin offerings (symbolizing substitutionary atonement), we should not link this with the New Testament demand that we offer our best to God but rather use typology to preach Christ as "the Lamb of God who takes away the sin of the world!" (John 1:29) — the same sense plus escalation.

Sixth, do not simply draw a typological line to Christ but *preach Christ*. Simply drawing a line to Christ is not preaching Christ. When one has drawn a line from the Old Testament text to Jesus of Nazareth, one should ask the question, "So what?" How does this line build up the congregation? Are they to admire the wonderful providence of God, or the intricate redemptive design of the Scriptures, or the ingenuity of the preacher? John Stott rightly insists, "The main objective of preaching is to expound Scripture so faithfully and relevantly that Jesus Christ is perceived in all his adequacy to meet human need. . . . The preacher's purpose is more than to unveil Christ; it is to unveil him that people are drawn to come to him and receive him."[78] Beginning with the Old Testa-

---

77. Cf. Fairbairn, *Typology*, 3, "The typical is not properly a different or higher sense, but a different or higher application of the same sense."

78. Stott, *Between Two Worlds*, 325. Cf. Daniel Lys, *Int* (1967) 406, "The preacher cannot be satisfied by merely *pointing to* Jesus Christ. . . . The Christ is not simply the chronological result after the OT; he is the axiological meaning of the OT where the

ment type, Christian preachers can proclaim the person or work of Christ so that people will commit themselves to this Savior and Lord, put all their trust for salvation in him alone, and seek to obey him in every area of life.

Examples of Types in Various Genres of Literature

To conclude this section on typology, it may be helpful to list a few more examples of genuine types as we discover them in various genres of Old Testament literature.

Types in the Narrative Genre

Most of the types are found in the narrative genre. Here we find the proclamation of redemptive *events*, such as the exodus from Egypt, the provision of manna and water in the desert, the conquest of Canaan, victories over Philistines and other enemies, the return from Babylonian exile — all of them types of the great deliverance God has prepared for his people in Jesus Messiah. Here we also find *persons* such as Moses, Joshua, judges, and kings through whom God delivered his people and sought to establish his kingdom (theocracy — "God rule"). This redemptive work of God through his anointed leaders qualifies them as types of Christ through whom God would ultimately deliver his people and establish his kingdom on earth. We also discover high priests and priests who are types of Christ in offering sacrifices to atone for the sins of the people and in interceding for them. Besides anointed priests and kings, the narrative genre also recounts anointed prophets who are types of Christ in proclaiming the will of the Lord to his people.

Before using any of these persons in a sermon as a type of Christ, however, we need to assess the situation carefully, for we cannot count on, "Once a type, always a type." These leaders of Israel are types only insofar as they enable God to do his redemptive work through them. Moses is not a type of Christ when he slays the Egyptian. Samson is not a type of Christ when he has sex with a prostitute. Aaron is not a type of Christ when he makes the golden calf, and the priests Hophni and Phinehas are not types of Christ when "they treated the offerings of the LORD with contempt" (1 Sam 2:17).

---

same God reveals himself as in the Word become flesh. . . . A sound appropriation of the OT should lead the believer to learn how to live in history, as the OT people did, between the basic salvation act and the Savior to come."

Types in Other Genres of Literature

In the legal material we find persons such as priests who may prefigure the person and work of Christ, but we discover primarily *institutions* which may be types of Christ. Think of the Passover feast, the Day of Atonement, the Year of Jubilee, and the tabernacle and its daily sacrifices. All of them and more find their typological significance and fulfillment in the person and work of Christ.

In the Psalms we also find persons who are types of Christ. We have already mentioned the Royal Psalms, which speak of the Davidic king through whom God rules his people. These anointed kings are types of the great Son of David through whom God will rule the nations. Typology may also become an option when we consider that "the speaker in many of the psalms is the Davidic king."[79] In giving expression to his pain, his anguish, his trust in God, the king may be a type of Christ, as we recognize retrospectively when Jesus utters these same words when he relives these experiences at an even more intense level.[80] In addition, the righteous sufferer crying out to God may be a type of Christ. As Stek explains, "These cries became the prayers of God's oppressed 'saints,' and as such they were taken up into Israel's book of prayers. When Christ came in the flesh, he identified himself with God's 'humble' people in the world. . . . Thus these prayers became his prayers also — uniquely his prayers. In him the suffering and deliverance of which these prayers speak are fulfilled (though they continue to be the prayers also of those who take up their cross and follow him)."[81]

In the genre of prophecy, the anointed prophets themselves are types of Christ as they declare God's will to his people and announce both judgment and salvation. In addition, the prophets begin to use typology as they speak of a new exodus, a new Moses, a new David, a new Elijah, a new covenant, a new temple, and new heavens and a new earth.

THE WAY OF ANALOGY

Analogy is less controversial today than are typology and promise-fulfillment. The reason may be that analogy does not claim to be, strictly speaking, exegesis or interpretation of a text but is a popular method of

---

79. Dillard and Longman, *Introduction*, 233.
80. On Psalm 22 as typology, see Douglas Moo, "Problem," 197.
81. Stek, *NIV Study*, 786.

applying the message of the Old Testament to the church today. Elizabeth Achtemeier frequently uses analogy, and remarks that "this is probably the most frequent method by which we relate the Old Testament to
contemporary Christian life. The preacher asks if Israel's situation in relation to God . . . is analogous to ours. . . ."[82] By analogy (parallel situations)
the word of God for Israel can be addressed to the church today.

Even as a homiletical method of application, analogy is based on
the unity of redemptive history and the continuity between Israel and the
church. Von Rad writes, "The church of Christ is again on the march from
a promise to fulfillment, and for this reason its situation is analogous to
that of the people of the Old Testament. . . . The manifold temptations,
consolations, judgments, and helps for Israel are also the temptations,
consolations, judgments, and helps of the church of Christ. . . ."[83]

The Way of Analogy for Preaching Christ
from the Old Testament

Our interest in analogy extends further than relevant application of Old
Testament messages; we are also interested in analogy as a way of
preaching *Christ* from the Old Testament. Therefore, we need to stress
that the unity of redemptive history adheres in Christ; the continuity between Old Testament Israel and the New Testament church is accomplished only in Christ. Paul formulates this clearly in addressing the Gentile Christians in Ephesus, "Remember that you were at that time without
Christ, being aliens from the commonwealth of Israel, and strangers to
the covenants of promise, having no hope and without God in the world.
But now in Christ Jesus you who once were far off have been brought
near by the blood of Christ" (Eph 2:12-13). How have Gentiles "in Christ"
been brought near to the commonwealth of Israel? In Romans 11:17 Paul
uses the vivid image of grafting: "You [Gentiles], a wild olive shoot, were
grafted in their place to share the rich root of the olive tree." But only
through Christ. "If you belong to Christ, then you are Abraham's offspring, heirs according to the promise" (Gal 3:29; cf. 1 Pet 2:9-10).

This pivotal position of Christ in redemptive history enables
preachers to use analogy to direct the Old Testament message to the New
Testament church. For through Christ, Israel and the church have become
the same kind of people of God: recipients of the same covenant of grace,

---

82. Achtemeier, *Preaching from the Old Testament*, 58. Cf. ibid., "Relevance of the
Old Testament," 20-23.

83. Von Rad, *God at Work*, 156.

sharing the same faith, living in the same hope, seeking to demonstrate the same love.[84] In addition, this pivotal position of Christ in redemptive history enables preachers to use analogy for preaching Christ from the Old Testament.

To accomplish this goal, preachers need to look for analogies in several key areas. They should inquire about the analogy between what God is and does for Israel and what God *in Christ* is and does for the church. They should inquire about the similarity between what God teaches his people Israel and what *Christ* teaches his church. And they should search for parallels between God's demands in the Old Testament and *Christ's* demands in the New Testament. Although there will be differences because of the progression in the histories of redemption and revelation, analogy concentrates on locating the continuity, the parallels, between what God is and does for Israel, teaches Israel, or demands of Israel, and what God in Christ is and does for the church, teaches the church, or demands of the church.

Examples of Using Analogy in Various Genres of Literature

Because analogy is more general than promise-fulfillment and typology, it can be used with a wide variety of texts. But its more general character also means that the Christ-centered focus can easily get blurred in the sermon. Therefore it would be well to make sure that the congregation catches the connection — only *in Christ*. This connection can frequently be made explicit by quoting words of Christ recorded in the New Testament.

Using Analogy in Preaching Narrative

In preaching on texts from Old Testament narrative, analogy can be used by focussing on what God was doing for Israel and what God is doing in Christ for the New Testament church. The emphasis here can be on God's acts of redemption as well as on the required response. For example, preaching on Jacob at Bethel (Gen 28:10-22), preachers can use analogy to make the point that as Israel learned about God's protecting presence from Jacob's experience at Bethel before his hazardous journey, so Christ promises to be with us on our dangerous journey through life (analogy combined with New Testament reference such as Jesus' promise in Matt 28:20). Or, as God guided and protected Israel through the cloud (Exod 13:21-22), so God guides and protects his church through Christ "to the

84. See Marten Woudstra, "Israel and the Church: A Case for Continuity."

end of the age" (Matt 28:20). Turning to the required response: as God called Abram to claim Canaan for the kingdom of God (Gen 12:1-9), so Christ calls us to claim the world for God (Matt 28:18-20). And as God called Israel to be a light to the nations (Gen 12:3; Isa 49:6), so God in Christ now calls the church to be a light to the nations (Acts 13:47).

Using Analogy in Preaching Law

In preaching Old Testament law, one can also make use of analogy. For example, in preaching on the Ten Commandments (Exod 20), one can note God's indicative before the imperatives, God's act of redemption (Exod 14) before any laws are given: "I am the LORD your God, who brought you out of the land of Egypt, out of the house of slavery; you shall have no other gods before me." Christ, similarly, pronounces a nine-fold blessing before giving his law (e.g., Matt 5–7).[85] Or, as God made covenant with Israel and gave them his law (again the pattern: first historical prologue of God's acts, then the covenant stipulations), so God through Christ makes covenant with us and gives us his covenant stipulations. Or, as Israel's motivation for obedience was gratitude for God's redemption, so our motivation for obedience is gratitude for redemption through Christ. Or, as Israel was forbidden to follow the abominable practices of the nations (Lev 18:24-30), so the church "must no longer live as the Gentiles live. . . . That is not the way you learned Christ!" (Eph 4:17-24). Or, as God required Israel to give the firstfruits in response to God's gifts of land and harvest (Deut 26:1-11), so God requires of us concrete gifts in response to his bountiful gifts in Jesus. Or, as God commanded Israel to love God (Deut 6:5) and their neighbor (Lev 19:8), so Jesus demands that we love God and our neighbor (Matt 22:37-39).

Using Analogy in Preaching Prophecy

In prophetic literature one can apply analogy as well. Preaching on God's promise to bring Israel back from Babylonian exile to the promised land (Isa 40:1-11), one can use analogy: As God promised to bring Israel home, so Christ in the New Testament promises to bring his people home (John 14:2-3; 2 Pet 3:13). Preaching on the Suffering Servant who ministers to Israel (Isa 50:4-11), one can use analogy for moving to Jesus, who as the Suffering Servant ministers to his people. Preaching on Israel in exile needing to wait for God's coming salvation (Isa 51:4-8), one can use analogy

---

85. See also the form of Paul's letters: first the indicatives (e.g., Rom 3–11), then the imperatives/exhortations (Rom 12–16).

for shifting to the church today needing to wait for God's coming salvation when Christ returns.

Using Analogy in Preaching the Psalms

Through Christ, the Psalms of Israel are now also the songs of the new Israel, the church. This assumption enables the church to read and sing and pray the Psalms directly as their doxology or lament. In preaching the Psalms, however, we begin with historical interpretation, that is, inquiry into the way Israel originally heard the Psalm. Historical interpretation is required for sound interpretation, but it also makes us aware of the difference between Israel's understanding of the Psalm and ours. Here analogy can help us bridge the distance and preach Christ. For example, preaching on Israel's confession, "The LORD is my Shepherd" (Ps 23), one can use analogy to make the point either that the Lord is *our* Shepherd only through Jesus Christ, or that Jesus claims, "I am the good shepherd" (John 10:11). Or, preaching on "Happy are those . . . [whose] delight is in the law of the LORD" (Ps 1), one can use analogy to proclaim, "Blessed are those whose delight is in the law of Christ" (Matt 5–7, the beatitudes followed by the law of Christ). Preaching on "God is our refuge and strength" (Ps 46), one can use analogy to proclaim that God is our refuge only when we are in Christ.

Using Analogy in Preaching Wisdom

Preaching Christ from wisdom literature is difficult because wisdom is based on observation of regular patterns in God's creation. But here, too, analogy can be of help, frequently by moving to the *teachings* of Jesus. For Jesus was considered a wise teacher; the people "were astounded at his teaching, for he taught them as one having authority, and not as the scribes" (Mark 1:22). In wisdom, he was "greater than Solomon" (Luke 11:31; cf. 2:52; 7:35). In fact, "his predominant teaching form was the parable (*parabolē*, in Hebrew *māšāl* [also translated 'proverb']), a wisdom form."[86] For example, preaching on seeking wisdom "like silver" and searching for it "as for hidden treasures" (Prov 2:4), one can use analogy to move to Jesus of whom Paul writes that in him "are hidden all the treasures of wisdom and knowledge" (Col 2:3). Preaching on "Do not wear yourself out to get rich. . . . When your eyes light upon it, it is gone" (Prov

---

86. Dillard and Longman, *Introduction*, 245. For a broader discussion on Old Testament wisdom literature and Christ, see Graeme Goldsworthy, *Gospel and Wisdom*, esp. pp. 147-90.

23:4-5), one can use analogy to move to Jesus' similar teaching, "Do not store up for yourselves treasures on earth, where moth and rust consume, and where thieves break in and steal" (Matt 6:19). Preaching on the intriguing prayer, "Give me neither poverty nor riches; feed me with the food that I need" (Prov 30:8), one can use analogy to move to Jesus teaching us to ask the Lord: "Give us this day our daily bread" (Matt 6:11).

THE WAY OF LONGITUDINAL THEMES

So far the ways of preaching Christ from the Old Testament have been directly linked to redemptive history: the ways of redemptive-historical progression, promise-fulfillment, typology, and analogy. The next three ways we shall explore are more closely associated with the history of revelation. The history of redemption and the history of revelation are closely related, of course, since the history of revelation accompanies the history of redemption.[87]

The history of revelation is the history of God's *kerygma*, that is, God's relevant proclamation to his people at different stages of redemptive history. This proclamation is relevant for Israel at each stage because it has a redemptive focus, that is, God's goal is to teach Israel about himself, his plan, and his will in order to save his people.[88] This *kerygma* is still relevant today, but because of progression in the histories of redemption and revelation, its themes need to be traced through the New Testament in order to establish the message for the church today.

Biblical Theology

In Chapter 5 we noted two Old Testament themes which the New Testament developed further: the themes of redemption and of required sacri-

87. Clowney, *Preaching and Biblical Theology*, 15, "The Bible records revelation given in the course of history. This revelation was not given at one time, nor in the form of a theological dictionary. It was given progressively, for the process of revelation accompanies the process of redemption. Since redemption does not proceed uniformly but in epochs determined by God's acts, so revelation has an epochal structure, manifested and marked in the canonical Scriptures."

88. Bryan Chapell, *Christ-Centered Preaching*, likes to speak of a "Fallen Condition Focus," that is, "the mutual human condition that contemporary believers share with those to or for whom the text was written that requires the grace of the passage" (p. 42). Note that the "Fallen Condition Focus" is the flipside of the "redemptive focus": the redemptive focus of the text addresses and meets the fallen condition of the hearers.

fices. The New Testament, of course, develops many other Old Testament themes. Today it is especially the discipline of biblical theology that helps us trace longitudinal themes from the Old Testament to the New.[89] Major Old Testament themes which function as highways leading to the person, work, and teaching of Christ are the kingdom of God (reign and realm), the providence of God, covenant, the presence of God, the love of God, the grace of God, justice, redemption, law, sin and guilt offerings, God's concern for "the poor," mediator, the Day of the Lord, and so on. Edmund Clowney suggests asking the following questions: "What truth about God and his saving work is disclosed in this passage? . . . How is this particular truth carried forward in the history of revelation? How does it find fulfillment in Christ?"[90]

Examples of Longitudinal Themes

A few examples may clarify how longitudinal themes can be used as a way to preach Christ from the Old Testament. In a sermon on Jacob at Bethel (Gen 28:10-22), the theme is that God will be with Jacob as he travels to a foreign country (vv 15, 20; cf. vv 16-17). We can trace this theme of God's presence with his people to the cloud and pillar of fire leading and protecting Israel during the exodus, to the cloud in the tabernacle traveling with the people through the desert, to the cloud in the temple in the midst of Israel, to the presence of God with his people in Jesus (Immanuel, Matt 1:23), to the promise of our risen Lord, "I am with you always, to the close of the age" (Matt 28:20), to the outpouring of the Holy Spirit (Acts 2), and to the new creation where "God himself will be with them" (Rev 21:3). In the sermon one need not mention all these points, lest the sermon become tedious or predictable, but the way to Christ is plain.

Or when preaching on giving the tithe (Deut 26:12-15), one can trace into the New Testament the theme of giving to the Lord. What does the New Testament prescribe regarding our gifts to the Lord? In 2 Corinthians, Paul encourages Christians to be generous in giving for the poor. Interestingly, Paul adds, "I do not say this as a command, but I am testing the genuineness of your love. . . . For you know the generous act of our

89. Cf. Hasel, "Biblical Theology: Then, Now, and Tomorrow," *HorBT* 4/1 (1982) 77, "A Biblical theology has the task of providing summary interpretations of the final form of the individual Biblical documents or groups of writings and of presenting the longitudinal themes, motifs, and concepts that emerge from the Biblical materials." Cf. my *Modern Preacher*, 67-72.

90. Clowney, "Preaching Christ from Biblical Theology," 59.

Lord Jesus Christ, that though he was rich, yet for your sakes he became poor, so that by his poverty you might become rich" (2 Cor 8:8-9). Here is a clear connection to Jesus Christ from the law of giving the tithe: after the sacrifice of Christ to save us, our giving should no longer be a matter of observing an external law but of giving generously from a grateful heart because of the astounding gift of Jesus Christ.

Preachers have always had difficulty preaching Christ from a book like Proverbs. But as we saw with the way of analogy, a fruitful connection can often be made by linking the teaching of Proverbs with the teaching of Jesus. Here, similarly, we can seek to link the theme of the passage by way of longitudinal themes with Jesus' own teaching. Suppose we wish to make a sermon on Proverbs 8:22-36, the passage that contains the famous section on wisdom's part in creation. We may be tempted, with the church fathers, to move straight to John 1:1-3, Colossians 1:15, or Revelation 3:14 to make the connection with Christ the eternal Logos. But this would be premature. "Proverbs 8 is a poetic representation of God's attribute of wisdom with no narrowly prophetic intention."[91] Before looking for a way to preach Christ, we should first establish the theme of the passage. The theme can be summed up, I think, in the words of verse 35, "Whoever finds me [wisdom] finds life." Checking a concordance on how Proverbs elsewhere links wisdom and life leads to Proverbs 3:18, "She [wisdom] is a tree of life to those who lay hold of her." The tree of life is a reminder of the tree of life in paradise (Gen 2:9) — the tree from which God barred humankind after the fall into sin (Gen 3:24). The theme of access to the tree of life goes practically underground at that point, to resurface fully only in the new creation (Rev 22:2). Yet the point of our passage is that finding wisdom, ordering one's life in accordance with God's creation order, is finding life — life similar to the life that was available in paradise. But the New Testament teaches us that only Christ can again open the door to the tree of life. Now a more fruitful connection for preaching Christ on the basis of Proverbs 8:22-36 opens up: not a connection to Christ the eternal Logos in John 1 but to Christ "the wisdom of God." Paul makes this connection in 1 Corinthians 1:30, where he writes, "He [God] is the source of your life in Christ Jesus, who became for us wisdom from God. . . ."[92]

---

91. Dillard and Longman, *Introduction*, 245.

92. Dillard and Longman, in their *Introduction to the Old Testament*, include for each Old Testament book a valuable section entitled "Approaching the New Testament." "Here one or more of the main themes of an Old Testament book are followed into the New Testament" (p. 36).

THE WAY OF NEW TESTAMENT REFERENCES

New Testament authors frequently use Old Testament passages to support their messages. Preachers can spot these references by checking the appendix of their Greek New Testament, a good concordance, a good cross-reference Bible, or *The Treasury of Scripture Knowledge*.[93] We must remember, of course, that we cannot always follow New Testament writers in their use of the Old Testament: when we preach on 1 Chronicles 3, we cannot use Matthew's number fourteen (David), and when we preach on Sarah and Hagar (Gen 21:8-21), we cannot use Paul's "allegory" in Galatians 4. With other references, too, we must keep in mind that the New Testament authors do not intend to give us a definitive interpretation of Old Testament passages but use (*usus*; see pp. 189-91) the Old Testament to support their own particular messages. Wilhelm Vischer's casual use of a "link to a New Testament text" (see p. 170) cautions us that New Testament references and allusions need to be used judiciously.

The Use of New Testament References

Many New Testament references consist of the ways of promise-fulfillment, typology, or longitudinal themes. If preachers had failed to discover these ways by themselves, these New Testament references are a good corrective of oversights. If preachers had already discovered any of these ways, the New Testament references serve not only as confirmation but can often be used as stepping stones in the sermon to make the point for the congregation. In addition, New Testament references and allusions may at times provide an unexpected link to Christ in the New Testament. For example, Matthew's interesting parallels between the lives of Elijah and John the Baptizer and those of Elisha and Jesus could possibly be used for preaching Christ from the Old Testament.[94]

Examples of Using New Testament References

Preaching on an Old Testament narrative, one can frequently find a New Testament reference or allusion that may serve as a link to preaching

---

93. *The Treasury of Scripture Knowledge: Consisting of Five-Hundred Thousand Scripture References and Parallel Passages from Canne, Browne, Blayney, Scott, and Others* (New York: Revell, n.d.). Also accessible on *Logos 2.1 Bible Software*.

94. For details, see Dillard and Longman, *Introduction*, 166-67.

Christ. For example, preaching on God's command to Abraham to sacrifice Isaac, "Take your son, your only son Isaac, whom you love, and go to
the land of Moriah, and offer him there as a burnt offering . . ." (Gen 22:2),
one should notice that John alludes to this passage in his famous, "God so
loved the world that he gave his only Son . . ." (3:16). John's allusion enables the preacher to make the point that the great sacrifice God stopped
Abraham from making, God made himself: he loved the world so much
that he sacrificed his only Son. Or, preaching on Jacob's dream at Bethel,
"there was a ladder set up on the earth, the top of it reaching to heaven;
and the angels of God were ascending and descending on it" (Gen 28:10-
22), a New Testament reference offers a way of preaching Christ on the
basis of this passage. For Jesus uses this image for himself: "Very truly, I
tell you, you will see heaven opened and the angels of God ascending
and descending upon the Son of Man" (John 1:51).

Preaching on Old Testament law, one can also use New Testament
references as a way to preach Christ. The link in law will usually be with
the teaching of Christ, the new Moses. The Sermon on the Mount (Matt 5–
7) provides many such links. To use another example, when preaching on
giving the tithe (Deut 26:12-15), one can move from this law to Jesus'
teaching in Matthew 23:23, "Woe to you, scribes and Pharisees, hypo-
crites! For you tithe mint, dill, and cummin, and have neglected the
weightier matters of the law: justice and mercy and faith. It is these you
ought to have practiced without neglecting the others."[95]

Preaching on prophecy also allows one to use New Testament references as bridges to preaching Christ. Sometimes Jesus himself cites the
very passage one is preaching on, and the way is clear. At other times the
reference may be more subtle. Preaching on Isaiah 50:4-11, we read in
verse 4, "The Lord God has given me the tongue of a teacher, that I may
know how to sustain the weary with a word." In Matthew 11:28 we hear Jesus say, "Come to me, all you that are weary . . . , and I will give you rest."
But verse 6 of this Isaiah passage has a clearer New Testament reference: "I
gave my back to those who struck me, and my cheeks to those who pulled
out the beard; I did not hide my face from insult and spitting." As Jesus and
his disciples head for Jerusalem, Jesus says, "See, we are going up to Jerusalem, and the Son of Man will be handed over . . . ; they will mock him, and
spit upon him, and flog him, and kill him . . ." (Mark 10:34). For the sake of
a unified sermon, one will probably wish to select only one of the New Testament references. In this case the reference to verse 6 is best since it is clos-
est in line with the theme of the Isaiah passage.

95. Another option for linking this passage with Christ is mentioned under longitudinal themes above, pp. 267-68.

Preaching on the Psalms, similarly, one may find New Testament passages referring to the very text one has selected. When Jesus uses expressions from the selected Psalm to express his own feelings, the way to preaching Christ is clear. For someone preaching on Psalm 22, for example, the words, "My God, my God, why have you forsaken me?" (v 1), necessarily lead to Jesus' forlorn cry on the cross, "My God, my God, why have you forsaken me?" (Mark 15:34). And for one preaching on Psalm 31, the words of verse 5, "Into your hand I commit my spirit," necessarily lead to Jesus' words from the cross, "Father, into your hands I commend my spirit" (Luke 23:46). Or, when one is preaching on Psalm 98, the words of verse 9 that the Lord "will judge the world with righteousness" can be linked to Jesus' words, "The Father judges no one but has given all judgment to the Son . . ." (John 5:22; cf. 2 Tim 4:1).

Preaching Christ from wisdom literature can also benefit from New Testament references. For example, if one's text is Proverbs 15:29, "The LORD is far from the wicked, but he hears the prayer of the righteous," the theme of "hearing the prayer of the righteous" brings to mind Hebrews 4:16, "Let us therefore approach the throne of grace with boldness, so that we may receive mercy and find grace to help in time of need." This New Testament reference would lead us to Jesus, who not only taught us how to pray but who, as high priest, opened the lines of communication with God so that we can be assured that God will hear the prayer of the righteous.

THE WAY OF CONTRAST

Because of the progression in the histories of redemption and revelation, it should not come as a surprise that the message of an Old Testament text will sometimes stand in contrast to that of the New Testament. One thinks immediately of Old Testament ceremonial laws, civil laws, and the so-called "imprecations" in some Psalms. But one can find contrast even in the foundational covenant ordinance which functioned for two thousand years: "Throughout your generations every male among you shall be circumcised when he is eight days old. . . . Any uncircumcised male . . . shall be cut off from his people; he has broken my covenant" (Gen 17:12-14). The contrast is almost total between this ancient ordinance and the decision of the first council of the Christian church: "It has seemed good to the Holy Spirit and to us to impose on you no further burden . . ." (Acts 15:28-29). Even the venerable, and presumably timeless, Decalogue is caught up in the progression in redemptive history when it prescribes for Old Testament times, "The seventh day is a sabbath to the LORD your

God; you shall not do any work" (Exod 20:10). In the New Testament we see a gradual change from the seventh day of the week to the *first* day, the Lord's day, to celebrate the resurrection of our Lord (1 Cor 16:2; cf. Rom 14:5; Col 2:16). This does not mean that such Old Testament passages cannot be preached in the Christian church today, but only that they need to be proclaimed in the light of God's final revelation in Christ and therefore in the light of possible contrast. If the contrast is extreme, however, it would be well to preach on a New Testament text and from that angle show the contrast with the Old Testament.

The Way of Contrast Centers in Christ

The way of contrast clearly centers in Christ, for he is primarily responsible for any change between the messages of the Old Testament and those of the New. It was Jesus' sacrifice, once for all, that filled up the ceremonial laws of sacrifice. It was his mission to the nations that moved the church beyond Israel's civil laws; this outreach to Gentiles also led to the decision to drop the requirement of circumcision. It was Jesus' teaching that changed the "imprecations" in the Psalms as commonly understood, for he taught, "Love your enemies, do good to those who hate you, bless those who curse you, pray for those who abuse you" (Luke 6:27-28). And it was Jesus' resurrection that changed the seventh-day sabbath to the first-day Lord's day. In short, the person, the work, and the teaching of Jesus Christ are the main reasons for the contrasts we observe.[96]

Under the way of contrast we can also include a road to Christ frequently traveled by Spurgeon — a road which begins with the problems encountered in the Old Testament and leads to the solution in Jesus Christ. For example, the Old Testament text may convict us of the gravity of human sin, it may confront us with a just and holy God, and it may remind us of the Day of Judgment. These plights cry out for a solution, and the solution is found in Jesus Christ. Christ is the answer to Old Testament problems.

---

96. Jesus also, when questioned about divorce (Matt 19:3-9), contrasted the teaching of Deuteronomy 24 with that of Genesis 1–2 and changed the Mosaic legislation in the process.

Examples of the Way of Contrast
in Various Genres of Literature

To conclude this final way of preaching Christ from the Old Testament, it may be helpful to list some examples from different genres of literature.

Contrast in Preaching Old Testament Narrative

In Old Testament narrative, contrast may become evident in several forms. For example, God instructs Israel at various times to attack Canaanite cities and annihilate their inhabitants: "You must not let anything that breathes remain alive. You shall annihilate them . . ." (Deut 20:16-17). The inhabitants were to be "devoted to the LORD for destruction" (*cherem*; e.g., Josh 6:17, 21; 10:28-40). But after the coming of Christ and in the light of his teaching, no nation has the right to conduct a "holy war" and commit genocide.

Often contrast can also be used in combination with one of the other ways. For example, in preaching on the judge Gideon, we notice that he is obedient to God in destroying the altar of Baal and saving Israel from the Midianites, but afterward Gideon builds an ephod and leads Israel away from God (Judg 6–8). A combination of typology and contrast leads to preaching Christ as the perfect Savior, who frees us from our sins and our enemies, including death, and who connects us with the Father in a covenant relationship that can never be broken (John 10:27-30).[97] To use another example: "Ezra-Nehemiah attests to the expansion of holiness beyond the confines of the temple to include the whole city of Jerusalem." But clear boundaries remain between the holy and the secular, clean and unclean, Jew and Gentile. "It is Jesus Christ who tears down the 'wall of separation.' First of all, he tears apart the veil that separated the Holy of Holies from the rest of creation. Second, he demolishes the division of humanity that separated Jew from Gentile (Eph 2:14-18)."[98]

Contrast in Preaching Old Testament Law

In preaching Old Testament law — for example, "You shall have no other gods before me" (Exod 20:3) — we are confronted with Israel's and our inability to keep God's law perfectly. The solution to this serious plight is to be found in Jesus Christ and his perfect righteousness. In fact, Paul

97. The contrast here can also be seen as the element of escalation which marks typology.

98. Dillard and Longman, *Introduction*, 187.

writes that the law was our disciplinarian (*paidagogos*) "to lead us to Christ" (Gal 3:24, NIV).

In preaching law, we can also use contrast in combination with one of the other ways. Although the Old Testament laws requiring blood sacrifices, for example, are fulfilled by Christ's sacrifice, in this New Testament era God still requires our sacrifices: "present your bodies as a living sacrifice" (a combination of typology, contrast, and longitudinal themes). Or, in preaching on the commandment, "Remember the sabbath day, and keep it holy" (Exod 20:8), one needs to contrast this seventh day in the Old Testament with the first day in the New Testament. One day in seven is still set aside as a special day for worshiping the Lord (1 Cor 16:2; Heb 10:25), but it changes to the first day of the week in celebration of Jesus' resurrection (a combination of contrast and New Testament references).[99]

Contrast in Preaching Prophecy

In Old Testament prophecy, contrast will often reveal itself in prophecies that confine themselves to the restoration of Israel as a national entity while the New Testament moves far beyond that to God's restoration of all nations and of the whole creation (e.g., Rom 8:19-21; Rev 22:1-2). But there are also more specific contrasts. For example, Ezekiel informs us that he saw "the appearance of the likeness of the glory of the LORD" (Ezek 1:28). Notice that he is two steps removed from seeing "the glory of the LORD." By way of contrast, John reports seeing the glory of the Lord directly in Jesus: "The Word became flesh and lived among us, and we have seen his glory . . ." (John 1:14). Further, Ezekiel proclaims the Lord's message to Israel: It is not the children of sinners, but "only the person who sins that shall die" (Ezek 18:4; cf. Jer 31:30). Although this message already contrasts with earlier Old Testament teaching (see Exod 20:5), contrast with New Testament teaching shows that we need not die for our sins because Christ died for them.

Contrast in Preaching Psalms

Contrast in preaching Psalms is usually associated with preaching the so-called "imprecatory" Psalms. In several Psalms we hear prayers to the Lord to avenge his people, to bring about full justice.[100] Such prayers are still heard in the New Testament, for example in Revelation 6:10, "Sovereign Lord, holy and true, how long will it be before you judge and avenge

---

99. See further, e.g., Moo, "The Law of Moses or the Law of Christ."
100. See, e.g., Pss 5:10; 55:15; 58:6-8; 59:11-13; 69:22-28; 83:9-12.

our blood on the inhabitants of the earth?" But some Psalms seem to give expression not just to the desire for God's justice but for retaliation. For example, Psalm 137 reflects on Israel's terrible experiences in Babylon and exclaims, "O daughter Babylon, you devastator! Happy shall they be who pay you back what you have done to us! Happy shall they be who take your little ones and dash them against the rocks!" (Ps 137:8-9). In Psalm 109 we hear the Psalmist's prayer about the person who "did not remember to show kindness, but pursued the poor and needy and the brokenhearted to their death" (v 16): "May his days be few. . . . May his children be orphans. . . . May his children wander about and beg. . . . May the iniquity of his father be remembered before the LORD, and do not let the sin of his mother be blotted out" (Ps 109:8-14). If these are indeed all-too-human desires for revenge and retaliation — scholars are not agreed on this[101] — then we need to contrast these thoughts with Jesus' teaching, "Love your enemies and pray for those who persecute you" (Matt 5:44; cf. 1 Cor 13:13), and his own prayer on the cross, "Father, forgive them; for they do not know what they are doing" (Luke 23:34).[102]

One can also use contrast with other Psalms, however. For example, Psalm 44 is a national lament regarding Israel's suffering. Israel cries out, "Because of you we are being killed all day long, and accounted as sheep for the slaughter. Rouse yourself! Why do you sleep, O Lord?" (vv 22-23). The Psalm ends with the urgent plea, "Rise up, come to our help. Redeem us for the sake of your steadfast love" (v 26). A Christian preacher can do more than reiterate this plea for help in a time of suffering. A New Testament reference shows that Paul quotes verse 22 in Romans 8, where he deals with the persecution and suffering of the church. But in contrast to the Psalmist's plea for help, Paul gives the assurance that in the very sufferings mentioned in this Psalm, "we are more than conquerors through him who loved us. For I am convinced that neither death, nor life, nor angels, nor rulers, nor things present, nor things to come, nor powers, nor height, nor depth, nor anything else in all creation, will be able to separate us from the love of God in Christ Jesus our Lord" (Rom 8:37-39). God

---

101. Compare Ronald Allen and John Holbert, Holy Root, 128, "An imprecation is an invocation of a curse upon one's enemies," and Stek, NIV Study, Ps 5:10, "Actually, these 'imprecations' are not that at all; rather, they are appeals to God to redress wrongs perpetrated against the psalmists by imposing penalties commensurate with the violence done (see 28:4) — in accordance also with normal judicial procedure in human courts (see Dt 25:1-3)." See also Achtemeier, Preaching from the Old Testament, 142-44, and George L. Klein, "Preaching Poetry," in Reclaiming the Prophetic Mantle, ed. George L. Klein (Nashville: Broadman, 1992), 90.

102. Cf. Jer 29:7, "Seek the welfare of the city where I have sent you into exile, and pray the LORD on its behalf. . . ."

is not asleep when we suffer. He *has* redeemed us for the sake of his "steadfast love" (Ps 44:26). This love and assurance is ours "in Christ Jesus our Lord" (Rom 8:39).

Contrast in Preaching Wisdom Literature

Ecclesiastes 11:7–12:8 enables one to preach on the important theme, "Enjoy your life, remembering your Creator before the days of adversity come." When I first made a sermon on this passage for a youth service, I fudged a bit by not preaching on verse 8, which concludes the passage with the observation, "Vanity of vanities, says the Teacher; all is vanity." At the time it seemed like this pessimistic conclusion would spoil a good message. Today I would include verse 8, not only because it is part of the textual unit[103] but also because it enables me to make the message more powerful by way of contrast. For the Teacher, death ends everything (see, e.g., Eccl 2:16, 21; 3:18-21; 9:2-6); hence the continual repetition of "vanity of vanities . . . ; all is vanity." But as New Testament Christians we know that Christ has overcome death, and that astonishing victory also gives us a different view of life. This passage clearly begs to be contrasted with Paul's powerful chapter on the resurrection, 1 Corinthians 15. Death has been overcome: "Thanks be to God, who gives us the victory through our Lord Jesus Christ." Then Paul concludes, "Therefore, my beloved, be steadfast, immovable, always excelling in the work of the Lord, because you know that in the Lord your labor is not in vain" (1 Cor 15:57-58). Paul discloses a staggering reversal, from "all is vanity" to "in the Lord your labor is not in vain" — all because Jesus rose from death.

*   *   *

This completes our discussion of the christocentric ways of preaching Christ from the Old Testament: the ways of redemptive-historical progression, promise-fulfillment, typology, analogy, longitudinal themes, New Testament references, and contrast. Because of overlap between these ways, our concern should not be whether we have stuck to the precise perimeters of a particular way. Our concern should rather be: Does this sermon preach Christ? Bryan Chapell suggests that "every preacher should ask at the end of each sermon: When my listeners walk out the doors of this sanctuary to perform God's will, with whom do they walk?" That's a good question to ask, for often we leave people to figure it out for themselves, or we may even have left the impression that they can do this

---

103. It also forms an inclusio with Ecclesiastes 1:2.

in their own strength. "If the sermon has led all persons within sight of the Savior and they now walk into their world with his aid firmly in their grasp, then hope and victory brighten the horizon. Whether people depart alone or in the Savior's hand will mark the difference between futility and faith, legalism and true obedience, do-goodism and real godliness."[104]

104. Chapell, *Christ-Centered Preaching*, 285-86.

CHAPTER 7

Steps from Old Testament Text to Christocentric Sermon

"There is salvation in no one else [than Jesus], for there is no other name under heaven given among mortals by which we must be saved."

Peter, Acts 4:12

SEVERAL SCHOLARS have proposed a number of steps preachers need to follow in order to move responsibly from text to sermon.[1] Fred Craddock observes, "It is vital that one's procedure lead smoothly into and through a text and that it be simple enough to be followed almost unconsciously. . . . A method will be most fruitful when it has become a habit as comfortable as an old sweater."[2] I suggest that the following basic steps are simple enough to become a habit for a lifetime of fruitful ministry of the Word.[3]

1. Select a textual unit with an eye to congregational needs.
2. Read and reread the text in its literary context.

---

1. For example, Haddon Robinson, *Biblical Preaching*, 151-209; Fred Craddock, *Preaching*, 99-209; Thomas Long, *Witness*, 60-188.

2. Craddock, *Preaching*, 99.

3. In teaching these ten steps from text to sermon and combining them with an expository sermon model (see Appendix), I have found that seminary students tend to be more faithful to the biblical text and more creative working within specified boundaries than they are without specific guidelines.

3. Outline the structure of the text.
4. Interpret the text in its own historical setting.
5. Formulate the text's theme and goal.
6. Understand the message in the contexts of canon and redemptive history.
7. Formulate the sermon theme and goal.
8. Select a suitable sermon form.
9. Prepare the sermon outline.
10. Write the sermon in oral style.

The number of steps is not as important as is their sequence, for putting questions to the text in the wrong sequence is asking for hermeneutical and homiletical trouble. In the context of this book on preaching Christ from the Old Testament, we need to learn primarily at what point in the interpretive process we should raise the questions concerning the ways of preaching Christ and how this functions concretely in preaching Old Testament texts. To meet this need, we shall first examine the ten sequential steps and then demonstrate with Genesis 22 how they work concretely in developing an Old Testament text into a christocentric sermon.

TEN STEPS FROM OLD TESTAMENT TEXT TO CHRISTOCENTRIC SERMON

First, Select a Textual Unit with an Eye to Congregational Needs

When tragedy strikes a church or community, people come to church seeking a word from the Lord on how to deal with the overwhelming grief. When church members have made material goods the god of their lives, they need a word from the Lord about the Creator's goal for human life. When church bells ring in Easter Sunday, people need to hear a word from the Lord about the resurrection.

Congregations, of course, have a wide variety of overlapping needs. One of their most basic needs is to be equipped "for the work of ministry, for building up the body of Christ" (Eph 4:12), and another to hear "the whole purpose of God" (Acts 20:27). One of their more routine needs is to hear sermons that relate to the church year: special seasons such as Advent or Lent, or special days such as Christmas, Easter, and Pentecost — a need well met when preachers use a lectionary. And one of their more general needs, in view of the increasing lack of knowledge about the Old Testament, is to hear more sermons based on the Old Testament.

For more specific needs one has to exegete the congregation and the culture in which it lives. Together with the elders one may detect such needs as confusion and doubt about the Christian faith, fear of the future, a lack of active involvement in God's coming kingdom, a lack of trust in God, a lack of assurance of salvation, a lack of love for each other, a lack of concern to promote justice in the land, a lack of knowledge about God and his will, the temptations of contemporary idols, illness, stress, sorrow, anger, insecurity, and a host of other needs.

Before selecting a text, we should decide which particular need should be addressed in this sermon. The congregational need provides the target. Next we need an arrow that will fly straight to the target — we need a biblical text that addressed a similar need in Israel or, in the case of the New Testament, in the early church. This strategy of matching texts with needs allows us to create sermons that are relevant from beginning to end — sermons which are of one piece, shifting back and forth only between the need addressed in Israel and the similar need in the church today. By contrast, selecting the text first and then belatedly trying to apply it to an acute congregational need can lead to unnatural and forced applications.

In searching for a text which met a similar need in Israel, we must be careful not to confuse the needs of Israel, the Old Testament church, with the needs of individuals such as Abraham or David. In contrast to those who engage in biographical and character preaching, we should see the stories about Abraham and David as messages that have been taken up in the Bible to meet certain needs in *Israel*. Preachers should focus on the question: What need in *Israel* did this text address? What was the question in Israel which this text sought to answer? What was the issue behind the text? If, upon further study, we find that the text met a different need in Israel than we first supposed, we must either look for a different text or develop the selected text into a sermon that will meet a different need than that which we first intended. The point is that preachers must at all costs do justice to the biblical text and not twist it into responding to a different issue than its author originally addressed.

The reason for selecting a biblical textual unit as preaching-text is to ground the sermon in the written Word of God. Expository sermons seek to expose for the present congregation a word of God originally spoken to Israel or, in case of the New Testament, to the early church. Preachers are like transmission towers who transmit the original biblical message from an earlier generation to the present generation.[4] Their calling is not

---

4. They are also like translators who transform the original message so that it makes its original point in a different culture.

to invent their own messages but relevantly to pass on the divine messages found in the Bible. This calling to be faithful to the biblical text makes proper text selection such a crucial first step. It is almost impossible to preach a sound, biblical sermon from a poorly selected preaching-text.

The selected text must be a message unit — not a clause, nor a fragment, but a literary unit. A message unit may sometimes be only one sentence (e.g., some proverbs) but usually will consist of one or more paragraphs (especially with narrative texts).[5] Further, since preaching is so crucial for the hearers, and since preachers have only a limited number of opportunities to preach, the selected text should proclaim a vital theme.[6]

Second, Read and Reread the Text in Its Literary Context

Using various Bible translations, read and reread the text in the context of the book. At this early stage our interest is to become aware of the big picture, to see the forest before we focus on the trees with detailed Hebrew analysis. Fred Craddock makes a strong case for this "spontaneous, even naïve, engagement with the text. All faculties of mind and heart are open, with no concern for what one ought to think, much less what one will say later in the sermon. This is the time to listen, think, feel, imagine, ask."[7] He warns against using other study aids such as commentaries at this point. "When used at the proper time they are indispensable, but if too early opened, they take over. They suppress and intimidate the preacher."[8]

As we carefully read and reflect on the text, we listen not only for ourselves but also for the congregation. We may involve the congrega-

5. For example, James Stewart, *Heralds,* 165, makes the following contrast: "Read Isaiah 6 analytically, and you may feel an urge to preach on the wings of the seraphim, or the smoke that filled the house. . . . Read it as a unity, and there will emerge, clear-cut and decisive, the outlines of a totally different kind of sermon: now, with the whole chapter as your text, you will preach on the three visions which came in rapid succession to the prophet and enter still into the experience of every true servant of the Lord — the vision of God, the vision of himself, and the vision of a waiting world."

6. "Any notion that the preacher is less than an ambassador of the kingdom of God reduces the pulpit from prophetic urgency to timid homilies on marginal matters." Merrill R. Abbey, *Living Doctrine in a Vital Pulpit* (Nashville: Abingdon, 1964), 124. For more details on text selection, see my *Modern Preacher,* 124-28.

7. Craddock, *Preaching,* 105.

8. Ibid., 106.

tion even more directly by reading the selected passage in pastoral calls. How does a parishioner dying in a hospice hear this text? How about a single parent? What questions does it raise for a troubled teenager? As we listen to the text by ourselves or possibly with a few members of the congregation, we should jot down these initial questions. Later in the process, these questions can guide our consultation of study aids such as commentaries. As Craddock puts it, "The text has raised the questions to be pursued in those books, and therefore those volumes are servants, not masters."[9] Moreover, we may be able to use some of these questions in the sermon, for our hearers on Sunday will probably have similar questions.[10]

Third, Outline the Structure of the Text

At this stage, it is time to zero in on the text itself and make use of our Hebrew language skills. We first need to probe below the text's surface meaning in order to discover and expose its structure. If the text is a narrative, we need to trace the story or plot line. Specific questions to ask are: What was the setting? What generated the conflict? What intensified the conflict? Where does the conflict reach its climax? When and how is the conflict finally resolved? And what is the outcome or conclusion?[11] We should seek to answer all these questions and note the appropriate verse references.

If the text is an argument, we should inquire about the flow of the argument: What are the major affirmations? How are these major affirmations related? What is the conclusion? We should list our findings again with the appropriate verse references. The sequence of major affirmations, like tire tracks in the snow, show the direction in which the argument is heading.

The use of the original Hebrew will enable us to be more precise than simply working with English translations. We will be able to chart the clausal flow with greater precision and note literary structures such as repetition, parallelism, and *ki* ("because") clauses which may or may not be evident in English translations.

9. Ibid.

10. Craddock, ibid., suggests, "It is also likely that these early notes will provide more than half one's introductions to sermons. And why not? After all, this is the way the preacher began to get into the text; the congregation could happily begin the same way." Although I agree that this is an intellectually catchy way to begin the sermon, I think preachers can often do better at an existential level. See Step 9 below.

11. See Tremper Longman, *Literary Approaches to Biblical Interpretation,* 92.

Outlining the structure of the text has several advantages: we begin to assimilate the text; we begin to understand the textual flow in its parts and the whole; and we may be able to use this outline later for the sermon outline.

Fourth, Interpret the Text in Its Own Historical Setting

In this fourth step most of the detailed analyses will be done. As we saw in Chapter 6, in interpreting the text we can distinguish three intertwined strands: literary, historical, and theocentric.

Literary Interpretation

Under literary interpretation we need to ask two basic questions: How does it mean? With this question we seek to give an account of the genre of the book, the form of the text, and the figures of speech within the text. The second question is, What did it mean in the context of this book? In the Hebrew text, we should note the rhetorical structures such as repetition or key word technique (A . . . A' . . . A''), inclusio (A . . . A'), or chiasm (A . . . B . . . C . . . B' . . . A'). All of these structures help to determine the textual unit (from the first A to the final A). They can also help to determine the focus or theme of the text: often the repetition of key words, the center of a chiastic structure, and sometimes the A's (bookends) of an inclusio.

In poetry (as well as some prose), we should pay attention to the parallelisms and whether they are synonymous, synthetic, or antithetic. Parallelism, too, may provide clues to the textual unit as well as the author's message.

In narrative, in addition to the plot line (Step 3), we should note the scenes and their interrelation, the characters, their description (infrequent, but important if present) and their dialogue, changes in a repeated speech, and contrasts between the characters. Further, we should try to spot the narrator, his point of view, his use of pace retardation to highlight crucial turns in the story, his evaluation of characters (seldom present), his conclusion and message. In nonnarrative prose, we should go beyond listing the major affirmations (Step 3) to adding the details of modifying clauses and phrases.

This literary analysis needs to be combined with grammatical analysis in which we raise questions about verbs, adverbs, nouns, pronouns, and adjectives (grammar) as well as sentence structure (syntax). After taking students through a detailed "rhetorical analysis" of the Hebrew text, Elizabeth Achtemeier concludes, "If a preacher studies a passage in such detail, it is very hard to miss its meaning. Above all, the message of the text shapes the thought of the preacher, rather than vice versa. It is out of such careful analysis of the text that all truly biblical sermons are born."[12]

Before we can decide on the message of the text, however, we need to determine the function of the passage in the context of the book. At this point literary interpretation merges with historical interpretation in seeking to understand the message of the text in its own historical setting.

Historical Interpretation

Under historical interpretation we need to ask two basic questions. First, What was the author's intended meaning for his original hearers? We can answer this question by seeking answers to the five familiar questions: Who wrote this text? To whom? When? Where? And why? For proper understanding, however, we need not know the precise answer to each of these questions, for frequently we can understand the message even though we may not know the author, or precisely when or where he wrote. But the questions "To whom?" and especially "Why?" are of crucial importance for preachers, for these questions have to do with the original life-setting *(Sitz im Leben)* of the text. Moreover, they provide information to answer the second basic question.

The second basic question is, What need of the hearers did the author seek to address? Every text has a question behind the text, an issue that called the text into being. It may be idolatry, or lack of knowledge, or lack of justice, or lack of love for neighbor, or foreign alliances, or exile, or misplaced trust in large armies. Combining the meaning discovered in literary interpretation with the clues to existential meaning provided by historical interpretation will give us a good idea of the author's original message.

Understanding this original message is vitally important, for it offers an objective point of control against subjective and arbitrary interpretations. Especially when our interest is in Christ-centered preaching, which, as we have seen, is open to subjective manipulation, understanding the original message can help prevent allegorizing, typologizing, and other arbitrary ways of preaching Christ from Old Testament texts. First and foremost, we need to do justice to the original message.

12. Achtemeier, *Preaching from the Old Testament,* 44. See pp. 39-44.

Theocentric Interpretation

The major question under theocentric interpretation is: What does this passage reveal about God, his redemptive acts, his covenant, his grace, his will for his people? The question about God in relation to his people is probably the most important question to ask to prevent the moralistic, imitation preaching so prevalent today. For basically the Bible is about God; it is his self-revelation to his people. This revelation naturally includes God's will for his people, but this is usually revealed in divine laws and directions for human behavior rather than in fallible models of such behavior. In addition to preventing moralistic preaching, theocentric interpretation also provides an important link to Christ-centered preaching, as we shall see in Step 6.

At this point in our steps from text to sermon, we have done enough personal study so that we can, with a measure of confidence, consult the usual study aids such as theological dictionaries, introductions, and commentaries. The best of these scholarly works reflect the careful thinking of the church over the centuries about the meaning of these biblical passages. In the light of the church's overall reflections on the message of these texts, individual preachers should naturally be open to correction and different conclusions. The blending of our own insights into the meaning of the text with the valid insights of others throughout church history is an exciting but responsible way of discerning God's message for his people.

Fifth, Formulate the Text's Theme and Goal

We are now ready to focus the various insights by formulating two single, related sentences: the text's theme and the text's goal.

The Textual Theme

The textual theme is a summary statement of the unifying thought of the text. It answers the question, *What* is the author saying in this text? What is his point for his original hearers? For the sake of the unity of the sermon, the theme should be a single statement. Since it is the heart of the message, the theme should be formulated as an assertion with a subject and predicate. J. H. Jowett contends, "I have a conviction that no sermon is ready for preaching . . . until we can express its theme in a short, pregnant sentence as clear as crystal. I find the getting of that sentence is the hardest, the most exacting and the most fruitful labor in my study. . . . I do not think any sermon ought to be preached, or even written, until that sentence has emerged, clear and lucid as a cloudless moon. . . . [Then] there will be no danger of unscrupulous text-twisting. . . . The word of God will dominate our mind, set fire to our hearts, control the development of our exposition and later leave a lasting impression on the congregation."[13]

The Textual Goal

The textual goal is a succinct statement of the goal the known or unknown author had in sending this message to his original hearers. It answers the question, *Why* is the author sending this message to Israel? Does he aim to teach Israel certain facts? to warn Israel against certain sins? to persuade Israel of God's steadfast love? to urge Israel to walk in God's ways? to encourage Israel to praise the Lord? to comfort Israel in exile?

Essentially, all biblical texts seek to teach. But most have a deeper goal than to teach, namely to teach in order to persuade, to warn, to correct, to encourage, to comfort, and so on. In general, the goal of law is to teach Israel the law in order to urge obedience. The goal of wisdom is to instruct Israel in the regular patterns observed in God's creation order so as to encourage people to walk wisely and be happy in following God's order. The goal of narrative is to teach Israel the story of God and his people in order to give people hope and encourage them to look for and work for the wonderful coming kingdom of God. With each text, however, we need to move beyond the general goal of the genre to the specific goal of this particular text.

The advantage of discerning the author's specific goal is that it reveals the relevance of the preaching-text. It exposes the question behind the text, the need in Israel the author sought to address. This insight transports preachers halfway to conceiving a relevant sermon. The other half is discovering the same or a similar need among the contemporary hearers, so that the word of the Lord for Israel may be proclaimed as a relevant word of the Lord for the church today.

Sixth, Understand the Message in the Contexts of Canon and Redemptive History

With the historical theme and goal for Israel firmly in mind, we can now broaden the scope and seek to understand the message in the contexts of the whole canon and all of redemptive history. At this all-encompassing

---

13. Jowett, *The Preacher: His Life and Work* (New York: Doran, 1912), 133.

level, literary interpretation becomes canonical interpretation. It asks, What does this passage mean in the context of the whole Bible, from Genesis 1 to Revelation 22? Historical interpretation at this level becomes redemptive-historical interpretation. It asks, What does this passage mean in the context of God's all-encompassing story from creation to new creation? And theocentric interpretation at this level becomes christocentric interpretation. It asks, What does this passage mean in the light of Jesus Christ? And, What is the road from this passage in the Old Testament to Jesus Christ in the New?

This, then, is the point in the hermeneutical sequence at which we raise the questions concerning the ways of preaching Christ.[14] Only after we have firmly established the historical meaning of the text and have struggled to focus this meaning in a clear statement of the textual theme and goal can we move on to the question, How does this passage proclaim the good news of Jesus Christ? Which of the seven ways provide a solid link to Jesus Christ? This is therefore the place to raise the questions, Does this message in the course of redemptive history lead to Jesus Christ, our Savior and living Lord? Does it promise his coming? Does it prefigure his person and work? Does it show by analogy who God in Christ is for us today? Does its theme lead into the New Testament to Jesus or his teaching? Does a New Testament author quote this passage or allude to it? Does New Testament teaching stand in contrast to this Old Testament message?

This process will probably lead to more links from the Old Testament text to Christ than we can effectively include in any one sermon. We should therefore be prepared to select a few decisive links which support the sermon theme and help to accomplish the sermon goal.

Seventh, Formulate the Sermon Theme and Goal

The Sermon Theme

When the New Testament assumes or confirms the message of the Old Testament passage, the sermon theme will usually be the same as the theme of the text. This offers a major advantage for designing the sermon, for now the outline of the text (discovered in Step 3) will support the sermon theme and can be used as the outline of the sermon. By contrast, when the progression in revelation examined in Step 6 changes the mes-

---

14. "A valid canonical interpretation will not stop at the grammatical-historical step but will seek the canonical and christological sense of the passage." David Dockery, *GTJ* 4/2 (1983) 203.

sage of the text in some way, the sermon theme may need to be adjusted to take into account the New Testament perspective. It is advisable, however, not to change the sermon theme radically but to stay as close as possible to the textual theme so that the outline of the text, at least in part, supports the sermon theme.

The sermon theme should be formulated as a single assertion, a clear sentence with subject and predicate. The sermon theme will help keep the sermon focussed and unified and thus provide movement.[15]

The Sermon Goal

The preacher's goal with the sermon must match the sermon theme and be in harmony with the goal of the author of the text. For example, if the author of Isaiah 40 intended to comfort Israel in exile, the preacher today should not use this text to warn the congregation about the effects of disobedience. Although the preacher's goal today cannot always be exactly the same as that of the original author, it ought to be at least in harmony with it.

The sermon goal is a succinct statement of what the preacher seeks to do in preaching this sermon, whether it be to encourage the hearers to commit or recommit their lives to Christ, or to warn them against certain sins, or to persuade the hearers of God's steadfast love, or to urge them to walk in God's ways, or to encourage them to have hope in God and his coming kingdom. The goal states *why* the sermon is being preached. It is a focussed response to a perceived need in the congregation.[16] The goal will guide the style of the sermon and can also be used to determine the content of the introduction and conclusion (see Step 9 below).

Eighth, Select a Suitable Sermon Form

In the last few decades, homileticians have become more aware of the significance of selecting a suitable sermon form, both for faithfully transmitting the biblical message and for reaching the hearers at more levels than merely the intellectual.[17] For faithfully transmitting the biblical message,

15. See further, Craddock, *Preaching*, 155-57, and my *Modern Preacher*, 136-40.

16. The need pinpointed in Step 1 in selecting the text, confirmed to exist in Israel in Step 4, targeted with the statement of goal in Step 5, and now focussed on the present hearers in Step 7.

17. "If the minister wants the sermon to do what the text does, then he or she will want to hold on to the form, since form captures and conveys function, not only during the interpretation of the text but during the designing of the sermon as well." Craddock, *Preaching*, 123.

we should select a sermon form that both respects the form of the text and achieves the goal of the sermon. For example, when the text is a narrative, we should seriously consider using a narrative form that follows the story line of the text rather than the standard didactic form which imposes its own structure on the text. Or when the text is a lament Psalm, we should consider following the form of the Psalm through its various moves from calling upon God, to description of distress, to complaint against God, to petitions to God for help, to professions of trust, to final praise.[18] Or when the text aims to teach, we should consider following its major affirmations to its conclusion to convey its meaning. The point is, in expository preaching we should not only expose the meaning of the text but also the form and structure that convey this meaning.[19]

Ninth, Prepare the Sermon Outline

As indicated above, the ideal sermon form follows the flow of the text. Here the work done in Step 3 pays additional dividends, for the main points or moves of the text can often become the main points or moves in the body of the sermon. But we must still work on a sermon outline, for sometimes there may be good reason for reversing the order of the text or for highlighting in the sermon a subsidiary point in the text or for adding a point from the New Testament. In addition, we do not want every sermon based on an Old Testament text to have a predictable final move to the New Testament. It may be possible to begin with the New Testament and then flash back to the Old Testament text, or to move to the New Testament in the middle of the sermon and then move back to the Old Testament text.

Moreover, in addition to working on the body of the sermon, we need to reflect on an effective introduction, a fitting conclusion, and clarifying illustrations. Elizabeth Achtemeier notes, "If we set down our sermon in outline form, we can shape it creatively, eliminate any [needless] repetitions, and plan the introduction and illustrations. Above all, we know the conclusion toward which we are driving; we know how the sermon is going to end."[20] A good outline is characterized by unity, balance (symmetry), and movement to a climax.[21]

---

18. For more details on these "prayers," see Stek, *NIV Study*, 783. Cf. Achtemeier, *Preaching from the Old Testament*, 51.

19. For more detail and references, see my *Modern Preacher*, 141-56.

20. Achtemeier, *Preaching from the Old Testament*, 59.

21. See, e.g., Hugh Litchfield, "Outlining the Sermon," in *Handbook of Contemporary Preaching*, ed. Michael Duduit (Nashville: Broadman, 1992), 162-74.

Our work on the theme and goal also pays dividends at this stage of preparing an outline. The theme controls and focusses the contents of the body of the sermon. In deductive development, each point of the body should be subordinate to and support the theme; in inductive development, each move should lead toward the theme. While the *theme* thus functions primarily to outline the body of the sermon, the *goal* can be used especially to design its introduction and conclusion. For the introduction, we can zero in on the need-side of the goal: Why is this sermon being preached? What is the need being addressed? Beginning with a contemporary illustration of this need will put the relevance of the sermon up-front, and the whole sermon, also when it deals with Israel, will be experienced as relevant because everything stands in the service of addressing the present need. For the conclusion, we can again look to the goal and ask ourselves, How can I best achieve this goal? Would a poignant quotation from Scripture help me clinch the goal, or a moving illustration, or the suggestion of concrete steps people can take?

Although our focus has been on preaching Christ, this does not mean that the conclusion will always be an invitation to "accept Christ as personal Savior." The type of conclusion depends on the text and the goal. Moreover, although there will be occasions to press for a decision, commitment to Christ is much broader than a momentary personal decision; it is a lifetime of living for Christ in every area of life. For Jesus is Lord of all and requires total commitment. Lesslie Newbigin contends, "A preaching of the gospel that calls men and women to accept Jesus as Savior but does not make it clear that discipleship means commitment to a vision of society radically different from that which controls our public life today must be condemned as false."[22]

To focus the sermon on Christ is not to narrow relevance. True relevance lies precisely in the biblical theocentric-christocentric message and its required response. Moreover, with the focus on Christ, the possibilities of application are as broad as life itself. John Stott gives us a hint of the relevance of Christ for all of life: "To encounter Christ is to touch reality and experience transcendence. He gives us a sense of self-worth or personal significance, because he assures us of God's love for us. He sets us free from guilt because he died for us, . . . and from paralyzing fear because he reigns. . . . He gives meaning to marriage and home, work and leisure, personhood and citizenship."[23]

22. Newbigin, *Foolishness to the Greeks*, 132.
23. Stott, *Between Two Worlds*, 154.

Tenth, Write the Sermon in Oral Style

Finally, the sermon should be written in oral style. In contrast to written style, oral style is characterized by short sentences, vivid words, strong nouns and verbs, the active voice, narration in the present tense, memorable images, and moving illustrations.[24] Writing out the sermon at least during the first ten years of one's ministry will enhance precision of expression, insure economy of words, and in general improve one's English style.

THE STEPS APPLIED TO GENESIS 22

To demonstrate concretely how these steps lead from an Old Testament text to a christocentric sermon, we shall take Genesis 22 through the first nine steps. I have selected Genesis 22 because the story of God commanding Abraham to sacrifice Isaac is such a powerful narrative while the history of preaching shows that it presents daunting difficulties for interpretation and preaching. We shall first look at some of the pitfalls to avoid in preparing to preach on this passage.

We should not begin our study by consulting commentaries, least of all the so-called "homiletical commentaries," which in their drive for application tend to lead preachers astray. On this passage, for example, the *Homiletic Commentary* suggests the following applications. For verse 2, as Abraham was called upon to sacrifice his son, "so we, in like manner, may be called upon to make sacrifices." For verse 5, "He [Abraham] wanted not to be interrupted. . . . Great trials are best entered upon with but little company." And for verse 11, "God delights to bring his people to the mount, to the very brow of the hill, till their feet slip, and then he delivers them."[25]

---

24. See the excellent suggestions in Mark Galli and Craig Brian Larson, *Preaching That Connects: Using the Techniques of Journalists to Add Impact to Your Sermons* (Grand Rapids: Zondervan, 1994), especially pp. 91-115.

25. T. H. Leale, *The Preacher's Complete Homiletical Commentary* (New York: Funk & Wagnalls, 1892), Genesis 22. Cf. Robert S. Candlish, *Studies in Genesis* (Grand Rapids: Kregel, 1979 [1868]), 381, "We are tried in the very same way with him [Abraham]. We are called to give up to God the desire of our eyes — the beloved of our hearts — some dear partner, or child, or friend. . . . It is a bitter parting. . . . But it is God's will; and we submit." Cf. James Hastings, *The Great Texts of the Bible* (Edinburgh: Clark, 1911), 198, "God's true children must climb their mount of sacrifice. When our own hour shall have come, may we arise forthwith, cleave the wood for the burnt-offering, and go unflinching up the path by which our Heavenly Father shall lead us. So shall the mount of trial become the mount of blessing."

Notice that the author does not inquire first about the message of this story for Israel; he simply stops at every verse and seeks to attach some practical applications to these elements of the story. No other literature is subjected to such abuse, but practical commentaries will frequently cut biblical narratives into little pieces for the sake of attaching to these pieces some morals or other "relevant" applications.

The contemporary, popular biographical preaching is another pitfall to dodge. Biographical preaching tends to look for attitudes and actions of biblical characters which the hearers should either imitate or avoid. One of the most outlandish examples of this genre of preaching is a sermon on Genesis 22 preached in 1984 under the theme, "Parents and children must worship the Lord together." The sermon, which the preacher considered worthy of publication, has four points:

  I. Father and son walked together.
 II. Father and son talked together.
III. Father and son worked together.
 IV. Father and son sacrificed together.[26]

In 1992 a fine essay was published analyzing Genesis 22, but, unfortunately, it also concludes with a disappointing sermon outline:

  I. God tests His saints so as to confirm their faith through enduring obedience.
 II. The righteous obey the Lord, trusting in His ultimate provision for deliverance.
III. The Lord rescues His saints, fulfills His promises, and rewards the righteous.[27]

Notice that in point I God's unique testing of Abraham is applied to the testing of all his saints — the error of generalizing or universalizing. In point II the author's *description* of Abraham's obedience and trust is for all practical purposes turned into a *prescription* for the righteous — the error of moralizing (like Abraham we must obey and trust the Lord). And

---

26. My translation. The preacher will remain anonymous, but an analysis of this sermon is found in Strydom, *Aard van die Prediking*, 216, 243-45.

27. Kenneth A. Matthews, "Preaching Historical Narrative," in *Reclaiming the Prophetic Mantle*, ed. George L. Klein (Nashville: Broadman, 1992), 45. In 1997 a pastor shared the following sermon outline on this passage with the cyberspace world: Sermon title, "The Journey of Faith." Sermon points: 1. Be in relationship with the Most High God; 2. Risk it all; 3. Be prepared and obedient; 4. Trust God to provide; 5. Receive God's blessing.

in point III the Lord's rescue of Abraham and his rewards are extended to all the righteous — again the error of generalizing.[28] Although the points made are not unbiblical, they are not the message the biblical author intended to send with this particular text. Let us see where the ten steps take us with this passage.

First, Select a Textual Unit with an Eye to Congregational Needs

I have selected this passage not with an eye to congregational needs but to demonstrate how we can move responsibly from an Old Testament text to a Christian sermon. This places us in the same position as a pastor who follows the lectionary: the text is given but the congregational need addressed may not yet be clear. If we had been able to let a congregational need guide us to a preaching-text, we might have thought of Genesis 22 in the season of Lent when a sermon related to the suffering and death of Christ is appropriate. Or perhaps the general need for more preaching on the Old Testament might have led us to this moving story. Whatever need might have led us to choose Genesis 22, once we have selected the text, we should temporarily set aside the congregational need so that we can first explore how Israel heard this text.

Sometimes the need for a text that fits a particular occasion, such as a wedding or a funeral, causes preachers to select not a textual unit but a mere fragment of the text. The story is told of a pastor who had accepted a call to another church and needed a fitting text for his farewell sermon. Since he shared this church with another pastor who would remain at his post, he announced as his text Genesis 22:5a, "Abraham said to his young men, 'Stay here with the donkey.'" From such an inauspicious start there is no recovery. Even the renowned preacher Spurgeon erred in not selecting complete message units. As we recounted in Chapter 4, at one point Spurgeon selected as his text only Genesis 22:1. He introduced the two points of his sermon as follows: "Let us look at our text. It is a kind of preface to this unique, this unparalleled story of Abraham's test. First, 'It came to pass after these things, that God did tempt (or "prove") Abraham' — here we see *the Lord's way with believers*. And, secondly, when God 'said unto him, Abraham,' the patriarch instantly answered, 'Behold, here I am,' — here we learn *the believer's way with the Lord*. These two heads will not be difficult to remember: the Lord's way with believ-

---

28. On the error of universalizing, see Ernest Best, *From Text to Sermon*, 86-89. On the error of moralizing, see my *Modern Preacher*, 161-66.

ers, and the believer's way with the Lord."[29] Although these two heads may not be difficult to remember, it is obvious that they are based on a textual fragment rather than the message unit.

What is the textual unit? It is clear that verse 1 begins a new unit with, "After these things," but where does the story end? We could conclude that verses 1-14 are a complete unit with a beginning, a conflict building up to a climax, and the resolution to the conflict. Verses 15-18 appear to be dealing with a different topic as they pick up a larger theme in Genesis by repeating the covenant blessings. Yet in the canonical text, these verses are also part of the narrative unit, for verse 19 relates that Abraham returns to his young men, they travel to Beersheba together, "and Abraham lived at Beersheba" — end of story. Verse 20 begins a new unit with, "Now after these things" (cf. 22:1).

The literary unit is therefore Genesis 22:1-19. But already we have spotted a complication. In terms of style and contents the passage appears to consist of two distinct parts: verses 1-14, the narrative of God testing Abraham; and verses 15-18, the monologue of God blessing Abraham. Verses 1-14 appear to have one message, while verses 15-18 seem to reiterate a theme from the larger Abraham cycle.[30] How can a textual unit with two distinct themes yield a unified sermon with a single theme? We will leave that question for now and concentrate next on reading the text in its literary context.

Second, Read and Reread the Text in Its Context

At this early stage we simply read the text and its context of the book of Genesis in our first language in order to apprehend the big picture. The details of the text must always be understood in the light of the whole.

The context of Genesis makes us aware of the setting of this story: after many years of waiting, Isaac, the child of the promise, was born, and a few years later Ishmael was sent away (Gen 21). Abraham and Sarah now have only Isaac. Then comes God's demand that Abraham offer this "only son Isaac." After the test we hear the Lord's last recorded words to Abraham (Gen 22). The next chapter (23) reports Sarah's death and burial

29. See p. 161, n. 201.

30. As we check some commentaries later, we will note that this issue is argued at length. Von Rad, *Genesis*, 237, argues strongly, "It is clearly noticeable that the narrative once concluded with v 14." Gordon J. Wenham, *Word Biblical Commentary*, vol. 2 (Dallas: Word, 1994), 102-3, and other commentators challenge the "secondary nature" of vv 15-18.

in the land of promise, followed by the search for a bride for Isaac (Gen 24).

At this stage we also look carefully at the selected text to spot questions that we, or our hearers, may have about it. This particular text raises many questions. One initial question is, Since God had forbidden child sacrifice in Israel,[31] why would God ask Abraham to offer his child as a burnt offering? Another obvious question is, Where is "the land of Moriah" (v 2)? And why did God select such a distant place (a three-day journey, v 4) instead of nearby? Why is there not a word about Sarah in this text? And how should we understand Abraham's words to his servants, "The boy and I will go over there; we will worship, and then *we* will come back to you" (v 5)? Or Abraham's response to Isaac's question, "God himself will provide the lamb for a burnt offering, my son" (v 8)? Is this a "white lie" or an expression of faith? Why would Isaac, probably a teenager by now, just allow himself to be bound and placed on the altar (v 9)? Who is "the angel of the LORD" (vv 11, 15)? Why would the Lord use a divine oath (v 16)? What is the meaning of "by your offspring shall all the nations of the earth gain blessing for themselves" (NRSV), "all nations on earth will be blessed" (NIV, v 18)? And, finally, why is Isaac left out in the concluding, "So Abraham returned to his young men" (v 19). We should jot down these initial questions and seek to answer them in further study of the text. Some of these questions will probably find their way into the sermon, both to convey the meaning of the text and to maintain the interest of the hearers.

Third, Outline the Structure of the Text

With the third step we begin to dig deeper into the text. At this stage we wish to expose the structure of the text. Finding the structure not only makes us aware how the author conveyed his message, but this structure may also become a major part of the sermon outline.

Since the text is a narrative, we need to sketch the plot line. Most biblical narratives have a simple plot (in contrast to complex). We have already noted the setting of the text: "after these things" (v 1) refers to the foregoing chapter, where we read of the birth of Isaac and the expulsion of Ishmael. The conflict is generated by God's demand, "Take your son, your only son, whom you love, . . . and offer him . . . as a burnt offering . . ." (v 2). The conflict intensifies with the three-day journey, father and son's lonely climb up the mountain, Isaac's question, "Where is the

---

31. See Lev 18:21; 20:2-5; Deut 18:10; 2 Kings 3:27.

lamb for a burnt offering?" and Abraham's ambiguous response, "God himself will provide the lamb for a burnt offering . . ." (vv 3-8). The conflict reaches a climax when Abraham builds an altar, puts the wood on it, binds Isaac, puts him on the altar, reaches for the knife, and is ready to kill his son (vv 9-10). At that excruciating pinnacle the angel of the Lord cries out, "Do not lay your hand on the boy," and the tension breaks (vv 11-12). The conflict is finally resolved when Abraham spots a ram and offers it up "as a burnt offering instead of his son," and names the place, "The LORD will provide" (vv 13-14). The angel of the Lord calls a second time, and the Lord repeats his covenant blessings (vv 15-18). The story ends with Abraham back in Beersheba (v 19).

To have the plot line clearly in mind, it is best to diagram it together with the verse references. The diagram would look like this:[32]

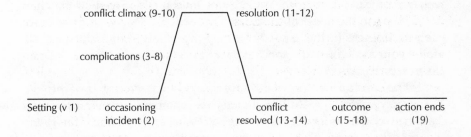

conflict climax (9-10)   resolution (11-12)

complications (3-8)

Setting (v 1)   occasioning   conflict   outcome   action ends
                   incident (2)   resolved (13-14)   (15-18)   (19)

Fourth, Interpret the Text in Its Own Historical Setting

To understand the text in its historical setting, we need to look at the three dimensions of the text: literary, historical, and theocentric.

Literary Interpretation

The text clearly is of the narrative genre, and we have already discovered the plot line in Step 3. We shall now work our way further into the text by checking some other narrative characteristics. We shall first examine the scenes and characters. Hebrew narrative usually has two characters in each scene: two individuals, or an individual and a group. Frequently God is either one of the characters or represented by one. The result of a quick check is as follows:

32. See the general diagram of "the structure of biblical narrative" in Tremper Longman, *Literary Approaches*, 92. Reproduced in my *Modern Preacher*, 204.

Scene 1: God and Abraham (vv 1-2)
Scene 2: Abraham and his servants (vv 3-5)
Scene 3: Abraham and Isaac (vv 6-8)
Scene 4: Abraham and Isaac (vv 9-10)
Scene 5: The angel of the Lord and Abraham (vv 11-14)
Scene 6: The angel of the Lord and Abraham (vv 15-18)
Scene 7: Abraham and his servants (v 19)[33]

The omniscient narrator lets his hearers know at the outset (v 1) that God is *testing* Abraham. Abraham, of course, does not know this; he only hears the command, "Take your son, your only son Isaac, whom you love, and . . . offer him. . . ." Hebrew narrators usually offer little character description, but this description of Isaac as "your son, your only son Isaac, whom you love" stands out and drives home the enormity of God's request. "Obedience to God and love for his son will tear him [Abraham] in diametrically opposed directions."[34] The immensity of God's request is further underscored by repetition of the same description, "your son, your only son," at the climax (v 12) as well as at the conclusion (v 16).

The narrator also slows the pace to a crawl at the climax of the conflict. Every action is carefully reported: "Abraham built an altar there and laid the wood in order. He bound his son Isaac, and laid him on the altar, on top of the wood. Then Abraham reached out his hand and took the knife to kill his son" (vv 9-10).

In literary interpretation we also check for rhetorical structures such as repetition and chiasm. In this narrative, certain repetitions stand out. We have already noted the repetition of "your son, your only son" in verses 2, 12, and 16. Another repetition begins in a rather ambiguous way. Isaac has just asked his father, "Where is the lamb for a burnt offering?" Abraham answers, "God himself will provide the lamb for a burnt offering, my son" (v 8). This is where we raised one of our initial questions: Does Abraham tell a white lie to avoid the devastating answer, or does he give expression to his unwavering faith in God?[35] The narrator

---

33. Kenneth Mathews, "Preaching Historical Narrative," 32, identifies vv 9-12 as scene 4 and vv 13-19 as scene 5. Wenham, *Word* 2.100, offers a chiastic structural division: v 1a, narrative; 1b-2, monologue; 3, narrative; 4-6b, dialogue; 6c-8, dialogue; 9-10, narrative; 11-18, monologue; 19, narrative.

34. Wenham, *Word*, 1.104.

35. Gordon Talbot, *A Study of the Book of Genesis* (Harrisburg, PA: Christian, 1981), 146, calls these words "a brilliant confession of faith." Wenham, *Word* 2.109, comments, "The organization of the story, which makes 'God will provide' the turning point of the story, does favor a positive reading, i.e., as an expression of hope, a proph-

leaves it open-ended for now. But as the story unfolds, God does indeed provide the lamb for a burnt offering, the ram caught in a thicket by its horns (v 13). Is it any wonder that Abraham called that place *Yahweh-yireh*, "The LORD will provide" (v 14)? There is the word *r'h*, "provide" or "see to," a second time. For good measure the narrator adds for a third time that to his day people use the popular saying, "On the mount of the LORD it shall be provided" (v 14), or, since this is the niphal of the verb, some scholars translate, "On the mount of the LORD he shall be seen" (NRSV note) or appear. The triple English translation of "provide" is true to the Hebrew repetition of the same verb root. Since repetition functions like tire tracks in the snow, the repeated "the LORD will provide" may well show us where the narrator is heading with his story.

Literary interpretation at this level is also concerned with understanding the text in the literary context of the book. One of our initial questions was why God used a divine oath in verse 16, "by myself I have sworn." Gordon Wenham points out that "this is the first and only divine oath in the patriarchal stories, though it is frequently harked back to (24:7; 26:3; 50:24; Exod 13:5; often in Deuteronomy)."[36] The fact that the repetition of God's blessing in 22:16-18 is the thirty-fifth and final time of God speaking to Abraham[37] may contain a partial answer to our question. Even more telling is the twofold reference to Abraham's obedience in the text itself: "By myself I have sworn, says the LORD: *Because you have done this*, and have not withheld your son, your only son, I will *indeed* [Wenham, "really"] bless you.... *because you have obeyed my voice*" (vv 16-18). Wenham speaks of "the meritoriousness of Abraham" and declares that "the central thrust of the story [is] Abraham's wholehearted obedience and the great blessings that have flowed from it."[38] Although these comments could raise concerns about preaching the "health-and-wealth gospel" or works righteousness, these concerns are premature, for our task at this stage is to disclose the Old Testament message as honestly and

---

ecy, or a prayer...." Claus Westermann, *Genesis 12–36* (trans. John Scullion; Minneapolis: Augsburg, 1985), 359, suggests that Abraham does not deceive Isaac, "but simply opens up to him as a possibility what for himself (since God gave his command) is a fact."

36. Wenham, *Word*, 2.111. But see John Stek, *CTJ* 29/1 (1994) 29 on Genesis 15, "The mysterious passing of the blazing torch between the halves of the slaughtered animals is best understood as symbolizing God's executing a self-maledictory oath ritual to ratify his covenant."

37. Mathews, "Preaching Historical Narrative," 31.

38. Wenham, *Word*, 2.111, 112. Cf. p. 116, "This last display of obedient faith was rewarded by an extension and endorsement of the original promises that not only exceeds every previous formulation but every subsequent statement of the promises."

candidly as we can. The time to consider such concerns, if necessary, is at Step 6, when we view the message of this passage in the context of the whole canon.

With respect to the more immediate context, it has also been suggested that the Abraham cycle is arranged as a chiasm.

A. Genealogy of Terah (11:27-32)
   B. Start of Abraham's Spiritual Odyssey (12:1-9)
      C. Sarai in foreign palace; ordeal ends in peace and success; Abram and Lot part (12:10–13:18)
         D. Abraham comes to the rescue of Sodom and Lot (14:1-24)
            E. Covenant with Abraham; Annunciation of Ishmael (15:1–16:16)
            E'. Covenant with Abraham; Annunciation of Isaac (17:1–18:15)
         D'. Abraham comes to the rescue of Sodom and Lot (18:16–19:38)
      C'. Sarah in foreign palace; ordeal ends in peace and success; Abraham and Ishmael part (20:1–21:34)
   B'. Climax of Abraham's Spiritual Odyssey (22:1-19)
A'. Genealogy of Nahor (22:20-24)[39]

For the selected text in Genesis 22, the important issue raised by this chiasm is the author's deliberate parallel development between Genesis 12:1-9 and Genesis 22:1-19 as well as further progression. In Genesis 12 God tells Abraham to "go" (lek-leka), offer up his past (relatives, friends, country), and receive the promise of a threefold covenant blessing. In this narrative God tells Abraham to "go" (lek-leka), but now to offer up his future, "your son, your only son, whom you love." The stakes are raised. Now Abraham has to rely on God even when God seems to go back on his covenant promise. But when he obeys God, he receives the threefold covenant blessing in even heightened form. Because Yahweh "provides."

Historical Interpretation

In historical interpretation we raise the well-known Who? To whom? When? Where? Why? questions. Answers to all these questions are helpful but, especially with Old Testament passages, not always available.

---

39. Mathews, "Preaching Historical Narrative," 30, with credit to G. Rendsburg, *The Redaction of Genesis* (Winona Lake, IN: Eisenbrauns, 1986), 27-52.

The important questions preachers need to answer are, To whom? and Why? Answers to these two questions help us understand how Israel heard this passage and what need it addressed. Some evidence in the text suggests that this narrative is addressed to the people of Israel living in the land of Canaan, for the author speaks about a burnt offering (see Lev 1) and alludes to the meaning of Passover in verse 13, where he informs his hearers that Abraham offered the ram "instead of his son" (see Exod 12:12-13).[40] If Israel in Canaan is the recipient of this message, our initial question is even more pertinent: Since God had forbidden child sacrifice in Israel (Lev 18:21; 20:2-5; Deut 18:10; 2 Kings 3:27), why would God contradict his own law by asking Abraham to offer his child as a burnt offering? To find answers to pointed questions like this, we probably need the help of a few good commentaries. Both Westermann and Wenham suggest that the answer to our question lies in another peculiar law for Israel.[41] God commanded, "The firstborn of your sons you shall give to me" (Exod 22:29; cf. 13:2). Therefore God's demand that Abraham offer his "only son" to God was within the parameters of his law. But in his grace, God had also specified for Israel a required alternative to this offering: "All the firstborn of your sons you shall redeem" (Exod 34:20; cf. 13:13). God had also prescribed how parents could redeem these firstborn with a substitute: a lamb at Passover (Exod 12), a lamb at the mother's purification rite, or, "if she cannot afford a sheep, she shall take two turtledoves or two pigeons" (Lev 12:8; cf. Luke 2:22-24 for the offering made for Jesus).

Good commentaries can also help us with other questions we raised. For example, Why did God select such a distant place (a three-day journey, v 4) instead of nearby? Calvin seeks an answer by focussing on the testing of Abraham: "God . . . compels him to revolve this execution in his mind during three whole days, that in preparing himself to sacrifice his son, he may still more severely torture all his own senses. . . . This tended to make him persevere, so that he should not obey God by a merely sudden impulse. . . . It hence appears, that his love to God was confirmed by such constancy, that it could not be affected by any change in circumstances."[42] By contrast, Westermann suggests a literary reason: "In Exodus 3:18; 5:3; 8:23, it is a journey of three days to the place where the Israelites want to offer sacrifice in the desert; there is a possible allu-

---

40. "In later Jewish tradition (e.g., the book of Jubilees, 100 BC) a connection is made between passover and the sacrifice of Isaac." Wenham, *Word*, 2.116.

41. Westermann, *Genesis 12–36*, 357-58; Wenham, *Word*, 2.105.

42. Calvin, *Comm. Genesis* (trans. John King; Grand Rapids: Eerdmans, 1948), 565-66.

sion to this. In any case, three days is the period of preparation for more important events in the Old Testament. . . ."[43]

Historical interpretation confronts us with another key question: With whom would the original hearers have identified? This is often a difficult question to answer with any degree of certainty.[44] In this story the choices are limited to Abraham and Isaac. Initially the hearers would probably have identified with Abraham and the excruciating choice he had to make. But at a deeper level, there can be little doubt that Israel would have identified with Isaac: Would Isaac die or live? If he had died on the altar, there never would have been a people called Israel; the ram died so that Isaac, that is, Israel, might live. Even in modern times, Jews identify with Isaac and read this story of what they call "The Binding of Isaac" on the Jewish New Year's day. This view is confirmed by von Rad: "When Israel read and related this story in later times it could only see itself represented by Isaac, i.e., laid on Yahweh's altar, given back to him, then given life again by him alone. That is to say, it could base its existence in history not on its own legal titles as other nations did, but only on the will of Him who in the freedom of his grace permitted Israel to live."[45]

Theocentric Interpretation

The key question here is what the passage tells us about God and his will for his people. In analyzing scenes and characters, we noticed that God is one of the main characters in scene 1 as well as 5 and 6; in terms of dialogue, God has the first word as well as the last. But not only at the beginning and the end but throughout the story we notice the centrality of God: "God tested" (v 1), Abraham assures Isaac, "God will provide" (v 8), God stops Abraham from offering Isaac (v 12), God provides the ram (v 13), Abraham names the place, "The LORD will provide" (v 14), the narrator adds, "as it is said to this day, 'On the mount of the LORD it shall be provided'" (v 14), and the Lord promises to bless Abraham, his offspring, and the nations (vv 15-18). The entire story highlights God's involvement with Abraham and Isaac.

---

43. Westermann, *Genesis 12–36*, 358, with further references to Gen 31:22; 34:25; 40:20; 42:18.

44. See my *Modern Preacher*, 175-81.

45. Von Rad, *Genesis*, 239-40. Cf. ibid., *Biblical Interpretations*, 39, "In Isaac the community saw itself represented; in Isaac it saw itself offered up to God; in Isaac it confessedly had received back from God's hand its entire existence and now knew itself to be living solely by his grace and entrusted to his will." Cf. Roland de Vaux, *Ancient Israel* (New York: McGraw-Hill, 1965), 443, "Any Israelite who heard this story would take it to mean that his race owed its existence to the mercy of God. . . ."

Fifth, Formulate the Text's Theme and Goal

We now face the hard work (especially with narrative) of formulating the textual theme in a brief sentence that summarizes the message of this text for Israel. Some have suggested the theme, God tests Abraham's faith and obedience. But this is more like a title which describes the event rather than a summary of the message. Others have suggested, "Abraham offers his son because of his faith in God's life-giving power."[46] But again, this is description instead of a theme. The question we need to ask is, What is God's message to Israel by way of this story? What is the point for Israel?

We have to choose between two possible themes. The first and most frequently used entrance into the text takes its cue from verse 1, "God tested Abraham" (see the two suggestions above). Von Rad maintains that one of the main thoughts in this narrative is "the idea of a radical test of obedience. That God, who has revealed himself to Israel, is completely free to give and to take, and that no one may ask, 'What doest thou?' (Job 9:12; Dan 4:32), is without doubt basic to our narrative. . . . Yahweh tests faith and obedience."[47] Wenham holds that "the central thrust of the story [is] Abraham's wholehearted obedience and the great blessings that have flowed from it."[48] From these comments we could conclude that Israel was supposed to learn from this story that God is sovereign and free to test his people's faith, and that he expects the unquestioning obedience and total trust that Abraham displayed. In fact, Westermann states that "the majority of interpreters . . . see the narrative holding Abraham up as an exemplar."[49] The ideas of God sovereignly testing Abraham's faith and Abraham modeling obedience for Israel can be merged into a single textual theme formulated like this: Whenever the sovereign God tests the faith of his people, he demands unquestioning, trusting obedience. Focussing on God and Abraham, this theme does justice to the fact that this story is located in the Abraham cycle of stories and that it brings closure to the ideas introduced in Genesis 12:1-3. A weakness, however, is the as-

46. J. L. Helberg, *Verklaring*, 118 (my translation).

47. Von Rad, *Genesis*, 239.

48. Wenham, *Word*, 2.112.

49. Westermann, *Genesis 12–36*, 364. Calvin, *Comm. Genesis*, 568, comments similarly that Abraham "shows himself to be entirely devoted to God," and that he passes the test "by taking refuge in Divine Providence, 'God will provide himself a lamb.' This example is proposed for our imitation. Whenever the Lord gives a command, many things are perpetually occurring to enfeeble our purpose: means fail, we are destitute of counsel, all avenues seem closed. In such straits, the only remedy against despondency is, to leave the event to God, in order that he may open a way for us where there is none."

sumption that in hearing this story Israel identifies with Abraham — an assumption which is contrary to our findings above. Another weakness is that although this theme captures a broader theme of the Abraham cycle of stories, it misses the specific theme of this particular story.

To hear the more specific theme of this story we need to hear it as Israel heard it. Israel, we have seen, would have identified intensely with Isaac. When Israel heard the story of Isaac lying on the altar, it heard the story of its very existence hanging in the balance. Isaac's death or life is the heart of the plot. At the climax, Isaac is only a knife-thrust removed from death; then he receives his life back and a ram is offered "instead of" Isaac. This entry into the text does better justice not only to the narrator's plot line in verses 2 to 14 but also to his explicit "tracks of meaning" given in the repeated key words, "God will provide." We hear these words first in Abraham's testimony, "God will provide" (v 8), next God's actual provision of a ram to be offered "instead of" Isaac (v 13), then Abraham calling that place, "The LORD will provide" (v 14), and finally the narrator's own testimony, "On the mount of the LORD it shall be provided" (v 14). This focus on Isaac is even supported by the concluding covenant blessings, which, in contrast to the blessings in Genesis 12:2-3, now deal not so much with Abraham as with his seed: "I will surely bless you and make your descendants [seed] as numerous as . . . the sand on the sea shore. Your descendants [seed] will take possession of the cities of their enemies, and through your offspring [seed] all nations on earth will be blessed . . ." (vv 17-18, NIV).

Analyzing the structure of the story, Wenham concludes that "God will provide" is "the turning point of the story."[50] It is that and more: "God will provide" is the heart of the message of this story for Israel. In the light of God claiming the firstborn in Israel and providing for their redemption by way of a substitute, we could formulate the theme as follows: The Lord reveals his sovereign grace by claiming and redeeming Isaac (Israel). But since it is beneficial to stick more closely to the wording of the text, it is better to revise that version into the following textual theme: *The Lord provides a lamb for a burnt offering so that Isaac (Israel) may live.*

The hermeneutical choice for this particular theme rather than the one that sees Abraham as a model of faith obviously has homiletical implications. One of these is that in the sermon we cannot with a good conscience induce our hearers to identify after all with Abraham and to imitate his faith and obedience. If that was not the point of this particular story for Israel, we should not make it the point of this story for the church today.

---

50. Wenham, *Word*, 2.109. Cf. Walter Brueggemann, *Genesis* (Atlanta: John Knox, 1982), 186, "There can be little doubt of the cruciality of this statement on structural grounds" — namely, a comparison of the three summons/response statements.

However, in another sermon on a different text, we can certainly use this story to illustrate the essence of faith. For example, when we preach on Hebrews 11:1, "Faith is the assurance of things hoped for, the conviction of things not seen," the sermon theme is "Faith is the assurance of things hoped for." Now we can illustrate this theme with the faith of Abraham evident in this story. In fact, the author of Hebrews does so himself (11:17-19). Biblical stories, as well as contemporary events, can illustrate many things. The Genesis text could be used to illustrate not only the essence of faith (as does Heb 11:17-19) but also that faith must reveal itself in works (as does James 2:21), or to illustrate God's prerogative to test people, or God's providence, or God's rich blessings in response to obedience, or even how people then sought contact with God on mountains and how they performed burnt offerings. Biblical stories can illustrate any number of things. To do justice to the preaching-text, however, and to keep the sermon focussed, we should concentrate on the original message for Israel, using only illustrations which support this theme, and avoiding others that might be derived from the story but make a different point.

Having formulated the textual theme, we should also formulate the author's goal as closely as possible. The goal is usually derived from the textual theme and the historical situation in which Israel heard this passage. In this case the historical situation is rather uncertain, but the literary structure has yielded the theme, the Lord provides a lamb for a burnt offering so that Isaac (Israel) may live. This theme suggests several possible goals that fit the general situation of Israel:

1. to teach Israel that it lives only by the grace of the Lord's covenant faithfulness.
2. to move Israel to gratitude for the Lord's grace in providing a substitute offering.
3. to encourage Israel fully to trust their faithful covenant Lord to provide redemption.

At this stage this listing of possible textual goals will suffice. When we formulate the sermon goal in Step 7, we will have to narrow these down on the basis of the need in the congregation.

Sixth, Understand the Message in the Contexts of Canon and Redemptive History

With Step 6 we seek to understand the Old Testament message, as focussed in theme and goal, in the contexts of the whole of Scripture and redemptive history. At this broader level, we can also distinguish three dimensions in our interpretation: literary, historical, and theocentric. But at this broader level they become canonical, redemptive-historical, and christocentric interpretation.

Canonical Interpretation

We now inquire about the meaning of Genesis 22 in the context of the whole Bible, from Genesis 1 to Revelation 22. This is the place to raise the concern about using verses 16-18 ("Because you have done this, . . . I will indeed bless you . . . because you have obeyed my voice") to preach a sermon involving works righteousness or the health-and-wealth gospel. The hermeneutical choice we made in formulating the theme of the whole text, "God provides," has virtually removed these issues from our consideration for this sermon. But if there is a lingering concern that verses 16-18 might feed into a health-and-wealth gospel mentality in the congregation, this would be the place to view this issue from a New Testament perspective, especially in the light of Jesus' description of true discipleship (e.g., Mark 8:34-38; Matt 10).

This is also the place to raise our initial question about "the land of Moriah." The only other time the Old Testament speaks of Moriah is in 2 Chronicles 3:1, where the author informs us, "Solomon began to build the house of the LORD in Jerusalem on Mount Moriah, where the LORD had appeared to his father David. . . ." Because of this identification of Mount Moriah with Mount Zion, some interpreters have been quick to identify the place of the offering of Isaac with the later temple mount. In fact, today tourists to the Dome of the Rock on the temple mount in Jerusalem are shown the very rock on which Isaac allegedly was placed. Preachers could draw interesting links from the ram Abraham offered on this rock to the many animals Israel's priests offered on the temple mount, to Christ who offered his life not far from there. But since "the land of Moriah" of Genesis 22 is not necessarily "Mount Moriah" of 2 Chronicles 3 (the author links it to David, not Abraham),[51] we had better not base too much on this tenuous link.

More certain than the place of Moriah is the theme of substitu-

---

51. See von Rad, *Genesis*, 235, "It is striking that the passage in Chronicles defines the place where the angel appeared to David and not the place of our story, which would, of course, have given the place a much more ancient consecration." The question, of course, is whether the author of Chronicles was interested in "a much more ancient consecration" or whether his intent was to highlight King David. Wenham, *Word*, 2.104-6, argues for a connection between "the land of Moriah" and "Mount Moriah."

tionary atonement as it develops from the ram offered "instead of" Isaac to the Passover lambs offered instead of the firstborn (Exod 12:12-13), to the lambs offered to redeem the firstborn (Exod 13:13-15; 34:20), to the lambs offered daily at the temple instead of Israel (Exod 29:38-42; Lev 4–7), to Christ offered instead of his people. There are many other links from our passage to the New Testament, but we will save them for our discussion of Christocentric interpretation below.

Redemptive-historical Interpretation

We now seek to understand the text in the context of the history God makes from creation to new creation. Gene Tucker remarks, "This pithy narrative is a chapter in the history of salvation — including Exodus, covenant on Sinai, wilderness wandering and settlement of Canaan. Awareness of this larger story heightens the drama — as if there were not drama enough already — for it is not only the life of a single child that is in jeopardy. The promised future is held captive to the outcome of the tale."[52] The history of salvation, of course, continues beyond the settlement of Canaan, all the way into New Testament times when Christ is born of Israel, offers his life "a ransom for many," and mandates his church to make disciples of all nations in fulfillment of God's promise to Abraham: "through your offspring all nations on earth will be blessed" (Gen 22:18, NIV). Ultimately, what is in jeopardy in this story is not only the life of Isaac nor the existence of Israel, but the coming of the Messiah and the entrance of the nations into the kingdom of God.[53]

Christocentric Interpretation

Finally, we ask, What does this passage mean in the light of Jesus Christ? How is this message related to the person, work, and teaching of Christ as revealed in the New Testament? In our survey of the history of preaching we noticed that the church fathers saw in Isaac carrying the wood for a burnt offering Christ carrying his cross. Some contemporary commentators continue to suggest this as a valid way of preaching Christ: "Even

52. Tucker, "Reading and Preaching the Old Testament," 44.
53. Cf. Calvin, *Comm. Genesis,* 560, "For the great source of grief to him [Abraham] was not his own bereavement, not that he was commanded to slay his only heir, the hope of future memorial and of name, the glory and support of his family; but that, in the person of this son, the whole salvation of the world seemed to be extinguished and to perish." Although Calvin, in my opinion, speculates on the knowledge Abraham had in his time, he has certainly understood the issue in the overall perspectives of Scripture and redemptive history.

as Christ was later to carry His own cross on the road to Calvary, so Isaac here was required to carry the wood for his own sacrifice."[54] But Isaac carrying the wood never functioned as a symbol in Israel, and therefore this detail cannot be extended into a type of Christ. Moreover, since this connection is laid between a detail in this story and a detail in the New Testament, it is a form of typologizing. For a legitimate connection to Jesus Christ, we should look not at textual details but at the central thrust of the passage as we have formulated it in the textual theme: The Lord provides a lamb for a burnt offering so that Isaac (Israel) may live. Which of the seven ways provide a solid connection with Jesus Christ? We shall explore each in turn.

The Way of Redemptive-Historical Progression

Redemptive-historical progression is the foundational and most general of the seven ways of preaching Christ from the Old Testament; it can frequently be explicated more precisely in one of the other ways such as promise-fulfillment, typology, or longitudinal themes. The initial question we raise here is, In the course of redemptive history, does the message of Genesis 22 lead to the person, work, or teaching of Jesus Christ? A first response might be: because Isaac did not die but lived, Israel could live; and because Israel lived, the Messiah could eventually be born of Israel. This line of thinking develops from the outcome of the story, Isaac lives. Though true, a better and more specific response would concentrate on the message of the text as focussed in the theme. The text relates that the Lord provides a lamb as a substitute offering for Isaac/Israel, that is, the Lord provides the ransom required for redemption. The message concerning ransom develops in Old Testament history into a whole series of laws with respect to Passover, burnt offerings, sin offerings, and guilt offerings to pay the penalty for sin. In the fullness of time, the Lord provides his Son as the final ransom required for redemption. John the Baptizer introduces Jesus as "the Lamb of God who takes away the sin of the world!" (John 1:29). Jesus himself proclaims that he came "to give his life as a ransom for many" (Mark 10:45). Thus the Lord providing a lamb as a ransom for Isaac progresses in redemptive history to the Lord providing his own Son to set his people free from the bondage of sin.[55]

---

54. Talbot, *Study of the Book of Genesis*, 145.

55. Cf. Clowney, *Unfolding Mystery*, 57, "God, not Abraham, paid the price of redemption. Indeed, only God *could* pay the price. He paid it, not in providing a ram or a lamb, but in providing His own Son. . . ."

The Way of Promise-Fulfillment

Promise-fulfillment raises the question, Does this passage promise Jesus' coming? The answer in terms of our theme is, Not directly. We can, therefore, move on to the other options.

The Way of Typology

Typology asks, Does a person, institution, or event in this passage prefigure the person and work of Jesus Christ? Although many would answer affirmatively, there is no agreement on whether it is Abraham,[56] Isaac, or the ram. In a sermon on Genesis 22, Chrysostom presents both the ram and Isaac as types: "All this . . . happened as a type of the Cross. Hence Christ too said to the Jews, 'Your father Abraham rejoiced in anticipation of seeing my day; he saw it and was delighted.' How did he see it if he lived so long before? In type, in shadow: just as in our text the sheep was offered in the place of Isaac, so here the rational lamb was offered for the world. . . . Notice . . . how everything was prefigured in shadow: an only-begotten son in that case, an only-begotten in this; dearly loved in that case, dearly loved in this. . . . The former was offered as a burnt offering by his father, and the latter his Father surrendered."[57] Spurgeon similarly

---

56. Without using the word "type," Brueggemann, *Genesis*, 192-94, suggests a form of Abraham-Christ typology. He writes, "The life of Abraham, then, is set by this text in the midst of the contradiction between the *testing* of God and the *providing* of God. . . . The dialectic of testing and providing, of taking and giving, may be linked appropriately to the reality of Jesus of Nazareth. . . . The crucifixion of Jesus is the ultimate expression of the testing of God. Like Abraham, Jesus in Gethsemane (Mark 14:32-42) is in a situation where he must choose. . . . Jesus, like Abraham, trusts only the promise. . . . The resurrection is the miracle by which God provides new life in a situation where only death is anticipated. The dialectic of *testing/providing* in our narrative becomes the dialectic of *crucifixion/resurrection* in the faith of the church." I judge that the dialectic which places the same weight on God's testing as on God's providing is a foreign structure which does not fit the text. In v 1, the narrator simply informs Israel, which knew of God's prohibition against child sacrifice, that this was a test, whereas in the story he puts all the emphasis on "God provides."

57. Chrysostom, "Homily 47 [Genesis 22]," 21-22. Justin Martyr, similarly, detected "double typology" in the battle with Amalek: "The two Advents of Christ were symbolically announced and told beforehand by what Moses and Joshua did. For the one of them, stretching out his hands . . . reveals a type of nothing else than the Cross; the other, [Joshua,] whose name was altered to Jesus, led the fight, and Israel conquered. Now this took place in both these holy men and prophets of God, that you may perceive how one of them could not bear up both the mysteries: I mean the type of the Cross and the type of the Name." *Dialogue*, 111, as cited in Daniélou, *From Shadows*, 235.

asks, "When did Abraham see Christ? . . . On the top of Moriah, when his own son was on the wood, and his own hand was lifted up, he must have seen the Son of God, and the uplifted hand of God offering the Great Sacrifice. When he took the ram from the thicket, and so saved the life of his son, how clearly he must have understood that blessed doctrine of substitution, which is the very centre of the gospel."[58]

Although not many today would follow Chrysostom and Spurgeon in presenting two figures in one passage as types of Christ, the decision on who is a type of Christ is by no means resolved today. Von Rad cuts through the knot by declaring, "Isaac is not simply a type of Christ. . . . Furthermore, it is best not to regard the ram caught in the thicket as a type of Christ."[59] Still, influential commentators teach that "Isaac is here a type (prefiguration) of Christ."[60] There is a weakness in this view, however, and that is that Isaac did not die on the altar. In other words, the Isaac-Christ typology breaks down on the decisive parallel. On the other hand, the ram that was offered does contain this crucial parallel; it was killed. Even more, it was offered "instead of" Isaac — thus a substitute offering, a ransom.[61] Therefore not Isaac, who represents Israel, but the ram is a type of Christ. The ram in this story functioned in Israel as a *symbol* of a substitute offering (think of the Passover lamb) so that Isaac/Israel might live. In the context of the whole of Scripture, therefore, the ram can function as a *type* of Christ, who, as a substitute, offers his life so that his people may live.[62]

The Way of Analogy

Analogy raises the question, Does the message show by analogy who God in Christ is for us today? The message of Genesis 22 clearly shows

---

58. Spurgeon, *Metropolitan Tabernacle Pulpit,* 37.500.

59. Von Rad, *Biblical Interpretations,* 39.

60. *NIV Study Bible* on Gen 22:9. Cf. Talbot, *Study of the Book of Genesis,* 144, "Abraham and Isaac serve as types of God and His Son in this particular incident." See also the references in Gerard Van Groningen, *Messianic Revelation,* 144, to John R. Rice, George Rawlinson, and Leopold Sabourin.

61. Cf. Van Groningen, *Messianic Revelation,* 145, "But Isaac was not sacrificed; he was not put to death. . . . The ram slain served as a symbol and was a type of Christ who died in the place of others."

62. We should stick to this major parallel and not drift into typologizing by looking for more parallels in details of the story. For example, both Tertullian and Augustine liken the ram caught by its horns in a brier-thicket to Christ receiving a "crown of thorns on his head." Jean Daniélou, *From Shadows,* 125-27, with references to Tertullian's *Adversus Judaeos,* 13 and Augustine's *City of God,* 16.38.

God's covenant faithfulness and grace for his chosen people Israel. God himself provided the required ransom: he provided the ram as a substitute offering so that Isaac/Israel could live. In Jesus Christ, God reveals the same faithfulness and grace for his people today, but in a far greater measure: God gave his Son as a substitute offering so that his people may live eternally.

The Way of Longitudinal Themes

Many Old Testament passages contain themes which track through the Old Testament and into the New to Jesus or his teaching. In tracing the theme of the Lord providing a substitute offering, many instances come to mind, as we saw under literary interpretation. We can begin with the Passover lambs slain in Egypt instead of Israel's firstborn (Exod 12:12-13), move on to the lambs and other animals slain to redeem the firstborn in Israel (Exod 13:13-15; 34:20; Num 18:15), and then note the daily burnt, sin, and guilt offerings of lambs so that Israel may live (Exod 29:38-42; Lev 4–7). Continuing into the New Testament, we hear John the Baptist introduce Jesus, "Here is the Lamb of God who takes away the sin of the world!" (John 1:29). Clearly, the theme of God providing a lamb leads directly to Jesus Christ and the sacrifice he makes so that his people may live.

The Way of New Testament References

Frequently the New Testament refers or alludes to the Old Testament passage selected as preaching-text. In checking these references, we should remember our findings in Chapter 5 that the New Testament often uses (the technical *usus*) the Old Testament in an impromptu way and does not intend to offer definitive interpretations of Old Testament passages.

The appendix in the Nestle-Aland Greek New Testament offers an unusually high number of New Testament references for Genesis 22:

> for our whole passage it lists Hebrews 11:17;
> for v 2, Matthew 3:17; Luke 3:22; James 2:21;
> for v 9, again James 2:21;
> for v 16, Romans 8:32; Hebrews 6:13;
> for v 17, Hebrews 6:14; 11:12;
> for vv 17-18, Romans 4:13; and
> for v 18, Matthew 1:1 and Acts 3:25.[63]

---

63. 27th ed., 1993. The changes in this appendix from one edition to the next are indicative of the tentative nature of spotting allusions.

The listing itself makes clear that the New Testament texts usually refer to verses, that is, elements, in the Old Testament passage and not necessarily to its theme. Still it is worthwhile checking these references for a possible bridge to the New Testament. The first reference is to Hebrews 11:17, a passage in which the author expands on his theme, "faith is the assurance of things hoped for" (11:1), with many illustrations from the Old Testament. Since this illustration of faith does not support the textual theme, this reference is not helpful for this particular sermon. The second reference is more promising: in Matthew 3:17, and its parallel Luke 3:22, God says of Jesus, "This is my Son, the Beloved"; these words may well allude to Isaac being Abraham's beloved ("your son, your only son, whom you love"). The next reference is to James 2:21, "Was not our ancestor Abraham justified by works when he offered his son Isaac on the altar?" Here James uses the Genesis passage to support his theme that faith without works is dead — which is quite different from the theme of the text. The next reference is more to the point: Paul's words in Romans 8:32, "He [God] who did not withhold his own Son, but gave him up for all of us," are an allusion to verse 16, "Because you have done this, and have not withheld your son."[64] The references to Hebrews 6:13 and 14 and 11:12 have to do with God swearing "by himself" and two quotations of parts of the promise. As such, these references offer no bridges to preaching Christ. The next reference, Romans 4:13, alludes to our passage to illustrate that the promise that Abraham "would inherit the world" did not come "through the law but through the righteousness of faith" — again, a different theme. The reference to Matthew 1:1, "the genealogy of Jesus the Messiah, the son of David, the son of Abraham," suggests that Jesus is the fulfillment of God's promise to Abraham, "through your offspring [seed] all nations on earth will be blessed" (v 18, NIV). This reference discloses another possible bridge from our passage to Christ which we somehow missed when exploring promise-fulfillment, probably because we were concentrating on the main theme of our passage. This shows how checking for New Testament references toward the end of our investigation can serve also to double-check our previous work. The final reference, Acts 3:25, is again a quotation of part of the promise but offers no direct link to preaching Christ.

Although we cannot use many of these New Testament references and allusions for our sermon, this search has brought to light two promising bridges to preaching Christ from this passage. The major one in the light of our theme of "God provides" is Matthew 3:17 (parallel Luke 3:22), where God says of Jesus, "This is my Son, the Beloved." Strangely,

---

64. Origen already suggested this link. See Daniélou, *From Shadows*, 120.

Nestle-Aland missed the even more prominent allusion to the repeated "your son, your only son" in John 3:16, "For God so loved the world that he gave his *only* Son."[65] This familiar verse proclaims that because of his love for the world (*kosmos*), God himself made the supreme sacrifice which he prevented Abraham from making: he gave his only Son, his beloved, in order to save his people. This idea, in turn, links up with the allusion we discovered in Romans 8:32, "He [God] who did not withhold his own Son, but gave him up for all of us, will he not with him also give us everything else?"

The Way of Contrast

The final way to check is that of contrast. The question here is whether progression in redemptive history and revelation, especially since the coming of Christ, places New Testament teaching in some form of contrast to this Old Testament message. Although it is better to move to Christ via the positive links between the Old and the New Testament established above, we should still take note of any contrast because of the coming of Christ.

In our passage, the major contrast is that since the offering of Christ "once for all" (Heb 10:1-18), the offering of animals to ransom human beings is no longer required. This progression in redemptive history and revelation is probably so obvious to present-day hearers that it needs no elaboration.

*   *   *

In exploring the seven ways we have discovered several possibilities for preaching Christ on the basis of Genesis 22. We can use *redemptive-historical progression* to move from the Lord providing a lamb as a substitute offering (a ransom) for Isaac/Israel to Jesus giving "his life as a ransom for many" (Mark 10:45). We have also discovered a possibility of moving along the road of *promise-fulfillment* from God's promise to Abraham, "through your offspring [seed] all nations on earth will be blessed" (v 18, NIV) to the fulfillment in Christ, "the son of Abraham" (Matt 1:1). But even though Matthew links up with a major theme in the Abraham cycle, this is not the specific theme of the selected text. We can also move along the road of *typology* from the ram that was offered "instead of"

65. A good cross-reference Bible or commentary will fill this gap. For example, Wenham, *Word,* 2.117, says that John 3:16 "makes the same comparison" as Rom 8:31-32.

Isaac to Christ who was offered instead of his people. We can possibly move along the way of *analogy* from God's faithfulness and grace for his people Israel in providing a substitute offering to God's faithfulness and grace for his people today in providing his son, Christ Jesus. We can also travel along the way of *longitudinal themes* from the ram slain as a substitute offering for Isaac to the Passover lambs slain annually instead of the firstborn sons, to the lambs slain daily at the temple for Israel, to Jesus Christ slain "once for all" (Heb 10) for his people. And, finally, we can use *New Testament references* not only to support some of the connections noted above but especially to link up with that profound allusion in John 3:16: God the Father accomplished the unthinkable; he did what he could not allow father Abraham to do: he walked with his son Jesus from Nazareth to Jerusalem and from Gethsemane to Golgotha, and then he gave him up to be killed in order to save his people; he "gave his only Son, so that everyone who believes in him may not perish but have eternal life."

The seven ways have opened up several inspiring possibilities for preaching Christ from this Old Testament passage. Naturally we should not use all of these roads and clutter up the sermon: in preaching, less is often more. We should, therefore, select a few key ideas that support the theme that "the LORD provides" and that help to accomplish the goal of the sermon. Out of several possible combinations, I favor a blend of the typology of the substitute offering (ram-Christ), of the longitudinal theme of substitute offerings (ram, Passover lamb, temple sacrifices, Christ), and the New Testament references regarding God himself offering his only Son (John 3:16; Rom 8:32).[66] But the final decision on this will have to wait till we are outlining and writing the sermon.

Seventh, Formulate the Sermon Theme and Goal

We are now ready to formulate the sermon theme. In order to do justice to the preaching-text, we should keep the formulation of the sermon theme as close as possible to that of the textual theme. The textual theme reads, *The Lord provides a lamb for a burnt offering so that Isaac (Israel) may live.* In the contexts of the whole of Scripture and redemptive history the message needs to be broadened considerably from Isaac (Israel) to all nations. If we change "Isaac (Israel)" to "his people," this covers both Isaac (Israel) and God's people today. The words "a lamb for a burnt offering"

---

66. These references as well as the theme "the LORD provides" will keep the sermon from the pitfall of Christomonism. As Paul puts it in Rom 5:8, "*God* proves his love for us in that while we still were sinners Christ died for us."

need to be amended to cover also the death of Christ. If we substitute "sacrificial lamb," this covers the ram for Isaac, the lambs for Israel, and the Lamb of God for all God's people. The resultant sermon theme is, *The Lord provides a sacrificial lamb so that his people may live.*

Next we need to state the goal we have in preaching this sermon. The sermon goal should fit the theme and be in harmony with the textual goal. The possible textual goals we listed in Step 5 were: (1) to teach Israel that it lives only by the grace of the Lord's covenant faithfulness; (2) to move Israel to gratitude for the Lord's grace in providing a substitute offering; and (3) to encourage Israel fully to trust their faithful covenant Lord to provide redemption. For the sake of a well-focussed sermon, we now have to decide on a single sermon goal that meets a specific need in the congregation. With a slight change we can keep the first goal, to teach God's people that they live only by the grace of the Lord's covenant faithfulness. This is very general, of course, and in some sense the goal of all biblical passages is to teach something. We can get to a deeper goal by raising the question, Why? Why do I wish to teach God's people that they live only by the grace of the Lord's covenant faithfulness? Is it to move them to gratitude? Or is it to encourage them fully to trust God for their salvation? To attempt to accomplish both of these deeper goals leads to a lack of focus in the sermon, so we must decide what is the greater need in the church addressed, a lack of gratitude or a lack of trust. We shall develop the sermon further to meet the lack of trust. Our sermon goal, then, can be formulated as follows: *To encourage God's people fully to trust their faithful Lord for their salvation.*

Eighth, Select a Suitable Sermon Form

It is now time to consider the form of this sermon. Shall we cast the message in a didactic form or in a narrative form, or in a combination of the two? Shall we develop it deductively or inductively, or as a combination of the two? Since in expository preaching we wish to expose not only the meaning of the passage but also the form that conveys this meaning, the part of the sermon dealing directly with the text should be in the narrative form, that is, it should follow the plot line. Further, the narrative form is usually most effective when it is developed inductively, that is, the theme is disclosed not at the beginning but at the end of the narrative. The power of the narrative form is that it can draw the hearers into the story so that they experience the message from inside the story. The risk of using the narrative form is that people may simply be entertained, ideally even moved, but never catch the point of the text. To counter this risk, we shall seek to use repetition to lay a track of the theme throughout the sermon just as the narrator did with his repetition of "God provides."

Ninth, Prepare the Sermon Outline

This is the final step before writing the sermon. It is important not to skip this step by beginning to write the sermon right away, for this may lead to poor organization and the preacher (and later the hearers) getting lost in the details. This is the point where we still have a clear view of the big picture: we know the central thrust of the message (theme), we know our goal with this sermon, we know the major moves in the text as well as the possible moves to preaching Christ from this text. This is the time when we can arrange all of these elements in good order for a powerful message. Just as an artist first sketches the outline of his painting, so the artist-preacher prepares an outline of the structure of the sermon before painting in the details. But also, as an artist feels free to deviate from his preliminary sketch, so the preacher, when writing the sermon, should feel free to deviate from his original outline if there is good reason for doing so. The outline is intended to be not a straitjacket but a guide.

Many preachers like to begin the outline by sketching first the introduction of the sermon, next the body, and then the conclusion. Although this sounds logical, when preachers start with the introduction, they could possibly skew the presentation of the biblical message and its conclusion to fit the introduction. In the interest of doing justice to the message of the text, therefore, it is normally better to think about an appropriate introduction only after we know exactly what message will be brought and how it will be concluded. The normal order of sketching the outline would therefore be: (1) body, (2) conclusion, (3) introduction.

But, as we shall see, our passage is an exception to the rule, so we shall first discuss the introduction. One of the functions of an introduction is to create interest in the message of the text. But introductions can do much more than simply create interest to listen. The best sermon introductions expose the existential *need* to listen to this message. Since our goal in this sermon is to encourage God's people fully to trust the Lord for their salvation, a good introduction would focus on the need-side of the goal, namely our lack of trust in the Lord for our salvation and the resultant insecurity. The preacher would begin to speak of this lack of trust and the resultant insecurity at a safe distance — this happens to others — and then relate it to our own lack of trust and insecurity. Now we *need* to listen to this message.

But our passage is an exception to the rule. Since this powerful biblical story will be read to the congregation before the preaching of the sermon, good interpretive reading will automatically draw people into the story. So we do not need an introduction to create interest. Although it may still be advisable to have an introduction that creates the existential need to listen to this message, the downside is that this will place people outside the story when the reading of the text has already placed them on the inside. In the light of these considerations, an effective introduction can continue within the story just read and pick up on a question that undoubtedly lives in people's minds, How could God ask Abraham to offer his son? If we raise this question through the character of Abraham, we do not break the spell of the story but can retell it together with explanatory comments that help the modern hearer understand the message. So we begin the sermon with the "occasioning incident" of the plot (v 2).[67] The introduction might go something like this:

> Abraham cannot believe his ears. In the quiet of the night he had heard God speak to him: "Take your son, your only son Isaac, whom you love, and go to the land of Moriah, and offer him there as a burnt offering. . . ." Has he been dreaming? Would God ask him to sacrifice his son Isaac? Abraham and Sarah had waited a lifetime for God to give them this promised son. Finally, when they were too old to get children, God had given them this miracle child. Their whole future is tied up in this child. Through him God's covenant blessings will be fulfilled: they will become a great nation, and all nations of the earth will be blessed through them. And now God asks him to burn this son on an altar? His only son Isaac, whom he loves? Impossible! It makes no sense at all!
>
> But Abraham still hears the words ringing in his ears: "Take your son, your only son Isaac, whom you love . . . and offer him as a burnt offering." "God, this makes no sense at all!" But early the next morning we find Abraham making preparations for the agonizing journey to offer his only son.

In the body of the sermon, we follow the major moves in the text, in other words, the plot line of conflict and resolution we discovered in Step 3. Further, although we shall develop this narrative inductively, we want to make sure that our hearers will hear the theme reverberate through the sermon the way Israel heard it in the text: "God will provide." And, of course, we need to sketch how we can best preach Christ on the basis of this text. In the light of these considerations, I suggest the following outline:

67. To begin the sermon with v 1, "God tested Abraham," would also pull people out of the story. We can save this information for later in the sermon.

Introduction: the beginning of the conflict, "Offer your only son" — v 2

I. The conflict about offering the son of the promise intensifies.

    A. Abraham's preparations: possible questions, doubts — v 3

    B. The three-day journey: possible questions, doubts — v 4

    C. Isaac's question, "Where is the lamb for a burnt offering?" — v 7

    D. Abraham's ambiguous answer, "*God will provide* himself a lamb" — v 8

    E. The height of the conflict: Abraham builds an altar, lays on the wood, binds his son Isaac, lays him on the altar, on top of the wood, reaches out his hand, takes the knife to kill his son — vv 9-10

II. Resolution: The Lord intervenes and provides a substitute.

    A. The angel of the Lord cries out the good news: "Do not lay your hand on the boy" — vv 11-12. It had been a test — v 1.

    B. *The Lord provides* a substitute offering, the ram, which Abraham offers as "a burnt offering instead of his son" — v 13

    C. Abraham names the place, "*The LORD will provide*" — v 14a
The narrator adds, "On the mount of the LORD *it shall be provided*" — v 14b

    D. The message Israel heard: *The Lord provides* a sacrificial lamb so that Isaac (Israel) may live.

III. The Lord provides sacrificial lambs so that Israel may live.

    A. The Passover lambs in Egypt for Israel's firstborn — Exod 12:12-13

    B. Lambs and other animals for the firstborn in Israel — Exod 13:13-15

    C. Daily sin and guilt offerings of lambs for all Israel — Lev 4–7

    D. The message Israel heard: *The Lord continues to provide* sacrificial lambs so that his people may live.

IV. The Lord provides his only Son as a sacrificial Lamb so that his people may live.

    A. John 1:29, "Behold, the Lamb of God who takes away the sin of the world!"

    B. John 3:16, "God so loved the world that he gave his only Son."

    C. The message for us: *The Lord provides* his only Son as a sacrificial Lamb so that "whoever believes in him may have eternal life."

Conclusion: Encouragement to trust God for our salvation: he provides! Romans 8:31-32, "If God is for us, who is against us? He who did not withhold his own Son, but gave him up for all of us, will he not with him also give us everything else?"

CHAPTER 8

Practicing the Christocentric Method

"Do your best to present yourself to God as one approved by him, a worker who has no need to be ashamed, rightly explaining the word of truth."

Paul, 2 Timothy 2:15

IN CHAPTERS 5 and 6 we examined seven ways of preaching Christ from the Old Testament: the ways of redemptive-historical progression, promise-fulfillment, typology, analogy, longitudinal themes, New Testament references, and contrast. In Chapter 7 we saw at what point in the steps of interpretation we should raise the questions concerning the text's witness to Christ and how this works out concretely with a specific biblical text. In this final chapter, we shall concentrate on working with the christocentric method by applying the seven ways to Old Testament passages which in the past have been interpreted allegorically and by providing exercises for practicing the christocentric method on texts from various genres of Old Testament literature. The objective of this chapter is to clarify further the use of this christocentric method and to make questioning the text about its witness to Jesus Christ an ingrained habit.

TESTING THE CHRISTOCENTRIC METHOD AGAINST THE ALLEGORICAL

The proof of the pudding, it is said, is in the eating. One proof of the effectiveness of the redemptive-historical christocentric method is to see whether it can replace the allegorical method, which frequently was, and is, used for preaching Christ from the Old Testament. To present this "proof," we shall apply the seven ways to several Old Testament passages which, in the past, have yielded Christ-centered preaching by way of allegorical interpretation: Noah and the flood, the water of Marah, the battle with Amalek, the ceremony of the red heifer, and Jericho and Rahab.

Preaching on Noah and the Flood (Gen 6:9–8:22)

Justin Martyr preached Christ from the story of Noah and the flood by using fanciful allegorical interpretation: "At the time of the flood the righteous Noah with his wife and three sons and their wives, making in all eight persons, were a figure of the eighth day, on which Christ appeared as risen from the dead. . . . Now Christ, the first-born of every creature, is become the head (*archee*) of a new race, which has been regenerated by him through water, faith and wood, which embraces the mystery of the cross, as Noah, together with his family, was saved by the wood of the ark carried on the waters."[1] Justin sees four links to Christ: the eight people and the day of the week Christ rose from the dead; like Noah, Christ becomes "the head of a new race"; the wood of the ark and the wood of Christ's cross; and the water of the flood and the water of Christian baptism. In establishing these links with Christ, Justin clearly focusses primarily on details of the story — number, wood, and water — and links these elements with elements in the New Testament story about Jesus. But by focussing on more or less incidental elements of the story, Justin ends up missing its essence and reading Christ back into this text.

The story of the flood is not about the number eight and wood and water, however; it is about God's judgment of human sin (Gen 6:13), God's grace in saving Noah, his family, and the animals, and God's promise to maintain the regular seasons on earth (Gen 8:22). Since these chapters and the next echo the creation stories, the context of redemptive history will place the message of these chapters into sharper relief.

In the beginning God created his harmonious kingdom on earth (Gen 1–2). With the fall into sin (Gen 3), violence enters the peaceable kingdom (Gen 4), and it takes only a full number of ten generations for the earth to be "filled with violence" (Gen 6:11). That is the broader setting of the flood narrative. The conflict in this narrative is generated with God's declaration

---

1. Justin Martyr, *Dialogue*, 138, as cited in Daniélou, *From Shadows*, 91. Other church fathers, such as Augustine, used an even more elaborate form of allegorical interpretation on this narrative. See p. 102 above.

to Noah, "I have determined to make an end of all flesh, for the earth is filled with violence because of them; now I am going to destroy them along with the earth" (6:13). God's declaration immediately raises the question, Will God's judgment result in the annihilation of his kingdom on earth? The conflict intensifies when the torrential rains begin pounding the earth for "forty days and forty nights" (7:11-18) and reaches a climax when all the land, even the mountains, are covered with water and every living creature on the face of the ground is blotted out (7:19-24). God's judgment has reversed his acts of creation (Gen 1), and chaos has returned to the earth. Is this the end of God's kingdom on earth? That is the issue.

The story, however, continues: "But God remembered Noah and all the wild animals and all the domestic animals that were with him in the ark" (8:1). As in Genesis 1, God again reins in the destructive waters, and gradually dry land appears, a home for human beings and animals. The story concludes with God's promise, "I will never again curse the ground because of humankind, for the inclination of the human heart is evil from youth; nor will I ever again destroy every living creature as I have done. As long as the earth endures, seedtime and harvest, cold and heat, summer and winter, day and night, shall not cease" (8:21-22). The conflict has been resolved: God has judged and cleansed the world of human sin, but in his grace God will still seek to build his kingdom on earth through Noah, the new Adam, and his descendants (Gen 9). The turn in the narrative is, "But God remembered Noah" (8:1). This focal point is confirmed by a probable chiastic structure which centers in, "God remembered Noah."[2]

We can, therefore, formulate the theme of this narrative as follows: *Even as God judges the world for human sin and violence, in his grace he continues his kingdom on earth by making a new start with Noah, his family, and the*

---

2. See Gordon J. Wenham, *Genesis,* vol. 1 (Waco, TX: Word, 1987), 156:

Transitional introduction (6:9-10)
   1. Violence in creation (6:11-12)
   2. First divine speech: resolve to destroy (6:13-22)
      3. Second divine speech: "enter ark" (7:1-10)
         4. Beginning of flood (7:11-16)
            5. The rising flood (7:17-24)
               God remembers Noah
            6. The receding flood (8:1-5)
         7. Drying of the earth (8:6-14)
      8. Third divine speech: "leave ark" (8:15-19)
   9. God's resolve to preserve order (8:20-22)
   10. Fourth divine speech: covenant (9:1-17)
Transitional conclusion (9:18-19)

animals with him. Possible goals for this message to Israel depend on the circumstances in which Israel heard this story: Was Israel living in peace and prosperity in the promised land? Was it undergoing God's judgment in the exile? Was it a disheartened remnant after the exile? The message will hit home differently under different circumstances. Some possible goals of this passage are: to teach Israel that its God is a God of justice as well as grace; to teach Israel about God's covenant faithfulness in building his kingdom on earth even through a remnant; to warn Israel against sin and wickedness; to encourage Israel to rely on God's saving grace. The theme and possible goals of this passage will help us select appropriate ways of preaching Christ from the options provided by the seven ways of preaching Christ.

1. The Way of Redemptive-Historical Progression

We first view this story in the light of redemptive history in order to get the big picture, for details must always be understood in the light of the whole. Genesis 1 relates that in the beginning God set boundaries to the endless darkness that "covered the face of the deep" and to the destructive waters, so that chaos became an ordered cosmos where all kinds of creatures could live in peace. But human sin and its ever increasing violence destroyed this peaceful environment of God's good creation. "The LORD saw that the wickedness of humankind was great in the earth, and that every inclination of the thoughts of their hearts was only evil continually. . . . So the LORD said, 'I will blot out from the earth the human beings I have created — people together with animals and creeping things and birds of the air, for I am sorry that I have made them.' But Noah found favor in the sight of the LORD" (Gen 6:5-8). Clearly, the verses just prior to our text sum up God's judgment as well as God's grace in the midst of his judgment (cf. the repetition in our text in 6:11-14).

God's judgment at this stage of redemptive history consists of releasing the destructive waters, which he had restrained in the beginning, so that chaos returned to earth and all that was wicked was destroyed. God's judgment of sin at the dawn of human history combined with God's grace for Noah and his family is a precursor of God's judgment and grace at the end of history. God's judgment and salvation with the waters of the flood and God's final judgment with fire and his salvation — like the beginning and end of a journey — provide us with a sense of the direction of this story in the sweep of redemptive history. At the midpoint of this history, God's judgment of sin falls on one person, his Son, Jesus Christ. Paul writes, "For our sake he [God] made him to be sin who knew no sin, so that in him we might become the righteousness of God"

(2 Cor 5:21). God's judgment and God's grace — both come together in the cross of Christ. But God's grace wins out. "Noah found favor in the sight of the LORD" (Gen 6:8). So did Abraham. So did Israel. So did and does the church. Even in the final judgment God's grace will win out, for the final judgment will purge this world of all wickedness and issue into God's glorious new creation.

2. The Way of Promise-Fulfillment

Although this passage contains God's promise to maintain the order of his creation "as long as the earth endures" (Gen 8:22), it contains no direct promise of Christ.

3. The Way of Typology

Noah is described as "a righteous man" (Gen 6:9; 7:1). He is also another Adam, a new head of the human race who receives similar blessings and instructions as those originally received by Adam (Gen 9:1-7). With Noah God makes a new start with the human race as it inherits a cleansed earth. As such Noah can be seen as a type of Christ, for in Christ God also makes a new start with his people as they look forward to inheriting a new creation. But the new start made in Christ in the end far exceeds that made with Noah: God's people will be given clean hearts and the cosmos will be set free from its bondage to decay once and for all (Rom 8:21) — analogy and escalation.

4. The Way of Analogy

One way of using analogy is to link the teaching of this passage with the teaching of Jesus about judgment and grace. But a more direct way is to transfer to the church today the thought of God's grace in the midst of judgment: As God in his grace saved a chosen remnant of humanity at that time, so God in Christ today still saves a chosen remnant. Also, as God in his grace upheld his creation and promised to maintain the regular seasons, so it is God in Christ who upholds his creation even today (Col 1:17). In other words, we live on this earth in the relative security of regularly changing seasons only because of God's grace in Christ Jesus.

5. The Way of Longitudinal Themes

For this passage we could trace through the Scriptures the theme of God's judgment and the theme of God's grace. Since both occur together in this passage, however, it is more valuable to track the combined theme of God's grace in his judgment. This dual theme can be traced from the flood and God's new start with Noah to God's judgment at the tower of Babel (Gen 11) and God's new start with Abram (Gen 12:1-3), to the prophets' warnings that the day of the Lord will be a day of darkness (Amos 5:18) and the promise, "In that day I will restore David's fallen tent" (Amos 9:11), to God's judgment of Israel with the deportation to Assyria (722 B.C.) and the exile to Babylon (587 B.C.) and God's new start with the remnant (538 B.C.), to God's judgment executed in Christ's death on the cross and God's grace revealed in Christ's resurrection, to God's judgment on "the day of God" when "the heavens will be set ablaze and dissolved, and the elements will melt with fire" and God's grace in establishing "new heavens and a new earth, where righteousness is at home" (2 Pet 3:12-13).

6. The Way of New Testament References

Any of the above roads to Christ may be confirmed and strengthened by New Testament references. The appendix in Nestle-Aland's Greek New Testament (27th edition) provides several references. Hebrews 11:7 uses Noah's action to illustrate true faith. In Matthew 24:37-39 (par. Luke 17:26-27) Jesus uses the unexpected coming of the flood as an illustration of the unexpected "coming of the Son of Man." Peter presents the flood as a type of baptism: "God waited patiently in the days of Noah, during the building of the ark, in which a few, that is, eight persons, were saved through water. And baptism, which this prefigured [antitypon], now saves you — not as a removal of dirt from the body, but as an appeal to God for a good conscience, through the resurrection of Jesus Christ . . ." (1 Pet 3:20-21). Second Peter uses this passage to assure his beleaguered readers of the reality of God's judgment and grace in their day: "If he [God] did not spare the ancient world, even though he saved Noah, a herald of righteousness, with seven others, when he brought a flood on a world of the ungodly . . . , then the Lord knows how to rescue the godly from trial, and to keep the unrighteous under punishment until the day of judgment . . ." (2 Pet 2:5, 9). The next chapter draws an analogy between the flood and the final judgment, "By the word of God heavens existed long ago and an earth was formed out of water and by means of water, through which the world of that time was deluged with water and perished. But by the same word the present heavens and earth have been reserved for fire, being kept until the day of judgment and destruction of the godless" (2 Pet 3:5-7).

7. The Way of Contrast

In Genesis 8:21 God himself says, "Never again." God says "never again," recognizing that "the inclination of the human heart is evil from youth." The "never again" is possible only because in the fullness of time Christ will bear God's judgment on sin.

The suggested roads to Christ disclose several appropriate ways of preaching Christ on the basis of this passage. The sermon theme and goal should be used to decide which ways will be used in the sermon. In any event, it is clear that we need not resort to allegorical interpretation to preach Christ from this passage.

Preaching on Israel and the Water of Marah (Exod 15:22-27)

Justin Martyr and other church fathers preached Christ from the story of Marah by understanding the wood that sweetened the bitter waters as the wood of the cross of Christ. For example, Tertullian wrote, "The bitterness of the water was changed and the water made fresh and drinkable by Moses' staff. This wood was none other than Christ himself who transformed the waters of Baptism."[3] Tertullian has taken a little liberty with the text by identifying the wood that was thrown into the water with Moses' staff, for the text speaks only of the Lord showing him "a piece of wood" or "a tree," which he threw into the water (Exod 15:25). The narrator gives no indication that there is something special about this wood; it appears to have been just a piece of wood lying on the ground. Centuries later, when Elisha and the company of prophets similarly faced death during a famine when they found "death" (poison) in a pot of stew, Elisha simply threw in some flour with the result that "there was nothing harmful in the pot" (2 Kings 4:41). Wood or flour — it is not the physical composition of what is thrown in that restores water or food and saves lives; the piece of wood in our passage is simply a sign for all to see that it is the Lord who restores the quality of the water and thus saves Israel. As God himself says, "I am the LORD who heals you" (Exod 15:26). At any rate, we again see that allegorical interpretation connects a detail in the story, wood, with a detail in the New Testament, the wood of the cross, which is then made to stand for Christ himself. And in the process the message of this Old Testament story is lost.

3. Tertullian, *De Baptismo* 9, as cited in Daniélou, *From Shadows*, 171.

A better alternative for preaching Christ from this story is to ask first what the story is about. Israel has just left Egypt by crossing the Sea of Reeds (Exod 14) and has celebrated God's redemption in the Songs of Moses and Miriam (Exod 15:1-21). "Then Moses ordered Israel to set out from the Red Sea [Sea of Reeds], and they went into the wilderness of Shur. They went three days in the wilderness and found no water" (Exod 15:22). That is the issue that generates the conflict: three days in the wilderness and no water. The conflict is heightened when they finally find water at Marah but cannot drink it because it is bitter. The people complain against Moses, and Moses cries out to the Lord, "and the LORD showed him a piece of wood; he threw it into the water, and the water became sweet" (v 25). The conflict is resolved. The next stop is Elim, where there is plenty of water, in fact, "twelve springs of water . . . ; and they camped there by the water" (v 27). The point of the story is that the Lord provides water for his people in the wilderness to keep them alive. In the next story, the Lord provides his people with food in the form of manna and quail (Exod 16). The theme of our passage is, therefore, *The Lord saves Israel in the wilderness by providing life-sustaining water.* Possible goals for later Israel in Canaan or exile might be: to teach Israel that only the Lord can sustain life; to encourage Israel to trust the Lord to provide water in times of drought or in returning from exile; or to motivate Israel to grateful obedience (see v 26) to this God who kept their forefathers alive in the wilderness and who still provides for them in Canaan.

1. The Way of Redemptive-Historical Progression

We should first look at the issue of this story in the context of redemptive history. At what stages in redemptive history do we find the Lord providing water to keep his people alive? In order to pick up the trail, we may have to broaden the issue somewhat, for water is a rather narrow focus. If we broaden the issue to the Lord providing the necessities of life, we find God making provision for food for Adam and Eve in paradise (Gen 1:29). Later God makes similar provisions for Noah and his family (Gen 9:3). Now, as Israel travels through the wilderness, the Lord provides water and food for his people, even as he brings them to "a land flowing with milk and honey" (Exod 3:8). In New Testament times Jesus feeds the hungry multitudes. Redemptive history ends with the marvelous picture of the new creation where, "They will hunger no more, and thirst no more . . . ; for the Lamb at the center of the throne will be their shepherd, and he will guide them to springs of the water of life . . ." (Rev 7:16-17).

2. The Way of Promise-Fulfillment

The passage contains God's conditional promise of healing Israel (v 26) but no direct promise of Christ.

3. The Way of Typology

Moses is the leader whom God used to bring his people out of slavery in Egypt and who now leads them to the promised land. As leader and re-deemer of God's people, Moses is a type of Christ who leads his people out of the slavery of sin and violence to the promised land of the new earth. But in this story the typology is more specific: when the people are dying of thirst and cannot drink the water of Marah, "the people com-plained against Moses, saying, 'What shall we drink?' He [Moses] cried out to the LORD" (v 25). Moses here functions as a mediator who speaks to God on behalf of the people and who on God's behalf provides the people with fresh water to keep them alive. As such Moses is a type of Christ the Mediator who speaks to God on behalf of his people and who on God's behalf provides people with living water to keep them alive for eternity — analogy plus escalation.

4. The Way of Analogy

Analogy could draw the following parallel between then and now: as God provided for the necessities of life for Israel in the wilderness, so God in Christ provides for our necessities of life today. A stronger parallel is to draw the analogy between the teaching of this passage that the Lord is Israel's provider and healer (v 26) and Jesus' teaching, "Do not worry, saying, 'What will we eat?' or 'What will we drink?' . . . Your heavenly Father knows that you need all these things. But strive first for the king-dom of God and his righteousness, and all these things will be given to you as well" (Matt 6:31-33).

5. The Way of Longitudinal Themes

The theme of God providing water for his people can be traced in our text right from Marah to Elim, "where there were twelve springs of water" (Exod 15:27). From there we can continue tracing this theme to the water from the rock at Rephidim (Exod 17:1-7), to the water from the rock at Meribah (Num 20:1-13), to the plentiful waters of the promised land, to the words of Psalm 23:1-2, "The LORD is my shepherd, I shall not want. He makes me lie down in green pastures; he leads me beside still waters," to Jesus, the Good Shepherd (John 10). How this theme carries on further in the New Testament may not be immediately clear, but the way of New Testament references (below) may help out.

6. The Way of New Testament References

The Nestle-Aland Greek New Testament lists two allusions to Exodus 15:23: Hebrews 3:8 and Revelation 8:11, neither of which supports the textual theme. *The Treasury of Scripture Knowledge* offers five New Testament passages, the most promising being a link to the teaching of Christ in Matthew 6:25, "Therefore I tell you, do not worry about your life, what you will eat or what you will drink. . . ." Checking the word "water" in a concordance leads to the intriguing passage in John where Jesus says to the Samaritan woman at the well, "Those who drink of the water that I will give them will never be thirsty. The water that I will give will become in them a spring of water gushing up to eternal life" (John 4:14). Further, in the book of Revelation "the one who was seated on the throne" says, "To the thirsty I will give water as a gift from the spring of the water of life" (21:6). And the book ends with the invitation, "Let everyone who is thirsty come. Let anyone who wishes take the water of life as a gift" (22:17).

7. The Way of Contrast

At Marah the Lord provided Israel with water that kept them alive at least for a few days. In contrast, Jesus Christ provides living water that keeps people alive for eternity (see John 4:14, cited above).

Questioning this passage according to the seven ways has again disclosed several ways of preaching Christ from this passage without resorting to the allegorical method. Again, the sermon theme and goal should determine which specific options will be used in the sermon to preach Christ.

Preaching on Israel's Battle
with Amalek (Exod 17:8-16)

Justin Martyr, Irenaeus, Origen, and other church fathers also used the allegorical method to preach Christ from Israel's battle with Amalek. Justin writes, "When the people waged war with Amalek, and the son of Nave, Jesus [Joshua] by name, led the fight, Moses himself prayed to God, stretching out both hands, and Aaron supported them the whole day. . . . For if he gave up any part of this sign, which was an imitation of the

Cross, the people were beaten, but if he remained in this form Amalek was defeated, and he who prevailed, prevailed by the Cross. For it was not because Moses so prayed that the people were strong, but because, while one who bore the name of Jesus was in the forefront of the battle, he himself made the sign of the Cross."[4] Justin's links to Christ are two: the name of Joshua, which in the Greek translation is Jesus, and Moses stretching out his hands in the form of a cross. In order to preach Christ, Justin again focusses on a few details of this story. In addition, he takes some liberties with the text when he claims that Moses stretched out his hands in the form of a cross, for the text says only that he "held up his hand" (v 11, NRSV), or "held up his hands" (NIV).

We should first determine the story's message for Israel. The first verse in this story reveals the conflict, "Then Amalek came and fought with Israel at Rephidim" (v 8). The Israelites have just been delivered from Egypt and now their very existence is threatened by Amalek, descendants of Esau (Gen 36:12, 15-16). What are they to do? "Moses said to Joshua, 'Choose some men for us and go out, fight with Amalek. Tomorrow I will stand on the top of the hill with the staff of God in my hand" (v 9). The next day, the battle seesaws back and forth: "Whenever Moses held up his hand, Israel prevailed; and whenever he lowered his hand, Amalek prevailed" (v 11). Complications set in when Moses' hands grow tired and Israel is about to lose the battle. A solution is found in Aaron and Hur supporting Moses' hands, which they do until sunset. The outcome of the battle is that "Joshua defeated Amalek and his people with the sword" (v 13).

The narrator makes clear that Joshua did not win this battle in his own strength but depended totally on Moses keeping his hands lifted.[5] In

---

4. Justin Martyr, *Dialogue*, 90, as cited in Daniélou, *From Shadows*, 233. For Irenaeus, see p. 79 above, and for Origen, p. 86 above.

5. Bernard P. Robinson, "Israel and Amalek," *JSOT* 32 (1985) 15, suggests a chiastic structure focussing on Moses' hands:

A. Amalek at war with Israel (17:8)
   B. Moses' instructions to Joshua
      What he (Moses) will do. Compliance of Joshua (17:9, 10a)
      C. Joshua smites Amalek (17:10b)
         D. Moses, Aaron, and Hur (17:10c)
            E. Moses' arms (17:11)
            E'. Moses' arms (17:12a)
         D'. Moses, Aaron, and Hur (17:12b)
      C'. Joshua smites Amalek (17:13)
   B'. YHWH's instructions to Moses
      What he (YHWH) will do. Compliance of Moses (17:14, 15)
A'. YHWH at war with Amalek (17:16)

his hands Moses held "the staff of God" — the staff which represented almighty God and which Moses had used in Egypt to perform God's miracles to set Israel free. The point of the story is, therefore, that *God* gives Israel the victory in the battle against Amalek, who threatened their very existence. In case we missed the point, the narrator adds, "Moses built an altar and called it, The LORD is my banner" (v 15). So we can formulate the theme of this narrative as follows: *When their fragile existence is threatened by Amalek, the Lord gives Israel the victory in battle.* Possible goals of this story for later Israel might be: to encourage Israel to trust the Lord to give them the victory in their battles; or, to provide Israel with a sense of security, even living in the midst of their enemies, because of the presence of the Lord.

1. The Way of Redemptive-Historical Progression

The theme of God giving his people the victory in battle echoes through much of redemptive history. It began right after the fall into sin when God "put enmity between you [the serpent] and the woman, and between your offspring and hers" (Gen 3:15). Our text in Exodus discloses an instance of God giving victory to the seed of the woman: Amalek threatens to destroy God's people on the way to the promised land, but the Lord gives Joshua the victory. As part of the ongoing battle between the seed of the serpent and the seed of the woman, this passage leads in redemptive history to Satan's attempt to kill the Christ-child through King Herod, but God provides a way of escape. The God-given victory surfaces again with Satan's apparent victory when Jesus is killed and buried, but God gives Jesus the victory when he raises him from the dead. It leads finally to the last day when God gives Jesus the victory and casts the devil "into the lake of fire and sulfur" (Rev 20:10). Redemptive-historical progression provides the broad brush strokes which will be filled in with promise-fulfillment, typology, analogy, or longitudinal themes.

2. The Way of Promise-Fulfillment

This text contains no direct promise of Christ.

3. The Way of Typology

Joshua is a type of Christ, not because his name translated in Greek is Jesus but because he is the leader of Israel in the battle against Amalek and through this leader the Lord gains victory for his people over the enemy. Thus Joshua prefigures Jesus Christ, who on the cross gains the decisive victory for his people over Satan and who will gain the final victory on the last day. Again we see analogy and escalation.

4. The Way of Analogy

Analogy could forge a link to Christ: As God gave his people Israel the victory over Amalek, so God in Christ gives us the victory over our enemies. But this analogy has been misused from Emperor Constantine's armies ("In this sign [the cross] conquer!") to the twentieth-century Nazis ("Gott mit uns") — each claiming victory over their enemies in the name of Christ or God. This misuse of analogy demonstrates concretely the importance of checking the way of analogy with the way of contrast — in fact, all seven ways should be checked before finalizing the sermon. For Christ never promised us victory over national or personal enemies. Instead, he commanded us: "Love your enemies and pray for those who persecute you" (Matt 5:44). Although human governments are God's way of promoting justice in a sinful world (Rom 13:1-7) and Christians must work for justice, the only victory Christians are promised is the final victory over sin and death (1 Cor 15:54-57). Therefore a better analogy is, As God gave his people Israel the victory over Amalek, so God in Christ will eventually give his church the victory over its enemies: sin, the Antichrist, and death.

5. The Way of Longitudinal Themes

The theme that God fights for his people and gives them the victory can be traced throughout the Old Testament and right into the New Testament. It is the theme of God as the warrior King — a title the New Testament gives to Jesus, the "King of kings and Lord of lords" (Rev 19:16). During his earthly life Jesus waged war against Satan and his cohorts as he cast out demons and healed the sick. On the cross, he won the decisive victory over the satanic powers, with the final victory to come on the last day.[6]

6. The Way of New Testament References

The Greek New Testament offers no references to this passage. The Treasury of Scripture Knowledge offers sixteen New Testament texts, all on de-

---

6. On God and Jesus as the warrior king, see Tremper Longman III, "The Form and Message of Nahum: Preaching from a Prophet of Doom," *Reformed Theological Journal* 1 (1985) 13-24. Cf. Tremper Longman III and Daniel G. Reid, *God Is a Warrior* (Grand Rapids: Zondervan, 1995).

tails of the Exodus passage and most on prayer, probably because Moses' uplifted hands are understood as prayer. However, since the theme of the passage is not prayer but the Lord giving victory in battle, we cannot use these New Testament references in this particular sermon. Checking a concordance on "conquer" provides a possible way for Christ-centered preaching: Paul writes in Romans 8:37-39 that "we are more than conquerors through him who loved us. For I am convinced that neither death, nor life, nor angels, nor rulers, nor things present, nor things to come, nor powers, nor height, nor depth, nor anything else in all creation will be able to separate us from the love of God in Christ Jesus our Lord."

7. The Way of Contrast

Tremper Longman points out the contrast between the battles fought by Israel and the battles fought in New Testament times. "Jesus' Holy War is different from the Holy War of Israel. While the latter, at the Lord's command, directed their warfare against earthly enemies, Jesus struggled with the forces, the powers and principalities, which stand behind sinful mankind (cf. his miracles and healings). . . . His [Jesus'] command is not to slay but to convert (Matt 28:16ff)."[7]

Checking this text for all seven possible ways of preaching Christ has again disclosed several options of preaching Christ on the basis of this particular passage. But it has also laid bare the danger of using analogy by itself and of putting too much stock into suggested New Testament references. All seven ways should be diligently explored before writing the sermon.

Preaching on the Ceremony
of the Red Heifer (Numbers 19)

The *Epistle of Barnabas* allegorizes the prescribed ceremony of the red heifer with great abandon. The links forged to Christ are three: "The calf [heifer] is Jesus," the "piece of wood" is a "type of the Cross," and the "scarlet wool" is the blood of Christ.[8] Although Wilhelm Vischer finds even more references to Jesus in the details of this law, all of them are related to the heifer: the requirement that the heifer is to be without blemish alludes to Christ being without spot; that it had never been under a

---

7. Ibid., 20.
8. See p. 73 above.

yoke alludes to Christ, "who never came under the yoke of sin"; that it was to be slaughtered outside the camp refers to Christ being sacrificed outside the walls of Jerusalem; and that some of the blood was to be sprinkled toward the tabernacle is linked with, "Nothing but being sprinkled with the blood of Christ can absolve us, and nothing but the transfer of the merit of His obedience to us can open the door to God's service."[9]

Unfortunately, linking a few details of this law to Christ by allegorizing or typologizing misses the point of this passage. This difficult passage contains many ceremonial symbols, and commentators are not agreed on the significance of each of these symbols for Israel. For example, what is the significance of the requirement that the heifer be red and that the priest throw "cedarwood, hyssop, and crimson material . . . into the fire in which the heifer is burning" (v 6; cf. Lev 14:4-6)? If we can only speculate about the significance of these elements for Israel, extending their significance to the cross of Christ and to his blood is extremely dubious. Nor should preachers link the sprinkling of some of the blood toward the tabernacle with the sprinkling of the blood of Christ, as Vischer does. That may be true for other sacrifices at the tabernacle in which blood is poured out at the base of the altar and sprinkled once a year on the mercy seat to atone for sins. But this particular "purification offering" (v 10) was to take place "outside the camp" (v 3). The only connection with the atonement sacrifices at the tabernacle is the requirement that the priest "shall take some of its [the heifer's] blood with his finger and sprinkle it seven times towards the front of the tent of meeting" (v 4). This particular law focusses not on the sprinkling with blood (most of it is burned) but on the sprinkling with water containing the ashes of the red heifer — "the water for cleansing" (v 10; cf. vv 11-22). God here provides the Israelites with a means of purifying themselves when they have become unclean through contact with a corpse. When they are unclean, they are not allowed to worship with God's people at the tabernacle/temple, for they would "defile the tabernacle of the LORD" (vv 13, 20). A person who is unclean has no part in fellowship with a holy God. Being unclean is, therefore, extremely serious. Ordinary water is not sufficient to clean a person who is ritually unclean. But in this law God provides Israel with special water — water into which the ashes of the red heifer have been mixed.

We can focus the message of this passage under the theme, *When you become unclean by contact with death, purify yourself with special water containing the ashes of the red heifer!* Possible goals of this message for Israel are: to teach Israel the distinction between clean and unclean, holiness and sinful-

9. See pp. 175-76 above.

ness; to persuade Israel of the seriousness of sin (being unclean), for it severs fellowship with a holy God; to urge Israel to use the means God provides for purification and restoration to fellowship with God.

1. The Way of Redemptive-Historical Progression

In looking for ways to preach Christ on the basis of this passage, we should again examine its message first in the light of the big picture of redemptive history. The passage has to do with being unclean through contact with death. Death first entered human history with the fall into sin: "You are dust, and to dust you shall return" (Gen 3:19). From the beginning death and sin have been connected: human sin led to death. Death, however, does not have the last word. John hears a voice from the throne in heaven saying, "Death will be no more" (Rev 21:4). But until that day, we still have to live with the reality of death as God's punishment for sin.

In this passage God provides his people with a religious rite to purify themselves from the defilement of death. Contact with death makes people unclean so that they must be "cut off" from fellowship with a holy God and his holy people (Num 19:13, 20). But God stipulates that sprinkling with this special water containing the ashes of the red heifer renders a person clean and restored for fellowship with God.

Throughout Old Testament history water is associated with ceremonial cleansing. At the tabernacle/temple the priests had a bronze basin filled with water for washing their hands and feet (Exod 30:21). On many occasions the Israelites were commanded to wash their clothes and bathe themselves to be ritually clean. In this passage, too, the priest that touches the red heifer is to "wash his clothes and bathe his body in water" (Num 19:7; see also vv 8-10). But here God also prescribes special water for removing this grave ritual uncleanness contracted through contact with death. Further, we find in Israel the development of baptism in water for proselytes. In the New Testament, John the Baptizer proclaims "a baptism of repentance for the forgiveness of sins" (Mark 1:4). From there it is but a step to Christian baptism: "Repent, and be baptized every one of you in the name of Jesus Christ so that your sins may be forgiven" (Acts 2:38). John's baptism is replaced by baptism "in the name of the Lord Jesus" (Acts 19:3-5) and "in the name of the Father and of the Son and of the Holy Spirit" (Matt 28:19).

2. The Way of Promise-Fulfillment

This passage contains no direct promise of Christ.

3. The Way of Typology

The water for cleansing is special because the ashes of the heifer have been mixed into it. The ashes of the heifer validate this sign of cleansing. Therefore, the red heifer is a symbol of cleansing from defilement and restoration to fellowship with God. As such the heifer can function as a type of Christ whose death provides the cleansing needed from the stain of sin and who restores his people once for all to fellowship with God — analogy and escalation.

4. The Way of Analogy

Analogy can virtually duplicate the analogy of typology above: As God provided Israel with a way to be ritually clean and restored to fellowship with God, so God provides his people today with his only Son to cleanse them from their sins and restore them to fellowship with God. But analogy can move beyond the analogy of typology by connecting the teaching of this law about clean and unclean to the teaching of Jesus or the apostles. For example, as God through this law taught Israel that they needed to be clean, that is, holy, for fellowship with God, so Jesus teaches God's people that they ought to be clean not just on the outside but on the inside (Luke 11:37-41; cf. Matt 15:10-20; 1 Pet 1:15).

5. The Way of Longitudinal Themes

We can trace the theme of purification of the ceremonially unclean from this law, which was to be "a perpetual statute for the Israelites and for the alien residing among them" (v 10), to the baptism of John the Baptizer, which was "a baptism of repentance for the forgiveness of sins" (Mark 1:4), to the Christian baptism of the apostles: "Repent, and be baptized every one of you in the name of Jesus Christ so that your sins may be forgiven" (Acts 2:38), to the teaching of the apostles. Not only does Christian baptism connect with Christ by being baptized into his name but the apostolic teaching about the significance of baptism reveals many links with concepts in our passage. For example, in Romans 6:4 Paul links baptism to death and life: "We have been buried with him [Christ] by baptism into death, so that, just as Christ was raised from the dead by the glory of the Father, so we too might walk in newness of life." Colossians 2:12-14 offers even more links with our passage — not only death and life but also sin and washing away ("erasing") in forgiveness: "When you were buried with him [Christ] in baptism, you were also raised with him through faith in the power of God, who raised him from the dead. And when you were dead in trespasses . . . , God made you alive together with him, when he forgave us all our trespasses, erasing the record . . . nailing it to the cross" (Col 2:12-14).

6. The Way of New Testament References

The Greek New Testament lists two references to this passage. The first is an allusion in Hebrews 9:19, which is not very helpful for our purposes. The second reference, to Hebrews 9:13, is much more promising because it confirms typology, "If . . . the sprinkling of the ashes of a heifer sanctifies those who have been defiled so that their flesh is purified, how much more will the blood of Christ . . . purify our conscience from dead works to worship the living God" (Heb 9:13-14).

Checking a concordance on the word "sprinkling" provides a further promising reference in Hebrews: "Therefore, my friends, since we have confidence to enter the sanctuary by the blood of Jesus . . . and since we have a great priest over the house of God, let us approach with a true heart in full assurance of faith, with our hearts sprinkled clean from an evil conscience and our bodies washed with pure water" (Heb 10:19-22).

Searching the concordance further on the word "water" leads to Ephesians 5:25b-27, "Christ loved the church and gave himself up for her, in order to make her holy by cleansing her with the washing of water by the word, so as to present the church to himself in splendor, without a spot or wrinkle or anything of the kind — yes, so that she may be holy and without blemish." This search also brings out the intriguing possibility of Acts 10:47 — intriguing because in the context God sent Peter to the house of the Gentile Cornelius and showed him that the ancient distinction between clean and unclean was no longer valid, especially as it was used to distinguish Jews and Gentiles. An angel of God said to Peter, "What God has made clean, you must not call profane" (Acts 10:15). When Peter arrives at the house of Cornelius and preaches Jesus Christ to them, the Holy Spirit falls on the Gentiles present. Peter responds, "'Can anyone withhold the water for baptizing these people who have received the Holy Spirit just as we have?' So he ordered them to be baptized in the name of Jesus Christ" (Acts 10:47-48).

Finally, checking the concordance under the word "unclean" provides two interesting passages. In 2 Corinthians 6:17-18, Paul combines several Old Testament passages to teach the Corinthians about holiness: "As God said, . . . 'touch nothing unclean; then I will welcome you, and I will be your father, and you shall be my sons and daughters.'" Further, in Romans 14:14 Paul asserts, "I know and am persuaded in the Lord Jesus that nothing is unclean in itself." This New Testament reference (as well as Acts 10 above) alerts us to the progression in redemptive history and revelation and thus to the way of contrast.

7. The Way of Contrast

With the coming of Christ, the Old Testament ceremonial laws are largely filled up and abrogated. We have already seen in the New Testament references that an angel of God said to Peter, "What God has made clean, you must not call profane" (Acts 10:15), and that Paul asserted, "I know and am persuaded in the Lord Jesus that nothing is unclean in itself" (Rom 14:14). Christ's one-time sacrifice on the cross offers cleansing once and for all. Moreover, Christ taught that we are defiled by sin not so much from without as from within: "Out of the heart come evil intentions, murder, adultery, fornication, theft, false witness, slander. These are what defile a person, but to eat with unwashed hands does not defile" (Matt 15:19-20).

Exploring the seven ways has opened up various avenues of preaching Christ on the basis of this passage without resorting to allegorical interpretation. Since various combinations of these options are possible, the sermon theme and goal should be used to select those options that will enable one to preach Christ persuasively.

Preaching on the Destruction of Jericho and the Salvation of Rahab (Joshua 2 and 6)

In A.D. 96 already, Bishop Clement of Rome preached Christ from the story of Jericho by focussing on the red cord: in directing Rahab to hang a red cord from her window, the Israelite spies "made manifest that redemption for all who believe and hope in God will come through the blood of the Lord."[10] Origen greatly expanded this link to Christ in his allegorical interpretation of this story. He proclaimed that "Joshua stands for Jesus, and Jericho for this world. The seven priests carrying trumpets represent Matthew, Mark, Luke, John, James, Jude and Peter. The prostitute Rahab stands for the Church, which consists of sinners; and the scarlet cord which she displayed to save herself and her household from the massacre stands for the redemptive blood of Christ."[11] Although not many preachers today would follow Origen's allegorical interpretation,

10. See p. 72 above.
11. See p. 87 above.

the move from Rahab's red cord to the blood of Christ is still a popular way of preaching Christ from this passage. This interpretation is usually dismissed as allegorizing, but Jean Daniélou points out that Justin Martyr, Irenaeus, Hilary, and Gregory all speak of the scarlet cord as a type of the blood of Christ in the context of the sign of the blood on the doorposts at the Passover feast. For example, Justin writes, "And as the blood of the Passover saved those who were in Egypt, so also the blood of Christ will deliver from death those who have believed. . . . For the sign of the scarlet thread . . . also manifested the symbol of the blood of Christ, by which those who were at one time harlots and evil persons out of all nations are saved. . . ."[12]

If the church fathers had made the case that Israel later read this story about Rahab's scarlet cord in the light of its Passover experience with the blood on the doorposts, they might have had a point. But it is not likely that the fathers used that kind of modern, historical thinking; it is more likely that they simply moved from the color red to the color of blood, just as they moved from any mention of wood to the wood of the cross. Moreover, there is no evidence that the scarlet cord ever functioned as a symbol of salvation in Israel; in fact, the chapter that relates the saving of Rahab and her family (Josh 6) not so much as mentions the cord. Instead of seizing immediately the detail of the red color of the cord, it is better to listen to the story as a whole.

Careful reading of these chapters shows that this story is primarily about the Lord *giving* the promised land to his people Israel. The spies return from their mission and report to Joshua, "Truly the LORD has given all the land into our hands" (Josh 2:24). But there is another theme running through these chapters: the spies had been saved by Rahab and had promised to save her and her family in turn. They told her to "tie this crimson cord in the window through which you let us down" (2:18), and Rahab did just that (2:21). The narrator continues the story by relating Israel's crossing of the Jordan and camping at Gilgal. We hear again about Jericho when Joshua approaches the city, perhaps to see how they might best attack it (5:13). Here "the commander of the army of the LORD" meets Joshua and tells him, "Remove the sandals from your feet, for the place where you stand is holy" (5:15). Joshua is another Moses (see Exod 3:5), who will lead God's people into the promised land. But Joshua does not have to do this in his own strength nor by the might of a powerful army. "The LORD said to Joshua, 'See, I have handed Jericho over to you, along with its king and soldiers'" (6:2) — again the emphasis on the Lord

---

12. Justin, *Dialogue*, 111.3-4, as cited in Daniélou, *From Shadows*, 247. See p. 248 for Irenaeus, p. 255 for Hilary, and p. 258 for Gregory.

giving the land. The chapter ends with the narrator's conclusion, "So the LORD was with Joshua; and his fame was in all the land" (6:27). The inclusio of chapter 6 shows that the main focus in this chapter is on the Lord and Joshua, and it is in this context that we hear again of Rahab.

The Lord literally gives Jericho to Joshua and Israel. They do not have to storm the walls of Jericho; all they have to do is walk around the city in a religious procession with the ark (the Lord) in the middle (6:9). The perfect number seven underscores the sacredness of this event: "Thus you shall do for six days, with seven priests bearing seven trumpets of rams' horns before the ark. On the seventh day you shall march around the city seven times. . . . Then all the people shall shout with a great shout; and the wall of the city will fall down flat, and all the people shall charge straight ahead" (6:3-5) — the city is a gift of God. But the gift will have to be returned to God: "The city and all that is in it shall be devoted to the LORD for destruction" (6:17a). This is a holy war. Already through Moses the Lord had commanded Israel: "You must utterly destroy" the seven nations living in Canaan (Deut 7:2), "so that they may not teach you to do all the abhorrent things that they do for their gods, and you thus sin against the LORD your God" (Deut 20:17-18). Every man, woman, child, and animal in Jericho must be killed. Amazingly, there is one exception to the destruction of the inhabitants of Jericho: "Only Rahab the prostitute and all who are with her in her house shall live because she hid the messengers we sent" (6:17b). The Canaanite Rahab and her family are saved from the total annihilation of Jericho. Twice this chapter gives the reason for saving Rahab and her family: "She hid the messengers." But there is not a word about the scarlet cord.

Since we hear about Rahab's salvation in two different stories in two separate chapters, Joshua 2 and 6, it is best to focus the sermon on one chapter or the other. I have elected to focus on Joshua 6 because it tells of the actual saving of Rahab, and the sermon can still refer to Joshua 2 as background. Even confining ourselves to chapter 6, it is difficult to formulate a single theme because the passage has two foci: the destruction of Jericho and the salvation of Rahab. These two foci are related to the fact that this narrative does not have a simple but a complex plot. The first issue is, Will Israel conquer the promised land while the strong fortress of Jericho is blocking its way? This conflict simmers for six long days while Israel obediently marches around the towering walls of Jericho. The conflict reaches a climax on day seven when Israel marches around Jericho seven times and Joshua gives final instructions (6:15-19). The conflict is resolved when the people raise "a great shout," the wall falls down, and Israel walks into Jericho and devotes it to the Lord as the firstfruits of the harvest of the whole land of Canaan (6:20-21).

But this resolution still leaves a second issue: What about Rahab and her family, who had earlier been promised life by the spies (2:14)? Joshua refers to this promise in his final instructions (6:17), but this issue is not resolved until Joshua specifically commands the spies to bring Rahab and her family out of the inferno of Jericho (6:22-24). This resolution results in an astonishing conclusion: the narrator tells us that while Rahab and her family were first put "outside the camp of Israel," Rahab's family "has lived in Israel ever since" (6:25). Amazingly, in God's grace, Rahab's Gentile family has become part of the special people of God.

To formulate a single theme for this passage, we need to subsume one theme under the other. Since the Lord giving Jericho to Israel appears to be dominant, I suggest the following theme for this chapter: *The Lord gives Jericho to Israel for total destruction, yet saves the Canaanite Rahab and her family.* Several goals suggest themselves for telling this story to later Israel: to assure the Israelites that the Lord has given them the promised land; to warn Israel of the consequences of idolatry; to demonstrate to Israel that Gentiles, too, can become part of the people of God. Having formulated the historical theme and possible goals of the chapter, we are now ready to check which of the seven possible ways offer a road from this passage to Jesus Christ.

1. The Way of Redemptive-Historical Progression

We shall first look at this message in the light of redemptive history. Israel is poised to conquer the land God promised to their father Abraham. When Abraham first came to this region, "the Canaanites were in the land" (Gen 12:6). Canaanites were descendants of Noah's son Canaan, whom he "cursed" for his sin (Gen 9:25). Now the land was occupied by Canaanites and other peoples who did "abhorrent things . . . for their gods" and were ripe for God's judgment. The Lord instructed Israel to "annihilate" these peoples (Deut 20:17-18), just as God himself had done on a much greater scale when he annihilated the wicked in the flood (Gen 6–7). It was to be a holy war in which all living creatures would be "devoted to the LORD for destruction" (Josh 6:17). Being "devoted to the LORD for destruction" is a precursor of the "day of the LORD" about which the prophets warn and of which Peter writes, "The day of the Lord will come like a thief, and then the heavens will pass away with a loud noise, and the elements will be dissolved with fire, and the earth and everything that is done on it will be disclosed" (2 Pet 3:10).

Israel is poised to dispense God's judgment upon Canaan. As God's people Israel replace the wicked people of Canaan, they will have to establish a beachhead for the kingdom of God — a place where God is honored as God and where his laws are obeyed. God gives them the first city in Canaan, Jericho, and Israel destroys the city and all its inhabitants. But there is a surprising exception to this total annihilation: Rahab and her family are saved because of her faith in Yahweh and her actions to protect the spies. These Canaanites become part of the people of God — a partial fulfillment of God's promise to Abram, "In you all the families of the earth shall be blessed" (Gen 12:3). But the redemption of the Canaanite Rahab and her family is only a small start. We meet Rahab again in the New Testament, where she is listed as one of the foremothers of Jesus (Matt 1:5). Jesus will mandate his disciples to "make disciples of all nations, . . . teaching them to obey everything that I have commanded you" (Matt 28:19-20). And so redemptive history continues throughout the church age until it ends in the new Jerusalem, of which we read: "the glory of God is its light, and its lamp is the Lamb. The nations will walk by its light, and the kings of the earth will bring their glory into it" (Rev 21:24).

2. The Way of Promise-Fulfillment

This narrative contains no direct promise of Christ.

3. The Way of Typology

There is a figure in this story who is clearly a type of Christ: Joshua, the leader of Israel. As Joshua conquered the enemy city and opened the way for Israel into the promised land, so Christ conquers Satan's stronghold (cf. Matt 12:28-29; Rev 20:2-3) and opens the way for his people into the new creation — analogy and escalation.

4. The Way of Analogy

In using analogy with Israel's victory over Amalek, we noticed that analogy must be handled with due regard for contrast or discontinuity. With this story, too, the analogy could easily be misdrawn if we were to concentrate on the first part of our theme: As the Lord gives wicked Jericho to Israel for destruction, so the Lord gives his people today wicked places (such as abortion clinics) to destroy. This analogy overlooks the discontinuity between Old Testament Israel and the church as well as New Testament evidence. A better place to draw the analogy is the second part of our theme: As God through Joshua saved the Gentile Rahab and her family from the judgment, so God through Christ saves us Gentiles from the judgment.

We can also look for an analogy between the teaching of this story for Israel and the teaching of Christ. Each of the possible goals we posited earlier becomes an option: As God assured Israel through this story that he would give them the promised land, so Christ assures his people that he will give them a place in his "Father's house" (John 14:2); or, As God through this story warned Israel of the dire consequences of idolatry, so Christ warns his church of the dire consequences of idolatry (e.g., Rev 21:8); or, As God through this story demonstrated to Israel that Gentiles, too, can become part of the people of God, so Christ teaches his church that the kingdom of God is for all nations (e.g., Matt 28:19).

5. The Way of Longitudinal Themes

Longitudinal themes also provide opportunities for preaching Christ from this passage. One could trace the theme of God's judgment upon the wicked to Christ's verdict in the final judgment. A more likely option, however, is to trace the theme of God's desire to save all nations, for a major theme in this story is the salvation from annihilation of this Gentile woman and her family and their incorporation into the people of God (Josh 6:25). The theme of God's desire to save Gentiles can be traced back to his covenant promise to Abram, "In you all the families of the earth shall be blessed" (Gen 12:3); and it can be traced forward to Ruth the Moabitess, who becomes part of the people of God; to the Psalms, which pray for the king's dominion "from sea to sea" (72:8); to the prophets, who remind Israel of her calling to be "a light to the nations" (Isa 42:6; cf. Jonah); to the servant of the Lord, to whom the Lord says, "I will give you as a light to the nations, that my salvation may reach to the end of the earth" (Isa 49:6). In the New Testament, Matthew picks up this theme by including the Gentile women Rahab and Ruth in Jesus' family tree (Matt 1), by reporting pointedly that Gentile wise men came to worship baby Jesus (Matt 2), and by including Jesus' commission to his followers to "make disciples of all nations" (Matt 28:19). From there this theme continues to the apostles bringing the gospel of Christ to the Gentiles, and it concludes in the book of Revelation with the visions of a great multitude "from every nation, from all tribes and peoples," praising God and the Lamb for their salvation (7:9-10), and people of all nations entering the New Jerusalem (21:24-26).

6. The Way of New Testament References

The Greek New Testament offers several references to this story. The first is an allusion to the seven trumpets in Revelation 8:2. The next two references are Hebrews 11:31 and James 2:25. Hebrews presents Rahab as an illustration of faith: "By faith Rahab the prostitute did not perish with those who were disobedient, because she had received the spies in peace." James, in contrast, presents Rahab as an illustration of the necessity of works: "Likewise, was not Rahab the prostitute also justified by works when she welcomed the messengers and sent them out by another road?" Since both Hebrews and James use the story of Rahab to illustrate their particular themes, and since neither of these is the theme of our passage, it is not likely that we can use these references in the sermon. Checking a concordance under the word "Rahab" turns up a direct link to Jesus Christ: in his genealogy of Jesus, Matthew (1:5) lists Rahab as one of the foremothers of Jesus.

7. *The Way of Contrast*

In searching for contrast we look for the discontinuities between the message of the text for Israel and the message of the sermon for the church — discontinuities created by progression in the histories of redemption and revelation, especially because of the coming of Christ. Since the coming of Christ, the church can no longer be identified with a particular nation, Israel, but includes all nations. Since the coming of Christ, the church has become not so much international as it has become supranational. No nation, not even an international coalition, can claim biblical support for conducting a "holy war" and committing genocide. Groups as radically different as the Crusaders and the Nazis disregarded the discontinuity between Israel and the New Testament church. But Jesus clearly teaches his disciples not to exterminate their enemies, not even to hate them, but to love them, pray for them (Matt 5:43-44), "do good" to them (Luke 6:35), and "make disciples" of them (Matt 28:19). In conformity with this attitude, Paul writes, "Do not repay anyone evil for evil, but take thought for what is noble in the sight of all. . . . Beloved, never avenge yourselves, but leave room for the wrath of God; for it is written, 'Vengeance is mine, I will repay, says the Lord'" (Rom 12:17, 19). The call to love one's enemies while leaving "room for the wrath of God" conforms to Jesus' teaching about the kingdom of God. In his parable of the weeds among the wheat, the slaves suggest that they tear the weeds out right away, but the master declares that it is best to "let both of them grow together until the harvest; and at harvest time I will tell the reapers, Collect the weeds first and bind them in bundles to be burned, but gather the wheat into my barn" (Matt 13:30). In the end, justice will prevail, for there is a final Day of Judgment.

Exploring the seven ways has again opened up many possibilities for preaching Christ on the basis of this Old Testament narrative. Naturally, we should not overload the sermon by using all of these possibilities but select a few key options that support the theme and help accomplish the goal. Since the theme is, The Lord gives Jericho to Israel for total destruction yet saves the Canaanite Rahab and her family, the object now is to combine those options that enable us with integrity to preach Christ as the one who today saves Jews as well as Gentiles from God's judgment and gives them eternal life in his new creation.

*   *   *

This completes our application of the seven ways to several texts which in the history of interpretation and preaching were often interpreted allegorically. By selecting the texts that surfaced in allegorical interpretation as covered in Chapter 3, we had to deal with texts that were not obviously christocentric.[13] If the redemptive-historical christocentric method can uncover ways of preaching Christ on the basis of these difficult texts, it should work for most, if not all, other Old Testament texts. It is important to remember that this method first seeks to understand the passage in its own historical-cultural setting; next it views this message in the contexts of canon and redemptive history and seeks to uncover specific roads from the Old Testament passage to Jesus Christ; and finally it requires preachers to decide, on the basis of the theme and goal of the sermon, which of the several possible ways will be used in the sermon. The object, as we argued earlier, is not simply to draw lines to Christ but to preach Christ so that people will entrust themselves to him for their salvation and commit their lives into his service.

This method, obviously, requires more time in sermon preparation than merely establishing the historical message for Israel and linking it to an analogous situation in our day. More time is also required for the message to percolate in preachers' thoughts so that the often surprising connections between the message of the text and Jesus Christ will spring to mind. But this extra effort is more than worthwhile if it will enable preachers to preach Christ authentically from the Old Testament text in its biblical context. Paul encouraged Timothy as well as preachers today, "Do your best to present yourself to God as one approved by him, a worker who has no need to be ashamed, rightly explaining the word of truth" (2 Tim 2:15).

---

13. One unexpected result of this survey is that none of these texts offered a way for preaching Christ by way of promise-fulfillment. This may indicate that messianic texts, from which Christ is preached rather easily by way of promise-fulfillment, were less likely to be interpreted allegorically.

EXERCISES IN USING
THE CHRISTOCENTRIC METHOD

The following exercises are based on texts from different genres of Old Testament literature. These exercises will be most beneficial if students or pastors work individually on each text or two and then meet together for group discussion. I have supplied the textual themes so that group discussion can proceed from them and focus on the specific ways of moving from the textual theme to a Christ-centered sermon.

For each text, answer two questions:

1. Which of the seven ways can be used for preaching Christ on the basis of this particular text and how?

2. Given the textual theme, which are your best options for preaching Christ while proclaiming the text's specific message?

Narrative:

Genesis 11:1-9: At Babel the Lord scatters the proud, who, building their own secular kingdom, threaten to thwart God's coming kingdom.

Genesis 37: God uses the evil deeds of Joseph's brothers to begin to fulfill his dreams of being king.

Law:

Leviticus 18: Do not sexually defile yourselves in the land as the nations around you do!

Or positively: Be sexually pure so that you may live in the promised land!

Deuteronomy 26:1-15: As a thank offering for God's blessings, give your firstfruits and tithes to the Lord!

Prophecy:

Isaiah 43:1-7: Fear not, for God will bring you safely back to the promised land.

Malachi 4:1-6: The day of the Lord is coming, burning the arrogant and healing those who revere the Lord.

Psalm:

Psalm 30: Thank the Lord for turning weeping into joy!

Psalm 72: Israel's king will establish God's justice in the whole earth.

Wisdom:

Proverbs 16:3: For your plans to succeed, commit your works to the Lord.

Ecclesiastes 11:7–12:8: Enjoy your life, remembering your Creator before the days of adversity come.

APPENDIX 1

Steps from Text to Sermon

1. Select the preaching-text.
Select the preaching-text with an eye to congregational needs. The text must be a literary unit and contain a vital theme.

2. Read the text in its literary context.
Read and reread the text in its context and jot down initial questions. These questions guide further investigation and may have to be answered in the sermon if your hearers have similar questions.

3. Outline the structure of the text.
In the Hebrew or Greek text, note the major affirmations, clausal flow, plot line, scenes, or literary structures. Mark major units with headings and verse references.

4. Interpret the text in its own historical setting.
   a. Literary interpretation
   b. Historical interpretation
   c. Theocentric interpretation
      Review your results with the help of some good commentaries.

5. Formulate the text's theme and goal.
   a. State the textual *theme* in a brief sentence that summarizes the *message* of the text for its original hearers: subject and predicate. What is the text saying?
   b. State the *goal* of the author for his original hearers. What is the text doing? Does the author aim to teach, to persuade, to urge, to encourage, to warn, to comfort? Be specific.

6. **Understand the message in the contexts of canon and redemptive history.**
   a. Canonical interpretation: interpret the message in the context of the whole canon.
   b. Redemptive-historical interpretation: understand the message in the context of God's story from creation to new creation.
   c. Christocentric interpretation: explore the ways of
      (1) redemptive-historical progression,
      (2) promise-fulfillment,
      (3) typology,
      (4) analogy,
      (5) longitudinal themes,
      (6) New Testament references, and
      (7) contrast.

7. **Formulate the sermon theme and goal.**
   a. Ideally, your *sermon theme* will be the same as your textual theme (Step 5). If Step 6 forces a change, stay as close as possible to the textual theme. Your theme will guide especially the development of the body of the sermon.
   b. Your *goal* must be in harmony with the author's goal (Step 5) and match the sermon theme. Your goal will guide the style of the sermon as well as the content of its introduction and conclusion.

8. **Select a suitable sermon form.**
   Select a sermon form that respects the form of the text (didactic, narrative, deductive, inductive) and that achieves the goal of the sermon.

9. **Prepare the sermon outline.**
   If possible, follow the flow of the text (Step 3) in the body of the sermon. Main points, derived from the text, support the theme. The conclusion should clinch the goal. The introduction should expose the need to hear this message.

10. **Write the sermon in oral style.**
    Say it as you write it. Write in oral style, using short sentences, vivid words, strong nouns and verbs, active voice, present tense, images, and illustrations.

APPENDIX 2

An Expository Sermon Model

A. Introduction (generally no more than 10 percent of your sermon)
1. Normally, begin with an illustration of the *contemporary need* addressed (Step 7b).
2. Connect this illustration to the need of the present hearers.
3. *Transition:* Show that this need or a similar issue was also the question behind the biblical text.
4. State the *theme* of the text/sermon, the revelatory point (Step 7). For the sake of maintaining suspense, you may postpone disclosing the theme at the beginning (inductive development), but by statement and restatement, you must make sure that the hearers catch the point of the sermon.

B. The Sermon Body
1. Expose the *structure of the text*.
   The main points, affirmations, moves, and scenes of the text (Step 3) normally become your main points in the sermon.
2. The *main points* should usually support the theme and be of the same rank.
3. Follow the *textual sequence* of the points unless there is good reason to change it, such as climactic arrangement (Step 9).
4. Use simple, *clear transitions* that enable the hearers to sense the structure of and movement in the sermon. For example, "Let us first see. . . . Now we see secondly. . . ." Or, "Look with me at verse 8. . . . Now look at verse 12." Or, "Not only . . . but also. . . ."
5. Use *verse references* before quoting key verses in the text so that the hearers can read along. Visual learning is nine times more effective than aural.

6. Use some personal observations to *illustrate* difficult concepts or to make the point. Personal illustrations are more natural and powerful than canned illustrations about Bishop Whately. Personal experiences may also be used but be careful not to preach yourself but Christ.

C. Conclusion
1. Be brief.
2. Do not introduce new material. Narrow the focus; do not expand it.
3. Clinch *the goal* (Step 7b).
4. Be concrete. Can you offer some concrete suggestions of what the hearers can do in response to the Word preached?

SELECT BIBLIOGRAPHY

Achtemeier, Elizabeth. *The Old Testament and the Proclamation of the Gospel.* Philadelphia: Westminster, 1973.

———. "The Relevance of the Old Testament for Christian Preaching." In *A Light unto My Path: Old Testament Studies in Honor of Jacob M. Myers.* Ed. Howard H. Bream, R. D. Heim, and C. A. Moore. Philadelphia: Temple University, 1974. Pp. 3-24.

———. "The Theological Message of Hosea: Its Preaching Values." *RevExp* 72/4 (1975) 473-85.

———. *Preaching from the Old Testament.* Louisville: Westminster/John Knox, 1989.

———. "From Exegesis to Proclamation." In *Studies in Old Testament Theology.* Ed. Robert L. Hubbard, Jr., *et al.* Dallas: Word, 1992. Pp. 47-61.

Adams, Jay E. *Preaching with Purpose.* Grand Rapids: Baker, 1982.

Aland, Kurt. "Luther as Exegete." *ExpT* 69 (1957-58) 45-48, 68-70.

Alexander, T. Desmond. "Messianic Ideology in the Book of Genesis." In *The Lord's Anointed.* Ed. Philip E. Satterthwaite, *et al.* Grand Rapids: Baker, 1995. Pp. 19-39.

Allen, Ronald J., and John C. Holbert. *Holy Root, Holy Branches: Christian Preaching from the Old Testament.* Nashville: Abingdon, 1995.

Anderson, Bernhard W. "Exodus Typology in Second Isaiah." In *Israel's Prophetic Heritage.* Ed. Walter Harrelson. New York: Harper and Row, 1962. Pp. 177-95.

———. "The Bible as the Shared Story of a People." In *The Old and New Testaments.* Ed. James H. Charlesworth and Walter P. Weaver. Valley Forge, PA: Trinity Press International, 1993. Pp. 19-37.

Augustine, *De Doctrina Christiana.* Ed. and trans. R. P. H. Green. Oxford: Clarendon, 1995.

———. *Concerning the City of God against the Pagans.* Trans. Henry Bettenson. New York: Penguin, 1972.

Baker, David L. "Typology and the Christian Use of the Old Testament." *SJT* 29 (1976) 137-57.

————. *Two Testaments, One Bible: A Study of Some Modern Solutions to the Theological Problem of the Relationship between the Old and New Testaments.* Downers Grove: InterVarsity, 1976.

Bandstra, Andrew J. "Interpretation in 1 Corinthians 10:1-11." *CTJ* 6 (1971) 5-21.

————. "Law and Gospel in Calvin and in Paul." In *Exploring the Heritage of John Calvin.* Ed. David E. Holwerda. Grand Rapids: Baker, 1976. Pp. 11-39.

Barclay, William. *Jesus As They Saw Him: New Testament Interpretation of Jesus.* New York: Harper and Row, 1962.

Barnard, Leslie W. "To Allegorize or Not to Allegorize?" *Studia Theologica* 36/1 (1982) 1-10.

Barr, James. *Old and New in Interpretation: A Study of the Two Testaments.* London: SCM, 1966.

Barrois, Georges A. *The Face of Christ in the Old Testament.* Crestwood, NY: St. Vladimir's Seminary, 1974.

Barth, Karl. *Church Dogmatics.* Vol. 1/2, 2/2. Trans. G. W. Bromiley and T. F. Torrance. Edinburgh: T & T Clark, 1956, 1957.

————. *The Preaching of the Gospel.* Trans. B. E. Hooke. Philadelphia: Westminster, 1963.

Bates, Gordon. "The Typology of Adam and Christ in John Calvin." *Hartford Quarterly* 5/2 (1965) 42-57.

Baue, Frederic W. "Luther on Preaching as Explanation and Exclamation." *LuthQ* 9 (1995) 405-18.

Beale, G. K. "Did Jesus and His Followers Preach the Right Doctrine from the Wrong Texts?" *Themelios* 14 (Spring 1989) 89-96.

Berkhof, Louis. *Principles of Biblical Interpretation.* Grand Rapids: Baker, 1950.

Berkouwer, Gerrit C. *The Person of Christ.* Trans. John Vriend. Grand Rapids: Eerdmans, 1955.

Best, Ernest. *From Text to Sermon: Responsible Use of the New Testament in Preaching.* Atlanta: John Knox, 1978.

Birch, Bruce C. *What Does the Lord Require? The Old Testament Call to Social Witness.* Philadelphia: Westminster, 1985.

Blackman, E. C. *Biblical Interpretation: The Old Difficulties and the New Opportunity.* London: Independent, 1957.

Bloesch, Donald G. "A Christological Hermeneutic: Crisis and Conflict in Hermeneutics." In *The Use of the Bible in Theology: Evangelical Options.* Ed. Robert K. Johnston. Atlanta: John Knox, 1985. Pp. 78-102.

Bock, Darrell L. "The Use of the Old Testament in the New." In *Foundations for Biblical Interpretation.* Ed. David S. Dockery, *et al.* Nashville: Broadman & Holman, 1994. Pp. 97-114.

Bonner, Gerald. "Augustine as Biblical Scholar." In *The Cambridge History of the Bible.* Vol. 1. Ed. P. R. Ackroyd and C. F. Evans. Cambridge: Cambridge University, 1970. Pp. 541-63.

Bornkamm, Heinrich. *Luther and the Old Testament*. Trans. Eric W. and Ruth C. Gritsch. Philadelphia: Fortress, 1969.

———. *Luther in Mid-Career: 1521-1530*. Trans. E. Theodore Bachmann. Philadelphia: Fortress, 1983.

Breck, John. *The Power of the Word: In the Worshipping Church*. Crestwood, NY: St. Vladimir's Seminary Press, 1986.

Bright, John. *The Kingdom of God: The Biblical Concept and Its Meaning for the Church*. Nashville: Abingdon, 1953.

———. "An Exercise in Hermeneutics." *Int* 20 (1966) 188-210.

———. *The Authority of the Old Testament*. London: SCM, 1967.

Broadus, John A. *Lectures on the History of Preaching*. New York: Sheldon, 1876.

Bromiley, Geoffrey W. "The Church Fathers and Holy Scripture." In *Scripture and Truth*. Ed. D. A. Carson and John D. Woodbridge. Grand Rapids: Zondervan, 1983. Pp. 195-220.

Bronkhorst, A. J. "In Memoriam Wilhelm Vischer [1895-1988]." *Kerk en Theologie* 40/2 (1989) 142-53.

Brown, Raymond E. *The "Sensus Plenior" of Sacred Scripture*. Baltimore: St. Mary's University, 1955.

———. "The *Sensus Plenior* in the Last Ten Years." *CBQ* 25 (1963) 262-85.

———. *Biblical Exegesis and Church Doctrine*. New York: Paulist, 1985.

Bruce, F. F. "Promise and Fulfilment in Paul's Presentation of Jesus." In *Promise and Fulfilment*. Ed. F. F. Bruce. Edinburgh: T & T Clark, 1963. Pp. 36-50.

———. *The New Testament Development of Old Testament Themes*. Grand Rapids: Eerdmans, 1968.

———. *The Time is Fulfilled: Five Aspects of the Fulfillment of the Old Testament in the New*. Grand Rapids: Eerdmans, 1978.

Bultmann, Rudolf. "The Significance of the Old Testament for the Christian Faith." In *The Old Testament and the Christian Faith*. Ed. Bernhard W. Anderson. New York: Harper & Row, 1963. Pp. 8-35.

Burghardt, Walter J. *Preaching: The Art and the Craft*. New York: Paulist, 1987.

Calvin, John. *Sermons from Job*. Trans. Leroy Nixon. Grand Rapids: Eerdmans, 1952.

———. *Institutes of the Christian Religion*. Ed. John T. McNeill. Trans. Ford Lewis Battles. Philadelphia: Westminster, 1960.

———. *Sermons on 2 Samuel: Chapters 1–13*. Trans. Douglas Kelly. Edinburgh: The Banner of Truth Trust, 1992.

Campbell, Charles L. *Preaching Jesus: New Directions for Homiletics in Hans Frei's Postliberal Theology*. Grand Rapids: Eerdmans, 1997.

Chapell, Bryan. *Christ-Centered Preaching: Redeeming the Expository Sermon*. Grand Rapids: Baker, 1994.

Childs, Brevard S. "The Sensus Literalis of Scripture: An Ancient and Modern Problem." In *Beitrage zur Alttestamentlichen Theologie*. Ed. Herbert Donner. Göttingen: Vandenhoeck & Ruprecht, 1977. Pp. 80-93.

------. *Biblical Theology of the Old and New Testaments*. Minneapolis: Fortress, 1992.

------. "On Reclaiming the Bible for Christian Theology." In *Reclaiming the Bible for the Church*. Ed. Carl E. Braaten, *et al*. Grand Rapids: Eerdmans, 1995. Pp. 1-17.

Chouinard, Larry. "The History of New Testament Interpretation." In *Biblical Interpretation*. Ed. F. Furman Kearley, Edward P. Myers, and Timothy D. Hadley. Grand Rapids: Baker, 1986. Pp. 195-213.

Chrysostom, John. "Homily 47 [Genesis 22]." In *Saint John Chrysostom: Homilies on Genesis. The Fathers of the Church*, Vol. 87. Trans. Robert C. Hill. Washington: Catholic University of America Press, 1992. Pp. 14-24.

Clowney, Edmund P. *Preaching and Biblical Theology*. Grand Rapids: Eerdmans, 1961.

------. "Preaching Christ from All the Scriptures." In *The Preacher and Preaching*. Ed. S. Logan, Jr. Phillipsburg, NJ: Presbyterian and Reformed, 1986. Pp. 163-91.

------. *The Unfolding Mystery: Discovering Christ in the Old Testament*. Colorado Springs: Nav Press, 1988.

------. "Preaching Christ from Biblical Theology." In *Inside the Sermon*. Ed. R. A. Bodey. Grand Rapids: Baker, 1990. Pp. 57-64.

Cosser, William. *Preaching the Old Testament*. London: Epworth, 1967.

Craddock, Fred. *The Pre-Existence of Christ in the New Testament*. Nashville: Abingdon, 1968.

------. *Preaching*. Nashville: Abingdon, 1985.

Criswell, W. A. "Preaching from the Old Testament." In *Tradition and Testament*. Ed. J. S. Feinberg. Chicago: Moody, 1981. Pp. 293-305.

Cullmann, Oscar. *Christ and Time: The Primitive Christian Conception of Time and History*. Rev. ed. Trans. Floyd V. Filson. London: SCM, 1962.

------. *Salvation in History*. Trans. S. G. Sowers. New York: Harper and Row, 1967.

Daly, Robert J. "The Hermeneutics of Origen: Existential Interpretation in the Third Century." In *The Word in the World*. Ed. Richard J. Clifford, *et al*. Cambridge, MA: Weston College Press, 1973. Pp. 135-43.

Daniélou, Jean. *From Shadows to Reality: Studies in the Biblical Typology of the Fathers*. Trans. Dom Wulstan Hibberd. Westminster, MD: Newman, 1960.

Dargan, Edwin Charles. *A History of Preaching*. Vols. 1 and 2. Grand Rapids: Baker, 1954 [1904].

Davies, W. D. *Invitation to the New Testament: A Guide to Its Main Witnesses*. Garden City, NY: Doubleday, 1969.

------. "The Jewish Sources of Matthew's Messianism." In *The Messiah: De-

velopments in Earliest Judaism and Christianity. Ed. James Charlesworth. Minneapolis: Fortress, 1992. Pp. 494-511.

Dekker, Harold. "Introduction." In John Calvin, *Sermons from Job*. Grand Rapids: Eerdmans, 1952. Pp. ix-xxxvii.

Dillard, Raymond B., and Tremper Longman III. *An Introduction to the Old Testament*. Grand Rapids: Zondervan, 1994.

Dockery, David S. "Martin Luther's Christological Hermeneutics." *GTJ* 4/2 (1983) 189-203.

————. "New Testament Interpretation: A Historical Survey." In *New Testament Criticism and Interpretation*. Ed. David A. Black and David S. Dockery. Grand Rapids: Zondervan, 1991. Pp. 40-69.

————. *Biblical Interpretation Then and Now: Contemporary Hermeneutics in the Light of the Early Church*. Grand Rapids: Baker, 1992.

————. "Typological Exegesis: Moving beyond Abuse and Neglect." In *Reclaiming the Prophetic Mantle*. Ed. George L. Klein. Nashville: Broadman, 1992. Pp. 161-78.

Dodd, C. H. *The Apostolic Preaching and Its Developments*. London: Hodder & Stoughton, 1936.

————. *According to the Scriptures: The Sub-Structure of New Testament Theology*. London: Nisbet, 1952.

Drane, John W. "Typology." *EvQ* 50 (1978) 195-210.

Duduit, Michael. "The Church's Need for Old Testament Preaching." In *Reclaiming the Prophetic Mantle*. Ed. George L. Klein. Nashville: Broadman, 1992. Pp. 9-16.

Dunn, James D. G. "The Use of the Old Testament." In *Unity and Diversity in the New Testament*. Ed. James D. G. Dunn. Philadelphia: Westminster, 1977. Pp. 81-102.

————. "Christology as an Aspect of Theology." In *The Future of Christology: Essays in Honor of Leander E. Keck*. Ed. Abraham J. Malherbe and Wayne A. Meeks. Minneapolis: Fortress, 1993. Pp. 202-12.

————. "Messianic Ideas and Their Influence on the Jesus of History." In *The Messiah: Developments in Earliest Judaism and Christianity*. Ed. James H. Charlesworth. Minneapolis: Fortress, 1992. Pp. 365-81.

Edwards, O. C., Jr. "History of Preaching." In *Concise Encyclopedia of Preaching*. Ed. William H. Willimon and Richard Lischer. Louisville: Westminster/John Knox, 1995. Pp. 184-227.

Eichrodt, Walther. *Theology of the Old Testament*. Vol. 1. Trans. J. A. Baker. London: SCM, 1961.

————. "Is Typological Exegesis an Appropriate Method?" In *Essays on Old Testament Hermeneutics*. Ed. Claus Westermann. Richmond, VA: John Knox, 1963. Pp. 224-45.

Ellis, E. Earle. *Paul's Use of the Old Testament*. Edinburgh: Oliver and Boyd, 1957.

————. "How the New Testament Uses the Old." In *New Testament Interpreta-*

tion: Essays on Principles and Methods. Ed. I. Howard Marshall. Grand Rapids: Eerdmans, 1977. Pp. 199-219.

———. "Biblical Interpretation in the New Testament Church." In *Mikra.* Ed. Martin J. Mulder and Harry Sysling. Philadelphia: Fortress, 1988. Pp. 691-725.

Ellison, H. L. *The Centrality of the Messianic Idea for the Old Testament.* London: Tyndale, 1957.

Ericson, Norman R. "The New Testament Use of the Old Testament: A Kerygmatic Approach." *JETS* 30 (1987) 337-42.

Fairbairn, Patrick. *The Typology of Scripture: Viewed in Connection with the Whole Series of the Divine Dispensations.* 6th ed. Edinburgh: T & T Clark, 1876.

Farrar, Frederic W. *History of Interpretation.* London: Macmillan, 1886.

Fee, Gordon D., and Douglas Stuart. *How to Read the Bible for All Its Worth: A Guide to Understanding the Bible.* Grand Rapids: Zondervan, 1982.

Filson, Floyd V. "The Unity of the Old and the New Testaments." *Int* 5 (1951) 134-52.

Florovsky, Georges. "Revelation and Interpretation." In *Biblical Authority for Today: A World Council of Churches Symposium on "The Biblical Authority for the Churches' Social and Political Message Today."* Ed. A. Richardson and W. Schweitzer. Philadelphia: Westminster, 1951. Pp. 163-80.

———. *Bible, Church, Tradition: An Eastern Orthodox View.* Belmont, MS: Nordland, 1972.

France, R. T. "The Servant of the Lord in the Teaching of Jesus." *TynBul* 19 (1968) 26-52.

———. *Jesus and the Old Testament: His Application of Old Testament Passages to Himself and His Mission.* London: Tyndale, 1971.

Frend, W. H. C. "The Old Testament in the Age of the Greek Apologists." *SJT* 26 (1973) 129-50.

Froelich, Karlfried. *Biblical Interpretation in the Early Church.* Philadelphia: Fortress, 1984.

Gamble, Richard C. "Exposition and Method in Calvin." *WTJ* 49 (1987) 153-65.

———. "Calvin as Theologian and Exegete: Is There Anything New?" *CTJ* 23 (1988) 178-94.

Goldingay, John. "Luther and the Bible." *SJT* 35 (1982) 33-58.

———. *Models for Interpretation of Scripture.* Grand Rapids: Eerdmans, 1995.

Goldsworthy, Graeme. *Gospel and Wisdom.* Exeter: Paternoster, 1987.

Goppelt, Leonhard. "Typos." *TDNT* 8.246-59. Trans. Geoffrey W. Bromiley. Grand Rapids: Eerdmans, 1972.

———. *Typos: The Typological Interpretation of the Old Testament in the New.* Trans. Donald H. Madvig. Grand Rapids: Eerdmans, 1982.

Gowan, Donald E. *Reclaiming the Old Testament for the Christian Pulpit.* Atlanta: John Knox, 1980.

Graesser, Carl, Jr. "Preaching from the Old Testament." *CTM* 38/8 (1967) 525-34.

Grasso, Domenico. *Proclaiming God's Message: A Study in the Theology of Preaching.* Notre Dame: University of Notre Dame Press, 1965.

Greer, Rowan A. "The Christian Bible and Its Interpretation." In *Early Biblical Interpretation.* Ed. James L. Kugel and Rowan A. Greer. Philadelphia: Westminster, 1986. Pp. 107-208.

Greidanus, Sidney. *Sola Scriptura: Problems and Principles in Preaching Historical Texts.* Toronto: Wedge, 1970.

―――. *The Modern Preacher and the Ancient Text: Interpreting and Preaching Biblical Literature.* Grand Rapids: Eerdmans, 1988.

Grogan, Geoffrey W. "The New Testament Interpretation of the Old Testament: A Comparative Study." *TynBul* 18 (1967) 54-76.

―――. "The Relationship between Prophecy and Typology." *Scottish Bulletin of Evangelical Theology* 4 (Spring 1986) 5-16.

Grollenberg, Lucas. *A Bible for Our Time: Reading the Bible in the Light of Today's Questions.* Trans. John Bowden. London: SCM, 1979.

Gundry, Robert Horton. *The Use of the Old Testament in St. Matthew's Gospel: With Special Reference to the Messianic Hope.* Leiden: Brill, 1967.

Gundry, Stanley N. "Typology as a Means of Interpretation: Past and Present." *JETS* 12/4 (1969) 233-40.

Gunneweg, A. H. J. *Understanding the Old Testament.* Trans. John Bowden. London: SCM, 1978.

Hanson, Anthony Tyrrell. *The Living Utterances of God: The New Testament Exegesis of the Old.* London: Darton, Longman and Todd, 1983.

Hanson, R. P. C. "Biblical Exegesis in the Early Church." In *Cambridge History of the Bible.* Vol. 1. Ed. P. R. Ackroyd and C. F. Evans. Cambridge: Cambridge University, 1970. Pp. 412-53.

Harrison, R. K. "The Pastor's Use of the Old Testament." *BSac* 146 (1989) 12-20, 123-31, 243-53, 263-72.

Hasel, Gerhard F. *Old Testament Theology.* Grand Rapids: Eerdmans, 1972.

―――. "Biblical Theology: Then, Now and Tomorrow." *HorBT* 4/1 (1982) 61-93.

Hays, Richard B. *Echoes of Scripture in the Letters of Paul.* New Haven: Yale University Press, 1989.

Hebert, Arthur G. *The Authority of the Old Testament.* London: Faber & Faber, 1947.

Helberg, J. L. *Verklaring en Prediking van die Ou Testament.* Potchefstroom: PTP, 1983.

Hendrix, Scott H. "Luther against the Background of the History of Biblical Interpretation." *Int* 37 (1983) 229-39.

Hesselink, I. John. "Calvin and Heilsgeschichte." In *Oikonomia: Heilsgeschichte als Thema der Theologie.* Ed. Felix Christ. Hamburg: Herbert Reich, 1967. Pp. 163-70.

Higgins, A. J. B. *The Christian Significance of the Old Testament.* London: Independent, 1949.

Hoekstra, H. *Gereformeerde Homiletiek.* Wageningen: Zomer & Keuning, 1926.

Holwerda, B. ". . . *Begonnen Hebbende van Moses.*" Terneuzen: D. H. Littooij, 1953.

Holwerda, David E. "Eschatology and History: A Look at Calvin's Eschatological Vision." In *Readings in Calvin's Theology.* Ed. Donald K. McKim. Grand Rapids: Baker, 1984. Pp. 311-42. (First published in *Exploring the Heritage of John Calvin.* Ed. David E. Holwerda. Grand Rapids: Baker, 1976. Pp. 110-39.)

————. *Jesus and Israel: One Covenant or Two?* Grand Rapids: Eerdmans, 1995.

Houlden, James L. *The Interpretation of the Bible in the Church.* London: SCM, 1995.

Hull, William E. "Called to Preach." In *Heralds to a New Age.* Ed. Don M. Aycock. Elgin, IL.: Brethren, 1985. Pp. 41-48.

Hummel, Horace D. "The Old Testament Basis of Typological Interpretation." *Biblical Research* 9 (1964) 38-50.

Irenaeus. *Proof of the Apostolic Preaching.* Trans. J. P. Smit. Westminster, MD: Newman, 1952.

————. *St. Irenaeus against Heresies.* Trans. Dominic J. Unger. New York: Paulist, 1992.

Jensen, Joseph. *God's Word to Israel.* Rev. ed. Wilmington, DE: Michael Glazier, 1982.

Juel, Donald H. *Messianic Exegesis: Christological Interpretation of the Old Testament in Early Christianity.* Philadelphia: Fortress, 1988.

Kahmann, J. *The Bible on the Preaching of the Word.* DePere, WI: St. Norbert Abbey, 1965.

Kaiser, Walter C. *Toward an Exegetical Theology: Biblical Exegesis for Preaching and Teaching.* Grand Rapids: Baker, 1981.

————. *Toward Old Testament Ethics.* Grand Rapids: Zondervan, 1983.

————. *The Uses of the Old Testament in the New.* Chicago: Moody, 1985.

————. *Toward Rediscovering the Old Testament.* Grand Rapids: Zondervan, 1987.

————. *The Messiah in the Old Testament.* Grand Rapids: Zondervan, 1995.

Kaiser, Walter C., and Moisés Silva. *An Introduction to Biblical Hermeneutics.* Grand Rapids: Zondervan, 1994.

Kepple, Robert J. "An Analysis of Antiochene Exegesis of Galatians 4:24-26." *WTJ* 39 (1976-77) 239-49.

Kingsbury, Jack Dean. *Jesus Christ in Matthew, Mark, and Luke.* Philadelphia: Fortress, 1981.

Klein, William W., Craig L. Blomberg, and Robert L. Hubbard, Jr. *Introduction to Biblical Interpretation.* Dallas: Word, 1993.

Knox, John. *Chapters in a Life of Paul.* Rev. ed. Macon, GA: Mercer University Press, 1987.

Koole, J. L. *De Overname van het Oude Testament door de Christelijke Kerk.* Hilversum: Schipper, 1938.

Kraeling, Emil G. *The Old Testament since the Reformation.* London: Lutterworth, 1955.

Kraus, Hans-Joachim. "Calvin's Exegetical Principles." *Int* 31 (1977) 8-18.

Kuiper, Rinck Bouke. "Scriptural Preaching." In *The Infallible Word.* Ed. Ned B. Stonehouse and Paul Woolley. Philadelphia: Presbyterian Guardian, 1946. Pp. 208-54.

Kuske, Martin. *The Old Testament as the Book of Christ: An Appraisal of Bonhoeffer's Interpretation.* Trans. S. T. Kimbrough, Jr. Philadelphia: Westminster, 1976.

Kuyper, Lester J. *The Scripture Unbroken: A Perceptive Study of the Old and New Testament.* Grand Rapids: Eerdmans, 1978.

Lampe, G. W. H. "Typological Exegesis." *Th* 51 (1953) 201-8.

———. "The Reasonableness of Typology." In *Essays on Typology.* Ed. G. W. H. Lampe and K. J. Woollcombe. Naperville, IL: A. R. Allenson, 1957. Pp. 9-38.

Larsen, David L. *The Anatomy of Preaching: Identifying the Issues in Preaching Today.* Grand Rapids: Baker, 1989.

LaSor, William S. "The Messiah: An Evangelical Christian View." In *Evangelicals and Jews in Conversation on Scripture, Theology and History.* Ed. M. H. Tanenbaum. Grand Rapids: Baker, 1978. Pp. 76-95.

———. "Prophecy, Inspiration and Sensus Plenior." *TynBul* 29 (1978) 49-60.

Leith, John H. "John Calvin — Theologian of the Bible." *Int* 25 (1971) 329-44.

Le Roux, Johann. "Die Betekenis van die Verhoudinge in die Goddelike Drie-Eenheid vir die Prediking: 'n Homiletiese Ondersoek vanuit Johannes 14–15." Th.D. dissertation. Potchefstroom: University of Potchefstroom, 1991.

Lienhard, Joseph T. "Origen as Homilist." In *Preaching in the Patristic Age.* Ed. David G. Hunter. New York/Mahwah, NJ: Paulist, 1989.

Lindars, Barnabas. "The Place of the Old Testament in the Formation of New Testament Theology." *NTS* 23 (1977) 59-66.

Lischer, Richard. *A Theology of Preaching: The Dynamics of the Gospel.* Nashville: Abingdon, 1981.

———. *Theories of Preaching: Selected Readings in the Homiletical Tradition.* Durham, NC: Labyrinth, 1987.

Long, Thomas G. *The Witness of Preaching.* Louisville: Westminster/John Knox, 1989.

Longenecker, Richard N. "Can We Reproduce the Exegesis of the New Testament?" *TynBul* 21 (1970) 3-38.

———. *Biblical Exegesis in the Apostolic Period.* Grand Rapids: Eerdmans, 1975.

———. "Who Is the Prophet Talking About: Some Reflections on the New Testament's Use in the Old." *Themelios* 13 (October-November 1987) 4-8.

Longman, Tremper, III. *Literary Approaches to Biblical Interpretation*. Grand Rapids: Zondervan, 1987.

Luther, Martin. *A Brief Instruction on What to Look for and Expect in the Gospels*. Trans. E. Theodore Bachmann. A selection reprinted in Richard Lischer, *Theories of Preaching: Selected Readings in the Homiletical Tradition*. Durham, NC: Labyrinth, 1987. Pp. 95-99.

———. ". . . Answer to the Superchristian, Superspiritual, and Superlearned Book of Goat Emser of Leipzig." Reprinted in Richard Lischer, *Theories of Preaching: Selected Readings in the Homiletical Tradition*. Durham, NC: Labyrinth, 1987. Pp. 151-58.

Lys, Daniel. "Who Is Our President? From Text to Sermon on 1 Samuel 12:12." *Int* 21 (1967) 401-20.

McCartney, Dan, and Charles Clayton. *Let the Reader Understand: A Guide to Interpreting and Applying the Bible*. Wheaton, IL: Victor Books, 1994.

McConville, J. Gordon. "Messianic Interpretation of the Old Testament in Modern Context." In *The Lord's Anointed*. Ed. P. Satterthwaite, *et al.* Grand Rapids: Baker, 1995. Pp. 1-17.

McCurley, Foster R. *Proclaiming the Promise: Christian Preaching from the Old Testament*. Philadelphia: Fortress, 1974.

———. "Confessional Propria as Hermeneutic — Old Testament." In *Studies in Lutheran Hermeneutics*. Ed. John Reumann. Philadelphia: Fortress, 1979. Pp. 233-51.

———. *Wrestling with the Word: Christian Preaching from the Hebrew Bible*. Valley Forge, PA: Trinity Press International, 1996.

McKane, W. "Calvin as an Old Testament Commentator." *NGTT* 25/3 (July 1984) 250-59.

McKenzie, John L. "The Significance of the Old Testament for Christian Faith in Roman Catholicism." In *The Old Testament and Christian Faith: A Theological Discussion*. Ed. Bernhard W. Anderson. New York: Harper and Row, 1963. Pp. 102-14.

Mackenzie, J. A. Ross. "Valiant against All." *Int* 22 (1968) 18-35.

Marshall, I. Howard. "An Assessment of Recent Developments." In *It Is Written: Scripture Citing Scripture*. Ed. D. A. Carson, *et al.* Cambridge: Cambridge University Press, 1988. Pp. 1-21.

Mathews, Kenneth A. "Preaching Historical Narrative." In *Reclaiming the Prophetic Mantle: Preaching the Old Testament Faithfully*. Ed. George L. Klein. Nashville: Broadman, 1992. Pp. 19-50.

Mayer, Herbert T. "The Old Testament in the Pulpit." *CTM* 35 (1964) 603-8.

Mays, James Luther. "Isaiah's Royal Theology and the Messiah." In *Reading and Preaching the Book of Isaiah*. Ed. Christopher R. Seitz. Philadelphia: Fortress, 1988. Pp. 39-51.

———. *The Lord Reigns: A Theological Handbook to the Psalms*. Louisville: Westminster, 1994.

Mellor, Enid B. "The Old Testament for Jews and Christians Today." In *The*

Making of the Old Testament. Ed. Enid B. Mellor. Cambridge: University Press, 1972. Pp. 167-201.

Meuser, Fred W. *Luther the Preacher.* Minneapolis: Augsburg, 1983.

Mickelsen, A. Berkeley. *Interpreting the Bible.* Grand Rapids: Eerdmans, 1963.

Miller, Donald G. *The Way to Biblical Preaching.* Nashville: Abingdon, 1957.

———. "Biblical Theology and Preaching." *SJT* 11 (1958) 389-405.

Moo, Douglas J. "The Problem of *Sensus Plenior.*" In *Hermeneutics, Authority, and Canon.* Ed. D. A. Carson and John D. Woodbridge. Grand Rapids: Zondervan, 1986. Pp. 175-211.

———. "The Law of Moses or the Law of Christ." In *Continuity and Discontinuity: Perspectives on the Relationship between the Old and New Testament.* Ed. John S. Feinberg. Westchester, IL: Crossway, 1988. Pp. 203-18, 373-75.

Mounce, Robert H. *The Essential Nature of New Testament Preaching.* Grand Rapids: Eerdmans, 1960.

Muller, Richard A. "The Hermeneutic of Promise and Fulfillment." In *The Bible in the Sixteenth Century.* Ed. D. C. Steinmetz. Durham, NC: Duke University Press, 1990. Pp. 68-82.

———. *Holy Scripture: The Cognitive Foundation of Theology.* Vol. 2 of *Post-Reformation Reformed Dogmatics.* Grand Rapids: Baker, 1993.

———. "Biblical Interpretation in the Era of the Reformation: The View from the Middle Ages." In *Biblical Interpretation in the Era of the Reformation.* Ed. Richard A. Muller and John L. Thompson. Grand Rapids: Eerdmans, 1996. Pp. 3-21.

Murphy, Roland E. "Patristic and Medieval Exegesis — Help or Hindrance?" *CBQ* 43 (1981) 505-16.

Newbigin, Lesslie. *Foolishness to the Greeks: The Gospel and Western Culture.* Grand Rapids: Eerdmans, 1986.

Newman, Elbert Benjamin, Jr. "A Critical Evaluation of the Contributions of the Hermeneutical Approaches of Representative Old Testament Scholars to an Appropriation of the Old Testament for Christian Preaching." Ph.D. thesis. Fort Worth, TX: Southwestern Baptist Theological Seminary, 1986.

Nixon, Leroy. *John Calvin, Expository Preacher.* Grand Rapids: Eerdmans, 1950.

Nygren, Anders. *The Significance of the Bible for the Church.* Philadelphia: Fortress, 1963.

Ogden, Schubert M. *The Point of Christology.* San Francisco: Harper and Row, 1982.

Olson, Dennis T. "Rediscovering Lost Treasure: Forgotten Preaching Texts of the Old Testament." *Journal for Preachers* 13/4 (1990) 2-10.

Oosterhoff, B. J. *Om de Schriften te Openen.* Kampen: Kok, 1987.

Origen, *First Principles.* In Karlfried Froelich, *Biblical Interpretation in the Early Church.* Philadelphia: Fortress, 1984. Pp. 48-78.

Parker, T. H. L. *Calvin's Old Testament Commentaries.* Edinburgh: Clark, 1986.

————. *Calvin's Preaching*. Louisville: Westminster/John Knox, 1992.

Petersen, Rodney. "Continuity and Discontinuity: The Debate throughout Church History." In *Continuity and Discontinuity: Perspectives on the Relationship between the Old and New Testament*. Ed. John S. Feinberg. Westchester, IL: Crossway, 1988. Pp. 17-34.

Piper, John. *The Supremacy of God in Preaching*. Grand Rapids: Baker, 1990.

Poythress, Vern S. *The Shadow of Christ in the Law of Moses*. Brentwood, TN: Wolgemuth and Hyatt, 1991.

Preus, James S. "Old Testament *Promissio* and Luther's New Hermeneutic." *Harvard Theological Review* 60 (1967) 145-61.

————. *From Shadow to Promise: Old Testament Interpretation from Augustine to the Young Luther*. Cambridge, MA: Cambridge University Press, 1969.

Preus, Robert D. "A Response to the Unity of the Bible." In *Hermeneutics, Inerrancy, and the Bible*. Ed. Earl D. Radmacher and Robert D. Preus. Grand Rapids: Zondervan, 1984. Pp. 669-90.

Preuss, Horst D. *Das Alte Testament in Christlicher Predigt*. Berlin: W. Kohlhammer, 1984.

Provan, Iain W. "The Messiah in the Book of Kings." In *The Lord's Anointed*. Ed. P. Satterthwaite, *et al.* Grand Rapids: Baker, 1995. Pp. 67-85.

Puckett, David L. *John Calvin's Exegesis of the Old Testament*. Louisville: Westminster, 1995.

Rad, Gerhard von. "Das Christuszeugnis des Alten Testaments." *Theologische Blätter* (1935) 249-54.

————. *Old Testament Theology*. Vols. 1 and 2. Trans. D. M. G. Stalker. Edinburgh: Oliver and Boyd, 1962, 1965.

————. "Typological Interpretation of the Old Testament." Trans. J. Bright. In *Essays on Old Testament Hermeneutics*. Ed. Claus Westermann. Richmond: John Knox, 1963. Pp. 17-39.

————. *Biblical Interpretations in Preaching*. Trans. John E. Steely. Nashville: Abingdon, 1977.

————. *God at Work in Israel*. Trans. John H. Merks. Nashville: Abingdon, 1980.

Ramm, Bernard. *Protestant Biblical Interpretation: A Textbook of Hermeneutics*. Grand Rapids: Baker, 1970.

Rendtorff, Rolf. "Towards a New Christian Reading of the Hebrew Bible." *Immanuel* 15 (Winter 1982-83) 13-21.

————. *Canon and Theology: Overtures to an Old Testament Theology*. Minneapolis: Fortress, 1993.

Reu, M. *Homiletics: A Manual of the Theory and Practice of Preaching*. Trans. Albert Steinhaeuser. Grand Rapids: Baker, 1967 [1924].

Richardson, Alan. "Is the Old Testament the Propaedeutic to Christian Faith?" In *The Old Testament and Christian Faith*. Ed. Bernhard W. Anderson. New York: Harper & Row, 1963. Pp. 36-48.

Ridderbos, Herman. *The Coming of the Kingdom*. Trans. H. de Jongste. Ed. Raymond O. Zorn. Presbyterian and Reformed, 1962; reprint St. Catharines, ON: Paideia, 1978.

————. *Paul: An Outline of His Theology.* Grand Rapids: Eerdmans, 1975.

Ridenhour, Thomas E. "The Old Testament and Preaching." *CurTM* 20 (1993) 253-58.

Robinson, H. Wheeler. *Corporate Personality in Ancient Israel.* Rev. ed. Philadelphia: Fortress, 1964 [1935].

Robinson, Haddon W. *Biblical Preaching: The Development and Delivery of Expository Messages.* Grand Rapids: Baker, 1980.

Roehrs, Walter R. "The Typological Use of the Old Testament in the New Testament." *Concordia Journal* 10/6 (1984) 204-16.

Rogers, Jack B., and Donald K. McKim. *The Authority and Interpretation of the Bible: An Historical Approach.* San Francisco: Harper & Row, 1979.

Rogers, John B., Jr. "The Foolishness of Preaching." *Int* 45 (1991) 241-52.

Rogerson, John, Christopher Rowland, and Barnabas Lindars. *The Study and Use of the Bible.* Grand Rapids: Eerdmans, 1988.

Runia, Klaas. "The Hermeneutics of the Reformers." *CTJ* 19 (1984) 121-52.

————. "Some Crucial Issues in Biblical Interpretation." *CTJ* 24 (1989) 300-315.

Russell, S. H. "Calvin and the Messianic Interpretation of the Psalms." *SJT* 21 (1968) 37-47.

Sabourin, Leopold. *The Bible and Christ: The Unity of the Two Testaments.* New York: Alba House, 1980.

Selman, Martin J. "Messianic Mysteries." In *The Lord's Anointed.* Ed. P. Satterthwaite, *et al.* Grand Rapids: Baker, 1995. Pp. 281-302.

Sharp, Jeffrey R. "Typology and the Message of Hebrews." *East Asia Journal of Theology* 4/2 (1986) 95-103.

Shires, Henry M. *Finding the Old Testament in the New.* Philadelphia: Westminster, 1974.

Smith, Dwight Moody. "The Use of the Old Testament in the New." In *The Use of the Old Testament in the New and Other Essays.* Ed. James M. Efird. Durham, NC: Duke University Press, 1972. Pp. 3-65.

Snodgrass, Klyne R. "The Use of the Old Testament in the New." In *New Testament Criticism and Interpretation.* Ed. D. Black, *et al.* Grand Rapids: Zondervan, 1991. Pp. 407-34.

Spurgeon, Charles Haddon. *The Metropolitan Tabernacle Pulpit: Sermons Preached by C. H. Spurgeon.* Vols. 37, 45, 47. London: Passmore & Alabaster, 1881, 1899, 1901.

————. *Christ in the Old Testament: Sermons on the Foreshadowing of Our Lord in Old Testament History, Ceremony and Prophecy.* London: Passmore & Alabaster, 1899.

————. *Lectures to My Students.* Selections reprinted in Helmut Thielicke, *Encounter with Spurgeon.* Grand Rapids: Baker, 1975 (reprint of Fortress 1963). Pp. 47-246.

Steimle, Edmund A. "Preaching as the Word Made Relevant." *LuthQ* 6 (1954) 11-22.

Stek, John H. "The Message of the Book of Jonah." *CTJ* 4 (1969) 23-50.

———. "Biblical Typology Yesterday and Today." *CTJ* 5 (1970) 133-62.

———. "Salvation, Justice and Liberation in the Old Testament." *CTJ* 13 (1978) 133-65.

———. "Introduction: Psalms." *The NIV Study Bible*. Grand Rapids: Zondervan, 1985.

———. "'Covenant' Overload in Reformed Theology." *CTJ* 29 (1994) 12-41.

Stewart, James S. *Heralds of God*. London: Hodder & Stoughton, 1946.

———. *A Faith to Proclaim*. The Lyman Beecher Lectures at Yale University. London: Hodder and Stoughton, 1953.

Storley, Calvin. "Reclaiming the Old Testament." *LuthQ* 1 (Winter 1987) 487-94.

Stott, John R. W. *Between Two Worlds: The Art of Preaching in the Twentieth Century*. Grand Rapids: Eerdmans, 1982.

Strydom, Marthinus Christiaan. *Die Aard van die Prediking oor Bybelkarakters*. Th.D. thesis. Bloemfontein: UOVS, 1988.

Talbert, John David. "Charles Haddon Spurgeon's Christological Homiletics: A Critical Evaluation of Selected Sermons from Old Testament Texts." Ph.D. thesis. Fort Worth, TX: Southwestern Baptist Theological Seminary, 1989.

Thielicke, Helmut. *Encounter with Spurgeon*. Trans. John W. Doberstein. Grand Rapids: Baker, 1975 [1963].

Thiselton, Anthony C. *New Horizons in Hermeneutics*. London: Harper Collins, 1992.

Thompson, John L. "Preaching as a Means of Grace in the Theology of Martin Luther." *Studia Biblica et Theologica* 12 (1982) 43-71.

Toombs, Lawrence E. *The Old Testament in Christian Preaching*. Philadelphia: Westminster, 1961.

Tucker, Gene M. "Reading and Preaching the Old Testament." In *Listening to the Word*. Ed. Gail R. O'Day and Thomas G. Long. Nashville: Abingdon, 1993. Pp. 33-51.

Unger, Merrill F. *Principles of Expository Preaching*, 1955. Grand Rapids: Zondervan, 1955.

VanGemeren, Willem A. "Israel as the Hermeneutical Crux in the Interpretation of Prophecy." *WTJ* 46 (1984) 254-97.

———. *The Progress of Redemption: The Story of Salvation from Creation to the New Jerusalem*. Grand Rapids: Zondervan, 1988.

Van Groningen, Gerard. *Messianic Revelation in the Old Testament*. Grand Rapids: Baker, 1990.

Van Leeuwen, Raymond C. "No Other Gods." *Theological Forum* 24 (November 1996) 29-42.

Van 't Veer, M. B. "Christologische Prediking over de Historische Stof van het

Oude Testament." In *Van den Dienst des Woords*. Ed. R. Schippers. Goes: Oosterbaan and Le Cointre, 1944. Pp. 117-67.

Van Zyl, H. C. "Die Nuwe Testament se Gebruik van die Ou Testament — Model of Norm?" *Fax Theologica* 6/1 (1986) 37-77.

Veenhof, C. *Predik het Woord*. Goes: Oosterbaan and Le Cointre, 1944.

Verhoef, Pieter A. "Calvyn oor Messiasverwagting in die Ou Testament." *NGTT* 31/1 (1990) 112-17.

Vischer, Wilhelm. *The Witness of the Old Testament to Christ*. Trans. of *Das Christuszeugnis des Alte Testaments*, vol. 1, 1935. Trans. A. B. Crabtree. London: Lutterworth, 1949.

————. *Das Christuszeugnis des Alten Testaments*. Vol. 2. Zurich: Evangelischer, 1944.

————. "Everywhere the Scripture Is about Christ Alone." In *The Old Testament and Christian Faith*. Ed. B. W. Anderson. New York: Harper and Row, 1963. Pp. 90-101.

Von Rad, Gerhard. See Rad, Gerhard von.

Vos, Geerhardus. *Biblical Theology: Old and New Testament*. Grand Rapids: Eerdmans, 1948.

Vriezen, T. C. *An Outline of Old Testament Theology*. Rev. ed. Trans. S. Neuijen. Oxford: Basil Blackwell, 1970.

Wainwright, Arthur. *Beyond Biblical Criticism: Encountering Jesus in Scripture*. London: SPCK, 1982.

Waltke, Bruce K. "Kingdom Promises as Spiritual." In *Continuity and Discontinuity: Perspectives on the Relationship between the Old and New Testament*. Ed. John S. Feinberg. Westchester, IL: Crossway, 1988. Pp. 263-87.

Westermann, Claus. "The Way of the Promise through the Old Testament." In *The Old Testament and Christian Faith*. Ed. Bernhard W. Anderson. New York: Harper and Row, 1963. Pp. 200-224.

White, James B. "A Critical Examination of Wilhelm Vischer's Hermeneutic of the Old Testament." Th.M. thesis. Grand Rapids: Calvin Theological Seminary, 1969.

Wiles, Maurice F. "Origen as Biblical Scholar." In *The Cambridge History of the Bible*. Vol. 1. Ed. P. R. Ackroyd and C. F. Evans. Cambridge: Cambridge University Press, 1970. Pp. 454-89.

————. "Theodore of Mopsuestia as Representative of the Antiochene School." In *The Cambridge History of the Bible*. Vol. 1. Ed. P. R. Ackroyd and C. F. Evans. Cambridge: Cambridge University Press, 1970. Pp. 489-510.

Williams, Mead C. "Preaching Christ." *Princeton Theological Review* 4 (1906) 191-205.

Willimon, William H. *Peculiar Speech: Preaching to the Baptized*. Grand Rapids: Eerdmans, 1992.

Wilson, Marvin R. *Our Father Abraham*. Grand Rapids: Eerdmans, 1989.

Wilson, Paul Scott. *A Concise History of Preaching*. Nashville: Abingdon, 1992.

Wood, A. Skevington. "Luther as a Preacher." *EvQ* 21 (1949) 109-21.

———. *Luther's Principles of Biblical Interpretation.* London: Tyndale Press, 1960.

———. *The Principles of Biblical Interpretation: As Enunciated by Irenaeus, Origen, Augustine, Luther and Calvin.* Grand Rapids: Zondervan, 1967.

Woollcombe, K. J. "The Biblical Origins and Patristic Development of Typology." *Essays on Typology.* Ed. G. W. H. Lampe and K. J. Woollcombe. Naperville, IL: A. R. Allenson, 1957. Pp. 39-75.

Woudstra, Marten H. "Israel and the Church: A Case for Continuity." In *Continuity and Discontinuity: Perspectives on the Relationship between the Old and New Testament.* Ed. John S. Feinberg. Westchester, IL: Crossway, 1988. Pp. 221-38, 376-80.

Wright, Christopher J. H. *Knowing Jesus through the Old Testament: Rediscovering the Roots of Our Faith.* Downers Grove: InterVarsity, 1992.

Wright, Nicholas Thomas. *The New Testament and the People of God.* London: SPCK, 1992.

———. *Jesus and the Victory of God.* London: SPCK, 1996.

Zimmerli, Walther. "Promise and Fulfillment." In *Essays on Old Testament Hermeneutics.* Ed. Claus Westermann. Richmond: John Knox, 1963. Pp. 89-122.

SCRIPTURE INDEX

Genesis
2:18-25   37
3:15   141, 239, 245-48
6:9–8:22   320-25
11:1-9   345
12:1-9   264
12:3   264
17:9-14   44, 232
17:12-14   271
18:2   79
22   157-58, 170
22:1   161
22:1-19   292-318
22:2   270
22:18   136, 247
24   253
28:10-22   263, 267, 270
32:22-32   35-36
37   345

Exodus
3:1-12   170
3:2   142
13:21-22   263-64
15:22-25   158
15:22-27   325-28
17:8-16   328-32
20:2-3   264
20:8   274
20:10   271-72

Leviticus
11   149

18   345
18:24-30   264
19:8   264

Numbers
19   175, 332-37
19:1-10   73
27:16-21   169

Deuteronomy
6:4   177
6:5   264
26:1-11   264
26:1-15   345
26:12-15   267-68, 270

Joshua
2   258, 337-39
6   338-44

Judges
6–8   273

1 Samuel
17   238-39

2 Samuel
5:1-12   251-52
7:16   245
7:21   156-57

2 Kings
5:1-27   43

Psalms
1   265
2:7   138
17:3   130
22   93, 271
23   265
30   346
31:5   271
44:22-26   275-76
46   265
72   138, 346
78   193
84   239-40
98:9   271
109:8-14   275
137:8-9   275
137:9   87n.81, 101-2

Proverbs
8:22-36   268
15:29   271
16:3   346
23:4-5   265-66
30:8   266

Ecclesiastes
11:7–12:8   276, 346
12:1-8   240

Isaiah
7:11-17   243
7:14   40, 139-40
7:14-16   210

40:1-11	264	5:17	45	**Romans**
43:1-7	345	5:21	133	5:12-19	217-18
49:6	264	5:21-48	225	8:21	206
50:4-11	264, 270	12:40-42	216-17	8:32	312
51:4-8	264-65	21:4-5	244	10:14-15	181
52:10	143	28:19-20	212	11:17	262
52:13–53:12	203			16:25-26	50
53	209	**Mark**		
61:1-4	242-43	1:1-4	58-59	**1 Corinthians**
63:1	137-38	1:13	219	2:2	6
		1:14-15	59	10:1-4	187
Jeremiah		4:3-20	88	15	205-6
31:31-34	134	4:39	224	15:3-4	58
31:33	216			
		Luke		**2 Corinthians**
Ezekiel		3:38	60, 204	3:6	99, 128
1:28	274	4:16-30	55-56	3:15-16	52, 201
18:4	274	4:18-21	194	
		4:21	209, 243	**Galatians**
Daniel		11:20	66	3:29	212, 262
7:9-14	64	14:25-26	100, 184	4:22-31	187
7:13-14	203, 209	24:25-27	56	
7:27	143	24:44	56, 60	**Ephesians**
				1:8-10	205
Hosea		**John**		2:12-13	262
11:1	93	1:1-14	61	
		1:14	219	**1 Timothy**
Joel		1:29, 36	219	3:16	50
2:31	242	3:14-15	217	
		3:16	313	**2 Timothy**
Zechariah		5:39	56, 61, 140-41	3:15-17	26
9:9-10	244	5:46	61	
		6:49-51	217	**Hebrews**
Malachi		14:2	66	Book of	219-20
4:1-6	345	14:9	49-50	1:1-2	49
		19:33-36	219	
				1 Peter
Matthew		**Acts**		1:12	136
1:1	59, 204	2:14-34	57	3:20-21	246
1:1-17	190	3:11-26	57	
1:22-23	210, 243	4:12	12	**Revelation**
2:4-6	210	8	57	21:1	212
5–7	219, 264	13:16-41	57	
5:5	212	17:1-11	57-58	

SUBJECT INDEX

Allegorical interpretation, 37, 70-90,
101-3, 104, 112-13, 128, 155, 158-59,
175-76, 187-88, 236, 320, 325, 328-
29, 332-33, 337-38
    allegorical equivalents list, 89n.85
Allegories, 88
Ambrose, 98, 99
Analogia fidei. See Rule of faith
Analogy, 220-22, 261-63
    examples of, 263-66, 310-11, 314,
    323, 327, 331, 335, 341-42
Anthropomorphism, 131
Application, 239, 248-49, 262, 280-81,
287, 291
Aquinas, Thomas, 106-7
Augustine, 99-103
Author, intention of, 36, 95, 100, 106,
107, 108, 129, 138, 140, 229-30, 233,
285. *See also* Holy Spirit: intention
of

Barnabas, Epistle of, 72-73
Bible, unity of, 31-32, 38, 44-53, 132-
33, 167-68, 174-75
Biographical preaching. *See*
Preaching: biographical
Bultmann, Rudolf, 21-22

Calvin, John, 127-51
Cassian, John, 103-5
Characters, biblical, 297-98
Chiasm, 284, 300, 321n.2, 329n.5
Christ. *See also* Preaching Christ
    as Angel of Yahweh, 142, 197

as God, 196-97
as link between the Testaments, 49-
    50
as Logos in Old Testament, 3, 54,
    74, 79, 141-42, 171-72, 174
as promise in Old Testament. *See*
    Promise-fulfillment
as Servant of Yahweh. *See* Servant
    of Yahweh
as Son of Man, 64, 209
historical Jesus, 202n.76
interpretation of Old Testament,
    202-3, 209, 216-17
preaching of. *See* Preaching: of
    Christ
resurrection of, 196
Christocentric method, 227-77, 319-46
Christological interpretation. *See*
    Interpretation: christological
Christomonism, 162, 176, 178, 228
Chrysostom, John, 94-96, 309
Clement of Alexandria, 81-82
Clement of Rome, 72, 337
Commentaries, 282, 286, 301
Congregational need. *See* Needs of
    hearers
Context
    canonical. *See* Interpretation: ca-
        nonical
    historical setting. *See* Interpreta-
        tion: historical
    literary, 130, 282-83, 295-96, 299-300
Continuity between Old Testament

and New Testament, 45, 48, 232, 263

Contrast, 134, 224-25, 271-72, 313, 331
   centers in Christ, 272
   examples of, 273-76, 313, 325, 328, 332, 337, 343

Corporate personality, 197-98, 246-48

Covenant of grace, 48, 132-33

Creation–Fall–Redemption–New Creation, 194, 235. *See also* Redemptive history

Creeds. *See* Rule of faith

Cross of Christ. *See* Preaching Christ: Jesus' cross

Decalogue, 131, 271-72

Discontinuity between Old Testament and New Testament, 23, 48, 224-25, 232

Eastern Orthodox interpretation, 105, 254

Eisegesis. *See* Interpretation: eisegesis

Figure(s) of speech, 91, 93, 115, 131, 229

Fourfold interpretation, 98-109

Fulfillment. *See* Progressive fulfillment; Promise-fulfillment

Fuller sense, 41, 233, 247, 252

Generalizing, 35, 161, 293-94

Genre(s)
   law, 261, 264, 270, 273-74
   narrative, 238-39, 245-48, 260, 263-64, 269-70, 273, 284, 290, 296-97, 320-21
   prophecy, 242-44, 261, 264-65, 270, 274
   psalm, 239-40, 244, 261, 265, 270, 271, 274-76, 290
   wisdom, 240, 265, 271, 276

Genre mistake, 36, 88, 162

Gnosticism (Gnostic), 18, 70

Goal. *See* Sermon: goal; Text: goal

God
   the Father, 179-81

Holy Spirit, 181-82
the Son, 196-97
sovereignty of, 127
Triune, 147, 181-82

Harnack, Adolf von, 20-21

Hearer identification, 302, 304-5

Hermeneutical circle, 52, 136-37, 201

Hermeneutical principles, 77-78, 113-20, 128-37, 228-34, 280-89

Historical context. *See* Interpretation: historical

Historical-critical method. *See* Interpretation: historical-critical

Historical Jesus, 202n.76

Historical narrative. *See* Genre: narrative

History of redemption. *See* Redemptive history

History of revelation. *See* Progression in revelation

Holy Spirit
   intention of, 107, 116n.21, 140
   preaching the, 181-82

Homily, 85, 147-48, 231

Identification. *See* Hearer identification

Individualism, 162

Intention of author. *See* Author: intention of

Interpretation
   allegorical. *See* Allegorical interpretation
   anagogical. *See* Interpretation: eschatological
   beyond literal, 131
   canonical, 51, 136-37, 230-34, 288, 306-7
   christocentric, 51, 140-45, 232-34, 288, 307-13
   christological, 111-26
   Eastern Orthodox, 105, 254
   eisegesis, 228, 252
   eschatological, 104, 235-37, 243-44, 248, 258
   fourfold, 98-109

grammatical-historical. *See* Interpretation: literal
historical, 77, 100-101, 129-30, 138-39, 148-49, 228-30, 257, 265, 284-86, 300-302. *See also* Interpretation: literal
historical-critical, 17, 38, 62, 165-66, 236, 240-41, 249
Jewish, 186-89
literal, 80, 81, 83, 91, 93-94, 95, 101, 104, 105, 106, 130, 154, 188, 257
literal-prophetic, 114-16
literary, 229, 284-85, 297-300. *See also* Context: literary
messianic, 55n.58
moral, 84-85, 104-5, 151
need addressed, 229-30
redemptive-historical, 230-34, 288, 307. *See also* Redemptive-historical progression
Roman Catholic, 45, 109n.168
spiritual, 80, 81, 83-85, 106, 152, 154-55, 156
theocentric, 137-49, 230, 232-34, 286, 302
threefold, 84-87, 98
tropological. *See* Interpretation: moral
twofold, 81
typological. *See* Typology
Irenaeus, 75-80
Israel and the church, 221-22, 262-63

Justin Martyr, 73-75, 320, 328-29, 338

Kingdom history. *See* Redemptive history
Kingdom of God, 12, 30, 66. *See also* Interpretation: eschatological

Law, third use of, 133-34
Law and gospel, 21, 116-19, 125-26

Lectionary, 16-17, 294
Logos. *See* Christ: as Logos
Longitudinal themes, 176, 222-24, 266-68, 274

examples of, 267-68, 311, 314, 323-24, 327-28, 331, 335-36, 342-43
Luther, Martin, 111-26

Marcion, 18-19, 24, 70-71
Messianic age, 195-96
Miracles. *See* Preaching Christ: Jesus' miracles
Moralizing(istic). *See* Preaching: moralistic

Narrative. *See* Genre: narrative
Needs of hearers, 280-81, 285, 289, 291, 294, 315, 316
New Testament
    not a textbook on biblical hermeneutics, 189-91
    use of Old Testament, 50-51, 185-89, 203-25
New Testament references, 50-51, 170, 185, 233-34, 269-71, 274
    examples of, 269-71, 311-13, 314, 324, 328, 331-32, 336-37, 342-43
Nicholas of Lyra, 105n.161, 107

Old Testament
    as Christian, 25-26, 44-46
    as law, 21, 116-19, 125-26
    as non-Christian, 37-40
    as open to the future, 46-47
    as pre-Christian, 40-44
    as related to New Testament, 29-32, 37-39, 41-42, 46-53, 116-19, 132-36, 148-49, 166, 167-68, 174-75
    benefits of preaching Christ from, 62-67
    difficulties in preaching, 22-25
    interpretation from New Testament perspective, 183-85, 199-203
    lack of preaching from, 16-25
    necessity of preaching from, 15-32, 62-67
    reasons for preaching, 25-32
    rejection of, 18-22, 39, 163-64
    teachings not in New Testament, 27-28
    theocentric, 177

witness to Christ, 53-62, 78-79, 119-20, 135-36, 168
Oral style, 292
Origen, 82-87, 337

Pairing, 42-44
Philo, 80
Preaching
  biographical, 34-36, 281, 293
  character-imitation, 34-36, 150-51, 161, 281, 292-93
  Christ-centered. *See* Preaching Christ
  expository, 231, 281-82, 290
  God-centered, 36-37, 145-48, 178-82
  human-centered, 34-36
  moralistic, 36, 150-51, 161, 293
  of apostles, 4-8, 56-58, 179, 183-85
  of Christ, 55-56, 180
  of gospel writers, 58-61
  textual, 43
  textual-thematic, 124
  Trinitarian, 181-82
Preaching Christ, 153-54, 182-83, 259-60, 276-77
  for salvation, 12-13
  in a post-Christian culture, 13-15
  incarnate, 53, 54
  Jesus' cross, 5-6
  Jesus' miracles, 66
  Jesus' person, 8-9, 64-65
  Jesus' resurrection, 6-7
  Jesus' teaching, 9-10, 66-67
  Jesus' work, 9, 65-66
  kingdom of God, 7-8
  mandate, 11
  meaning of, 2-10
  necessity of, 1-15
  reasons for, 10-15
  to the glory of God, 179-81
Preaching-text. *See* Text
Presuppositions, 31, 236, 249
Progressive fulfillment, 208, 212, 242-44
Progression in redemptive history. *See* Redemptive-historical progression

Progression in revelation, 48, 76-77, 97, 141, 266, 271, 313
Promise-fulfillment, 142-44, 156-57, 206-12, 240-49
  examples of, 242-49, 312, 313
  in New Testament, 209-12
  in Old Testament, 207-8
  relevance of, 248-49
  rules, 242
Prophecy. *See* Genre: prophecy
Providence, 213, 249
Psalms. *See* Genre: psalm

Redemptive-historical progression, 203-6, 234-40, 245, 271
  examples of, 237-40, 308, 313, 322-23, 326, 330, 334, 340-41
Redemptive history, 5-7, 26-27, 47, 48, 99, 191-95, 234-36, 255, 262-63. *See also* Creation–Fall–Redemption–New Creation
  God-centered, 236
  progression in, 48, 52, 76. *See also* Redemptive-historical progression
  unity of, 236, 262
Relation between Old and New Testaments. *See* Old Testament: as related to New Testament
Relevance, 280-82, 287, 291
Repetition, 284, 298-99, 304
Roman Catholic interpretation, 45, 109n.168
Rule of faith, 78, 101, 182

Schleiermacher, Friedrich, 20
Sense of Scripture. *See* Interpretation
Sensus plenior. See Fuller sense

Sermon
  form, 289-90, 315-16
  goal, 289, 315
  introduction, 316-17
  model, 349
  outline, 290-91, 316-18
  theme, 234, 288-89, 314-15

Servant of Yahweh, 65, 203, 209, 211, 264

Servant songs, 65, 198

Sola scriptura, 113-14, 127

Son of Man, 64, 209

Spiritualizing, 35, 36n.8. *See also* Interpretation: spiritual

Spurgeon, Charles, 151-62, 309-10

Steps from text to sermon, 279-318, 347-48

Suffering Servant. *See* Servant of Yahweh

Symbol(ism), 257-59

Ten Commandments. *See* Decalogue

Tertullian, 78, 325

Text
  goal, 287, 305
  selection, 160-61, 280-82
  structure, 283-84, 296-97
  theme, 286-87, 303-5
  unit, 281-82, 294-95

Theme. *See* Sermon: theme; Text: theme; Longitudinal themes

Theoria, 92

Theodore of Mopsuestia, 92-94

Threefold interpretation. *See* Interpretation: threefold

Type(s)
  as predictive, 250-52
  characteristics of, 255-57

Typological interpretation. *See* Typology

Typologizing, 97, 157-58, 175, 253, 308

Typology, 90-98, 100, 126, 144-45, 146, 154-55, 157, 169-70, 187, 195, 212-20, 245, 249-61, 274
  examples of, 260-61, 309-10, 313, 323, 327, 330-31, 335, 336, 341
  in New Testament, 217-20
  in Old Testament, 215-16
  Jesus' use of, 216-17
  rules, 257-60

Universalizing. *See* Generalizing

Vatican Council II. *See* Roman Catholic interpretation

Vischer, Wilhelm, 163-76, 236, 332-33

Wisdom literature. *See* Genre: wisdom

Worldview, 28, 31, 191-95, 235, 236. *See also* Rule of faith